ART

Edited By
Emma Hardinge Britten

Mrs Emma Hardinge Britten.

Table of Contents

Part First

Author's Preface

Introductory

Part Second

Part Third

2

Epilogue to the Drama of Art Magic

Author's Preface

--

The following pages were written at the solicitation of highly esteemed European friends, who deemed that the author's long years of experience as a student and adept in the Spiritism of many lands might furnish to the world some valuable information concerning the mysteries of that spiritual communion now so prevalent throughout the civilized world.

In order to gratify these too partial advisers, the author at first collated his personal experiences into a series of autobiographical sketches, the first few chapters of which were published under the title of "Ghost Land; or Researches into the Realm of Spiritual Existence," in Emma Harding Britten's high toned American Magazine, the "Western Star." As the calamitous fires which devastated the city of Boston some five or six years ago caused the suspension of Mrs. Britten's excellent periodical, the author determined to lay his papers aside, for any use posterity might derive from them, but the same friendly spirit of appreciation which had dictated the transcription of the autobiography subsequently pleaded for its continuance, or the preparation of a still more occult work, in which the much needed desideratum of a comprehensive philosophy, covering the principles which underlie spiritual existence should be given to the world, as a basis on which to found the superstructure of spiritual science.

This suggestion was too much in accordance with the author's habits of thought to be lightly rejected. A hasty and fragmentary sketch of the work was drawn up, but when compared with the vast fields of untrodden revelation that yet remained to be gleaned, the author would fain have committed his abortive attempt to the flames, and trusted to time to unfold that mighty realm of magical philosophy which can never be disclosed in a single life-time much less condensed into one volume. But the all-too-appreciative friends to whom the author's despair of purpose was revealed thought otherwise.

They deemed the broken gleams of light submitted to them were all-sufficient for the age in which they were to be given, and urged that the suggestions rendered, belonged to humanity, and could not fail to throw light upon many of the mysteries of spiritual manifestations.

Whilst wandering incognito through the cities of the United States, still seeking to add fresh records of Spiritualistic interest to an already full treasury of facts, the author had the pleasure of meeting with his highly esteemed English friend, Mrs. Emma Hardinge Britten. In addition to urgent appeals from this authoritative source to publish his book of magic, the author was farther tempted by the generous promise that he would be relieved of all the vexations and technical details of this publication.

Shrinking with unconquerable repugnance from any encounter with those butchers of human character, self styled "critics," whose chief delight is to exercise their carving-knives upon the bodies of slain reputations, without regard to qualification for the act of dissection, and equally averse to entrusting the dangerous and difficult processes of magical art to an age wherein even the most sacred elements of religion and Spiritualism are so often prostituted to the arts of imposture, or mean traffic, the author's reluctance to the proposed publication, even with all the advantages of his English friend's invaluable cooperation, would hardly have been conquered, had not loved and trusted spirit friends taken the helm of the storm-tossed mind, and advising the excision of such passages as would be dangerous to the half-informed spirituality of the present age, those well-trained counselors themselves suggested the conditions of publication which they deemed most in harmony with the author's wishes and position, conditions subsequently embodied in the circular which announced the publication of this volume.

The reception which that circular met with, the unworthy jibes, sneers, and cruel insults which have been leveled against the excellent lady who volunteered to stand between the author and his shrinking spirit, have caused him the deepest remorse for having placed her in such a position, and induced a frequent solicitation on his part that the publication of the book should be abandoned. In confiding the management of this work to his friends, the author had entire confidence that the invaluable services rendered by the noble editress to the Spiritualists of America, which would have been sufficiently appreciated to protect her against misrepresentation and unjust attack.

That these expectations have been so rudely disappointed, only proves how much better the spiritual intelligences who dictated the conditions of publication understood the elements to be dealt with than the trusting mortals they counseled.

That Emma Hardinge Britten has found five hundred friends in America, who put faith alike in her judgment and honesty, is deemed by her as a sufficient trimph for one lifetime. Should the author of "Art Magic" find five hundred readers who can appreciate its occult pages, that shall be esteemed as an equal meed of recompense for his share of the work.

Having already made confession of inefficiency to cope with so vast a subject in so small a space, acknowledging that a mere sketch is here presented instead of the full length portrait of Art Magic the author's mind had conceived, and given to all whom it may concern, the rationale of how this publication came to be launched upon the world, we shall conclude in the quaint words of Robert Turner, the translator of Cornelius Agrippa's fourth book of "Occult Philosophy" into English, who in presenting his introductory words to the public, says:

"There be four sorts of readers – sponges, which extract all, without distinguishing; hour-glasses, which receive and pour out as fast; bags, which retain only the dregs of spices, and let the wine escape; and sieves, which retain the best only. Some there are of the last sort, and to them I present this Occult Philosophy, knowing that they shall reap good thereby." A conclusion in which Dr. Robert Turner is cordially joined by

Introductory

--

Standing as we do upon the sublime heights to which the progress of ages has elevated us, we are enabled to look aback upon the footprints left by the ascending feet of those who have preceded us, and take account of every obstacle they have surmounted, every impulse that has swayed them to the right or the left, and almost hear the pulse-beats of the pilgrim hearts that have throbbed in response to the eternal cry of Life's Marshals, "Onward and Upward!" The piercing and analytical eye of science can investigate these footprints, and determine almost with mathematical precision the physical characteristics of the beings who have made them. The species or class to which the toiler belonged, becomes a letter in that alphabet, whereby science as clearly unravels the unwritten past, as the scale of a fish, or the fossiliferous imprint of a vanished organism can interpret the species and class to which the relic belonged; but the far more penetrating gaze of the soul looking into the metaphysical causes which underlie all physical effects, beholds an outstretched panorama of being, which transcends those spheres of knowledge bounded by physical horizons; hence it can pierce not only the causes, but master also the ultimates and controlling forces of mortal existence.

To arrive at a complete apprehension of truth, or that which is, we must call up the witness of that which was, that which shall be, and that which moves, as well as that which is moved upon. The anatomist who numbers up the bones, recites the names and describes the forms and functions of the tissues, organs and apparatuses which constitute the physical structure, explains nothing of the true man except the house he lives in.

The physiologist who explains the motions which proceed throughout the wonderful housekeeping processes of human life, supplements in one degree the science of anatomy, but does no more than his contemporary by way of unveiling the mystery of that being which inhabits the many-sided structure. Oh, how long! How wistfully, and yet in what agonizing yearning for light – light upon the mystery of self-knowledge, light upon the problems of who am I? what am I, whose am I? whence do I come? And whither am I bound? – has the I am of moral existence waited! Can the answer ever be rendered? If so, it must come from the realm of true knowledge, the esoteric innermost, from whence and to which the exoteric is but a temporary pilgrim! Those who have stood face to face with this esoteric sunbeam, who have beheld it vanishing behind the clouds of matter for the span of a mortal term of existence, but emerging again into the clear noonday radiance of a day which knows no night, a firmament whose unbounded vistas enshroud no mysteries, a realm of being limited only by the capacity of finite perception – such an one surely has the right to say, I know, and such an one writes and alleges he will reveal the order of Divine wisdom as manifest in human □xistence, and declared by the souls who have lived and struggled behind the veil, broken their way by the sword of death through its misty envelopment, and finally attained to that breadth of vision where cause and effect cohere like pearls on the unbroken thread of destiny, where past and future lie outstretched in the boundless panoramas of a never beginning, never ending present.

Any attempt to elucidate the problems of being, conducted in one direction, and by one method alone, must fail.

Those philosophers who reason from induction alone, only arrive at a mayhap perception of truth, nor do they fare any better who conduct their arguments through the half-declared processes of deduction. Both methods are essential to master the entire situation.

Theory must prompt the possibility of new discoveries, and facts must goad us on to the evolvement of new theories – even phenomena are needed to startle our self-conceit from the arrogant assumptions of half-enlightened, half-blind belief, and failures must follow on the heels of successes ere we can presume to erect a milestone on the path of destiny for the guidance of others. When every method has been exhausted, and all avenues to the way of light have been carefully traversed, then, and not till then, can the soul of man venture to affirm, I know; then, and not til then, are we in a position to challenge the bigoted adherents of a single school or a solitary method, and say, "I have entered upon a grander vista of truth than you – follow me!" Emerging from the many branching avenues of knowledge which the study of spirit and matter, fact and theory, intuition and phenomena afford, let us lay out our scheme of the Universe, and then proceed from its underlying principles to such results as their action have given shape and organic life to.

Section I
Spirit, The First Great Cause
--

The Solar Universe, of which the earth is a part, consists of Matter, Force and Spirit.

Matter is an aggregation of minute, indestructible atoms, existing in the four states known as solid, fluid, gaseious and ethereal. The general attributes which distinguish matter in the three first conditions, are indestructibility, extension, divisibility, impenetrability, and inertia.

By indestructibility is meant that property which is the antithesis of annihilation, and utterly prevents the assumption that a single atom of matter, however minute, whether in the finest condition of air or the hardest of crystal, can ever be wholly put out of existence.

Extension is the property by which an atom of matter can be changed so as to occupy more or less space.

Divisibility is the property by which an atom can be divided or reduced to the smallest known particles, and yet each particle preserve some capacity for farther subdivision.

Impenetrability implies the impossibility of one atom occupying the space of another; an inertia is the tendency of matter to continue either in that condition of rest or motion in which it has once been set by the application of force, until another force changes the former direction. There are many other definitions applicable to matter; such as crystalline, porous, dense, elastic, etc.; but the five general properties enumerated above, will sufficiently explain its nature for our present purpose.

Ether is matter in so rare and sublimated a condition, that its divisibility into particles is no longer possible to man in his present stage of scientific attainment. It far transcends the rarefaction of the finest of gases, hydrogen, and filling up every space of the solar universe explored by man, not occupied by particles matter, may with propriety be called unparticled matter.

Force is the life principle of being. It is the second of the grand Trinity of elements which constitute existence, and ranks, therefore, next to matter, which it permeates, vitalizes, and moves. It is motion per se, and though matter is never exhibited without it. Force, as we shall hereafter prove, can exist without a material body for its exhibition.

Its attributes are dual, and should be named Attraction and Repulsion.

The vast and extended orbits of planetary bodies are marked out and regulated by Force, with its dual attributes, now attracting the revolving satellite to the centre, now forcing it off into a relative point of distance, but always maintaining it in a given path or orbit between the oscillations of its contending motions.

Force is the unresting life which charges every atom of matter, and fits inorganic masses to become organic. It is Electricity in the air; Magnetism in the earth; Galvanism between different metallic particles – cohesion, disintegration, gravitation, centripetal and centrifugal forms of motion; Life in plants, animals, and men, the aural, astral, or magnetic body of spirits.

Spirit is the one primordial, uncreated, eternal, infinite Alpha and Omega of Being. It may have subsisted independent of Force and Matter, evolving both from its own incomprehensible but illimitable perfection; but Force and Matter could never have originated Spirit, as its one sole attribute comprehends and embraces all others, must antedate, govern, and surpass all others, and is itself the cause of all effects. That attribute is Will.

As there are but two attributes of Force, namely, attraction and repulsion, yet many varieties of modes in which attraction and repulsion are perceived, so, whilst there is but one attribute of Spirit, namely, Will, there are many subordinate principles emanating from Will, such are Love, Wisdom, Use, Beauty, Intelligence, Skill, etc. The most marked and distinctive procedures are, however, nine; namely, Love, Wisdom, and Power; Creation, Preservation, and Progress; Live, Death, and Regeneration.

In Matter, Force, and Spirit, then, is the grand Trinity of Being, which constitutes the solar universe and its inhabitants.

Reasoning from analogy, and still more, founding upon the assertions of wise teaching angels and the vague shadows of antique beliefs, founded in a spiritual enlightenment far in advance of the present, we have authority for supposing that the astral, and all other universes included in the illimitable fields of being, may have proceeded from and include the same primordial Trinity of elements, and that Spirit, Force, and Matter form that stupendous Ego, the totality of which, to finite beings, is vaguely called God, the separated units of which include Astral and Solar Systems, Suns, Satellites, Worlds, Spirits, Men, Animate and Inanimate Things, and Atoms.

Section II
Speculation Regarding the Origin of Man
--

All human beliefs that are derived from oral, traditional, monumental, or sacerdotal sources, incline to ascribe the origin of man to a purer and more spiritualized cause than that of human generation.

The favorite and widely diffused idea of the ancients, that man incurred the penalty of mortal birth and the discipline of a mortal existence by disobedience, pervades so universally the foundations of all religious system, that it demands from philosophy some more rational explanation than the contemptuous stigma of "myth." Whence comes myth, and can it any more explain the origin of ideas than a shadow can account for form without a substance? We can accept nothing, learn nothing, hope for nothing, from modern theology; for it teaches no philosophy, owns allegiance to no science, and is amenable to no requirements of reason or justice. And yet even she cherishes, in her usual materialistic way, the dogmas of original sin and the fall of many from a state of primeval innocence.

Who can render account of these opinions? And since time cannot quench them, nor the devotees of classical lore and antique philosophy blot them out from the "wisdom of the ages," why not seek to harmonize them with those glimpses of an inner and higher life with which all human records are so mysteriously illuminated?

The Fall of Man is but the shadow of a still diviner truth, the substance of which is – The Fall of Spirit. All existence originates in Spirit. As the curious mechanism of the clock, the ship, the steam-engine, are all creations first of the mechanical mind, in which their several parts are contained ere they can become reduced to a material expression, so the clockwork of the sideral heavens, the worlds which sail through the oceans of space, and the mechanism of every organized form, from the rounding of a dewdrop to the complicated structure of a man, must have had their origin in mind. Since mind is but an attribute of Will, and Will is Spirit, we cannot escape from the conclusion that the creation of the physical universe is but the expression of a spiritual idea. The creation of a physical man is no more, no less. The human race is the external expression of a spiritual idea, because ideas must originate with spirit ere they can be expressed in matter. The watch, the ship, the steam-engine are as much genuine creations of the soul before as after they are modeled out in matter. Should they never be thus incarnated, they have been, and are, and ever will remain, in the imperishable realm of spiritual entities.

Matter creates nothing. It is only the mold which Spirit uses to externalize its ideas for the sake of external uses.

The things which will appear as new inventions, the methods of science which will take their places as new discoveries on earth in ages yet unborn, are all in imperishable existence now and ever have been in the eternal realms of spirit. Can man be exempt from this universal law of procedure?

Man, who is the microcosm of being, the conservator of all forms of force, all varieties of matter – can he be the sole exception to the all-embracing order of Divine procedure? Only in the superstitious and unscientific belief of the bigot, or the scarcely less unreasonable blindness of materialism. Man was a spirit ere he was born into matter.

In the primordial conditions of planetary life, creatures so finely organized as man could not be sustained, hence long ages of preparatory growth were essential to fit this or any earth for his reception.

When matter had been sufficiently laborated by the successive births and destructions of millions of generations of organized beings in the vegetable and animal kingdom, the earth awaited the advent of a still higher and nobler creature than any that had yet appeared; one who should in its perfection and microcosmic powers finish the work of creation, cap the climax of animated being, and close up the succession of mortal forms by the introduction of an immortal being. The earth called for a man, and he came. He was already an immortal existence, a spirit; not a perfected, self-conscious, individualized entity, but a bright, luminous emanation of the Divine mind. He was the Divine idea in the shape of the man that should be. Angelic in essence, spiritual in substance, he lived in a paradise appropriate to him, pure and innocent, but still wholly lacking in those elements of love, wisdom, and power which can be perfected alone through incarnation in a material body, and progress through probationary states.

That man existed as a pure spiritual being, a sinless paradisiacal unit, previous to his incarnation in a material body, is not only the opinion of those sages of antiquity who studied from the original books of life, rather than from records made and altered to suit the purposes of successive generations of interested priests, but it is the witness of the human spirit itself ere it became bent and perverted by theological myths, or its memories were dimmed by time and the more vivid impressions of mortal experiences. In every primordial condition of the human family the belief in a fall or descent of the spirit from heaven to earth from purity to transgression, is an unquenchable element in man's nature. Belief it can scarcely be called; it is a memory, growing fainter and fainter as it recedes from its source, but still an indestructible link of connection in that chain of destiny which has finally incarnated the soul in a mortal body.

We shall close this section by citations from some few out of the countless host of authoritative minds who have favored the opinions herein announced as the rationale of the first act in the Divine drama of human existence.

Section III
Is There One or Many Gods?

--

It is easier for the imagination to rest upon the idea of one God than many, and still more natural for the soul of man to accept of Polytheism than Atheism.

The utter insufficiency of any argument which attempts to shut out an idea because its magnitude baffles the finite mind, has never been more completely demonstrated than when man, the puny, shadowy phantom who flits through a few sand grains of time, and then disappears for an eternity, attempts to argue against the existence of any higher being than himself, simply because he, by his sensuous perception, cannot apprehend it.

No man can, by sensuous perception, apprehend the existence of his own soul. Socrates well understood this truth when he said, "I respect my soul though I cannot see it," and the Apostle Paul equally well appreciated its force when he declared that the spiritual man alone could judge of the things of the spirit.

From the revelations of spirits who are in the experience of spiritual entities, and the sublime imaginings of those who in the childlike faiths of antiquity were nearer to God than are the mammon-worshippers of today, we will erect our scheme of the Divine Godhead, surrounding the noble temple with such a scaffolding of testimony as will enable every reader to climb to the highest pinnacle of a thought which the finite mind can reach.

That "God is a Spirit," and the eternal, uncreated, self-existent, and infinite realm of Spirit is God, none can deny who profoundly analyze the depths of being pointed to in our first two Sections; but as to the mode in which God can be apprehended, or whether there be one or many Gods, remain questions open to much broader fields of speculation.

Were it not more in the order of these writings to present the results of vast mental struggles, and the conclusions drawn from researches which have only permitted the panting Soul to pause for breath at the gates which lead from one stage of infinity to another, we should precede our own definitions of Godhead, by the opinions of the authorities we propose to cite; but the responsibility of affirmation is ours, and surrounded as we are "by a cloud of witnesses," who wave the lustrous banners of spiritual truths above our page, how can we hesitate, or, in the cold world's materialistic phrase, why fear to commit ourselves to opinions we know in our Soul to be Divine truth?

The Solar System of which our earth is a part, moves around the physical sun as a centre of light, heat, and attraction.

By well defined astronomical laws we know that this Solar System forms only a part of a larger and far grander aggregation of starry worlds, called the Astral System.

The exact centre of this system is not arrived at, yet all the observations of astronomy point to such a pivotal centre, and the known laws of Science determine that in the visible universe, all motions proceed in and are sustained by the dual modes of centrifugal and centripetal force. That the stars discovered by astronomical Science are only a part of an array of systems which occupy the spaces of infinity, is an axiom universally acknowledged; hence, indeed, the terms "infinity" and "boundless," as applied to the sidereal heavens; but in the midst of that unknowable which stretches away into vistas where the glass of the astronomer cannot penetrate, and the mind of the most aspirational becomes palsied, even there, the steadfast helm of physical science guides the ship and prophesies of an inevitable port of knowledge yet to be reached.

"The law which rounds a dew-drop shapes a world," and the principles which inhere in one System prevail throughout space. We cannot find a telescope that will pierce into the Astral Centre nor resolve all the floating masses of nebulae that crowd the galaxy into blazing Suns; but we know by analogy that that Centre and those Suns exist, and that the only horizon that shuts them out from human discovery, is human ignorance and incapacity.

In the midst of all our baffled wisdom and enlightened ignorance, physical Science and spiritual revelation supplementing each other, assure us there is one grand central Sun of being.

Physical Science tells us it must be so. Spiritual revelation affirms it is so. That central Sun is God. This perfection of being exists in the form of a globe, the only point of union between mathematics and geometry, and occupies the centre, the only position whereby revolving universes can live, move, and have their being and life, be born, sustained and renewed.

God is the dispenser of heat and light, the two elements in being which account for generation and revelation, love and wisdom, life and sense. This Spiritual Sun throws off from the centre the elements of new-created worlds by centrifugal force, and draws them back and keeps them in determinate orbits by centripetal force. Its nature is Spirit; its attribute, Will; its manifestations, Love, Wisdom, Power. This is God.

13

Supplement to Section III
Early Conceptions of the Hindoos
--

The best of Philologists agree in attributing to the nations or peoples called Aryan, or Indo-European, the first linguistic records we possess:

"Men do not invent names for things of which they have no idea."

"The Word has always been recognized as the fittest Symbol of Truth, and the purest manifestation of Deity." The Aryan name for God was Div, which signifies "The clear light of day;" and this word has become the root-word of all worship for untold ages until we arrive at its modern appellative, Deity.

In fragmentary accounts given of the most early historic people, classified as Aryan, it is asserted that they kept fires constantly burning as their chief element in religious worhip. Fustel de Coulanges in his fine epic (for such it is), entitled "La Cite Antique," published in Paris, in 1870, clearly proves that the Aryan's religious belief, recognized in fire the symbol of God – in light his wisdom – in material forms an expression of his potential word – and in Guardian Spirits his Ministering Angels or tutelary deities.

When we trace the early conceptions of the Hindoos – that most ancient of contemplative men, those children of the Spirit, who communed with Nature's God through the profoundest study of Nature herself – we find they cherished ideas so exalted of the First Great Cause, that they ventured not to embody their thought of Him in any form, symbol, or even to assign Him a name.

The Supreme Being was with them, the Unknowable, and only became typified as Brahm, which, interpreted, signifies The Void, The Silent Region which cannot be pierced – the unfathomable which cannot be gauged or understood. That the human mind might rest on a Providential scheme, the Sages of India taught that there were three Subordinate emanations from the First Great Cause, who embodied the Grand Trinity of his Deific attributes. This primordial Trinity consisted of Brahma, the Creator; Vishnu, the Preserver; and Siva, the Destroyer and Reproducer.

Each of these Deific emanations were so intimately connected in the Hindoo mind with the attributes of heat and light, that the earliest Hindostanee worship may with truth, be assumed to have laid the foundation of that stupendous systems known, in later ages, as the astronomical religion. A large proportion of the Vedas – the oldest of the Hindoo Scriptures – consist of epics in praise of Light; accounts of the miracles outwrought by the mighty Sun-God; invocations to the spirits of the air, moon, stars, and sacred fire, and different elements. Many are the prayers addressed to Indra, the starry-robed Ruler of the constellated heavens, as well as to the spirits of different departments of the Universe. Fire was held sacred in every household, and employed in all sacerdotal rites. The very shape of the pyramidal Temples, or the blunted pylons, signified the all-pervading reverence of the Hindoo mind for the symbol of the tapering flame

In one of the most ancient of the Vedic hymns, addressed to the Heranyagarbha, occurs the following passage:

"In the beginning there arose the Source of golden light, He was the only born Lord of all that is. He established the earth and the sky. To what other God shall we offer sacrifice? He through whom the sky is bright, and the earth is firm; who measured out the light in the air. To what other God, etc., etc.

"Wherever the mighty water clouds went; where they placed the seed and lit the fire; thence arose He who is the only life of the bright Gods. To what other God, etc., etc.

There was neither entity, nor non-entity then – neither atmosphere nor sky beyond. Death was not, nor therefore immortality; nor day nor night. That One breathed breathless by itself. There was nothing different from it, nor beyond it. The covered germ burst forth by mental heat; then first came Love upon it, the Spring of mind. The rays shot across, and there were mighty powers producing all things. Nature beneath, and Energy above.

The Vedic hymns are nearly all invocations to the Solar and Astral sources of light and heat; the Vedic philosophy, speculations on the origins of Being, ever re-affirming the influence of Solar and Astral agency in Creation.

The following passage, descriptive of the Hindoo's God, will convey an idea of his sublime conceptions of Deity:

"Heaven is his head; the sun and moon are his eyes; the earth his feet; space his ears; air his breath. He is the Soul of the Universe. The Sun of all luminaries. All Creation derives light from him alone. The wise call him the Supreme Light-giving Spirit."

In the Egyptian and Persian Theogony, the direct acknowledgment of one Supreme Being corresponding to the Sun and its attributes, is as marked as in the Aryan and Indian records. The elaborate woof of Grecian and Roman Mythology partake of the same golden threads of belief, and whilst ramifying into a complete system of Polytheism, still refer back to the Indian and Egyptian idea of Creation springing from one Supreme Source, and this a spiritual centre of heat or creative energy, and light or creative wisdom.

In the Orphic Songs, the one first Great Cause celebrated as Zeus is more completely associated with the Egyptian idea of a Sun-God, a spirit "without parts of passion, sex or nature," than in the theories of later philosophers. Orpheus, the Sage, to whom the introduction of Egyptian Theogony into Greece is mainly due, chants thus of the Supreme Being:

"Zeus is male, Zeus is female. Zeus is the spirit of all things. Zeus is the rushing of uncreated fire. Zeus is the king; he is the sun and moon. Zeus is the mighty power, the demon, the one mighty frame in which this universe revolves. He is fire and water, earth and ether, day and night. All things unite in the body of Zeus"

Pythagoras, Plato, Socrates, Aristotle, and other of the most distinguished Grecian sages, taught more directly of God as a Spirit, and as the source from which all subordinate gods proceeded.

Passing on to the mediaeval, and still later ages, we find the most illuminated of the Mystics either reaffirming the ancient beliefs of India and Egypt in the Great Central Sun, or claiming to receive confirmation of this truth from spiritual inspiration, direct revelations, or intercourse with superior orders of being.

Cornelius Agrippa, Paracelus, Jacob Behmen, and Swedenborg, taught this idea of Deity with more of less distinctness. Swedenborg, in particular, who elevates his conception of Jesus Christ into the Lord, from whom, and to whom, all the activities of the Created Universe proceed and return – clearly teaches that "The Lord" is only seen as a Sun. In his essay on "Creation by Two Suns," he affirms that, "The Sun of Heaven is the Lord, the light there is Divine truth, and the heat there is Divine good, which proceed from the Lord as a Sun. From that origin are all things which exist and appear in the heavens." Again he says: That the Lord actually appears in heaven as a Sun, has not only been told me by the angels, but has also been given me to see several times, wherefore what I have seen and heard concerning the Lord as a Sun, I would here describe, etc., etc.

Of still more recent date are the teachings of certain spirits claiming to have had a mortal existence, many thousands of years ago, but who found themselves impelled to return to earth during the great spiritual outpouring of the last quarter of a century, in the United States of America. We shall quote from those who manifested their presence at the spirit house of Jonathan Koons, a farmer residing in the remotest wilds of Athens County, Ohio, and who gave their testimony, speaking through trumpets, with an audible voice, under circumstances which defied the probability of collusion or imposture, and with a power and spirituality of tone and presence acknowledged by all who heard them to have been truly sublime and authoritative.

The communications given by these spirits orally were transcribed by those present, and subsequently corrected by themselves – others were written by spirit hands in the presence of many witnesses, or found in locked drawers. From the MSS. Preserved of these wonderful writings, the history of the Athens County manifestations are elaborately described in "Hardinge's Twenty Years' History of Modern American Spiritualism," and it is from the pages of this highly authentic work that we submit the following excerpt.

The author says:

"These spirits declare that 'there is an electric element, divided through space by another element, which bears no affinity to it; that spirits, at least such as communicate with earth, cannot themselves penetrate this interior element; in fact, to their apprehension, no one in the universe can do so, save only God; and this mysterious innermost, with all its hidden and impenetrable glories, is called by the spirits the 'subter fluid.' They declare that the electric element forms the various paths in which planets and all other known bodies in space travel and move in their respective orbits, but that nothing visible to spirits, or comprehensible to them as of an organic nature, can penetrate the realms of the 'subter fluid,' yet it divides and permeates all space, and seems to hold in control the infinite realms of the electric element. 'Rays of light,' however, they say, 'can and do penetrate the 'subter fluid,' as they appear to issue from and return to it incessantly.' Also, 'There is a grand central territory in the universe, known to exist by all spirits, and in all worlds. It embraces illimitable though unknown realms; yet its position as a vast central point is defined, from the fact that from thence, and to thence, seem to strand all the illimitable lines of attraction, gravitation, and force, which connect terrestrial bodies, and link together firmaments teeming with lives and systems. All the innumerable firmaments, spangled with an infinitude of solar and astral systems, seem to revolve around, and derive attractive and living forces from this unknown centre. Sometimes it is called 'the Celestial Realm.' Again 'The Central Sun,' 'Heaven,' 'God,' 'The Infinite Realm,' 'The Eternal Life!' While firmaments thickly sown with suns and revolving satellites, appear but as specks of light in comparison with the inconceivable vastness of this celestial laboratory, invisible and boundless as it is, from which flows out, through all universes, the centrifugal and centripetal forces of being."

In Cahagnet's "Celestial Telegraph," several spirits, communicating through celebrated Somnambules, startled their hearers' preconceived opinions on the subject of Deity by affirming positively that he was seen and known by highly exalted angels as a Grand Central Spiritual Sun.

Through the ecstatic Bruno it was asked; "Do angels, such as you describe your Guardian Gabriel to be, see God?" A. "Yes." Q. "In what form?" A. "In that of the Sun." Q. "Is it our terrestrial Sun?" A. "No; there is in the heaven of heavens but one Sun, which is the Spiritual Sun, the form in which God appears. Our terrestrial sun is but the reflection of the rays dispensed from the Great Central Spiritual Sun, which is God."

The Hindoo child seeress Sanoma, heretofore referred to also affirmed, when in ecstatico, at the tender age of five years, when her infant mind had never been impressed with one single idea of theology, that the God of the universe was a Spiritual Sun, whilst all the suns and stars, visible or invisible to the naked eye, derived their light and heat only from Him. When questioned by Sir James Mackintosh, the eminent astronomer, whether the sun of our solar system was not an incandescent body, and the originator of all light and heat received by his satellites, she emphatically denied that it was so, and exposed, with wonderful acumen, in her lisping, child-like tone, but with penetrating scientific arguments, the fallacies of those astronomers who endeavor to defend the incandescent theory of the sun's body.

This youthful ecstatic affirmed that all the light and heat in the universe proceeded from the great Central Spiritual Sun, and was reflected from thence to every body in space, according to its size, situation, and the energy of the centrifugal and centripetal forces operating between suns, satellites, and systems.

During an unbroken system of communication, extending over a period of nearly half a century, between the author of these pages and spirits of various degrees – during perceptions of angelic spheres observed by his liberated spirit amongst the realms of the wise and blest, similar testimony to the existence of a Deity who is no mystery to His creatures, has been rendered.

It seems strange, and not in the order of the Providential scheme, that the one sole mystery of the universe would be the Being most capable of originating revelation, namely a First Great Cause. But has this Supreme One been a mystery from the beginning? Or would He have continued so, if man, in his egotism and pride, had not flattered himself with the assumption that subordinate beings, tutelary spirits, and even specially inspired men, were the real Gods of the Universe, condescending to come and minister in person to humanity? Did not the first men of the earth, fresh in their primitive inspiration from Deity, rightly apprehend Him in the beginning? Have not the Prophets, Seers, Magians, Mystics, and modern Ecstatics, ever perceived and known God in gleams of the original brightness, dimmed by ages of materialism, and perverted by gloomy, earth-made theologies? Wherever the voices of the angels find reverberating echoes in human inspiration, there this Great Mystery of God is solved in the revealment of the uncreated, self-existent, infinite, and eternal Spiritual Sun, from which emanate, and to which return, all rays of light, light, heat, germinative, creative, and sustaining power.

Wherever we see the people of earth straying away in search of human idols, striving to discover in their God man-made, man-shaped, and man-like personalities; wherever we see an interested ignorant and selfish priesthood, enslaved by their own passions and prejudices, aiming to keep the people enslaved to their opinions – there look to find the face of the Infinite veiled in mystery; the truths of Godhead, natural science and spiritual inspiration crowded back into the realms of mystery; and mystery, the mother of all abominations, setting up idols for human worship, which change with the customs of the age, and the fashion of the hour. To drown the voice of Spiritual science, and that reason which insists that the most obvious existence in Creation must be Creation's Author, the epithets of "Pagan, Heathen, Infidel, Heretic, Fire Worshiper and Blasphemer" have been shouted through the highways of life's common places, and still echo in our ears even in this analytical nineteenth century' for the rule of Mystery, Babylon the Great, the Mother of Harlots and Abominations of the Earth, is not yet broken, and until it is, her votaries will fight for her and perish soul and body for her, and all the while the light will be "shining in the darkness, though the darkness comprehendeth it not."

Man, in his primitive appearance on earth, came only as a poor, untutored savage, the mere form of the being he was to become – only a prophecy of the Lord of Creation he should be. As he emerged from savagism to the dawn of an intellectual morning, the perception of his descent from an antecedent sphere of spiritual existence possessed his memory, and a perception of his return to that blest state of purity and happiness inspired his power of prevision.

His gradually awakening intellect taught him to analyze and understand himself. Casting about for the causes of existence, that supports on which it rested and the aims for which he lived, man dedicated all his earliest powers of mind to religion. Even his earliest triumphs in the arts of civilization were but used as means to the one end. His superb temples of worship, his solemn preparations for another life, and his colossal monumental records of his religious beliefs, remain almost imperishable evidences of his deep and undivided interest in the problems of religion; whilst of his social and commercial pursuits, only the most fragmentary and unimportant vestiges can be found. India, Egypt, Arabia, the recesses of the mighty Himalayas and the giant Koh Kas, the lovely vales and smiling plains of Asia – vales blooming like glimpses of the fabled Eden, and savage wilds, deserted now, desolate and ruined – all bear witness to the unquenchable devotion of the early man to his religious belief; all are thickly strewn over with colossal remains of that stupendous system in which that belief found expression. The burning lands of the Orient are one vast bible overwritten with distinct asseverations that to the early man God was not the Unknowable, and religious faith was no mystery. Whence came this faith if not from man's intuitive knowledge and the obvious facts of creation? Sun, moon, stars, the constellated glories of the heavens, their eternal order and their majestic march through infinity – these were scriptures in which the natural instincts of an unspoiled nature recognized God's own writing, and interpreted it without failure or effort.

The ancient man did not vainly exhaust his intellect to discover God. Untrammeled by creeds, unfettered by priestcraft and unbiased by inherited prejudices, he did not seek God, he simply found Him – knew Him in the love which engenders life; the wisdom that sustains it; the power that upholds it – knew Him in the sacred flame, which is heat; the splendor of light, which is revelation. He discovered the reflection of his dwelling-place in the majesty of the blazing sun, and perceived his own destiny – God's Providence and Nature's profoundest harmonies – in the constellated paths of the starry heavens and the movements of the fiery legions of space.

Priestcraft, Kingcraft, Artificial Civilization, with their long train of crime and disease, want and woe – an over-strained devotion to the idols of ecclesiasticism and physical science, have alienated the soul of man from pure, natural, spiritual religion, interrupted the precious communication which pure, spiritual natures alone can enjoy with angelic spheres of existence, and driven the soul off into the baneful mysticisms of idolatrous faiths or blank materialism.

It is a hopeful and significant sign to behold the spiritual standards once more set up on earth. It is a hopeful and significant fact to note how the best of the modern Seers tend towards ancient faith in the Divine Spiritual Law as the Author and Centre of being, and the prophecy of a better, more truthful, just and reasonable theology is continually renewing itself in the air, as the lips of the most inspired teachers of the time re-affirm the sublime utterances of old: "God is a Spirit, and they who worship Him, must worship Him in spirit and in truth."

Section IV
How Traditions Become Scriptures
--

The shelves of any ordinary sized library could be entirely filled with fragments of literature concerning the worship of the ancients, and the peculiar character of those myths which have been preserved from the remotest days of antiquity, and now underlie all the present systems of theological belief. It is a remarkable fact that, notwithstanding the vast collection of writings extant on this subject, there is no one compendious and accessible text-book from which the masses generally could derive reliable information and assimilate the knowledge thus widely diffused; and it is no less worthy of observation that, whilst the mythical character of early worship is stamped with unmistakable fidelity upon every form of modern theology, this damaging fact seems to make no difference in the idolatrous veneration with which the modern worshiper clings to the items of his faith; on the contrary, whilst the evidence accumulates around him, that the ideas to which he renders divine homage are paraphrases of ancient fictions, he all the more sturdily battles for his idol, and denounces every attempt to shake the authenticity of legends which he translates into divine revelations.

Perhaps it is for want of an authentic text-book; perhaps because the literature of the subject is too widely diffused and broken up into too many scattered fragments, that this apathy of idolatry prevails so universally, and that the common sense and intelligence of the nineteenth century is contented to bow down with purse and person before lifeless husks from which the spirit has departed; the husks which at best only contained in their original form the spirit of an impersonated myth.

It is not for the sake of converting one single idolator of the nineteenth century that we now write. It is not with the desire of proving to any sincere worshiper of the name of Christ that he is adoring the Sun-God of the ancients, that we now collect the torn fragments of the great Osiric body, and present a concrete, though necessarily microscopic view of the original structure. When the idolatries of fire-worship have done their work, their perversions will die the natural death which the divine order of the universe demands; until that time arrives we write for the truth's sake alone; let who will accept or reject us. Truth is "the Master's Word," which unlocks all mysteries, furnishes the clue to all religious beliefs, underlies the magical history of the race, and therefore its free enunciation is demanded in this work.

At what period the early man first commenced to worship the starry host of heaven, or in what nation the germ was first planted of that stupendous system which overlaid the earth with temples and survived all the wrecks of chance, change and time, none can say. We find the manifestations of its completeness only when humanity had acquired the art of recording its opinions in picture-writing, symbolical engravings, hieroglyphical and alphabetical Scriptures.

Traditions come wafted down the ages on the tongues of men with an impress as authoritative as graven Scriptures; for, ere men had learned to record their thoughts, they depended on memory for their preservation; hence they cultivated and strengthened this faculty, held its integrity sacred, and hence the perpetuity and universality of oral traditions.

Tradition affirms that when the mind of man rose out of the lethargy of savagism to the dawn of reason, and became fired with all those anxious inquisitions into the nature of cause and effect which reason prompts, he began to perceive that all the grand machinery of nature was coincident with the apparition and disappearance of the resplendent lights which spangled the canopy of the over-arching heavens. The God whom his earliest perceptions recognized in the majestic Sun, was unquestionably the source of those climactic changes which formed the principal theme of his primal studies.

To cultivate the ground, feed and protect his flocks, and determine the best times to perform the simple duties of agriculturist and herdsman, it became necessary to study the succession of the seasons, and consider not only the familiar alternations of night and day, but the equally important order which marked the changes in tides and times, together with all the variations of climate, and their effects in heat and cold.

None could fail to observe that every change on the face of nature kept step with the succession of certain solar and astral phenomena

From the early dawn of these perceptions, up to the maturity of the stupendous astronomical religion, man learned to read the fiery Scriptures of the skies, and the ever mobile face of nature, with a profound depth of understanding.

How many ages it required to outwork a complete theology from the book of nature and the starry heavens, man may never determine.

Thought grows fast or slowly according to the amount of momentum that is imparted to it. The world is very old in relation to that succession of changes we call time.

Millions of years have been consumed in laying down the rocky walls that extend from the circumference to the interior of the earth's crust. It occupied the world builders untold ages to develop a spear of moss or a tuft of lichen, from a mass of primary granite. Time is nothing in the issues of divine purposes; a second or a billion of years are but indices on the dial plates which mark the rounds of eternal progress, and since the first human worshipper veiled his adoring eyes in the passion of his soul's communion with the Spirit who dwells in the orbs of primal light, up to the age when reverend scholarly men were set apart by the busy multitude to watch the order of marching worlds from the high towers of the early "episcopacy," many successions of times, seasons, generations and ages had come and gone. The constellated heavens had been studied out; charts had been drawn; numerical Bibles written. The starry legions had been divided into geometrical proportions, and their motions calculated with mathematical precision. Even the forward movement of the entire solar system around what science now asserts to be an undiscovered but inevitable centre, had been perceived and the precession of the equinoxes was understood. The whole grand scheme, involving the awful majesty of the

Sun-God, the mild radiance of the moon, the glory of the fixed stars, the erratic motions of the wandering planets, the terrific apparition of fiery comets, flashing meteors, and the deep and unfathomable mystery of floating nebulae - all these, no less than their influence upon the fair, green earth, with its lofty mountains and shoreless seas, its sombre forests and quiet vales, its half-savage, half-divine inhabitants - all this realm of power and mystery, sublimity and littleness, solemn silence and restless eloquence, the ancient mind discovered, by thousands of years of patient and untiring study, to be all in motion - motion of one continuous and correspondential order - motion which swept "the heavens, and the earth, and all that in them is," through regions of space, unknown and unknowable, but still defined to the piercing intelligence of the astronomical priesthood as one grand and interblended universe of Love, Wisdom, and Power.

From the results of our forefathers' sublime discoveries, from the mass of varied records they have left, an the fragmentary collections that we have gathered up of their wisdom, we give in the following pages a brief and most imperfect compendium of their religious belief. It is only necessary to consult the diagram of the heavens, as mapped out on any common almanac, school atlas or celestial globe, to perceive that the apparent path of the sun is laid down in an imaginary waving track called the Ecliptic. This path (assuming as did the ancients, that the sun moves around the earth), crosses the equator or fanciful belt encircling the earth at two periods of time, which by the relative positions of the sun towards the earth, divide up the solar year into winter and summer, and place the sun in the aspect of south and north towards the earth.

The path of the Sun on the Ecliptic was defined by ancient astronomers between two lines, parallel to each other, sixteen degrees apart, the sun's march being between them.

This space was, and still is, called the Zodiac. The Zodiacal circle was divided into three hundred and sixty degrees, these again into four right angles of ninety degrees each, and the whole into twelve signs, consisting each of thirty degrees.

These signs were, with the ancients, arbitrary divisions of certain groups of stars called constellations. They were named chiefly in accordance with the climactic changes transpiring on the earth at the period when the sun was passing through them.

In January, now called the first month of the year, the sun passed through the constellation or group of stars called, from the season of storms and heavy rains that then prevail, Aquarius, the washer, or the Greek Baptizo. In February he enters the sign of Pisces, or the Fishes, a time of famine, dearth, and distress, when the fruits and roots are consumed, and little is left to the primitive man but the spoil of the accumulating waters.

In March the sun enters Aries the Lamb, significant of the young and tender products of the approaching Spring. In April, when the energy of the agricultural season is to be typified, the constellated group through which the sun passes is called the Bull. In May, when Summer and Winter are reconciled, and the sweet genial period of flowers and bloom seems to knit up the opposing seasons in fraternal harmony, the constellation then prevailing is called Gemini, or the Twins. In June, when the sun appears to undergo a retrograde motion significantly explained in astronomy, the sign in the ascendant is termed Cancer or the Crab. In July, the raging heat of the burning Summer suggests for the ascendant sign that significant title of the Lion, whilst the Virgin of August, the Scales of September, the Scorpion or Great Dragon of October, the Archer of November, and the Goat of December, are supposed to have somewhat more direct reference to fancied resemblances in the shapes of the constellations, than for the physical correspondence between their names and the climacteric conditions of the earth. Besides these subdivisions of the Zodiacal path, there were two other methods of marking the astronomical year. The first was the division of the whole twelve months into four seasons, each of which contained ninety degrees, and were symbolized by a special emblem, as - an Ox, a Lion, an Eagle, and a Man. The Ox denoted the agricultural pursuits of the Spring, the Lion the fierce head of the Summer, the Eagle was adopted for certain symbolical reasons as a substitute for the Scorpion of Autumn, and the Man was still retained as the Winter emblem of Aquarius, or the water-bearer. Added to this quarternial division of the year, were the two primal and opposing conditions of Summer and Winter, always held significant by the ancients of good and evil principles.

The most solemn and important periods of the astronomical year were when the Sun descended from the North at the close of Summer to cross the plane of the autumnal equinox, and that when he ascended from the South in the Spring to cross the vernal equinox. The first motion heralded death of the great light-bringer, famine and desolation to the earth; the second inaugurated the rejuvenating power of his triumph and glory in the promise of Spring, and the fulfillment of Summer.

Slight as seems this foundation for a theology, it is on this only, that the superstructure of every theological system of the earth has been upreared.

Besides the general titles assigned to the twelve Zodiacal constellations, each separate star visible in the heavens, had its name, and was supposed to exert an influence peculiar to itself for good or evil upon mankind. Thus all the stars through the plane of, or near which the sun passed in Summer were deemed to be beneficent and in harmony with the celestial traveller of the skies, favorable also to the inhabitants of earth to whom they aided in dispensing seed-time and harvest, fruits, flowers, and all manner of blessings. On the other hand, the stars of Winter were assumed to exert a malignant influence not only on the mighty Sun-God, whom they opposed, but also upon man and his planet, causing storms, tempests, pestilence, and famine. By these malignant astral influences the gracious Sun was shorn of his heat-dispensing powers, and the hours of his illumination upon earth were shortened. The majesty of Day was so obscured by the hosts of malignant Spirits, supposed to inhabit the wintry stars, that he vainly strove to contend against them. On the opposing spiritual forces inhabiting the Summer and Winter constellations, was founded the apocalyptic legend of "the war in heaven," and endless flights of visionary astronomical myths.

In this celestial scheme every star became a symbol of some good or evil genius; every constellation was a realm, peopled by innumerable legions of beneficent or malignant angels, and the entire field of the sidereal heavens was made the battle-ground of infinite squadrons of opposing angelic influences.

On the earth the solar year was mapped out into grand subdivisions of time, in which the impersonated stars and their rival influences enacted a mighty drama with the Sun-God for its hero, the inhabitants of earth for an adoring audience, and a royal astronomical priesthood for its historians.

These ancient priests, called from their custom of studying the face of the heavens from high watch-towers, Episcopacy, became in ages of practice familiar with every phase of the sublime epic they wrote. They occupied centuries in correcting their calendars and amending their Zodiacal charts. They invented thousands and tens of thousands of allegorical fables descriptive of the scenes, incidents and angelic personages of the celestial drama. They varied names, images and symbols to suit the progress of ideas in revolving ages, and invested their astral Gods with all the attributes which fervent Oriental fancy could suggest.

As an example of the leading ideas which prevailed throughout this stupendous system, it is proper to recite some of the main features which clustered around the supposititious history of the magnificent Sun-God. When this light-bringing luminary entered the sign of Aries, or the Lamb, in March, he was assumed to have crossed the vernal equinox and become the Redeemer of the world from the sufferings and privations of Winter. Then the earth and its inhabitants rejoiced greatly. The young Savior had entered upon his divine mission, bringing the earth out of darkness into light; miraculously healing the sick; feeding starving multitudes, and filling the world with blessing.

This triumphant career culminated to its fullest glory between the months of July and August, which, in the figurative language of the astronomical religion, was sometimes called the betrothal of the Virgin, sometimes the marriage feast of the Lion, of July, and the Virgin, of August. This was the season of the grape harvest, the time when the Sun converted, by his radiant heat, the waters which had desolated the earth in Winter into the luscious wine of the vintage. Then it was, as the ancient astronomers proclaimed, that the great miracle of the solar year was performed, the Sun manifested forth his most triumphant glory.

From thence the constellation of the Scales, or the Balances, seemed for a time to maintain the celestial hero in a just and even path; his miraculous power and life-giving presence was hailed with feasts and rejoicings, which lasted until the fatal period when the Great Dragon of the Skies, the mighty Scorpio of October, appears in the ascendant. Then sorrow and lamentation possessed the earth. The Savior of men must cross the autumnal equinox and from thence descend into the South - the Hades, Acheron, Sheol, Hell, Pit, of many ancient nations.

To announce the dire calamity at hand, the Dragon, of October, is preceded by a bright and glorious star called in the Spring Vesper, or the evening star; in autumn, Lucifer, or "the Son of the morning." In the sweet vernal season this splendid luminary is the herald of Summer, the brightest and most beautiful of all the heavenly host. Then it appears high in the heavens, and occupies what is significantly called the seat of pride. Appearing in the boding season of Autumn, low on the edge of the horizon, and shining only in the early dawn, its name is changed with its station - it is now the fallen Angel; the mighty rebel, who seduced by pride and vaulting ambition, has been dethroned and cast down to the ominous depths of the lowest hell. Transformed into Lucifer, "Son of the Morning," this star becomes the herald of the darkest ill that can beset the path of the celestial Savior. As it appears in advance of the great constellation of the Dragon, it is assumed to be the rebel Angel that incited "a third of the host of heaven to disobedience;" hence it is often confounded with the Dragon, of which, however, it is only the prototype.

The constellation of the great Dragon is the most powerful of the entire Zodiac. From its peculiar form, and the immense group of shining stars that extend in the convolutions of its resplendent train, it has been called the Starry Serpent of the Skies. Its attendant luminaries are assumed to be third of the host of heaven seduced by the rebel Angel from their allegiance, and its position as the inaugural constellation of the much-dreaded wintry season impresses upon it the ominous name of Satan, or the adversary. And thus, from the position of a group of stars, and their apparition in the season deemed fatal to the prosperity of earth and its inhabitants, has arisen that stupendous myth, that legend of world-wide fear, the supposititious existence of an incarnate spirit of evil, the Satan of the Persians, the Typhon of Egypt, the Pluto of the Greeks, the old Serpent of the Jews, and the most popular of all objects of alternate fear and worship, the Devil of the enlightened Christians.

Following up the astronomical legend, we find the great Dragon of October waging its annual war against the Sun-God. By the influence of its leader, Lucifer, the celestial Sun-God has already been put to death in his crossifiction of the autumnal equinox; from thence he is cast down into the power of the two evil months - November and December - who are crucified with him on the autumnal equinox.

It is just at midwinter when Capricorn, the Goat - signifying in ancient mythical language the renewer of life - is in the ascendant, that the Sun-God reappears as a new-born babe.

In the fanciful imaginings of the astronomical historians, the cluster of stars which appear in the midwinter sky bear a resemblance to a manager or stable, whilst the fertile minds of the "episcopacy" discover the reappearance of the Virgin of Summer with her companion, Bootes, or the constellation called Joseppe, or Joseph. For three days at midwinter the feeble radiance of the Sun appears to remain stationary, yet so greatly obscured, that the legend declares he descends to the nethermost parts of the universe and is lost to sight.

In the Greek theology this three days of solar obscuration is accounted for by the descent of Orpheus into the realms of Pluto, where, by the magic of his sweet music, he is supposed to rescue lost souls from the very jaws of Hades. In the astronomical legend the vanished God is represented as going on a mission of mercy, to illuminate with his radiance the darkened souls who have been held captive in the realms of perdition. At

length, on the 25th day of December, he reappears, and amidst the figurative
paraphernalia of constellated stars then in the ascendant, he is declared to have been born
in a manger through the maternity of the Zodiacal Virgin.

The women who have wept for Tammuz, the Syrian Sun-God, the mourners who have
lamented with Isis for the Egyptian Osiris, the Greeks who have wandered with Ceres in
search of the lost Proserpina, the devotees who have wailed for the slain Chrishna, one of
the Sun-Gods of the Hindoos, and the Marys who weep at the sepulcher for the Christ of
the Jews, all the nations of antiquity throughout the Orient - each of whom, under many
names and in many forms, have adored the Sun-God, and believed in his annual birth,
life, miracles, death and resurrection - all have united to celebrate the new birth of their
idol on the 25th of December, the period at which the solar orb actually passes through
the constellation of the Zodiacal sign Capricorn, or the "renewer of life." After the 25th of
December, the legend again loses sight of its new-born Savior.

In all Eastern theogonies Egypt is represented as the land of darkness and the symbol of
obscurity. During the prevalence of the two constellations of January and February, it is
supposed that antagonistic influences threaten the young child's life. The royal power of
Winter, with its storms and tempests, is in the ascendant, hence the world's Redeemer is
in danger from a mighty King. To avert the evil, the young child is carried by stealth to
the land of Egypt; there in concealment he remains until the season of danger is passed,
when he recrosses the equator at the vernal equinox, ascending from the southern depth
of Egypt into the light and glory of an acknowledged worker of miracles. Again the earth
rejoices in the presence of the young Lamb of Spring, who "taketh away the sins of the
world," and redeems it from the famine, desolation and evils or the past Winter. From
this time forth the Sun-God proclaims "peace on earth, and good will to men," and fulfills
his promise in miracles of healing, feeding the hungry, clothing the naked and bringing
life and plenty to all.

On taking a retrospective glance at this famous myth, it will be seen that the Sun-God is
its central figure, and his passage through the constellated stars of the Zodiac, together
with the peculiar changes of atmosphere, climate, and natural productions effected on
earth by solar and astral configurations, form the connected woof of the celestial drama.

Next in importance in the mythical history is the impersonation of the Virgin Mother of
the Sun-God. This constellated figure is assumed to hold in her hand a sprig, flower, or
fruit which she extends in the attitude of invitation to a minor constellation, named
Bootes, Jo-seppe, or Joseph, who from its proximity to the Virgin of Summer, is
sometimes impersonated as her betrothed, sometimes as the Father of men, Adam,
yielding to the seductions of Eve, tempting him by the extended fruit she holds in her
hand. The next, and not least important figure in the legend is the impersonation of the
evening star of Spring, transformed from an angel of light into Lucifer, the leader of the
rebel hosts and the morning star of Autumn.

This evil star is followed by another important actor in the Astral Drama, namely, the
Great Dragon, the antagonistic power of all systems, by whom the beneficent Sun-God is

put to death on the cross of the autumnal equinox; crucified between the two evil wintry constellations prevailing in November and December. According to an ancient Sabean tradition, one of these evil angels, symbolized by the Goat of December, repented him of the wrong done to the sinless God who was crucified with him, hence he becomes at first the hoary sign of Winter, the Goat, who participates in the death of the beloved Sun, and then the friend of the dying God, sheltering him in his manger, and protecting the fruitful Virgin in her hour of parturition. This phase of the legend, like thousands of others, is doubtless an attempt to reconcile the antagonistic characteristics of the wintry sign, during which the Sun is lost, with the favorable aspect of the same constellation in the last part of his month of power, when he is represented as ushering the new-born God into being, under the title of the renewer of life.

Endless are the fantasies of this kind interwoven with the Zodiacal legend. The discoveries of each succeeding age afforded to the astronomical priesthood a boundless field for the exercise of their favorite method of symbolical expression, thus, whilst we always find the main ideas of the scheme preserved intact, the divergent branches of ideality which spring forth from the parent root are in truth a realization of the parable of the mustard seed of the Jewish Scriptures. In the paraphrase of the Christian history of the Sun-God, the writers represent one of the thieves crucified with the Savior of mankind as becoming penitent at the last dread hour of death - Jesus, in allusion to his approaching new birth, answers him, "to-day shalt thou be with me in Paradise." This is a highly ingenious and creditable mode of disposing of the difficulty which ancient astronomers experienced in representing the constellation of December at once antagonistic and favorable to the dying God. The Capricorn of Winter shares the Sun-God's evil fate, but becomes favorable to him in the hour of his new birth in "Paradise." We have now brought the legend up to that point when it is to recommence with the renewal of Zodiacal history.

The Sun of righteousness is now to be re-born in the stable of the Goat, through the maternity of the immaculate Virgin, and thus the light of the world, the Lamb of Spring, the Lion of the tribe of Judah, the good master of the twelve Zodiacal Apostles, is ever sacrificed, that he may take away the sins of the world, and ever restored to life, that all may have hope of immortality in his resurrection, etc., etc., etc.

It would indeed be "vanity and vexation of spirit" to attempt to discover the exact order in which the antique mind first clothed the starry heavens with these fantastic symbolisms, and yet we must not suppose that the exoteric meaning of which we have given a brief sketch, is the all of this ancient and most wonderful faith. Later on in this volume we shall see that every symbol has a correspondential spiritual meaning, and that the esoteric philosophy veiled under this mass of symbolism is the real heart of its religious significance. These explanations, however, we must reserve for the present. How the ancients ultimately evolved an exoteric scheme from the external face of nature and its correspondential relations to the spangled heavens, can be no marvel to those who will consider their wisest and best minds as devoted, during the course of thousands of years, to this one grand field of observation. The origin, growth and perfection of such a system is far less problematical than is the conduct of modern theologians in reference to it. So long as the famous astronomical religion was practiced and taught amongst these nations whom Christians contemptuously denominate "the heathen," it was denounced by them as the vilest of idolatries, but at the point where they attempt to build up a theology of their own, they first begin by stealing the astronomical myth, then transpose its origin to a far later date, rechristen its personages, locate them in fresh birth-places, declare them to be genuine personalities, invest them with the most sacred names and attributes, fall down and worship them, and then call upon the name of the Most High God as a witness to the credibility of their audacious fictions.

In consideration of the vast and cumulative mass of testimony which the discoveries of archaeology and philology supply us with, concerning the foundation of all theological systems, the idolatry of the nineteenth century puts to shame the devotion of humanity's infancy to myth and mysticism.

The antique man would blush for the mendacity of the modern Priesthood, who not only steal the images of their forefathers' creation, but, reclothing them with the tinsel and varnish of ecclesiastical trumpery, set them up in shrines to worship as the legitimate offspring of divine inspiration.

With those who have dared to dispute the authenticity of these monstrous fabrications, the Christian world has offered no other arguments than fire an sword, torture and denunciation; and as the culminating point of the monstrous wrong which modern Priestcraft has perpetrated on the people, by foisting on them the myths of antiquity as genuine subjects for worship, it hesitates not to affix the awful name of that God, who is a spirit, not only, as above stated, in witness of their blasphemous plagiarisms, but as an actual participator in a Drama, which, if removed from the realm of myth to actuality, would subvert every law of reason, decency, justice, or morality, that has ever been promulgated since time began.

We commenced this section by affirming that if all the fragments that have been written on the history of the Sun-God an the order of the astronomical religion were gathered together, they would fill a library.

Our only regret is, that the present hour does not furnish us with the opportunity to give to the world a thorough but compendious aggregation of these severed fragments in one concrete body of testimony. We can only glance at them now; but we may not altogether omit to notice them, for, ere we can describe the origin, progress and development of the spiritual idea of which Art Magic is, in part, the external form, we must give the outlines of that religious system in which the human spirit took shape, as in a matrix; in which its conceptions were first unfolded, and from which its aspirations radiated forth in the insatiate demand for spiritual bread. At this present writing, we only feel justified in raising the veil sufficiently to show the first point of contact between God and Man, the Creator and the Creature, Religion the Body and Spiritualism the Soul of the Universe' but we reserve to ourselves the duty (God inspiring and mortal span of life permitting) of inscribing a volume in the future, wherein shall be shown, in its completeness, how the Teraphim of the ancients were fashioned, and how the moderns have stolen and worshipped them; when, and in what mode, ideas descended to man in the past from the starry heavens, and in what absurd perversions the Priesthood of the present endeavor to plant those ideas in divine soil, until the abomination of desolation sits in the holy places of human thought, and scientific, reasoning men, and pious, pure-minded women, worship a God whose example, if imitated, would fill the earth with monsters of injustice, impurity and wickedness.

Supplement to Section IV
Biographies of Chrishna and Buddha Sakia
--

The Hindoos - the oldest nation that possesses scriptural as well as monumental records, dating back to the highest antiquity, even to pre-historic ages - believed in one Supreme Omnific Central Source of Being, and from Him descending emanations corresponding in many respects to the mythical personages of the astronomical religion.

The biographies of two of their principal Avatars or incarnated God-men, Chrishna and Buddha Sakia, are closely accordant with the history of the Sun-God. The births of these Avatars through the motherhood of a pure Virgin, their lives in infancy threatened by a vengeful king, their flight and concealment in Egypt, their return to work miracles, save, heal and redeem the world, suffer persecution, a violent death, a descent into hell, and a reappearance as a new-born Savior, are all items of the Sun-God's history, which have already been recited, and maintain in every detail the correspondence between the Hindoo faith and the Sabean system. The feasts, fasts, seasons of lamentation and rejoicing, the reverence paid to fire, flame, heat, light, and even the minutest details of ceremonial rites practiced in the most ancient astronomical worship, are scattered through the varying forms of Hindoo theology, until the parity of the two systems cannot be questioned. An equally faithful adherence to the Sabean legend is to be found in the story of the Indian Dyonisius, subsequently repeated in Egypt, and forming the basis of the Osiric legend.

Egypt taught the Sun-God's history, and that in a series of myths and mysteries still more elaborate than those of India.

The stories of Osiris, Isis, Horus and Typhon, are direct transcripts of the astronomical scheme. The myths of the Gods Zulis and Memnon, the worship of Heliopolis, the gorgeous order of the famous mysteries, and the mythical personages scattered throughout the wonderful woof of Egyptian Theogony, are but elaborations of the Zodiacal table, and the worship of the powers of nature.

The Chaldeans, Ethiopians, Phoenicians and the most settled of the Arabian tribes, taught the same basic idea in their varied systems of worship.

The disinterred ruins of the once mighty city of Nineveh, is one complete inscription of the Sun-God's history and worship.

The most ingenious and varied symbolisms of Astral and Solar worship, speak in unmistakable tones of evidence from the magnificent remains of Babylon, from the ruins of Tadmor in the Desert, and in innumerable groups of once famous, though now unknown vestiges of human habitation, scattered throughout Central Asia. Even the Troglodyte remains bear witness to the prevalence of Solar worship, in rude carvings and grotesque imitations of the heavenly bodies.

From the ruins profusely scattered throughout Asia Minor, from the land of the Phascanna, Iberians, Albanians, Phrygians and Ionians, the author of this work has collected an immense number of photographic representations of planetary and Solar worship.

The Scythian nations generally worship fire, and preserve traditions of a crucified Sun-God. They celebrate the Sun's birthday on a 25th of December, and amongst some tribes of the Tartars the author has attended all the festal ceremonies described as appertaining to the astronomical religion.

The religions of China and Japan were originally founded on the mythical history of the Sun-God. Many additions and interpolations upon the basic legend have obtained in Chinese and Japanese worship, but the foundation is unique, and the feasts, ceremonial rites and seasons of observance, all prove the parity of worship amongst these people, with the Sabean system.

In the Islands of Ceylon, Java, the Phillipine and Moluccas, various forms of Solar and Astral worship have existed for ages.

The Druidical system of worship, though largely interspersed with other ideas, to be hereafter described, was firmly planted on the Sabean system, and recognized a Sun-God Mediator with a complete Zodiacal history in the incarnated deity they called Hesus.

The entire of the splendid imagery of Grecian and Roman mythology was but a paraphrase of Egyptian Solar worship, enlarged, embellished and beautified by the poetic mentality of Greece and Rome.

The idea of the Great Spiritual Sun of the ancients, the unknown and unknowable, finds its perfect correspondence in the Greek Zeus - the God who dwells alone, and from whom proceed, as subordinate emanations, all the impersonated powers of nature, planetary and astral spirits, who figure in the famous Pantheon. Apollo, Mercury, or Hermes, Bacchus, Prometheus and Esculapius were Sun-Gods, Mediators, Saviors; Ceres, Proserpina and Pluto played their special parts in the Astral Drama, but all derive their names and histories from the same source. Hindoos, Egyptians, Arabians, Parsees, Greeks and Romans, all drank at the same celestial fountain, and only varied their rites, ceremonials, names and figures to suit the ideality of the land whose age or climactic influence determined their intelligence.

The Jews, whose records of war, bloodshed, violence, laws, customs, dresses, upholstery and cuisine, the Christians hold sacred as the inspired word of God, worshiped a Deity who was only one of the Eloihim or astral tutelary spirits of the Egyptians. Bel, Belus, Baal, Baalpeor, Moloch, Dragon, Jehovah, Jah, I am, etc., etc., etc., these, and the names of the various other Gods, or tutelary Deities worshiped by the various nations of Arabia and Asia Minor, including the Jews, are only so many synonyms of the one Mediatorial Sun-God, who, under every conceivable variety of form and title, reappears in the stupendous system of Astral and Solar worship, itself an external expression of the sublime and harmonious order of the universe.

Section V
Sex Worship - Its Antiquity and Meaning

--

Ever interpenetrating the signs and symbols of the astronomical religion, ranging beside its emblems, yet never entirely losing its own individuality, or merging its identity in that of its companion, appears a system of worship, looming up from the antique ages, whose origin and meaning has, until recently, been involved in mystery. The repulsive nature of the subject has, in all probability, caused even the philosophers who had mastered its meaning and understood its symbols, to shrink from exposing their knowledge to the vulgar mind. This will be better understood when we intimate that the esoteric system, to which we allude, is sex worship, or religious belief founded on the assumed sacredness of the order of generation.

Amongst the emblems most commonly seen in this connection are the Phallus or Lingham, the Triangle, all the different methods of exhibiting the Cross, the Serpent with his tail in his mouth, and a vast number of such geometrical signs as include the triangle, cross and circle. Many learned archaeologists are of opinion that sex worship, if it did not actually antedate, is still of as ancient an origin as that of the stars.

The author of this work deems that the primal faith of humanity was unmixed solar and astral worship, but the authoritative reasons for this belief are of little consequence to the general reader. It is enough to say that the emblems of solar and sex worship are so constantly combined in the same monumental remains, that we must infer both were understood, and in a measure reduced to systematic expression, at this earliest period where man began to leave records of his thoughts.

There are no shadows without a substance, no fables without a genuine idea to allegorize upon.

The fable of the Garden of Eden, the temptation and fall of man, is very generally assumed by materialistic writers to have a purely astronomical origin, and to have been founded on the following astral order. The August constellation of the Virgin, represents a woman holding a flower, sprig or fruit in her hand, beckoning to Botes or Joseph, the constellation a little to the north of the Virgin, but in close proximity to her. This configuration of the heavenly signs, it is alleged, may be as often interpreted into the fabled relations of Adam and Eve as the Virgin Mary and Joseph. The radiance, bloom and beauty of the season in which these constellations appear, signifies the earthly Eden. The astral woman tempts the astral man, she herself is tempted by the Serpent, who presently appears in the skies as the Great Dragon. The woman gives of the fruit she holds to man, he eats and falls. The Cherubim and Seraphim of the skies (the typical signs of constellated stars), drive them forth from the Eden of Summer into the gloom and famine of Winter. To restore the fallen man to a future paradise, a Savior must be found, and this is effected in the birth of the Sun-God, at midwinter, and his renovating influence during the succeeding Spring and Summer.

To accept of this fable without allowing for a spiritual significance concealed beneath it, is equivalent to the assumption that the ancients actually worshiped the sun, moon and stars as personal Gods; but the ancients never enunciated sacred ideas except in allegorical forms of speech, and never mapped out the scheme of an allegory without a profoundly spiritual meaning veiled by it.

"As it is above, so it is below," "On the earth as in the skies," were the sentences by which the mystics of old were accustomed to affirm the universal correspondence between the harmonies of the natural and spiritual in every department of being.

To understand how the ancients interpreted these astral hieroglyphics into such a system as would explain the fall of man, and yet preserve the correspondence between his estate on earth and the movement of the heavenly bodies, it is necessary to revert to the theory enunciated in Section I, where it was shown that the Soul originally dwelt in a purely spiritual state of existence; but being tempted by the craving desire for earthly knowledge, it became attracted to this planet - incarnated in the form of man - and hence " the fall" of spirit into matter. With all that reverence which finite being must feel when it presumes to speculate on infinity, we may imagine that the form of the highest spiritual existences may admit of no parts or angles, but may be, indeed, like the perfection of the spiritual Sun, a globe; but all organic forms are sections of the perfect sphere, and man is obviously a complex assemblage of lines and circles, united in himself all the details of mathematical proportion, subordinate to the perfection of figure assumed to exist in the Spiritual Sun.

In taking on a material existence, therefore, and changing from a purely spiritual entity to become an organized material being, the first principle of earthly life to be evolved must needs be the means to produce and reproduce it.

This, in an earthly state of being, is just as sacred and paramount a theme as the formation of worlds, and the birth of suns and systems in the aggregate of the Universe.

As the function of creation is the highest and most wonderful with which the mind can invest Deity, so the imitative law must become the noblest and most sacred function of God's creatures. In the beginning of earthly existence, we believe it was thus esteemed, and in those remote ages when sex worship was incorporated into a religious system, the highest and noblest elements of human thought clustered around the subject of generation, elevating it to the topmost pinnacle of human worship.

As the clear intuitions of the early man carried him back to his state of primeval, spiritual innocence, and recognized in his birth into matter a descent in the scale of being synonymous with the idea of a fall, so he imagined he perceived the order of this scheme mapped out in the constelled Zodiac of the skies. As he recognized the generative functions to be the immediate means of the Soul's birth into matter, so he elevated them into divine significance and set up the emblems as fit subjects for religious reverence. In process of time the instinctive appetites of man's sensual nature stimulated sex worship into excess, and degraded a holy idea into gross licentiousness. But this was the abuse, not the true origin of sex worship. Physical generation was once esteemed as the gate by which the Soul entered upon the stupendous pathway of progress, and became fitted for its angelic destiny in the celestial heavens; but, like all sacred ideas when translated into matter, the law of physical generation came to be regarded as mere physical enjoyment; it sank into sensuality, and hence the necessity which the wise and philosophic priesthood of old perceived, of veiling all teachings on this subject in mysteries, and expressing all ideas in its connection in obscure symbolism.

There are marked evidences in the vestiges of antiquity as to how the sexual idea encroached upon the forms of Solar worship.

The primitive conceptions of creation were exalted, sublime; but when the idea of sex worship became universal, even the Astral religion became imbued with its materialistic influence. The impersonations of the stars and the powers of nature were divided into male and female.

The story of creation was woven into romantic legends of amorous Gods and Goddesses; the emblems of generation were profusely interspersed with astronomical signs and any description of animal, however loathsome, as long as it was remarkable for procreative power, became deified as a type of the creative energy.

To those who esteem the spiritual idea as antagonistic to the material, and believe with the most exalted of the Essences, that in heaven, angelic essences are pure and free from all the impulses and attributes of matter, it must indeed have seemed a fall for the Soul to descend to earth and become incarnate only through the process of physical generation. And yet such is obviously the law of physical being. In the order of the Universe, spirit is the primal essence in which there is neither sex, age, sin, nor capacity for pain.

With the descent of Soul into physical life, man becomes dual, male and female, with sex as the dividing line between them. Then, too, ensues that mysterious transformation of the soul's faculties which converts spiritual love into material passion, institutional knowledge into human reason, boundless perception into dim memory and vague prescience, eternal things into temporal, and a creature without parts or passions, into one all organs, and swayed by every emotion that ranges from the depths of vice to the heights of virtue.

The brief race on earth run, spiritual spheres of progress opening up fresh avenues of purification to the pilgrim Soul, still preserving all the faculties acquired by its birth and association with matter, the celestial Angel stands related to the germ spirit, as the fully unfolded blossom to the embryonic seed. In this order of progress it is clearly shown that the means whereby the spirit-dweller of the original Eden becomes the perfected Angel of a celestial heaven, are: mortal birth, a pilgrimage through spheres of trial, discipline and purification, and an organism made up of separate parts with appropriate functions, the due and legitimate exercise of which constitute the methods of progress. In such a scheme, every trial and suffering has its meaning, and every passion (even the tendencies to vice and crime), their use in shaping the rudimental Angel, through remorse and penalty, into ultimate strength and divine proportion.

A familiar but apposite illustration of the relative difference between the germ spirit that descends from realms of primeval innocence to be born into matter, and that same spirit unfolded through spheres of discipline into the perfected Angel, is found, if we liken the two states to those of the acorn and the full-grown oak.

The one is still the oak in germ, but the noble proportions of the tree, its overshadowing branches, the vast girth of its mighty trunk, the splendor of its Briareus arms wide-stretched to the winds, with its ten thousand leafy hands tossed abroad on the ambient air; its rich harvest of countless germs, and the unborn forests that are to be furnished from their reproductive powers, all grow out of the association of the primal acorn with the formative matrix of earth.

Even so it is with the Soul. To become an Angel it must first be a Man, then a Spirit, struggling on through spheres of graduated unfoldment, and when all is done, the Soul originally expelled from its Eden of innocence and ignorance will regain it with the strength, wisdom and love with alone can constitute it an Angel of God.

It was with this perception of the Soul's destiny that the ancients esteemed the generative functions as divine, and the deification of their emblems as an act of religious duty. Whilst we believe this view of the origin of sex worship the true one, those who regard it simply from the standpoint of results, and contemplate the abominations practiced in its celebration, might well believe it to be the offspring of man's merely animal and instinctive nature; such it undoubtedly became when it sank into that corruption and abuse which too often attends the decadence of ideas, however exalted in their source. There was much, too, in the Jewish Theogony to favor the tendency to excess in sex worship.

Throughout the writings of the Pentateuch the utmost importance is attached to the production of offspring. Every means was adopted by the priestly law-givers to promote the propagation of the species.

Childless women were branded with the bitterest reproach. Dunuchs or persons afflicted with personal blemishes were forbidden to hold sacred offices. Every inducement which a stringent law could hold out to compel the people to "multiply and replenish the earth" was an essential of the Jewish religion. On the other hand, the prophetic writings of the Jews abound with fulminations of the Divine wrath against those who carried their ideas of sex worship to excess and sensualism. The unsparing denunciations of the Hebrew prophets against the practice of sacrificing to "strange Gods," are accompanied by the plainest descriptions of what those sacrificial rites were, and give color to the belief that the religious veneration which had once sanctified the idea of the generative functions as a divine mystery, had sunk into an all-pervading and soul-corrupting sensualism.

In comparison with Egypt, Chaldea, Assyria and Hindo-stan, Judea was but a modern nation.

The nomadic tribes of the Jews had made no mark on the world's history when Egypt was hoary with age, and India had recorded cycles of time, lost in the night of antiquity. The exoteric remains of solar and sex worship, together with all their signs and symbols, presented to the Jews only a dying vestige of faiths of whose resplendent maturity no historic epoch, however remote, can show an authentic record.

We only know it must have been so. Maps of the heavens, and perfected charts of astral motions, involving intricate calculations, which must have required thousands of years to arrive at, were all handed down from pre-historic to the commencement of historic times, and that with a completeness which fully sustains the enormous claims of the Hindoos for the existence of their dynasty during cycles of time which baffle the human mind to conceive of.

How many times have the silent but most eloquent catacombs of the old earth, in the form of upturned plains, the beds of rivers, the depths of artesian wells, and the recesses of newly discovered caverns, brought to light conclusive testimony that man lived, labored, wrought in clay, stone, pottery and metals, tens of thousands of years ago, on the face of the earth!

The author has himself spent years in India studying out that wonderful system of numerals which point to the antiquity of man, and the fact that he commenced astronomical calculations more than twenty thousand years ago. Some of these silent voices indicate axial changes in this planet which could not have transpired in less than a hundred thousand years. Others prove that the Hindoos clearly understood the precession of the equinoxes ages before the Christian era.

About the commencement of that period the colossal forms of the mystic Sphinx might have been found in long and majestic rows in the various temples of old India, and yet the mystery of the Sphinx could only have been solved by a people who had correctly understood the precession of the equinoxes. To effect a change in the position of the sun in the Zodiacal path from one sign to another must occupy at least 2140 years; and yet such changes had occurred, been fully calculated and recorded in the astronomical riddle of the Sphinx, a composite figure, designed to celebrate the sun's passage from the sign of the Virgin to that of the Lion, when the Jews were unknown as a people.

What amount of intellectual power had the mind of man arrived at ere these records of astronomical lore, mechanical skill and artistic power were achieved?

The remains of tropical plants now found amidst the awful desolation of the Arctic and Antarctic regions - the constant stream of revelation silently but surely upheaving its mystic writings from the superincumbent debris under which the earth of a million years ago lies buried - the stony voices that thunder through the colossal remains of ruined cities, and the swift but immutable footprints of the fiery squadrons whose march through the skies, the mind of man has followed up through ages of unrecorded time, all proclaim that the movements of the Universe transpire in spiral and ever-revolving cycles.

Like the path of the sun on the Ecliptic, now ascending on the royal arch of the northern hemisphere, now descending into the southern bow, but ever moving in gyrating circles upward, typifying the march of planets, nations, ages of time and human souls, so that those who study the part may comprehend the whole, all these stupendous witnesses figure out the laws by which cycles of civilization are born, grow, ascend to their culminating point of splendor, then turn the hill of time, descend lower and lower into engulfing depths, lower and lower into corruption, degradation, death! And yet they rise again, and, Phoenix-like, spring from the funeral ashes of their pyre to be reborn in nobler, higher forms of younger civilizations.

So has it been with man and his religious beliefs. Solar and sex worship, born of man's highest conceptions of the Divine plan, rose into an almost perfect science, the science by which the antique man perceived the correspondence between the earth and the heavens, the Creator and his creatures. This famous era of ancient civilization culminated, crossed the equinox of prophetic death, descended into the night of corruption and sensualism, and perished with the closing up of Oriental dynasties.

The real spiritual truths of antiquity have never died; but yet their exhibition has only at times illuminated the ages with coruscation of light, so little understood that their holy radiance has been mistaken for the baleful glare of "Supernaturalism." They have never died; but, as yet, they only give promise, not a full assurance, of the resurrection that is at hand.

Mankind, absorbed in its devotion to the pursuits of material science, has ignored its spiritual interests, or carelessly committed them to the charge of an ignorant and selfish Priesthood; but when the day of true spiritual awakening comes, then the Soul of the Universe shall be known and felt in the Souls of His Creatures, the light of this spiritual revelation will shine upon husks and figments of the dead past, of which reason, no less than intuition will be ashamed. It will show the lifeless bodies of ancient faiths, from which the soul has long fled, leaving nothing but dust and ashes, forms and ceremonies, surplices and shaven crowns behind.

It will show the painted Clown and many colored Harlequins of an ecclesiastical circus still performing their dreary tricks in an amphitheatre from which the stately personages of the grand Drama have vanished, where the curtain has fallen, the lights are quenched, on which the eternal midnight of a dead age has set in, with nothing to relieve the silence but the fluttering wings of the spectral ideas which already begin to flit forth into the morning of a new day, seeking the resurrecting life and light of a new Spiritual religion.

Supplement To Section V
Sex Worship – Continued

--

The explorers of ancient India, Egypt, Greece and Rome have wisely distrusted the propriety of giving very graphic representations or close descriptions of their monumental remains.

Most of the popular writers on these lands have contented themselves with hinting that Phallic worship prevailed amongst the ancients, and that its emblems are abundantly interspersed with other records; but the truth is, that all the records are overlaid with emblems of Phallic worship, and that there is scarcely a monument or inscription of antiquity which does not, in some form or other, perpetuate the idea of Solar or Sex worship, or both.

Nearly all the Scriptural names have a direct bearing upon sexual ideas. Every title, including the syllables El, Om, On, Di and Mi, signify the same ideas. The titles ascribed to the Sun and the Generative Gods are mutually convertible, and both are continually bestowed upon the Gods of the ancients.

Adonis, Elijah, Elisha, El, Bael, Belus, Jehovah, Jah, Abraham, Samson, Jachin, Boaz, Adam, Eve, Mary, Esau, Edom, Zeus, Jupiter, Thor, Odin, Sol, Helios, Asher, Dyonisus, etc., etc., etc., are all names significant of sexual ideas.

Most of the names bestowed on Hindoo, Egyptian, Greek, Roman and Hebrew Gods bear the same interpretation, or else are applicable, in a double sense, to Solar and Sex worship. The names of the twelve tribes of Israel have direct reference to the generative functions; and thus are Bible names and Bible terms put into the mouths of innocent, lisping children as "the word of God," a word which, if interpreted in all the fullness of its meaning, would crimson the cheek of every virtuous matron with shame.

Up to the days when European civilization prevailed, and the influence of a temperate, equatorial climate moderated the excessive energy of that emotional nature which man inherits from his association with matter, stimulated to immense activity in the fervid heat of tropical climes, his religious aspirations were all tinctured with the idiosyncrasies of his physical nature. He deemed of his God as of himself.

The sublime beauty of the spangled heavens, the obvious correspondence of heat, light and planetary influence with his material well-being, and the final mystery and power of the generative functions, were the most direct and natural appeals that he could find in the universe to his sense of reverence and his ideas of power. Is it any marvel that he worshiped the heavenly host and deemed the laws of generation the most direct representations of Deific action in creation?

The chief symbols of these interblended systems are found in the various forms of crosses extant; in the Phallus or Lingham, and the Yoni, the male and female emblems of generation; in the triangle or Tau, the origin of the cross, the Serpent who in so many ways was esteemed as a deific emblem, and every object, natural or artificial, which bore the least resemblance to the figures enumerated above.

As regards the cross, it has frequently been attempted to show that it owes its sacred character to the instrument of punishment upon which the Christian's God was supposed to have suffered death.

Ages before the Jews were known as a nation, the cross was regarded all through the East as a sacred symbol.

To remove the obscenity of the idea attached to its original meaning, from the image, which modern civilization so devoutly cherished, it has been urged that it was reverenced by the Egyptians, because it was used as a Nileometer or measure of the river Nile. Granting this, and admitting that the Nile was held sacred by the Egyptians as the source of plenty and irrigation, hence, that the Nileometer, with its upright post and cross-piece to mark the height to which the water attained, was also held sacred as an emblem of redemption from famine, or a sign of possible destruction, still this does not account for the prevalence of the cross nor the reverence attached to it in lands where no Nileometer was required, and in distant ages ere Nileometers were invented.

Sculptured over every temple of the East, the cross in many forms was used to signify the generative power.

It was originally designed to represent a Trinity, and thus gave rise to the sacredness attached to the number three, with all its multiples, and in all the varieties of form in which the cross is found from the plain letter T, the Tau of the Scandinavians, or the hammer of Thor, to the eight-sided cross of the Templars, and in all its variousness it signified and does signify, nothing more or less than the fertility, fecundity and creative structure of the masculine principle of generation. The fact that the sun's two chief incidents of Zodiacal travel were the crossings of the Ecliptic plane at Spring and Autumn, deepened the reverence which antique nations cherished for this all-prevailing symbol, but instead of removing it from the earth to the skies, it simply showed in this dual significance, the unity of design expressed throughout the cosmic motions or the universe.

The female emblem was signified by an unit, a circle, a boat shaped shell, a lozenge, or any object, animate or inanimate, that resembled these figured, or implied receptivity, fruitfulness or maternity. The union of the female unit with the male triad, was designed by the sacred and mystic number 4, or symbolized by a serpent with his tail in his mouth, two fishes bent to form a circle, the rite of circumcision, and many other symbolical rites and figures.

The origin of Serpent worship arose first from the universal prevalence of these creatures throughout the Orient; the extreme subtlety of their natures implying wisdom, the custom of casting their skins denoting renewed youth and immortality, their tremendous and deadly powers of destruction, analogous to the "wrath of God," their supposed healing virtue indicative of the life-giving power of the sun, the glory of their shining scales imitating light; but, above all, the Serpent was deified as the antagonistic power of the skies, defined in the great constellation of the Dragon, which did annual war with the heavenly legions of the sun.

Endless were the fables invented to typify the wisdom and life-giving properties of serpents; endless the myths in which they figured as the representatives of good and evil Genii.

Serpent worship is, in all probability, as old as Sex and Solar worship, and a thorough understanding of the three systems forms a clue to all the signs, symbols, allegories and mysteries of all the ancient faiths that prevailed before the Christian era.

The ideas indicated by these symbols, and the legends attached to them, underlie all those stupendous rites, solemn mysteries and gigantic monuments of art that have overlaid the once splendid Orient with ruins that will remain the mystery and admiration of the race till time shall be no more. The myths and symbols of these interblended systems prevailed indeed long after the Christian era, and were preserved by the Gnostics, Manicheans, Neo Platonists, and many of the early sects amongst Christians and Philosophic Greeks; they are preserved and prevail amongst the most civilized of sects to-day, but alas! without any real appreciation of the ideas that once vitalized the images.

Much of the mysticism of the "Divine Plato," and the numerical wisdom of Pythagoras, owed their identity to the esoteric meaning veiled in Oriental symbolism.

The famous mysteries of Eleusis, the Bacchic and Dyonisian rites, the feats in honor of Ceres, the orgies of Cybele, and other mythical personages of the Greek Pantheon; ancient masonry, both speculative and operative, and its degraded and imbecile descendant, modern masonry, founded their origin upon the basic principles of these ancient systems of worship, and the mass of legendary lore to which they gave rise.

Curious as would be the tracery of these primitive roots through all the tendrils, branches and reproductive germs that have overlaid the world with theological systems, the work must be reserved for another place and time, and this part of our subject must close with a few words in evidence of the lamentable tendency to degeneracy which all great ideas suffer when they outlive their day and usefulness; whilst the ark of the tabernacle survives through the sacred flame that of old dwelt between the Cherubim and Seraphim is quenched in eternal night.

Throughout the churches of Christendom, the name of the Most High God, the Alpha and Omega of Being, the Great Spirit who dwells alone and unknown in central orgs of primal light, is scarcely remembered, and ever subordinated to the worship of the Cross, with all its varieties of expression and form.

The myth of the Sun-God reappears in every phase of the Christian's creed.

The surplices, robes and fantastic adornments of high ecclesiasticism, are simply imitations of the women's garments which the priests of antiquity wore to indicate that God was both male and female.

The bells and holy candles, the Lambs, Bulls, Eagles, Men, Lions, and twelve apostolic personages, the Serpents, etc., etc., which cast their prismatic glory from costly painted windows on the chequered marbles of the floor beneath, are all but so many astronomical signs of antique fire worship, or emblems of sexual religion. The very shape of the steeples that crown the "houses of God" are mementos of the reverence accorded to the sacred flame, or veiled effigies of the "divine Lingham."

It would be equally painful and humiliating to analyze the mythical character of every sign and symbol of modern ecclesiasticism, were we not deeply, reverentially conscious that the spirit that no longer vivifies the dead husks of extinct faiths, still pervades the earth, still manifests its undying love for poor, idolatrous humanity, still illumines the heart, and sustains the drooping tendrils of that religion which erects its altar in the soul, and finds its most imperishable shrine in the depths of man's spiritual consciousness.

Witnesses, too - witnesses on the sensuous plane of life - are not wanting to the truth of this undying spiritual influx, permeating every age, and adapting its revelations to all forms of faith that recognize spiritual existence.

Like the waving lines of the shining Ecliptic, over bounding yet ever sustaining the sun-like progress of human destiny, comes down the ages the tracery of an all-pervading realm of spiritual existence, at once the cause and effect of earthly being.

Soul and spiritual essence is the God and the procedure, the Creator and the creature; all things else are phantasmagoric shapes, born of the hour, as formative moulds in which the soul essences grow, perishing with the hour when their office is ended.

Were it not for the assurance that there is a realm of spirit adequate to produce, sustain and guide the tangled woof of creation, the pictures we have drawn, however faithful to the exoteric history of the race, would be but a temporary assemblage of dust and ashes heaped together into grotesque and incomprehensible images. With this compass to steer our way through the restless billows of life's storm-tossed ocean, we may rise and sink, drift far and wide of our mark, stagnate for awhile on the sluggish sea of materialism, or seem to founder amidst the foam-crested upheavals of convulsed opinions, but we are in the hands of that Love that will never forsake us, that Wisdom that is all-sufficient to direct us, that Power that is almighty to save us.

"God lives and reigns!" said stout-hearted Martin Luther, when, standing alone, he bore testimony to his faith before princes, potentates and the opposing force of earth's assembled great ones.

His strength is ours, and in that strength we can afford to stand by and watch the wreck of empires and dynasties, ecclesiastical faiths and man-made dogmas.

We are immortal parts of the immortal Soul of the Universe, and we never can be lost, or perish out of his hand.

Section VI
Subordinate Gods in the Universe
--

When the Spiritual in human history first dominated the mind, is as impossible to ascertain as who was the first man.

A celebrated materialistic writer of the eighteenth century says: "The idea of subordinate Gods becomes a necessary sequence to the acknowledgment of deific existence at all, and it would be as useless to search for the country or time when Gods, Spirits and Angels were first believed in, as to attempt ascertaining the locality and period where and when religious worship began." This is essentially true, though an adversary writes it.

The origin of man's belief in Deity must be supplemented by his acceptance of intermediate spiritual existences, for the Soul which is the witness of the one, proclaims the other, and the chief difference between the opinions on these points is, that whilst the deepest and most incommunicable emotions of the Soul rest on its Author and Finisher, Deity, the senses may bear witness to the presence and operation of subordinate Spiritual existences in the phenomena that attend their ministrations.

It is enough to affirm that the vestiges of humanity in every country and age, bear testimony to man's belief in the ministry and interposition in human affairs of orders or beings both superior and inferior to mortals, operating for good and evil, but always through methods beyond the power of mortal achievement, appealing to the senses through modes of action not possible to man without their aid, and after a fashion which proves them to be limited by none of the known laws of nature.

From the days when the most ancient Sanscrit writings laid down modes of invoking spirits, described their qualities and influences, and prescribed the conditions under which mortals should hold communion with them, up to the nineteenth century, when the "spiritualists who permeate every land of civilization, point their little tracts descriptive of the best means of forming 'circles' for the purpose of evoking spirit presence and communion, there never was an age or time when man in some form or other did not believe in Spiritual existences subordinate to the Deity; in the means of communing with them, and in their influence on human action for good or evil."

From the collected opinions of the Hindoos, Chaldeans, Persians, Jews, Hebrew and Oriental Cabbalists, Talmudists, Greeks and Romans, as well as from the author's own personal experience with spirits of different orders and grades, we present the following special summary of ideas concerning the various degrees of Spiritual existences in the Universe.

Whilst nearly every nation of antiquity deemed of God as the Demiurgus; neither male nor female, yet both; as of a Central Source of life, light, heat and creative energy, one alone, yet incomprehensible, uncreated and indestructible, all taught of subordinate procedures from Him. The first of these was a Divine Being corresponding to the Bramah of the Hindoo Trinity, the Osiris of Egypt, the Ormuzd of Persia, the Logos of Philo, the Adam Kadman of the Cabbalists.

The idea embodied in this Eheogony was that in the Deity resided the masculine principle of Power, and the feminine of Wisdom, called by the Cabbalists En Soph and Sophia. From the incomprehensible union of these two proceeded a third, the Logos, or Word, through which the will of God became manifest in expression -that is, in the evolution of forms - worlds, suns, systems, reproductive germs, and realms of progressive being. In this stupendous system, the superior emanations were Gods, directing the birth, formation and destinies of worlds; then came Archangels, charged with missions of Almighty power and wisdom. To them succeeded legions of Angels, some entrusted with the direction of Planets, Earths, Nations, Cities and Societies, hence called "Tutelary Angels," and worshiped as Gods. Others, exercising rule in specific groups, and classified by Hebrew Cabbalists as "Thrones, Dominions, Powers."

The division of Angels and Spirits into grand Hierarchies, Legions, and specific offices of divine ministration, would occupy a volume, and give a vast and exalted perception of the antique view of Spiritual existence. Descending from the grander scale of angelic ministration recited above, we notice that the Sages and Seers of antiquity identified certain spirits as the inspiring agencies of art, science, different branches of industry, and all the occupations of social, artistic, and even commercial life. The Hebrew Scriptures continually declare that God put it into the heart of such and such individuals to work in brass or wood, fine linen, or rich coloring. In the direct and intuitional communion with Spiritual existences enjoyed by the Hebrews, it was assumed that all good or exceptionally great powers resulted from inspiration, and, as explained in the New Testament, those were called Gods, to whom the word of God came; so when the terms God, or Lord, were made use of to signify the source of the idea, Spiritual influence was the kernel implied in the expression.

Below all the inspiring agencies for good were assumed to exist legions of evil spirits, almost as numerous, and scarcely less powerful to tempt and destroy, than good Angels were to bless.

Between these two realms of opposing powers were ranged human Souls, not only in their incarnate forms of mortal being, but also as disembodied spirits, vast realms of spiritual existence being assigned to them, interpenetrating and surrounding the earth, through which, in successive stages of growth and progress, the pilgrim Soul was permitted to win its way back to the celestial state from which it had fallen by mortal birth.

Every human Soul was supposed to attract to itself from the moment of birth two Spirits, the one powerful to influence for good, the other for evil. These Spirits were called by the ancients good and evil Genii; and the natural proclivities to vice or virtue in the individual to whom they ministered were supposed to be stimulated or exalted, according as the Soul gave head to the inspiration of the tempter, or the counsellor.

Besides the realms of being above enumerated, it was claimed that other orders existed, neither wholly good or purely evil; neither entirely spiritual, nor actually material in their natures; creatures of the elements, corresponding in their state, power and function, to the different elements in the universe, and filling up all the realms of space with uncounted legions of embryonic and rudimental forms.

These being were, by reason of their semi-spiritual nature, invisible to man, and, because of the gross tincture of matter in their composition, unable to discern any orders of being but themselves, except through rare and exceptional rifts in their atmospheric surroundings. They corresponded to the ether, air, atmosphere, water, earth, minerals, plants and different elements of which the earth and the universe generally is composed. Some of these beings were malicious and antagonistic to man, and others harmless and good. All exerted power, especially in the direction of the element to which they corresponded; they were said to be endowed with graduated degrees of intelligence, and to have bodies subject to the laws of birth, growth, change and death.

From being invisible to man, except through rare or prepared conditions, they were termed spirits; from being embryonic, rudimentary and attached only to certain fragments of the universe, they were termed Elementaries. Every plant and every world, every dew-drop and every sun, sustained swarms of this parasitical life, so that there was not an atom of matter but what was redolent of it. Had the ancients been acquainted with the powers of the microscope, they would doubtless have classed the infusoria and animalculae revealed by this wondrous instrument with the realms of elementary spirits. Be this as it may, it was assumed that, as their existence was only rudimentary, and the evidences of that divine trinity which in man constitutes an immortal being, namely, matter, force and spirit, was lacking, so they had no soul and were not immortal. It was also taught of the Elementaries, that though they propagated their species, were animated by will and some share of intelligence, lived their term of life, and died, still they possessed no concrete, self-conscious principle of being sufficiently developed to enable the spiritual essence that escaped at death to become individualized, and retain a recollection of its past, or a personal consciousness of its own identity. Thence it was taught that the spiritual essence of the disintegrated organism was gathered up in death and passed into some more advanced form of being; that each successive birth purified its nature and enlarged its capacity; in fact, that it was life, instinct, and matter, in progressive stages of existence, and that this progress continued until the most rudimental sparks of spiritual being expanded into fully developed spiritual blossoms, attained to the glory and dignity of self-conscious spiritual entities, gravitated to spiritual spheres, and from thence became attracted to earth, entered into the Soul principle of man, and thus united him in essence with all the lower forms of being, and themselves commenced a self-conscious and immortal stage of fresh ascending pilgrimages.

"The spheres of elementary existence," says a famous Oriental Cabbalist, "are as numerous and their orders as rife with variety and function as are the earth's planets, suns, systems, and realms of ether."

There cannot be a grain of matter but has its corresponding spiritual counterpart. Ranging from the infinitely large to the infinitely little, from a world to a monad, all things in the universe of matter are supplemented by an universe of spirit, and it is as unreasonable to suppose that mighty suns and resplendent planets should be destitute of Providential law, order, guidance and maintenance, through deific tutelary Angels, as that a sand-grain or a dew-drop should be left to the direction of its own unaided and non-intelligent movements. All, all, are but external expressions of the immortal soul, which in fragments and atoms suited to the thing it vitalizes, animates, permeates and sustains all being, even as the Soul of man vitalizes his material structure."

We have given this teaching as a compendium of antique and chiefly Oriental thought; but we now preface all farther attempts at elucidating the subject matter of this work, by claiming every iota of this philosophy to be the truth, as it appears to the mind of the author.

From long years of communion with spirits of every grade, high and low, perfected and rudimental; from the privilege of wandering in their spheres in the clairvoyant condition, from visits made spiritually to the realms of elementary being where the poor, imperfect dwellers beheld in the astral body of their visitant an imaginary God, from dreams, trances, visions, open and oral communication with angelic beings and ministering spirits, and author insists that the doctrines herein enunciated are transcripts of the order of the Universe, as clearly laid down as the half-prophetic, half-bedimmed vision of humanity can apprehend it, and that, whether accepted or rejected, it contains holy truths, which belong to the best interests of humanity to comprehend; revealments which our fathers understood, and we have lost sight of, from our undue devotion to material interests, and our blind fanaticism in ignoring all spiritual research save such as comes through an effete and materialistic ecclesiasticism.

We are quite aware that if this volume should fall into the hands of one-idead, self-styled scientists, the avowal of faith just recorded will amply justify such readers in committing the work to the flames as the ravings of a lunatic. Should it be read by any of those presumptuous and narrow-minded Spiritualists who assume that there is no other realm of spiritual being than that occupied by their own particular familiars, we anticipate the wail of denunciation they will raise, insisting that no theory can be true, or worth studying, that has not been spelled out by their rapping spirits, declared in doggrel rhymes through their semi-tranced media, or lisped out in comical broken English, by the spirits of "little Indian maids," or "big braves," once renowned for eloquence and wisdom, but transformed through mediumistic witchery, into imbeciles and buffoons. Should it be read by the too devoted followers of the soul-illuminated Seer of Sweden, who cannot admit of any truth which the mind of Swedenborg failed to grasp, they will say, these writings are dictated by lying spirits, and that, because he, the conservator and revelator of all truth to the minds of the bigoted, affirmed, that all angels, even the highest that moved around the throne of God, "had once been men."

Should these pages fall into the hands of the intelligent modern Spiritualist whose incessant watch-word is "light, more light!" his comment will be, "this may be true or false, but because I don't know it to-day, I will endeavor to prove it to-morrow, and accept or reject it, only as I can prove it."

Should the work fall into the hands of a learned "Pagan," well-read "Heathen," or instructed Orientalist, he will say, "Surely this writer has heard the voices of the Oracles; beheld the glories of the mysteries; and sat at the feet of the Sages, who quaffed from the eternal fountain of revelation!

"He is an initiate - a Hierophant - a Brother who speaks the word of truth known only to the few; the Master's Word is whispered in these pages, thrilling through the bones to the very marrow of humanity."

According to some, but not by any means the most intelligent or best educated of the American Spiritualists, there is no God at all, only a "principle," and nothing higher in the scale of being than the spirits of their deceased friends and kindred; but these materialistic philosophers form but a small part of that intelligent nation of thinkers, and their teachings have but little weight beyond a few score of poor people, who gather together, and in grandiloquent phraseology congratulate each other on being the great I Ams of the Universe.

The majority of persons convinced by wonderful signs and tokens in America, that the souls of men live and communicate to their friends on earth, have seemed to the author to be waiting for some philosophy or revelation that should carry them beyond this one isolated fact, and reduce spiritual existence and human life to correspondential and appreciable doctrines of science.

Would that these humble writings might aid to practicalize their noble aspirations!

The sacred books of Hermes, once supposed to have been the most ancient writings in the world, but now more generally deemed to have been copies of the Hindoo Vedas, transplanted from India into Egypt, give most elaborate accounts of the different orders of angelic beings in the Universe, and render descriptions of the spiritual counterparts of every plant, mineral, raindrop or speck of dust in the earth and its atmosphere.

Eusebius, the Christian Bishop of Caesarea, who wrote in the fourth century of the Christian era, claimed to have been familiar with these famous Hermetic writings. He says they often repeat the question: "Have you not been told that all spirits are sparks from the Divine Soul of the Universe; Gods, Demons, Souls, yet in their variousness all emanations from Him?"

Jamblichus, quoting from the same source, writes: "From this one came all Gods that be; all souls, all spirits, good and bad, and many that be neither very wicked nor yet good.

"There be many kinds of spiritual essences besides soul, as spirits of the earth, the sea, running waters, and even some that do inhabit the holes of reptiles that live on the banks of rivers, or the depth of mines......Their abiding places cannot so much as be named, without enumerating all the secret corners of the earth......That these spirits are often under the dominion of man, is as true as that they may be transformed by the arch enemy of mankind into instruments of ill, to work the deeds of darkness, in which he delights."

Lao-Kiun, a contemporary of the great Chinese Sage Confucius, founded a school, which, for the spirituality of its doctrines, far transcended the teachings of Confuscius. His text of religious faith was: "Tao (meaning God) produced one; one produced two, two produced three, and three produced all things."

During the lifetime of this philosopher, a book containing the names and offices of innumerable companies of spirits was found, as it was asserted, suspended on the royal gate of Pekin, placed there by no mortal hand and supposed to be full of direct revelations from heaven.

This miraculous volume is said to have contained magical formulae for the evocation and control of spirits; directions how to cast out devils and heal diseases; also the profoundest secrets of alchemy, namely the composition of the philosopher's stone and the elixir vitae.

To satisfy the bigotry and superstitious fears of succeeding generations, this book, together with all other magical writings, was destroyed. Still, it was asserted that private copies had been made and circulated of its contents. From a curious and very ancient roll of MSS, in the royal library of Pekin, the author has had the privilege of copying a fine astrological chart, and a magical evocation of elementary spirits, assumed to have been first written in the aforesaid book.

In Chaldea, the only great nation of antiquity in which Phallic and Yonic emblems are not found, proving by the universal prevalence of pure astronomical symbols, the extreme antiquity of the worship there practiced, a belief in various ascending and descending grades of spirits and angels, everywhere speaks out from the mighty and stupendous ruins. The same belief, only on a much more elaborate scale, was cherished amongst the Medes and Persians, and taught in all its minutiae by Zoroaster.

The universal prevalence of image worship throughout the East is due to the idea that the spirits of Stars, Planets, Angels, Seraphs, Chrubs and Elementary Spirits could be attracted to their images, when consecrated under magical formulae, and not only fix the worshipers' minds upon the spirits represented in the images, but actually draw them into these material receptacles. The strange and grotesque forms of consecrated images may thus be accounted for.

The winged Bull of Nineveh was the personification of the Cherubim. The winged Serpent represented the Seraphim.

The immense number of insects, birds and animals esteemed as sacred, and rendered homage to in animal images, were all supposed to be attended by spiritual essences, whose power resided in the particular shape of the creatures venerated.

The Persian Theogony not only includes all the ideas we have dwelt upon in other systems, but is divided by Zoroaster into interminable chains of Spiritual existences, two of whom, one good and another evil, is assigned as an Attendant "Ferver," to every living creature. Besides these, are hosts of Elementary Spirits, assumed to exert a beneficent or malignant influence upon every particle of the vegetable and animal kingdoms. Zoroaster's system, like that of the ancient Hindoos and Egyptians, was full of high moral teachings, and, save for the cruelty and reckless waste of life manifested in its system of sacrificial rites, forms a code of ethics not inferior to the sweetness and beauty of the teachings ascribed to Jesus of Nazareth. here as in Cabalism, Spirit is assumed to be a primal essence, containing the archetypes of all ideas. God is the one central source of light. Ormuzd the first Divine emanation, the King of Light. Mithra and Arimanes, the next procedures, are representatives of the resplendent God of Light, heat and goodness, and the terrific prince of cold, darkness and evil. All created forms are patterned after the archetypal ideas existing in the Divine Mind, and endless chains of good and evil Spirits, Angels, Genii and Elementaries, fill up all spaces in the invisible realms in which matter floats.

As in Chaldea, the most renowned methods of interpreting the will of God were by soothsaying and divination, so in Persia the favorite resort was to Astrology. The Persians claimed that the Stars were divine Scriptures, in which the order of visible nature was plainly mapped out; that the numerous changes and configurations of the heavenly bodies produced relative changes in the simplicity of the scheme indicated on the path of the Zodiac. That each star had its special influence upon the plant or living creature which was born during its ascendency.

Minerals, earths, waters and places, were directly governed by planetary influence. The mind was governed by the phases of the moon. All colored objects or glittering stones by the sun or one of the six planets; in fact, the rise and fall of nations and the destinies of individuals were spelled out by Persian Astrologers on the starry heavens, and he would have been considered an ignoramus or audacious skeptic, worthy of death, who should presume to dispute the prophetic dictum of any well-versed Persian Astrologer.

The Priests of this nation were called Magi, and it seems probable that this term, signifying Wise men, was used for the first time in this connection. Besides the Art of Astrology and Soothsaying, in which the Persian Magi were instructed as part of their education, they practiced in later days enchantment and divination, and as these arts began to be used popularly in other nations, and were often combined with Sorcery, Necromancy and phases of Magic of the most questionable character, the term Magician was at length applied to those who abused the power of Magic, exercised it for unholy purposes, or by aid of evil spirits. It was in this sense that the writers of the Pentateuch designated those Priests of Egypt who contend with Moses. They called them Magicians, whilst Moses in their phraseology was the Servant of God. They (the Magicians) acted under the influence of "Demons," Moses under that of the Hebrews' Tutelary "Deity." It is thus that we learn how the title of Magician - originally synonymous with superior wisdom and divine knowledge - may be used as a term of reproach by rival practitioners.

To the egotistical translators of the Septuagint, the performances of Moses with frogs, serpents, lice and other abominations were the work of "God," acting through his chosen servant; that of the Egyptian Priests, "Magic," a word as abominable in Jewish lips as it was honorable amongst Egyptians or Persians.

There is a Sanscrit word signifying worship, which somewhat resembles Magus, or Enchanter, a term synonymous in Chaldaic, with the Persian Magian. The translators of the Septuagint allege that the Babylonian High Priest was called Rab Mog, or Mag; hence it seems that Magic, Magian, Magician, and all their derivatives were, in the first instance, significant of deep religious meaning; but subsequently become corrupted into base and injurious terms, by the misuse that was made of the power they referred to.

In a curious old treatise, by Godwyn, on the manners, times and theological worship of the ancient Romans, published in 1622, there are the following items of information concerning the subdivisions of their Gods and Spirits, etc.:

"Though Satan had much blinded the hearts of men in old times, yet was not the darkness so great, but that they did easily perceive that there was some governor, some first mover, as Aristotle saith; some first originall of all goodnesse, as Plato teacheth; so that if any made this question whether there was a God or no, they were urged to confess the truth that there was a God; yet were they very blind in discerning the true God, and hence hath been invented such a tedious catalogue of Gods, that, as Varro averreth, their number hath exceeded thirty thousand. ......The second kind of Gods were called Semides id est demi-Gods; also, Indigites id est Gods adopted or canonized, or, men deified. For, as the select Gods had possession of heaven by their own right, so these Gods canonized had it no other way than by right of donation, being, therefore, translated into heaven, because they lived as Gods upon earth." ......Then follows a description of the rights of canonization, unnecessary to quote. The author goes on to say: "But that we may understand what is meant by these Semones (Gods of the third order), we must remember that by them are signified - not the Gods that appertain to us - but the necessaries of man's life, as his victuals, clothing and the like - to the which well-being of man were Gods of good and evil fortune, inclining to give or withhold.

"We read, likewise, of divers names given to many Gods who did severally afford help unto many, so that they were called tutelares, such as had undertaken the protection of any City or Towne, and thence are named for the City or Towne, as St. George, of England; St. Denis, of France; St. Patrick, of Ireland, etc., and the Romans, being fully persuaded of this kind of guard, held by tutelares, when they went about to besiege a Towne by certain enchantments or spells, they would first call out the Tutelar God, because they deemed it impossible to captivate the City as long as these Gods were within, and least others might use the same means in besieging Rome, therefore, as divers authors have thought, the true name of the Roman City was never known, least thereby the name of their Tutelar God might be descryed......And as they supposed some Tutelar spirit to have the charge of whole countries, so did they believe that others had the charge of particular men, and that so soon as any man was born, two spirits did presently accompany him invisibly, the one termed the good Angell, or bonus Genius, persuading him to that which is goo; the other called the Malus Genius, or evil Angell, tempting to that which should be hurtful, insomuch that they thought all the actions of men were guided by these Genii, so that if any misfortune befell a man they would say, 'We have grieved our Genius,' or 'Our Genius being displeased with us, or opposed to us.'"......"These Genii were thought to be a middle essence between Gods and men."......"They appear in divers forms, but oftener as a fierce tragical man, as did the evil Genius who warned Brutus of his fate, or a decrepit old man, or a sad one, or in many such forms of anger or woe as mankind doth assume."

Supplement to Section VI
The Jewish Caballa
--

One of the most curious compendiums of ideality and truth, allegory and veiled mysticism extant, is to be found in the ancient Caballa of the Jews.

This celebrated work is a collection of writings and allusions to traditions of still more authority, supposed to have been communicated by God to Adam, by Adam to Seth, by Seth lost or parted with in some mysterious manner, but renewed again in oral teachings from the God of SInai to Moses, from him revealed to Joshua, thence given to the seventy Elders, and thus transmitted to divers of the learned Jews, who dissented from the more direct assertions of the Talmud. There is another collection of writings and traditions bearing the title of Cabbala, attributed to Oriental scholars, but as this remarkable work is of little or not value without a key which can only be furnished by certain Oriental fraternities, its transcript would be of no value to the general reader.

Passing over the sources from whence the Jews pretend to derive their Cabbala, it is well to notice one peculiarity in its mode of inscription which may serve to explain the many confused and contradictory statements to which it has given rise.

The writers of the Jewish Cabbala evidently labored, and with remarkable success, too, to conceal the true meaning of what they wrote.

Thus some letters are so shortened as to leave the word intact, but the meaning masked; others are lengthened, crooked, or interpolated with seemingly unmeaning points, all with the same design; for example, in the sentence, Abraham came to week for Sara, the letter Caph is smaller than the others, by which Cabbalistic readers understand that as Sara was old, her spouse only wept for her a little.

In a certain passage the syllables Isch, signifying a man, and Escha, a woman, will be found with a point against the word man, absent in writing the word woman; next there occurs a point in the word woman, lacking in writing the word man; when the two points are combined in the same sentence, they signify God; when one alone is there, the word fire is implied. Without the pointing the idea conveyed is, man and woman do agree well together. With the interception of the subtle points in the peculiar mode of Cabbalistic writings, the sentence would read, When man and woman agree together, God is with them; when they disagree, fire is between them.

The study of a lifetime would fail to master all the subtleties with which these writings abound, and the determination which the authors of the Jewish Cabbala manifest to veil the meaning of their sentences under the mask of cypher; and hence it is doubtful how much the popular translations of this celebrated collection can be relied on, especially when they are given to the world by Mystics, as much interested in reserving Cabbalistic ideas, as their original authors.

The Talmud very probably contains a fair digest of the Cabbala, although the latter is richer in occult lore. From a comparison of the two we may glean the following summary of ancient Jewish opinions, concerning the Divine order of cosmogony.

"God is a Trinity," to-wit; Light, Spirit and Life. His first emanations are also triune, namely: En Soph, the masculine of Infinity; Sophia, the feminine of Wisdom and the Word, the divine Activity proceeding from the union of the two. A third triad of principles is indicated, namely: Matter, the formative mould; Life, the active principle of formation; and Soul, the eternal and infinite form of Spirit. Much stress is laid on the ineffable mystery of Triune being - that is, "Three in one, and one in three;" also on the science of numerals, the exact principle of mathematics, and the immutable order by which creation is designed, on geometrical proportions. Mathematics and geometry are as inextricably interwoven with Cabbalistic ideas as Spirit and matter.

The first man - Adam Kadman - is mysteriously mixed up with the Jewish Christ - the Adam of the fall; King David, and the original "only begotten Son of God." It would take all the craft of the unscrupulous Eusebius to disentangle the exact relations of Adam Kadman with his subsequent appearances on earth, and all the faith of the most unquestioning of Christian believers to swallow the Cabbalistic methods of interpreting the scheme of unaccountable perdition, and unaccountable salvation for man. There is some probability that the wild and unsustained theories of modern reincarnationists borrow their fantasies from these Cabbalistic ramblings; still there is much of beauty, much, too, of scientific value, in the suggestions thrown out concerning the just proportions of the universe, and the profound mathematical bases on which the structure of creation rests. To a great extent the scheme of descending emanations in creations, and ascending spheres providing for the progress of fallen spirits and elementary existences, agrees with the views of other ancient Theologians, whose opinions we have cited. Cabbalistic writers are very diffuse in their descriptions of different orders of "Resplendent Angels," Tutelary Spirits, Guardian Angels of every grade and function, Souls of men, Spirits, and legions of Elementaries, filling all space, crowding all elements, and peopling the universe with realms of Spiritual existence corresponding to the Archetypes, Spiritual principles and ultimates of form.

We shall have occasion to draw from the Cabbala again in our sections on Magic; meantime we close this brief notice by affirming that the very best and most reliable digests of Cabbalistic wisdom are to be found in the songs of Orpheus, the philosophy of Plato, the doctrines of Pythagoras, Appolonius of Tyana, and the modern mystics, Van Helmont and Behmen. Many others have borrowed fragments from this collection of writings, and though we are unprepared to assert that the celebrated Greek sages named above derived their ideas from the Cabbala, we are satisfied that they all and each drew from the same source, and that the fountains of wisdom that supplied them, poured forth their treasures from the grand old ranges of the mighty Himalayas, and trembled in the dewy chalices of the white lotuses that fringed the shores of the sacred Nile.

The more we pursue the wisdom of the ancients, through all their ramifications of varied speech, allegorical forms, and the symbolic representation, the more surely we shall come to the conclusion that they are all tributary streams from one central source; that this source was the Book of Nature, written over with flowers and bloom on the fair green earth, with suns and stars in the spangled vault of Heaven - that the great Schoolmaster, who first instructed men and angels in the letters of this divine alphabet was God, the Father of Spirits; that the means of teaching were intuition, inspiration, and direct communion with Angels, the messengers of God; - magic, as the artificer of a new form of communion, when the child-like early man lost the power of intuition, and broke the links of direct communication, by the corruptions of a materialistic civilization, and all means combined, when the pure heart and the clear brain can elevate the soul to its native heavens, and learn to master the occult forces of nature by science. Perhaps we may never return to the simple and child-like attitude which the early men of the earth sustained towards their God.

They conversed with their tutelary spirits as a man speaks with his friend. They looked, and saw that God was. They listened and God's Angels spoke to them in voices as clear as the sighing of the breeze or the murmuring of the brook. They reflected and their past spiritual origin and present destiny cast their images on the mirror of their minds as truthfully as the limpid waters of the lake reflects the lustre of the stars.

Had you asked the intuitional man of old, how he knew these things, he would have gazed upon you with astonishment, and questioned back, "How is it possible that you should fail to know them?" Socrates said, "I respect my own soul, though I cannot see it."

The men of our purely materialistic and external age doubt the existence of their own souls because they cannot see them.

How, then, can they expect to see spirits, hear their voices, or apprehend the nature of that God "who is a Spirit?"

Section VII
Man's Earliest Communion With Spirits
--

Man's earliest religious history is also the history of Spiritism, or his communion with the realms of Spiritual existence.

To effect this communion, the human organism must be adapted to the perception of Spiritual entities, or else means must be found to promote this adaption.

We have mis-spent our time in sketching out the ancient forms of religious belief, if we have failed to show that men once communed with their Tutelary Gods and ministering spirits intuitively, inspirationally, and even directly, but that in process of time, either by reason of changes in man's receptivity, or from the altered conditions which civilization imposes, that communion became interrupted, then more and more difficult; in some periods it ceased altogether, and finally became limited to a few exceptionally endowed individuals, in which category (with occasional irruptions of a more diffusive character) it has continued down to the present day.

The spontaneous and natural communion with spiritual beings, whether it be exercised by communities or individuals, we may term Spiritism. The arts by which this communion is procured through prepared conditions, should with equal propriety be designated Magic, and whether these arts be practiced for good or evil purposes, their methods must involve a knowledge of the occult forces existing in nature, and the means of calling them forth and utilizing them. If the understanding and application of Nature's laws in any one department of being is a science, then must all knowledge and all arts, which are but the application of knowledge, be included in the term science, hence magic, however ominous its name may sound in superstitious ears, and however much it may have been perverted to purposes of evil, is still a branch of science, and as such, should be studied and legitimately used.

Magic may be termed the science of Spiritism, and whilst it would be as idle to tender it to the acceptance of those whose natural endowments supply them with the art it professes to teach, as to paint the cheek of the rose, or blanch the lily white, its careful study may furnish us with a clue to the better use and guidance of natural gifts, and where there are lacking, instruct us in the methods of supplying the deficiency. In order to point out the spheres of power in which magic operates, it is necessary to define the order of communion which nature permits, through the exceptional endowments of her highly gifted children, the world's Seers, Prophets, Sybils, and Mediums.

The first gift included in the discernment of Spiritual beings is that of vision, or the faculty of seeing Spirits, recognizing their signs in aerial pictures, their writings when inscribed in spiritual substances, also of perceiving the spirits of fellow-men, reading the thoughts and characteristics masked to the mortal eye, and taking cognizance generally of the spiritual part of things in the Universe.

The second gift of the prophetic order is, the faculty of hearing sounds, whether in the form of spirit voices, music, or other vibrations made on the ethereal medium in which spirits live, rather than on the atmosphere which mortals breathe and dwell in.

The power of seeing and hearing spirits, opens up two of the principal avenues of intelligence to our Souls, and in like manner, the spiritual senses of smell, taste, and touch can be operated upon.

Through one or other of these gates to the inner consciousness, all spiritualistic phenomena must act, but the phenomena themselves are very various.

Something the Soul of man itself, looks forth through its material encasements, acting from within, and sees, hears, tastes, smells, and touches spiritual entities.

Sometimes ministering spirits produce effects acting from without upon the inner senses of man. Both methods are common, both belong to the one gifted individual.

Sometimes the influx of spiritual ideas is so silent, natural, and unmarked by physical disturbances, that their subject knows not that an Angel speaks, or that the soul has transcended the laws of sensuous perception, and derived ideas unconsciously from its near proximity to the realms of spiritual entities.

To account for the operation of the powers describe above, it is necessary to revert to the last section of the First Part, and bear in mind, that the realms of spiritual being are very near, in fact, all around and about us; that, though spirits of every grade and class swarm through the universe, ranged in their different spheres and orders, yet that the "spirit world," or the spheres through which the souls of men are making pilgrimage upwards and onwards to heaven are approximate to this earth, even as the soul of man is related to his body; that these spheres interpenetrate every atom of matter on this globe with a spiritual element, and again, as the disembodied spirits of earth are in the most direct, natural, and harmonious proximity to their still embodied friends, it is to the spirit spheres of humanity, that the most ready access to the human soul is obtained, and through which the most constant influx into the natural world transpires. To expect that the realms of disembodied human spirits should be the nearest in atmospheric proximity to man, the most in accordance with his grade of intelligence, and the most prompt to serve, bless and instruct him by ties of love, kindness, and adaptation, is just as rational as to suppose that the human mother would be the first to render aid to her suffering child, or that the child would be more likely to appeal for that aid to a tender parent than to some unsympathizing stranger. This phase of intercourse between spirits and mortals, we distinguish as Mundane Spiritism, and this we claim to be the most natural, direct, and spontaneous product of that divine plan which connects all conditions of being, from the highest to the lowest, in one unbroken chain of love and harmony, the links of which are millions of spheres of super-mundane, and sub-mundane spiritual existences.

There are but few analogies discoverable on the surface of mundane life, between the laws which separately govern Spirit and matter, but the closer we pursue our researches, the more clearly we recognize correspondence, if not actual analogies, between those elements. Amongst these are the laws of physical and moral gravitation.

As the heaviest and grossest bodies sink to the centre, so the least intelligent and exalted conditions of spiritual being obey the same law, and hence, sub-mundane Spiritism consists in communion with these lower orders of being, who are in point of position in the Universe, no less than in moral and mental unfoldment, lower than man, and whom the philosophers and mystics of old have significantly denominated, "the Elementaries."

It would be impossible to do justice to the immense multitudes of those beings who crowd the elements, and exist in all grades of semi-spiritual, semi-material bodies, from such progressed, but still rudimental conditions, as almost impinge upon the perfection of manhood, down to the "Pigmies," who emerge from rude, almost inorganic life, evolved from minerals, plants, water, earth, atmosphere and fire.

There are luxuriant and enormous growths, gigantic forms, exceeding the proportions of humanity, who abound in forests, mountains, hills, and desert places; stunted, dwarfish beings who frequent mines, caverns, and the deep recesses of earth, corresponding to the undeveloped elements of inorganic nature.

Beautiful, though still embryonic existences there are, who belong to the finer spheres, corresponding to flowers and air. Fantastic and diffusive shapes of elementary life crowd the waters, and resplendent globular unparticled essences exist, and can be detected in the realms of light and heat represented by fire. All are included in the title of Elementaries. All possess different functions, exert power in the particular elements to which they belong, are neither good nor evil per se, but malignant or beneficent in part, to those whom they affect or dislike; they possess, in short, varied powers and characteristics; and communion with them may be classed in the category of Sub-mundane Spiritism.

Myriads upon myriads there are in whom special animal instincts prevail, giving to their embryonic forms a similarity to the creatures whose natures they correspond to. These elementary spirits are all ranged and classed in the divine order of creation, under the same law of adaption that is manifest in the plants, animals and other products of different countries and climes. Every creature is as much in its place, and an inhabitant of its appropriate sphere, as is the material particle to which it corresponds. Hanging on the same divine thread of beneficence which binds man to the heart of Deity, these Elementaries could no more be riven away from the interminable chain of being, than the Planetary order of the skies could afford to part with Mercury, the youngest child of the solar system, because it is not so perfectly developed as Mars, nor yet cast out of the shining, starry family that circles round the parent sun, the planet Earth, because it has not attained to the size, lustre and glory of Jupiter.

"I number up my Jewels!" says the God of the sparkling sky; and which of his blazing sons of light could he disperse with, without throwing the whole scheme of revolving worlds out of eternal harmony?

"I number up my Jewels!" cries the Tutelary Angel of Earth, in the tender and merciful tones of divine Fatherhood; and which of his immortal soul gems could he afford to annihilate as his vision ranges, and his justice prevails, from the monarch on his throne, to the dying wretch in the cell of earthly condemnation?

"I number up my Jewels!" cries the Archangel of the grand solar system, and which of his minutest sparks of spiritual fire could he afford to extinguish, whether it blazed in the soul of a Copernicus, or glimmered in the uncouth form of a pigmy Elementary, on the lowest round of the ladder of sub-mundane pilgrimage?

Oh proud, disdainful man! disdainful and proud only in your ignorance! Which of you can say from whence you came, or deny what you might have been, however you may rejoice in the heigh to which you have now attained; however you may rest in the assurance that there is no such thing as retrogression, and that you cannot sink lower than you will to fall? Which of you who so cheerfully accept the vague theory of inductive science, that teaches you to believe men were once apes, need shrink back with contempt from the idea that your spirits were as rudimental as your bodies? Which of you that so fiercely reject the Darwinian theory, yet offer no better hypothesis for human origin - who would rather fancy you were nothing, than anything lower than you arrogance deems worthy of you - which of you can believe that from nothing sprang something, or that you suddenly appeared on the theatre of existence, a full-fledged immortal Soul, with a hitherward, but no whence - a heavenly goal to attain to, but no beginning to spring from?

The world that sees its Julius Caesars and Napoleon Bonapartes commence life as helpless, wailing babes, and end it as Masters of Europe and Lords over millions of their fellow-creatures, still scoffs at the idea that the race of man ever had a similar infancy.

The full-grown man of the nineteenth century repels with indignation the idea that he could have ever been related to the world of elementary being, and can see no justice, divinity, beauty, or order in the scheme that sows a germ of spiritual life in the most rudimental of material forms, and then expands it through a natural series of births and deaths, until it becomes fitted to take its place as a purely perfected and self-conscious spirit entity, in those realms where it awaits, in common with myriads of other spirits, a mortal birth on this or some other earth in the Universe. Yet such is God's plan, at least such does it appear to the most patient of students; those who have toiled through the esoteric significations of human history, and learned their spiritualistic lessons from the very beings who are in the experience of the truth they reveal. Such is God's plan, unless the philosophic minds, who have gathered up the accumulated wisdom of past ages, and studied nature and the mysteries of spiritual existence in their profoundest depths, have learned less than modern theorists, who never study such subjects at all.

Either the wisdom and occult knowledge of cycles of ages is wroth less than the scornful denial of utterly uninformed skepticism, or our brief review of sub-mundane Spiritism is a correct one as far as it goes.

Reserving more particular descriptions of the elementaries for further sections, we now proceed to notice the realms of supermundane Spiritism.

Here, legions of Archangels and Angels throng the Universe, of whom the imagination may conceive, but to whose being and nature the power of language can do no justice.

In whatever realms of spiritual life the entranced soul of the ecstatic may wander, with whatever resplendent beings that would may be permitted to hold converse, the mind is always directed to higher states, and higher individualities still. Like the revelating Angel addressing the Apocalyptic writer John, every Spirit or Angel that has ever communed with man, ignores worship, and ascribes all power and all glory to something still beyond - to Deific existences, incomprehensible, but ever felt in the understanding, and ever holding that central point of all devotion and worship, which we vaguely call God. Bear this fact in mind, and we shall be held guiltless of presumption when we write of what the eyes of Seers have beheld, of spirits with whom our fathers, like John of old, have identified even the Lord of life and light, and striven to worship as God; of mighty Angels, who, like the spirit that spoke through the thunders of Sinai, or from the midst of the burning bush, seem to man the last apex of glory on which the finite mind rests its conceptions of God. Higher and still higher, ever stretching away where roads are made of star dust, and paths are strewn with glittering Suns; where time is no more, and space is lost in infinity; stretching away into hemispheres where new sideral heavens form the boundary walls and gateways to the new corridors of an Universe wherein, end there is none.

Loose the reins of the imagination, and let the fiery steeds of a new mental Phoebus seek to traverse these high-roads of infinity! People them all with Angels ascending and still ascending in the scale of grandeur, power and immensity, and then question of the highest still, and still the choiring worlds will answer, "Higher yet! higher yet! There still are realms of being higher yet!"

We veil our presumptuous eyes against these vain speculations, retreat to our spheres of littleness, content to find that Angels, Guardian spirits, and Spirit friends, surround us, minister to our earthly powers and functions only as our minds can grasp and comprehend them, and thus we may concentrate our wandering thoughts on the firm assurance that God is, though man may never know Him, and rest in the certainty that all we hope and strive for, will yet be ours, as the heirs of immortal progress.

Super-mundane Spiritism teaches of Tutelary Spirits or Gods, and Planetary Angels.

The Jehovah of the Jews affords a well marked definition of the ancient belief in Eloihim, or Tutelary Gods.

The revelating Angels so often described by the Hebrew Prophets, and He who was claimed by the authors of the Apocalypse to have mapped out the masonic order of creation in that gorgeous vision, said to have been shown in the Isle of Patmos, or the isolation of the entranced Soul, clearly illustrate the nature of these celestial visitants who in the Oriental dispensation, talked with men, face to face. In our degenerate and unspiritual age, we have little to illuminate our prosaic lives, save the revelations of our Fathers. From time to time, bright beings flash athwart our path, more glorious than the forms of men or spirits, and the assurance that the realms of space must be filled with the messengers of God, induces us to yield acceptance to the Cabbalistic division of the higher orders of Angels into "Thrones, Dominions, Powers; - Angels of the Planets, Tutelary Spirits, Guardians of Nations, Cities, Men, the Souls of Ancestors, and beloved Spirit friends." The reader will remember the description so often rendered by Swedenborg in his ecstatic wanderings through Celestial spheres, or his having seen God as a Spiritual Sun. The same statement is made by several of the best modern Brahmins who are Seers. It was re-affirmed by Cahagnet's Somnambules under the control of many spirits who professed to have beheld the glory of this Spiritual Sun, and it was stated in opposition to all the preconceived opinions of surrounding listeners, by the Spirits who spoke with human voices at Koon's Spirit room in the opening of the American Spiritual Dispensation.

It has frequently been stated to the author by teaching Spirits, that the Tutelary Angel of every planet appears only as a Spiritual Sun, himself deriving light, heat, force, and being, from the Central Sun of the Universe; that these stupendous and sublime centres, the Spiritual Suns of Earths, Planets, and Satellites, impart their life-giving light, radiance and gravitating forces to the Physical Suns of the systems to which they belong; - that these Physical Suns are the most progressed aggregations of world matter in the Universe, hence become centres and parents of revolving Satellites, who derive a certain measure of light and heat from the Sun of their system, but like that material body, they would fade, perish and dissolve into their original elements were they not vitalized by the Spiritual Sun, which is to that system, as the Soul to the human body.

To the true Hierophant who can connect ancient mysteries with personal spiritual endowments, those who wear the Prophet's mantle, yet analyze its fabric by the light of modern science, Tutelary Spirits and Planetary Angels reveal themselves as distinctly now, as when they spoke from between the Cherubim and Seraphim of the "Ark of the Covenant," or reflected their lustrous rays from mimic skies, outstretched above the Hierophants of ancient mysteries.

Planetary Spirits respond to invocations from the sincere Spiritualist, and often hold watch and ward over the favored ones of earth to whom, through prepared conditions, they communicate many of the great truths of the Universe unattainable to mortals without their aid. Few of them are inferior to the highest of human intelligences, save the Spirits of Mercury and Venus, who should seldom be invoked and encouraged to commune with Earth.

Generally speaking, the Planetary Spirits are not attracted to earth, except on special missions, or by evocations procured as above states, through prepared conditions, of which more hereafter.
Ranging under the category of Super-mundane Spiritism, we place the Souls of men who

have attained to the highest conditions of Angelic exaltation, and who are attracted to Earth as messengers of beneficence, beauty, and goodness.

Souls of men that have enjoyed ages of progress, and attained to radiant conditions of celestial happiness, sometimes return to earth for material knowledge, to study lower conditions of being, and gather elements of use, imparting in return the noblest teachings, and very generally associating their mission with some master mind of earth, through whom they become, by inspiration and heavenly influence, the promoters of mighty reforms, great upheavals of human thought, culminating in social, political, or religious revolutions.

On every round of that visionary ladder, whose foot is on earth, whose apex in heaven - Angels who have once been men, Spirits who have lived and labored on earth and risen from the ashes of death, victor-browed, to a triumphant inheritance beyond; household "lares" - heart loves who have just left us, but still hover on the threshold they have crossed to smooth our rough and rugged path over the stones their torn feet have trod - all such ministers of live and blessing as these, ascend and descend on this mystic ladder, forming an interminable chain of love and harmony between the highest and the lowest, connecting each and all by the links of sympathy, bearing up the tired hands that are dropping life's burdens for very weariness - catching at the outstretched arms that are tossed abroad in the agony of frantic supplication to the God of many creeds and nations, tenderly wafting up to heaven the piteous prayers that long ago they lisped forth in accents as faltering as our own, and returning inspiration for aspiration, peace and blessing for the incoherent appeals of human ignorance and impotence.

These are the beings that fill up the sum of man's limited and finite span of knowledge, concerning Super-mundane Spiritism.

Section VIII
Man the Microcosm of the Universe

--

The modus operandi by which the worlds invisible to the outer senses of man can become so manifest as to convince him of their existence, must depend first on some element resident in the human organism, and next upon correspondential means operating upon man, from the invisible realms of being.

Were there not such operations mutually subsisting between the worlds of spirit and matter, all man's imaginings however sublime, all his intuitive faculties, however penetrating, and even the witness of his own interior nature, would never be susceptible of demonstrating God in the light of reason, never bring him face to face with Spirit as the absolute esse of being, never enable him to construct such a religious belief as the Father could communicate to the child, or the Priest impart to the People. There can be no doubt that the Soul's deepest and most intuitive perceptions of truth, are its own most acceptable witnesses, still these are incommunicable, and the spirit's witness of itself, its Deity, and its faith in immortality, can never ben fully translated into human speech. Happily, however, for those blunted natures which are not developed up to the transcendent heights of spiritual truth, the realms of invisible being approximate to earth, have found means to establish processes of communion which place their existence, varies offices of ministry, even their very natures beyond all shadow of doubt or denial to those who care to consult the occult, as well as the material side of human history.

Setting the question of evidence aside, however, or leaving it only as a subject of warfare between contentious factions of materialists and creedists, our part is to examine into the methods by which the communion between man and the invisible worlds of being transpire.

Mere opinions concerning the facts of the phenomena, furnish no clue to their means of occurrence.

Spirits come and go, apparently by no law analogous to those which govern human action.

Beings of an order wholly different in their essential nature, and similar only in form and intelligence to man, interpenetrate his atmosphere like the magical appearance of the lightning's flash, and disappear in the same inexplicable mystery.

Sounds, sight, movements, impressions, sometimes appealing to man with the subtle semblance of a vision, sometimes compelling him by a force he cannot resist, all captivate his senses, sway his soul, and fill him with awe and wonder.

The commonplace and secularizing modes of spiritual intercourse that have prevailed throughout the second half of our present century, have doubtless tended to strip the world of supernaturalism of its terrors, as well as much of its exaltation and spiritual beauty, still it has effected a wonderful revolution in man's intellectual appreciation of spiritual existence, confirming him in knowledge upon subjects that were before divided between myth and superstitious credulity, and bringing under the dominion of reason and judgement problems that were deemed heretofore insoluble upon any other ground than the assumption of miracle.

In treating of nature as of the visible and sensuous universe, and super-nature as of the invisible and spiritual, we are no longer driven to the necessity of premising our philosophy with an if, and such events really transpired, or leaning upon the authority of some great Sage or world-renowned Pundit, before we can demand acceptance for our facts.

However commonplace or even puerile many of the phases of modern Spiritual communion may be, however foolishly that communion may have been abused, by making it the shibboleth for the introduction of all sorts of subversive ideas into social, religious, and even political life, the immense flood of light it has diffused upon the great problems of life, death, immortality and the nature of the human spirit, rank it as one of the most revolutionary and powerful revelations that have been vouchsafed to man since the closing up of the Oriental and Mythological Dynasties.

It is as much by the positive, sensuous demonstrations afforded to us in this great modern Spiritual outpouring, as through a study of ancient or mediaeval records, that we are enabled to present the composite but absolute philosophy of Spiritism recited in this Section; but here let us premise, that we do not propose to pause in our definitions to say - this is Artephius, and that is Plato; thus argued the Fire Philosophers of the middle ages, and thus mused the Cabbalists of antiquity. Now as heretofore, our reference to authority must be sought for in the context of the work, rather than in the list of names cited.

Man is a Microcosm or Universe in little - as such, he is the conservator of all forces, the image of all objective forms, the embodiment of all subjective ideas, and the connecting link between all existences, higher and lower than himself.

In himself, taken to pieces by chemistry and analyzed by the display of his powers and relations to the invisible world, he is a trinity of elements, namely: Body, spirit and soul. His body is a conservator of all the powers and functions of matter; his spirit, the animating principle, is made up of all the forces we vaguely call life; his soul is the pure Deific, and immortal essence whose attribute is Will or Intelligence. It is the attempt to analyze these three elements, which has formed a groundwork of philosophy, and a theme of learned speculation, for thousands of years.

Judging from effects rather than assumed causes, may we not believe with the "Fire Philosophers" of the middle ages, that the soul is like its source - the Central Sun of being - in its nature and essence pure, unalloyed, Spiritual Light?

That it is the invisible and infinitely sublimated Spirit of Fire - not the gross visible element that can be seen, felt, and apprehended by the senses - but that wonderful innermost light, which, whilst it reveals and proves all things in its own manifestation, is itself invisible, unknown, and uncomprehended?

It is this essential, innermost and divine principle of soul which survives all change, which is neither subject to decay nor disintegration; which is the spark derived from Deity - the Alpha and Omega of being - and the link which unites the Creature to the Creator.

Encompassing this divine essence of soul, and clothing it as a spiritual body, is the subtle and refined element which, in its effects, is force; in its action, through organic bodies, is life; and in its all-pervading influence throughout the realms of space, is vaguely termed magnetism and electricity.

It is the second of that grand trinity of principles, whose union constitutes man a living being.

It is this element which we described in our first section, as recognized throughout the Universe, by the apparent duality of its modes, called attraction and repulsion, or centrifugal and centripetal force. As it is in the realm of this all-pervading life principle that we find our sole explanation of the various magical operations of a spirit power, we must dwell somewhat at length upon a description of its character and functions.

It has often been stated by Seers and illuminated "Sensitives," that there were many layers or strata of this spiritual body, of more of less attenuation, in proportion to their distance from the soul, or nearness to the physical body. These rings, or spheres, are called, collectively, the Astral Spirit, from the fact that the element itself is derived, like the pure essence of the soul, from the great Spiritual Sun of the Universe, from whom emanate, and to whom return all rays of light, heat, force, motion, power and being that fill the Universe of forms. This Astral Spirit is often mis-called in modern phraseology, the "magnetic body," the "nerve aura," "magnetism," "electricity," etc. Paul, the Apostle of the Gentiles, who writes equally in the spirit of ancient Cabbalism, and still later Gnosticism, terms this element in man, "The Spiritual body," a phase which corresponds well to the still more correct expression of "The Astral Spirit." In organic bodies we shall continue thus to term it; in the realms of space it is more proper to speak of it as the "Astral light." It is to the Universe of inorganic forms, what the Soul is to the body, its spirit - life or animating principle.

The Rosicrucians - a sect who obtained much notoriety about the fifteenth and sixteenth centuries, but of whose actual origin, tenets and very existence, no reliable information has ever been generally circulated - maintained that the last analysis of the Supreme Being would fail to discover any other existence than that of a Central Spiritual Sun - an Infinite, Eternal, uncreated and incomprehensible One alone, whose attributes were light and heat, whose manifestation was the Universe, revealed by light, energized into forms, suns, systems, worlds, men and things, by that spiritual heat whose last gross external exhibition is fire.

In this sense, the term repulsion, which has been treated as an attribute of matter, is accounted for by the energy with which heat burns, consumes, disintegrates, and drives off one particle from another; whilst attraction, also supposed to be an attribute of matter, is but the natural cohesion of particles, upon which the restless energy of heat either does not act, or becomes modified by the solidarity of the masses acted upon. Thus then, repulsion is the one universal law of motion, which itself is produced by heat; and attraction is only the absence of heat, not a true force.

Inertia is the only property of matter in this category - heat or repulsion its counteracting force attraction, the exhibition of the vis inertia of atoms.

We do not care to dismiss these propositions without a farther elaboration of their basic idea, and for this purpose we propose to offer a few excerpts from one of those writers who has assumed the office of describing the principles of the Rosicrucian Brotherhood. As far as the opinions of this remarkable association can be defined in language, the quotations selected will give a fair idea of their views on the subject under discussion:

"If the above abstractions are caught by the thinker, it will appear no wonder that the ancient people considered that they saw God, that is, with all their innermost possibility of thought - in Fire - which Fire is not our vulgar, gross Fire, neither is it even the purest material or electric fire, which has still something of the base, bright light of the world about it; but it is an occult, mysterious, supernatural Fire - not magnetic - and yet a real, sensible mind. It is the inner Light, the God, containing all things, the soul of all things, into whose inexpressibly intense, all-consuming, all-creating, divine, though fiery essence, and all the worlds in succession will fall back into whose arms of Immortal Light on the other side, as again receiving them, the worlds driven off into space and being heretofore, by the Divine energy will again rush back to him." ......

"The hollow world, in which that essence of things called Fire, plays, in its escape in violent agitation - to us combustion - is deep down within us, deep sunken inside of the time stages of which we are, in the flesh, rings of being, subsidence of spirit."

......"Narrowly considered, it will be found that all religions transcend up in to this spiritual Fire-floor, on which, so to speak, the phases of time were laid. Material Fire, which is brightness, as the matter upon which it preys is darkness - is the shadow of the true Spirit Light, which invests itself in fire as a mask, in which alone it can act possibly on matter. Thus material light being the opposite rather than the expression of God, the Egyptians - who were undoubtedly acquainted with the Fire revelation - could not represent God as light - material light. They therefore expressed their idea of Deity by darkness. Their adoration was paid to darkness, for in this they bodied forth the image of the Eternal." ......"Though fire is an element in which everything inheres, and of which it is the life, still it is itself an element existing in a second non-terrestrial, non-physical, ethereal fire, in which the first, or terrestrial coarse fire, flickers, waves, brandishes, consumes, destroys. The first is natural, material, gross; but this familiar element, seen and known in the natural world as fire, is contained in a celestial unparticled, infinitely extended medium - which celestial fire is its matrix, and of which, in this human body, we know nothing."

We here interrupt these excerpts - rendered chiefly as fragmentary representations of Rosicrucian ideas on the Deity - to interpret the obscure language of the writer, and state that the celestial fire referred to in the above passage, is the all-pervading element we have described, which, in its action through space, is termed the Astral Light, and in its investiture of the soul as a spiritual body, is termed the Astral Spirit. The innermost of the Rosicrucian Celestial Fire, like that of the human spirit, is the incomprehensible essence of light, not its substance, Soul. Robert Fludd, a Rosicrucian mystic of the middle ages, teaches that the Macrocosmos, or great Universe of intelligible and intelligent forms, is divided into three principal regions, which are denominated the Empyreum, the Aethereum, and the Elementary region. Each are filled with Celestial Fire, and traversed by innumerable oceans of Astral Light, but the quantity and quality of these divine elements diminishes as these subdivisions of space recede farther from the Central Source of all.

It is the union of the Celestial Fire and astral Light which constitutes the Soul of the Universe.

The Rosicrucian biographer proceeds to say:

"There are three ascending Hierarchies of beneficent Angels whose nature is of the purer portion of the Celestial Fire, and these are divided into nine orders. - These threefold Angelic Hierarchies are: The Teraphim, the Cherubim, and Seraphim; also, there is a correspondential realm of darkness, divided into nine spheres- the residuum of being, peopled with mighty but adverse Angels, who boast still, of the relics of their lost or eclipsed condition, once all light and heavenly glory." ......"The Elementary region includes the earth, man, and his belongings, also the lower creatures. This sphere is the flu, subsidence, ashes of the ethereal fire, and man himself is the microcosm or indescribably small copy of the macrocosm, or the great world. This earth having been produced by the contention of light and darkness, has denseness in its innumerable heavy concomitants, which contain less and less of the original divine light and heat, and thicken and solidify, until it is rent apart, torn, disintegrated and distributed into forms, by the still prevalent action of the Divine element of invisible fire.

"The inner jewel of light is never absent, even from the grossest atom, and though it may take ages to evolve, still will this divine light, ever tending to purify, refine, and elevate, alchemically convert base things into fine, gross matter into ethereal, and the earth itself into a radiant and gloriously spiritualized planet. Unseen and unsuspected, there is a divine ethereal spirit, an eager fire, confined as in prison, struggling through all solid objects, which are imbued with more or less of this sensitive life, as they are more or less refined, through the changing purgations of fire. Thus all minerals in this spark of light have the rudimentary possibility of plants, and growing organisms; plants have rudimentary sensibilities, which might in distant ages transmute them into locomotive creatures, and all vegetation might pass off, into new and independent highways of being, as their original spark of life-light, thrills, expands, and urges nature forward with more informed force, and directed by the unseen Angelic Ministers of the Great Original Architect."......"it is with terrestrial fire that the Alchemist breaks asunder the atomic thickness of visible nature, which, yielding up its secret destiny, of unlimited progress, sinks into the fiery furnace, in its basest proportions, to arise thrice purified, and forced upwards on the pathway of a higher round of the ladder.

"It is with the celestial fire that the Rosicrucian bursts asunder the bonds of error and darkness that hold the soul in a material prison-house. He becomes the Pontifex (bridge maker), which conducts the Soul across the dark waters of ignorance from the realms of the known to the unknown, from the gates of matter to the bright roads of Spirit; from earthly blackness to celestial light, from the visible fires of purgation to the invisible soul light of eternity."

Our readers may pardon us for interblending so many fragments of Rosicrucian musings with the practicalities which we profess to aim at, but to the genuine student of the occult sciences, it may not be uninteresting to learn something of the real opinions of a sect to whom so much that is false and mythical has been attributed. As God is the solvent for all the problems of pious ignorance, so electricity plays the same part in the realm of unexplained phenomena. The name of the Rosicrucians seems to have been borrowed in the same sense, and applied by superstitious and utterly misinformed babblers to cover up all the occult mysteries which science could not explain, and bigotry feared to tamper with.

It is something to know ourselves - not less to be truly known by others.

We do not press these fragments of Rosicrucianism on the reader's attention for the mere purpose of citing abstract opinions with which we have especial sympathy, but we feel that, to the interior sense of the profound thinker, they have a deeper significance than any other theories that have yet been advanced concerning the wonderful phenomena of Deity, life and being. Allowing for the varied modes of expression which prevail in different countries, and at various epochs of time, these opinions present a very fair, though necessarily condensed abstract, of the philosophies of the Cabbalists, Gnostics, Pythagoreans, Platonists, and many of the most enlightened of the Greeks, Romans and early Christians.

In giving a brief and practical summary of these theories, we find that, whilst the soul or innermost of the man is a Divine emanation from Deity, the body or outermost is an aggregation of material atoms, vitalized by the Astral Spirit, which serves as the life principle to the body, the ethereal body of the soul, and forms the connecting link between the soul and the body. This Astral Spirit accompanies the soul at Death, when the union of the two forms the spirit. The more sublimated portions of this Astral body adhere to the soul, and grosser and coarser layers form the outer covering or body of the spirit.

It is in this luminous Astral Spirit, this concentration of all force, life, heat, motion and imponderable essence, this invisible, "supernatural fire," as the ancient Theosophists termed it, that the power resides to make spirits visible to mortal eyes, to exhale force, so that they can lift bodies, make sounds, and produce all the manifestations by which spirits and mortals commune with each other. The heat generated in this Astral Spirit gives life and motion to the body; the light, which is its substance, colors the various tissues and fluids, and causes them to reflect the grosser rays of light in the atmosphere, so that they can become visible.

Once more we will suggest, that the Astral Spirit in the human structure is analogous, though differing in degrees of attenuation and force, to the Astral light in the realms of space. It is the spiritual principle of the earth, galvanism, magnetism, motion throughout its rocks, plants, minerals, waters, and gases.

It is the restless, ethereal fire that forces asunder the most mobile particles of fluid, and disperses them into gases; it separates the still finer particles of gases, and distributes matter into ether. it is not, as some have asserted, ether per se, but it is the principle of motion which rolls oceans of ether into undulatory waves, and causes it to become the carrier of light and heat. When its swift winged rays encounter opposite currents, when moving with inconceivable energy through one body it meets with its counterpart in opposing motion, the fierce concussion results in combustion; this mighty shock eliminates flame or lightning, and in the all-devouring action of the material fire, the surrounding particles are consumed. Destruction by fire, or what is called electricity then, is the material exhibition of two contending bodies, moving in opposite directions under the energetic action of the spiritual fire. In its primal condition, the Astral light of the Universe is like that of the Spiritual body in man, invisible, latent, inscrutable, unknown, except by its effects in life, warmth, and motion. In its external and last analysis, it is the consuming fire, and its action is to reduce all things back again into their own invisible essence; thus it is the Alpha and Omega of being, the first and the last; Deity.

The Astral Spirit in man is not a single original element, like the Soul, it is a combination of all the imponderables of the Universe. its first derivation or original essence is from the Sun and planetary system. Ether, air, atmosphere, earth, with all its freight of organic and inorganic life, combine to send off emanations which make up the sum of the wonderful structure called the Astral Spirit in man. It is a true cosmos of the Universe, and upon its exterior form is engraved all the sand grains of character, motives, powers, functions, vices, virtues, hopes, and memories, which the Soul has gathered up in its process of growth through the material body; hence it is as much a perfect microcosm of the individual's mind within, as of the visible and invisible Universe without. Not a deed, word, or thought which has helped to make up the sum of a human life, but what is photographed upon the spiritual body of the man, with as much fidelity as the mind of the Creator is written, in starry hieroglyphics upon the glittering skies. it keeps as faithful a record, as true a doomsday book, and pronounces as sure a judgment upon human life and conduct as ever the Egyptian Osiris could have done, in his sternest moods of God-like justice.

In many layers of graduated ethereal essence are felt by Sensitives as rings, or spheres. Those nearest the body are perceived as life spheres, and these change with the body's changes, and in its decay and death, recede, and become the outermost of the new born Soul's envelope. Those most interior to the body, and nearest the Soul, are the Sun spheres, and connect the Soul with the Solar and Astral influences, under which the individual was launched into being.

These interior spheres, too, change in response to Solar and planetary changes, and thence they affect the mind, influence the character, and constitute the links of connection by which the stars act upon the individual's destiny. As man's Astral Spirit is aggregated from so many forces in the Universe, so it is subject to the influence of changes occurring in every department of Nature.

The state of the earth, atmosphere, and aromal emanations given off in different seasons of the year - all these, with their changing influences, contribute to form the essence of the embryonic being ere it sees the light. The inherited tendencies of mind, body and spirit imposed by parental law, impart to the life germs their own peculiar idiosyncrasies. The physical sustenance, mental temperament, the very employments and thoughts of every mother, combine, also, to impress, with fateful images, their unborn offspring; but above all, the order of the planetary scheme, and the conjunction with every star sustains, first to the Sun, next to the earth, and finally to each other at the moment of mortal birth, must determine the nature of every spirit, and shape the springs upon which hinge the framework of human character.

Admitting then, the Soul's origin in Deity, and the Astral spirit's origin in the solar system, how vastly momentous upon the newly-born being's character and organization must be the solar and planetary influences which prevail in the hour of the germ's inception, through every stage of embryonic life, and at the very moment when, drawn by solar and planetary influence from the darkness of its embryonic prison, it is launched in space as a living creature!

Ages ago, the ancient astronomer discovered that all the vast crystal vault of the skies, the illimitable fields of space dotted over with millions of fiery blossoms, seemingly so fixed, so calm, so immobile in their solemn silence and mysterious beauty, were all moving! Moving on in constant but still ever-changing orbits. The certainty of these stupendous changes was absolutely determined by the discovery of that remarkable motion called "the precession of the equinoxes," a motion which, in a given period of time, varying between two and three thousand years, swept the blazing sun of the solar system, with all its planetary hosts, from one sign of the Zodiac to another. Later on - in fact, up to our own time - astronomical observations have determined that all the stars of the sidereal heavens, gorgeous field of space, filled with the march of suns and systems, speed on with a momentum so tremendous, that the mind of man shrinks back, awestruck, at the attempt to trace, those footprints of fire through spaces, wherein millions of miles are measured by hours and minutes. Whilst the external aspect of these spangled heavens changes but little to the eye of the observer during many centuries of time, the real permanence of the scheme is only apparent. "Only constant in eternal unrest," might be traced in every glittering point of the sideral heavens. Ever the same in the fixidity of matchless order, ever changing in the spiral circles of ascending progress. If this be so, as Science proves it is, how inevitably must the endless changes of the Macrocosm affect the nature of the Microcosm, and man, the world in little, partake of the infinite variousness which discourses so eloquently through the epic of the starry skies!

There cannot be two planetary conjunctions in the field of space which, in all respects, exactly duplicate each other; and this is the reason why those creatures, launched every second into human life, under the influence of ever-varying astral changes, must differ so widely from each other in all the essentials of physical, mental, intellectual and spiritual states. As the planets seem to return to stated points, and re-enact their mystic conjunctions in the shining pathway of the Zodiac, so there seem to be recurrences of certain types of character, and duplicates of certain facial lineaments.

Viewing the valley of the then from the mountain heights of the now, we are fain to give up this stereotyped opinion, and own that history only repeats itself in generalities, not in particulars, and that there is not a wave which beats on the shores of earth that ever returns with just the same force as those that have gone before - no never! And all this change in the planetary order is effected by the unceasing energy of the life that is throbbing, and burning, and blazing on in its mad career of eternal unrest, in the midst of every starry road, and thrilling down and pulsating through the very central heart of every starry world; and all this ceaseless movement, heard in the echoing feet of the tramping ages, is due to that same life spirit, burning up, shriveling into ashes, and scattering into dust the forms of the past, in order that their liberated spirits may become incarnate in all the fresher, fairer forms of the ages that are to be!

The consideration of these diffusive generalities are not irrelevant to our subject; on the contrary, they need to be thought out and appreciated ere the unaccustomed thinker can apprehend why the motions of a single point of fire, gleaming through the immensity of space, can affect the character and destiny of an individual removed from its orbit by incalculable sums of distance; why all nature, animate and inanimate, moves, acts and speaks with an universal chord of sympathy connecting the whole' why flights of birds, wheeling high in air, the motions of a dancing butterfly, a quivering sunbeam, a crawling worm, humming insect, or even the falling of a leaf, or the murmur of a wave, may discourse deep meanings in the ear of a true student of nature, and utter portents of immutable fate to illuminated scholars who have learned to interpret all the undertones of creations, and spell out its hieroglyphical inscriptions.

When we hear how Chaldean Soothsayers perceived the destines of nations, in the smoking ashes of the burnt offering; how Roman Augurs interpreted the issues of life and death from the flight of birds; how Persian Magi read the words of fate inscribed on the starry pages of the skies; or Hebrew priests discovered mystic meanings in the glittering luster of Urim and Thummim; we know that these men were simply natural philosophers, and had studied the occult side of nature with as much understanding, and perhaps more devotion, than the nineteenth century Scientists accord to the mastery of the known and the visible.

For thousands, perhaps for tens of thousands of years, it was the office of the best and wisest men of every succeeding generation, to devote a lifetime to the study of nature, and that in her profoundest depths, and through all the mazes and windings of her supernatural relations with the visible and invisible spheres of being around her. Ever let it be remembered, too, that the ancient philosopher brought to this sublime study a body as thoroughly prepared as a mind; a physique fitted by temperances, chastity and purity to allow full sway to the mind which inhabited it, and is so often cramped by inharmonious physical states.

When we come to lay down the conditions under which alone magical rites can become effective, and describe the life-long discipline which the powerful magian must pursue, in order to become one, we shall put to shame the self-indulgent, intemperate, and too often dissolute habits of the present age - habits which not even the sacred assumption of Priestly office seems always to impose restraint upon. And yet this same self-indulgent and luxuriant age, looks back with contempt on the asceticism of the ancient Priest, whilst those who profess to believe in all the miraculous records of Jewish history, treat those of every other nation of antiquity with scornful denial. As to Magic, why as something which can be taught, "it may be true," and perhaps even become a fashionable amusement, provided always that book-learning, and a superficial digest of the opinions of others, can point out the royal road to power, and convert tinsel drawing-rooms into the halls of Walhalla, wine and cigars into the Alembic of Alfarabi, gilded mirrors into the divining crystal of Dee, and extrait de bouquet into the elixir vitae of St. Germain. A few pages of Cornelius Agrippa, which no modern "Exquisite" would take the trouble to translate himself, ought, in modern estimation, to be quite sufficient to make a magician, and teach fine ladies to summon Slyphs and Undines for the amusement of an idle hour, just as a few pigments of Latin, an essay done into bad Greek, and worse Hebrew, by a professional college drudge, for the benefit of his rich paying patron, is sufficient passport to those holy orders of our modern priesthood in which God, Angels, Spirits, the immortal soul's origin, destiny, and powers, together with all the glories, marvels and mysteries of the boundless and eternal Universe, are the themes which demand interpretation.

The most supervidial retrospect of the lives, education and preparatory methods of discipline enforced upon the ancient priesthood, invest that body with the true dignity of men in "holy order;" but how do these compare with the careless, laxy system of mere book-learning, which in our own time is deemed all-sufficient to grind out a priest, the man who, of all others, should be bound by his sacred office to interpret the mysteries of being, nay, who should be deemed unworthy of that office, so long as mysteries remain unsolved.

Nature has not secrets from her true votaries. She sternly veils spiritual entities from the rude gaze of materialism, and refuses to render up any knowledge beyond the plane from which the inquiry originates. The Chemist, Geologist, Astronomer, and other disciples of the natural sciences, coldly set to work to examine Nature through her known formulae of physical laws; aught that transcends these they will none of, hence the occult side of Nature is an unexplored realm to them, and yet they are prompt enough to acknowledge that that occult side exists, through their sneer is loud and long against those who claim to have mastered its mysteries.

It is because the experience of past ages, conducted through thousands of years of study, by aid of carefully prepared conditions, has been devoted to the occult in Nature, that the ancients transcend the moderns in this respect, as much as modern science, in the direction of utilitarianism, transcends the colossal but cumbrous grandeur of antique civilization. There lives not now upon the face of the earth, one human being, save perchance, a solitary adept of the old order, or a very pure and highly endowed spirit medium, who, in respect to the understanding of true Theosophy, Theurgy, and every department of spiritual science, is fit to hold the office of Priest to the people, or instruct humanity in those grand truths which lie beyond the ken of physical science. It is to show the results of opinions which arise from countless ages of research into occult truths, that this section has been written. It is to present to the candid and bold thinker, the fruits of that knowledge which was gathered in through the discipline of asceticism, fasting, and prayer, and the study of the whole Universe, not less in the realm of soul and spirit, than in body and function, that we now write. Despite these treasures of mind, garnered up through thousands of years, if ye will, but it is thus alone that the Universe has ever yielded an answer to the soul's urgent questioning; thus alone can man ever solve the mystery of his being, and that of his planet.

To point the way, we have written; to show the kernel of the mighty fruit of the tree of occult knowledge, will these pages be devoted. But he who would eat of that fruit understandingly, must first plant the tree with his own hands, tend and culture it with a philosopher's patience, and then, and then alone, will it yield to his taste the true knowledge of good and evil, then only will he eat for himself, and not through the senses of another.

We shall conclude this section by another brief excerpt from the pages of the author whose definitions of Rosicrucianism we have given above:

"It is reasonable to conclude, at a period when knowledge was at the highest, and when human powers were, in comparison with ours at the present time, prodigious, that all these indomitable physical efforts - such gigantic achievements as those of the Egyptians, were devoted to a mistake? That the myriads of the Nile were fools, laboring in the dark, and that all the magic of their great men was forgery? or that we, in despising that which we call their superstitious and wasted power, are alone the wise? Not so. There is much more in these old religions than in the audacity of modern denial, in the confidence of these superficial science times and in the derision of these days without faith, we can in the least degree suppose.

"We do not understand; then why should we venture to deride these ancient times?"

Section IX
Ancient Priests and Prophets
--

The chief duties of the ancient Priesthood were first, to find out the points of contact or unity between man and higher existences than himself; next, to discover the laws of man's being, and teach him to adjust his actions to the will of those higher existences; and finally, to invoke or solicit their aid for man in the performance of his earthly mission. These were the duties of the ancient Priest, and should be no less obligatory upon officials of the same order to-day, but whilst we see some attempt in the external rites of ecclesiasticism to perform the third part of these priestly offices, we look in vain to discover any religious body which faithfully emulates the ancient Priest in the performance of the two first named duties.

It is enough for the historian to record that it has been done, and show that it was upon the performance of the solemn offices of spiritual ministry, that the structure of ancient Priesthood was upreared.

Amongst the Hindoos, Egyptians, Chaldeans, Persians and Hebrews, frequent mention is made of the Prophets, as a class distinct from the Priesthood, although at times associated with it. When the Prophets did take part in the temple services, they were esteemed the most honored of the Priestly order, and their dictum was received with unquestioning reverence as the voice of Deity.

Some authoritative writers intimate that it was upon the foundation of true prophetic gifts, that the Priesthood was instituted, and when it was found that Spiritual gifts belonged to special individuals - not to an office or caste - artificial means were resorted to, to supply the deficiency of natural endowments. Nature has studied to find out occult means of including vision, trance, seership and prophecy. The Priests were carefully instructed in astrology, theurgic rites, and the occult virtues of drugs, minerals, plants, words and ceremonial observances, and hence arose the art of magic, an art practiced simply as a substitute for spiritual gifts.

Amongst the Hebrews, the Prophets, as a class, acted independently of the Priesthood. They were often persons outside of the consecrated tribe of Levites, to whom the Priestly office was limited, when they were not only excluded by their birth from temple service, but they frequently acted in opposition to the Priesthood, and included them in their bold and unsparing denunciations against the corruptions of the time. Nothing can be more aggressive than the diatribes of Isaiah, Jeremiah and Ezekiel, against the abominations sanctioned by a corrupt and idolatrous Priesthood. Isaiah particularizes even the ceremonials of the Jewish faith, such as the observance of new moons, Sabbaths, fasts, feasts, times and seasons, as "abominations before the Lord," when they were practiced for impure of unholy purposes.

The contrast between the bigotry and conservatism of the Jewish Priesthood, and the bold, high-toned morality of the Hebrew Prophets, is one of the most remarkable specialties of the books of the Old Testament, and speaks in most significant language of the universal faith in good works inculcated by true Spiritism, and the dependence upon magical rites of mere ceremonial religions.

It will be observed that whilst several of the most renowned of the Greek Philosophers, such as Orpheus, Thales, Solon, Pythagoras, Appolonius, and others, studied in Egypt, or claimed to have obtained their occult knowledge in that land, their biographies prove, that they were naturally endowed with the true prophetic afflatus before they graduated in Egyptian Magic, and this is a comment upon the difference between natural and acquired gifts, which we desire our readers to bear in mind.

The Greeks must have fully recognized the superiority of natural over acquired gifts of the spirit, when they were so constant in selecting women to serve as the oracles between Gods and men. Women made famous the oracles of the Pythian Apollo, and the responses of Dodona. Women's special gifts, of inspiration, have transmitted the fame of the Sybils to all ages, and made their name synonymous with spiritual gifts. Even amongst the conservative Jews, whose contempt of women is one of the chief blots on their national credit, women were perforce admitted to certain prophetic offices in the temple, and several ladies of rank amongst the Romans and Egyptians, including the daughter of the famous Egyptian Monarch, Sesostris, were renowned for their prophetic endowments.

The elevation of woman to conditions of perfect equality with man, is now acknowledged to be the highest evidence of a true and rational civilization, but whether we are treating of ancient or modern conservatism, God in nature has proved through the unbroken lines of history, that spiritual gifts are innate, intuitional, and feminine in quality, and belong to those more rare and precious attributes of being, which particularly distinguish the female sex. If Soul essence is unique, and matter is shaped and determined chiefly by the energy and quantity of the Astral Spirit, it is to that realm of being that we must look, in order to analyze the specialty that constitutes natural prophetic endowments, or spiritual gifts, whether in the male or female sex.

At the very outset of our inquiry, we find two specialties of organism which more commonly belong to the male than the female, the study of which is important to a clear understanding of our subject. The first of these representative physiques, discloses an individual with a compact self-centered, well-knit frame, inclining to the nutritive in temperament, and the adipose in tissue. In manner these individuals are generally straightforward, somewhat authoritative, occasionally egotistic, and fond of display; kind-hearted, benevolent, and especially attracted to sick persons.

They generally have a clear eye, direct glance, and sometimes a piercing expression withal. With such peculiarities of temperament, the Astral fluid exists in excess, endowing the individual with good health, a vigorous frame, a moderately active mind, and a general tendency towards social life and material enjoyment.

These persons are almost always what is popularly termed "good magnetizers," and the excess of Astral fluid which develops itself in the above described idiosyncrasies, ordinarily induces the wish to use their gift, and impels them to magnetize sick people. It was from this class that the ancients selected their Therapeutic healers and the Priests who were employed in the magnetic healing rites of Temple service. The eye as the window of the Soul, and the hand as the prime conductor of the Astral fluid, are always well developed in these natural mesmerizers.

Where the first is full, clear, and luminous, and the second soft and warm, the astral fluid is invariably of a healthful and unifying character.

Where the eye is piercing, brilliant, or distinguished by the long Oriental shape of the almond, and the hand is damp and moist, or hard and dry, look to find a stronger mental than physical impression produced, but in all varieties of this type of man, the person may be esteemed as a good mesmerizer, and the more expansive the frontal region of the brain, the better will be the effects, and the more healthful the power produced.

As the magnet or loadstone only yields up the potency to the direction of skill, so these magnetic structures require the action of well-informed mind, and concentrated will, to render them serviceable; with these mental attributes to guide their powers and direct the projection of the Astral fluid, they may become admirable healers of the sick, or skillful "biologists" over sensitive subjects.

The second individuality to which we would introduce our reader, is a more concentrated and energetic type of the first, and one in whom the intellectual temperament prevails over the nutritive or social.

In the type of man now under consideration, a vast amount of the Astral fluid circulates, but it clusters chiefly about the crowning portions of the cerebrum, elevating the cranial apex in a remarkable degree. The cerebrum and nervous system absorb the surplus of the Astral fluid, rather than the fibrous and muscular tissues. Such persons exhibit many varieties of form and feature; but their specialty is a large and finely developed head. Persons of this type become fine psychologists, or in ancient phraseology, such are "Adepts, Master Spirits, or Priestly Hierophants." In both types described above, it is the abundance of the Astral spirit, infused by inheritance and planetary and solar influence during embryonic life, and at the period of birth, which determines their characteristics; and it is the distribution of this Astral fluid, in that one, throughout the whole system, and in the other, in certain regions of the brain, which constitutes the difference between the mere magnetic healer and the psychologists. Neither of these individuals may technically recognize the peculiarities with which they are endowed, but the one will always bring a powerful and soothing influence to the sick, and the other prove a controlling and masterful mind in whatever spheres of life he may be placed. If these persons understand their soul's capacities, they will know that, by mustering the excess of Astral fluid, permeating their systems, to the dominion of the will, they can induce a self-magnetized condition, in which the body sleeps, and the soul goes forth and traverses space, as in the phenomenon of somnambulism, natural clairvoyance, or in the exit of the spirit from the body when it is seen and termed the "Double," or "Wraith." They can induce these powers in others by magnetic and psychologic contact, and it only needs self-knowledge and the exertion of strong and concentrated will to call them into exercise.

There are no phenomena produced by disembodied spirits, which may not be affected by the still embodied human spirit, provided a correct knowledge of these powers is directed by a strong and powerful will. The conditions will be described in our sections on Art Magic, but the potency of the will can never be too strongly insisted upon in all Spiritualistic operations. In the physique above described as No. 1, the excess of the Astral fluid generally clusters around the epigastric and cardiac regions, rendering the person thus endowed highly powerful in physical magnetization and healing operations, but, as before hinted, the cerebral development is rarely proportionably marked, and the best of physical magnetizers are not the giants of intellect and psychological control.

The reverse of this position obtains in the organisms classed as No. 2. In them, the Astral fluid inheres more closely to the soul than the body; exalts the top of the cranium rather than the front; compels a predominance of the organs of command and ideality; projects its sphere of indomitable influence on all around, and unfolds the intellectual faculties into singular prominence, in whatever direction they exist, rendering the individual remarkable as a Statesman, General, Author, Priest, Physician, or, if devoted to the study, irresistible as an "Adept," Magician and controller of mundane and sub-mundane spirits. Such individuals are generally as eager as they are capable of penetrating into nature's profoundest depths.

We might rank the amiable and highly gifted Anton Mesmer as a type of the organism No. 1, and the noble sages of Greece, Apollonius and Pythagoras, as shining illustrations of the type described as No. 2.

Prophets, or Mediums, are persons in whom, from inherited causes, and Astral influences prevailing at birth, an immense amount of the Astral fluid exists, but who, by the peculiar conformation of the tissues which make up their physical structures, are too ready to part with their super abundant life principle. In powerful psychologists, the Astral fluid is concentrated, the tissues of the body firm and compact, and the efflux of magnetic power is due only to its superabundance. The medium with the same excess of magnetic force is totally lacking in the concentration and solidity which distinguishes the other class. The one in physique as in character is wholly positive; the other purely negative. The one the operator, the other the subject. The physical structure of the two may present little or no external signs of difference to those who do not study physiological types, rather than surface varieties, but the arrangement of the molecules in the two organisms, are structurally dissimilar, and this dissimilarity exhibits itself thus:

The magnetizer imparts strength from the abundance of his strength. The medium exhales the life principle to depletion, and, in the loss sustained, insensibly draws upon the forces of others. The medium is emphatically a "Sensitive." Every nerve is laid bare, every pore is a conductor of the too rapidly ebbing life fluid. When the brain is small, and the generating power of this life fluid is weak (the brain being its source), the intellectual faculties are limited and dull; the mind, incapable of drawing from the brain, becomes inactive, and the nature is stolid and unimpassioned. it is from such types as these that the superficial remark has arisen, that media should be, or always are, "very passive," unintellectual persons. There, however, are only one type of the class. A great many person, highly charged with the Astral fluid, and losing it in such rapid streams as to constitute them good mediums, are in consequence exceedingly sensitive, restlessly nervous, and susceptible to every influence they come in contact with. The life principle flows off all too rapidly through their tissues, leaving them irritable, weak and despoiled.

As nature abhors a vacuum, these organisms necessarily attract the Astral spirits of all things and persons around them, hence others in their presence often experience a sensible diminution of strength, whilst the media themselves are frequently affected painfully or pleasurably by the mere approach of certain individuals, realizing also the special influences which attach to scenes, places, houses and garments, which would produce no effect upon less susceptible persons. It is this extreme susceptibility and the negative condition produced by the loss of Astral fluid, which renders such persons fine instruments for the control of spirits.

These beings, clothed with the same Astral element which forms the spiritual body of mortals, readily effect a rapport with the class of organisms we have described. This rapport, however, most generally transpires between the spirits who are in the nearest proximity to earth.

It must be remembered that the atmosphere is as full of spiritual life, as the water is of animalculae. The Astral fluid - the element in which spirits live, and of which their external bodies are composed, permeates this atmosphere, like oceans of light, hence spiritual life is to this planet, what the Soul is to the body, only that the strata of spiritual life nearest the earth are graduated from the spirits of those who are most in rapport with earth, to elementary beings, who in reality constitute no inconsiderable portion of the earth itself, hence it is, that mediumistic persons - susceptible to the influences of varied life that swarms around them - are often moved by nameless and incomprehensible monitions of danger, the presence of evil, or the tendency to actions from which their own better natures and judgment would revolt.

The chief points of difference between the ancient Prophet, the Mediaeval Witch, and the modern Medium, consist in the aims and influences which severally actuated them, and inspired the spirits that surrounded them. The prophetic men and women of old were intensely religious persons. They lived in devotional ages, too, when their exceptional gifts marked them out for a species of reverence which almost amounted to worship. Separated from their fellow men by the peculiar sanctity attached to the prophetic character, their religious aspirations, and the asceticism of their lives, attracted to them beings of a far higher order than those whom we now invoke in the communion with family spirits and kindred ties.

Most of the ancient Prophets, Seers, and Sybils, prepared for the communion with higher intelligences than earth, by methods to be hereafter described, hence their powers were more concentrated, and phenomenally greater than those of the work-a-day trading media of the present time.

As to the Spiritism of the mediaeval ages, unless it existed in the persons of learned mystics, who cultured it after the ancient fashion, or it fell as a mantle of inspiration on poets, painters, musicians, inventors, religious reformers, etc., it degenerated into ugly and often injurious obsession, by ignorant spirits, attracted to media of a character kindred with themselves. Thus the study of different phases of spiritual influx proves how much its representation is determined by the age, spirit of the time, and character of the communicating intelligence.

Europe and America are at present in the heyday flush of materialistic civilization.

Utilitarianism is the genius of the nineteenth century. If religion could be put to some practical use, or reduced to a scientific analysis, it would be as much the fashion now as it was five thousand years ago; but whatever comes in the shape of religious belief, even scientific discoveries concerning the occult side of nature, must conform to the materialistic and utilitarian spirit of the age, or the age will none of it. Such is the crucible of human opinion through which the Spiritism of this century has to pass, and hence mediumship is a trade, an amusement, or a curiosity; Spiritism, a marketable commodity, or a fashionable mode of beguiling an idle hour. As inspiration invariably descends from the same plane to which aspiration ascends, spirit answers spirit from correspondential realms of thought and intelligence.

As it is below, so it is above; in the skies as on the earth.

Having briefly depicted the general characteristics of those through whom spirits communicate, we shall proceed to classify the groups into which prophetic or mediumistic gifts resolve themselves.

Premising that each mediumistic person is so by inheritance, or the awakening of latent but still functional powers, and that we are not now treating of that magic which compensates by art for the lack of natural endowments, we shall render such definitions of our subject, as practical experience suggests.

The Trance state ranges from that of Ecstasy, in which visions of the highest and most transcendental nature are revealed, through all the various stages of Somnambulism, to that semi-conscious sleep-waking condition, in which the ego is not lost, but wherein the origin of the thought, whether from the subject's own mind, or the impression of another's is not clearly discerned.

Inspiration is the addition of higher mentality to that of the subject's own individuality. It does not necessitate any abnegation of self-consciousness; it only stimulates that consciousness to extraordinary exaltation.

In all these states the influence of spirits is more than likely to be the superinducing cause. That influence is exerted in precisely the same fashion as the simply human processes of electro-biology, and by operators, who have either practiced this method of control on earth or been endowed with the power by nature to do so. The spirit projects his Astral spirit in the fashion of the earthly magnetizer upon his mediumistic subject; by this fluid the system becomes charged and the magnetic sleep, semi-conscious trance, or the exaltation of inspiration is induced.

These graduated conditions represent the amount of passivity or mental activity of the subject - total unconsciousness usually falling upon a very receptive and passive mind, and inspiration stimulating rather than subduing the powers of an already highly unfolded intellect. When the system is sufficiently saturated with the spiritual magnetizer's Astral fluid, as to be subject to control, the operator, by strong will, infuses high thought into the subject's mind; but whatever the specialty of thought may be, it becomes shaped, tinctured and not unfrequently marred to a greater or less degree by the idiosyncrasies of the medium's habits of speech and methods of expression. There must always be an adaptation between the subject on earth and the operator of the spheres. A spirit of a totally foreign and unsympathetic nature to the medium could not obtain control, except in the case of obsession, and that transpires through the brutal and resistless power of a gross, strong, earth-bound spirit, acting upon a generally frail, susceptible and most probably sickly organism.

In the ordinary exercise of spirit control, the spirit acting as a good magnetizer, chooses a well-adapted subject, whose mind and physique are calculated to assimilate with his own, and thus presents his ideas through the aid of a borrowed vehicle of thought. This mode of influence corresponds in many respects to the vaticinations of the Sybils and Prophetesses of old, only that the utterance of the Spirits termed Gods, or Demons, commonly took place in bodies which had previously been prepared by fastings, ablutions and sometimes by the inhalations of vapors, which subdued the senses, stimulated them to "mantic frenzy," or prepared the system for the infusion of a superior consciousness to their own.

These modes of control by spirits, speaking through the lips of entranced or inspired media, are not limited in their effects to the exhibition of merely curious mental transformations. In ancient, as in modern times, these oracular utterances have been productive of a far wider range of good and revolutionary thought than is dreamed of by those who listen, go hence, and deem they have simply been interested for the moment, and will certainly forget the ideas they have heard.

The Soul never forgets. The over-laden brain of humanity retains the impression of every image presented to it. As each fresh succession of images photographs itself on the mind's tablets, the last seem to crowd out and efface the impress of the earlier ones. They vanish from sight truly, but they are still there, and there they remain forever. Unconsciously to their possessors, they enter into every phase of character. They linger like a subtle perfume in the sphere of unconscious cerebration, pervade the sentiments, enter into the mental structure, shape the motives, externalize themselves in words which linger in others' ears, in deeds which affect others' destinies, and silently interweave themselves into invisible but indestructible images, reflected upon the Astral light of the Universe. Could this most subtle, but most potential realm of being be thoroughly explored, all the thoughts, words, and deeds, that have ever moved the race would be found in ineffaceable pictures engraved upon the billows of Astral light that heave and swell through the oceans of infinity. Nothing is lost in nature, nothing blotted out in eternity, and future generations, living, moving and breathing in the Astral realms of life imprinted with the Soul images of vanished ages, inhale them, grow in them, re-combine them into the elements of their own characters, and thus live over again, in ever rolling, but ever ascending cycles of time, every sand-grain of ideality that has ever been launched into space. hence, too, the universality of ideas; the spontaneous affection of two kindred minds unknown to each other, and removed apart by long intervals of distance, and yet how often are such at the same moment of time inspired by the same thought, moved to execute the same work, and even construct the same, yet apparently original, piece of mechanism; write the same stanzas of poetry, or arrange the same strains of melody into duplicate forms! This is the source of thought epidemics, mental contagions and infectious opinions.

The gross atmosphere of earth traversed by the seas of Astral light cannot but become charged with the images they bear, and whenever two waves of this Astral fluid unite to form an idea, some receptive mind seizes upon it. The wave flows on, the idea strikes another, and yet another mind, until the force of one leading thought sweeps on its grand career of influence, from pole to poke, and traverses the mental girth of an age, although, perchance, none but the constructive genius of a few can assimilate and utilize it. Trance mediums of the New Dispensation - Prophets of the old! Nothing is lost in Nature. Fear not for the results of they labors! Whatever is false or worthless will fade and perish - the beautiful and true never die!

The next class of media who represent the power of spirits to communicate with earth, are those impressed with artistic and intellectual ideas. They are moved to draw strange patterns, groups of flowers, portraits of deceased persons, symbolical or emblematical pictures, to write messages, words of love, poems, often containing tokens of memory which identify the controlling power with some individual who once inhabited a mortal body. Music totally foreign to the medium's mind or capacity has been thus given; foreign languages spoken and written by those unacquainted with them; pantomimic representations have been made, depicting the peculiarities of some deceased friend; and thus every sense is used, and every faculty brought into play, to prove the presence and influence of a world of being rising up like immortal blossoms from the ashes of the vanished dead.

Spirits making use of the Astral light which permeates all space, sometimes impress upon it visionary pictures of future events; sometimes shadowy representations of their own forms, and always in such shape as will identify them with those who have been deemed dead, and laid away in the quiet grave.

Spirits are full of ingenious resource, highly constructive and far more widely informed upon the arcanum of nature than mortals, hence can produce a greater variety of effects, and in much shorter period of time than we can conceive of, hence their methods of representation strike us as abnormal and magical. They are simply due to magnetization of the medium's spirits by the invisible operator, and psychological impressions produced through will upon the medium's spiritual consciousness.

The third order of media who specially distinguish themselves in the modern spiritual movement are those through, whom strong, powerful, earthbound spirits can act upon material bodies, and cause them to become telegraphic signs of their presence.

The persons through whom these theurgic signals are made, for the most part absorb the Astral fluid which is their life, through the cerebellum, the epigastric nerves, and the great solar plexus. Though not necessarily deficient in cerebral development, they are rarely distinguished in this region, and, in some instances, the preponderance of nervous force in the ganglionic or sympathetic system is greatly in excess of the cerebro-spinal, thus stimulating the instinctive appetites, especially those which correspond to animal tendencies.

This is not invariably the case, but it has and does characterize much mediumship of this order. It is also a significant fact, and one which should commend itself in the attention alike of the physiologist and psychologist, that persons afflicted with scrofula and glandular enlargements, often seem to supply the pabulum which enables spirits to produce ponderous manifestations of physical power.

Frail, delicate women - person, too, whose natures are refined, innocent and pure, but whose glandular system has been attacked by the demon of Scrofula, have frequently been found susceptible of becoming the most remarkable instruments for physical demonstrations by spirits. In some instances mediums for this class of phenomena are persons in the enjoyment of rude health and vigorous constitutions. The author has witnessed manifestations of the most astounding character eliminated through the mediumship of rugged country girls and stout men, especially the natives of Ireland and Northern Germany; but a close and careful scrutiny of those remarkably endowed media, will often reveal a tendency to epilepsy, chorea and functional derangements of the pelvic apparatus, which proves that the cerebellum and the ganglionic system of nerves are unduly charged, and that the magnetism of spirits of a similar temperament to their own may exaggerate these constitutional tendencies into excess and disease. It is a fact, which we may try to mask, or the acknowledgment of which we may indignantly protest against, yet it is a fact nonetheless, that the existence of remarkable medium powers, argues a want of balance in the system; and whilst the theory of too rapid ebb of the life forces and their excess, and unequal distribution, renders physical and scientific causes for this structural inharmony, it also proves what is the character of the pabulum which spirits use to produce the magnetic, psychologic and physical effects which are rendered through these unevenly balanced organisms.

It has frequently been asked whether there is any philosophy to explain these aberrations of nature, to which we reply, assuredly there is. The Astral fluid becomes characterized by every material atom through which it passes. It is at once the cause and effect of all varieties in nature. Its abundance, and the energy of its action, is determined by the quantity and quality of the atoms through which it flows; but once incorporated in organic bodies as their attribute, its own quality becomes materially affected by the quality of the particles it vitalizes; and here it is proper to recur to the opinion of many illuminated Seers, namely that there are several layers, or strata, of these Astral currents, forming as a totality one spiritual body. Those nearest the Soul are the finest in quality and represent the spheres related to the Solar and Astral systems. Those layers on the outer surface of the spiritual body, most nearly inhering to the material atoms, form the life spheres, permeate the body, partake of its quality, deteriorate or improve with it, are gross, coarse or dense, as the body's habits or mind's tendencies characterize it; in a word, it is this portion of the Astral spirit, which streams forth from the medium in a flood of emanation, and hence becomes the exact gauge of the medium's physical and mental state. It is particles of this latter description which form the life principle of plants and minerals.

It is these fiery elements of universal life force, which are struck out in radiant sparks from the hard flinty rock, or crystalline iron. Violent action will drive forth the lambent flames of life from every solid body, and cause them to quiver between the strokes of every concussion. They stream forth in odic lights from shells, crystals, magnets, and all magnetic bodies. They reach out their fingers of latent fiery force, to gather up kindred particles around the loadstone. They stream up in pencilled rays of many colored glory, painting over the northern skies with gorgeous illuminations in the wonderful Aurora Borealis. They form the electric paths in which rolling worlds, suns and systems are held in innumerable lines of force. They flash in the wild fires of contending cloud armies. They discharge solemn peals of heavenly artillery in the roar of the battling tempest.

They shout their anthems of power in the heaving billows, and sob away the last echos of sound in the murmur of the half slumbering waves. These invisible, latent, all-pervading flames of life, these direct emanations from the Central Sun of all being, connect suns and planets, earths and satellites by the stupendous chains of force, and fill all space with oceans of invisible, but ever living fires. They fill all creation with life, but take on the protean forms of every atom through which their living currents are forever ebbing and flowing.

Then need we not marvel that the Astral fluid which flows through the refined particles of a pure and healthful human organism, might afford intellectual spirits an opportunity of impressing the brain with high inspirational ideas, yet fail to give off that superabundance of quantity or denseness of quality, which is requisite to produce manifestations of a ponderable character - on the other hand, remembering the almost infinite varieties of exhibition which the Astral fluid assumes in accordance with the variousness of the particles through which it flows, we need not feel surprised that a human body abundantly endowed with this same life fluid, so constituted as to eliminate it through every pore, but giving off a quality which is especially redolent of influences generated in the vital and nutritive system of nerves, should furnish that pabulum which enables spirits to construct forms, and produce manifestations of a purely physical character.

In this scheme of natural order, disease must impress itself upon every imponderable particle of the Astral sphere, and since the body laboring under disease is really being disintegrated, and parts too rapidly and freely with its life principle, so do sick persons give off in the most abundance, and of the most dense quality, the element which spirits can use for the production of strong physical manifestations.

The same philosophy with certain modifications, applies to the mediumship of little children.

Endowed with a superabundance of that vital force which is necessary for the purposes of growth, young children disprove of this excess in general by violent exercise, exercise which would exhaust more mature bodies, but which nature impresses them to undertake as a safety-valve, for the escape of the vital currents, with which their young fresh frames are charged to repletion. Unscrupulous spirits who perceive the powerful aromal essences which flow forth so freely from the young, take advantage of its existence, to produce manifestations of their presence, and thus, it so often happens, that children, like sick persons, become potent media for spirits. It should be added that the practice of permitting children thus to be exercised as mediums, should only be indulged in to a very limited extent, the excessive draught procured from their tender and susceptible frames, rendering them liable to lose health, strength, and perhaps life itself, under its action.

We do not now enlarge upon the good or evil results of this kind of rapport between spirits and mortals, we simply write of its modes, and the means of ready access which spirits find for its performance.

The physical force medium is often endowed with a great variety of gifts, because the Astral fluid, charging the whole body to excess, and flowering through every pore with a profuse expenditure of the life principle, constitutes all the organs mediums. The skin is charged, rendering it liable to be impressed with fleshy letters. The eye becomes a ready conductor to the spiritual eye beneath, imparting the faculty of clairvoyance. The entire of the spiritual senses find ready expression through a physique which is all mediumistic, and a complete battery for the action of controlling spirits. Let it be remembered that in all magnetic operations every particle of the life fluid represents the whole; thus a sensitive by coming in contact with a lock of hair, a handkerchief, or the smallest piece of fabric touched by another, can psychometrically discover the entire of that other's nature. This alone would prove (were there other facts wanting), that one particle of the subtle fluid of life represents the whole, and this can only be accounted for by acknowledging the truth of a curious hypothesis, presented to the world by a celebrated physiologist, who says:

"Through the perspiratory ducts, and all the other methods by which nature supplies to the organism an apparatus for the dual functions of absorption and evaporation, the human body exhales the imponderable portions of blood, bone, nervous and muscular tissue, even the effete exhalations of hair and nails which go to make up the totality of the structure.

"All those vaporized elements are in the atmosphere, carried by the gasses, exhaled from the lungs, and swept off from the photosphere of the human body, into the atmosphere that surrounds it. If we could arrive at any method of separating the organic from the inorganic particles that fill the air, and charge the atmosphere with living emanations, where human life abounds, we might crystallize them back again into human bodies, and hence the claim of the Spiritualists to have found in spiritual magnetism that crystallizing element by which they can re-clothe the spirit with a material body, gathered up from the atmosphere which surrounds a circle of investigators, is neither so wild or improbable after all."

It would be a fact in spiritual phenomena, even if it were "wild and improbable" in hypothesis; but to those who are acquainted with the nature of the Astral fluid - its identity with the universal element we call force - its existence in man as a spiritual body, in the spirit's organism as an external body, and in the atmosphere as force per se; it only needs an appreciation of the physiological idea above suggested, as to the character of our emanations, to understand why spirits, having at command a dense and powerful stream of the Astral fluid exhaled from peculiar organisms, can easily use that as a force for crystallizing the imponderable elements, which abound in the atmosphere, into a temporary physical covering for themselves.

The medium's very flesh, and all the fluids and solids of his physique, are given off by exhalations, and remain in the atmosphere. These exhalations from the physical medium are abundant in quantity, powerful and magnetic in quality, and so long as they can be extracted by the magnetism of attendant spirits, and sustained by the combined magnetisms of other human beings, their crystallization by the aid of spiritual chemistry, can be readily effected, and spirits can thus temporarily re-clothe themselves in atoms of actual flesh and blood. They pass sparks of electricity through these imponderable exhalations, just as chemists can crystallize gases into fluids, and fluids into solids, by the same process. By aid of strong will, and having all the elements held in solution in the atmosphere, spirits can even communicate objective solidity to the images in their minds, and thus present again the ponderable semblances of ornaments, clothes, and other physical fabrics; nay more, by imparting to these temporarily formed substances a sufficient amount of the Astral fluid to produce cohesion, they can be kept in being for a considerable time after the first formative process has been effected.

There is no witchcraft or sorcery in these transformations, although they may with propriety take rank as spiritual magic; the Spirit is the Man, the Soul the designer; the Astral body the force, the mover, the motion, the executant.

The material body is only a vehicle, enabling the Soul through the Astral body or spirit to come into contact with matter. In the above necessarily brief description of spiritual phenomena, we only touch on the results of communion effected between spirits and mortals, where the former find conditions spontaneously prepared by nature for their use. We shall conclude this section by reviewing the possibilities which exist in every human being for producing extra-mundane effects through the application of natural laws to spiritual forces.

The gifts of the spirit are spiritual sight - hearing, taste, smell and touch, wholly independent of the material avenues of sense. The power of projecting the Astral fluid from one individual to another, through magnetic manipulations, contact or will, and the power of impressing the will of one individual by the superior force of another. The soul also possesses the power of so concentrating its own astral spirit, as to temporarily subjugate the other senses, steep them in forgetfulness, and then withdraw from the body, wander forth at will, preserve the body from death by leaving a sufficient portion of the Astral fluid to maintain its integrity, and subsequently return to and resume its occupancy of the body. There are still other powers of the embodied human Soul of which we shall yet speak more in detail, suffice it for the present to sum up by saying the Soul cannot only perform all the phenomena now executed by the aid of disembodied spirits, but it can command the assistance of inferior grades to man, and compel their aid in subjugating the forces of matter.

Man can read the hidden things of another's mind, and even temporarily obsess it, and by aid of inferior spirits, psychologize many persons at once, compelling them to see, hear, taste or feel the subjective images of his creation.

He can envelope some objects in the Astral fluid, rendering them invisible to the material eye; create disturbances in the atmosphere, or calm them by the same means; promote rapid and spontaneous growth in the vegetable world; wound the body and heal it in the same minute of time; render himself insensible to pain, fire, and the effects of gravitation, and so float in mid-air; cause himself to be buried alive during entrancement, and resume the functions of life when disinterred.

All these things we positively affirm men can do, through the operation of his own will, and the aid of powerful spirits, and all those things the author positively affirms he has witnessed, and proposes in the forthcoming sections to give the philosophy of, as gathered from personal experience, and the descriptions of Fakeers, Yogees, Dervishes, Bramins, and the adepts of Oriental systems of magic.

Whether our readers will observe the conditions necessary for the performance of these extra-mundane acts of spiritual power, is a question which we do not propose to decide upon; but we commend our closing remarks to special consideration.

The Soul is an emanation from Deity; therefore Deific in power and attributes. The Astral spirit which clothes the Soul and vitalizes the body, is a part of all the great motor power of the Universe, the source and cause of all motion.

The two combined, though temporarily shrouded in matter, and limited by the encasements of a material body, still form a Deific, and therefore all-powerful existence, which only requires the light of spiritual science to render its functions as Deific as its source. Something of this is shown, then the soul is emancipated from the body and returns to earth manifesting its astonishing and extended powers through what is called "spiritual phenomena."

Other glimpses of these powers shine forth, through the lives of ecstatics, seers, and magians; but what illimitable possibilities yet remain unfathomed and unheard of?

Who can say where the terminal line is drawn between God and His creatures, or why man should not manifest as a microcosm, all the creative attributes which belong to the Divine Author, the Macrocosm?

The superiority of ancient over modern Theosophy, does not arise from any retrogression in man or his planet. It is no arrest or backward step in the march of intellect; but it results from the profound devotion with which the ancient man regarded spiritual things, and the cold materialism of the present day; from the unceasing aspiration of our forefathers towards spiritual light and knowledge, and the universal contempt or indifference with which such subjects are regarded now.

The people of antiquity generally, and the priesthood in particular studied into the laws of spiritual forces, and spent generation after generation in analyzing their principles, and the relations they bear to visible nature.

Those thinkers of the nineteenth century, who strive to master the occult in nature at all, aim at doing so, by seeking for the spiritual through the laws of the material and expect to push their way upward, from the known, to the unknown, from matter to spirit.

Let those who would emulate the Divine plan, and work from the center to the circumference, from Deity to His creatures, and from Soul essence to created forms, despise not the results of human experience, and the strivings of the human mind for light and knowledge in any age, ancient or modern. Regarding the past as a stepping-stone to the present, and the lower chambers and galleries of the great Temple of humanity as the foundations upon which the integrity of the superstructure depends, let us with humble and reverent spirits avail ourselves of the successes and failures of our ancestors, as the warnings and encouragements by which our own steps may be safely guided, and boldly push on in those transcendent paths of research, in which Angels are our guides, ministering spirits our strength, the elevation and culture of the Divine Spirit within us our goal, and God the Spirit, the quenchless beacon-light by which our faltering footsteps will be ever illuminated, until we find our rest at last in Him.

Section X
Art Magic

--

General Summary of the Condition and Processes of Magical Practices - The Line
Between Ancient Theosophy and Occultism - Application of Theories

We adopt the caption of "Art Magic" for this section, because we desire to draw the line
between that vast amount of speculative philosophy, which is inextricably mixed up with
ancient Theosophy, and the occult practices which constitute much of that Theosophy in
application.

Hitherto we have written chiefly of the theories by which the ancients explained the order
of being, and the elements of life power and motion, by which being itself becomes
operative. Until the principles thus laid down are thoroughly well digested, our attempts
to show their application to the practices of magic will fail.

With the most sincere desire to explain the modes by which artificial means can be
induced to evoke the occult powers in nature, or in other words, to practice the art of
magic, our efforts will be in vain, if the reader fails to apprehend what nature is; to
comprehend the structure of man in his threefold character as a material, magical, and
divine being; to follow us in our definitions of the Astral fluid which vitalizes all things
in nature, and the Astral spirit, which constitutes the spiritual body of man; of the
connecting links between Men, Angels, Spirits, and Deity, and the difference between
Prophets and Magicians - the adept who commands spirits, and the medium who is
commanded by them.

Without these preparatory steps for acquiring occult knowledge, magic will remain magic
in its lowest and most obscure sense, and Magic it will be to the end of the chapter.
Magnetism and Psychology are the two pillars that support the Temple of Spiritism.

They are the Herculean columns through which the understanding leads the soul into
supernal realms of power; the "Jachim and Boaz" by which the over-arching vault of the
heavens is upheld, which canopies the Grand Lodge of Spiritual Masonry.

By magnetism the imponderable, all-pervading life element termed Astral fluid is
communicated from one body to another. By psychology the power of one mind
subjugates and controls that of another, and it is in these two spheres of operation that all
the marvels of magic transpire. The difficulties which oppose the scholar's mastery of this
art, as practiced by the ancient and mediaeval philosophers, arise from a concatenation of
causes, all combining to darken knowledge rather than to promote it, and tending to
obscure whatever light could be thrown upon the subject.

In the first place the Priests of antiquity, who were the chief repositories of occult
science, maintained their authority over the populace by reserving its understanding
exclusively to their own order. It was not alone that they deemed such knowledge too

high for vulgar minds, they felt that their own exclusive possession of its secrets was essential to the continuance of their authority, hence it would have been suicidal to entrust the multitude with that reserved force by virtue of which they held their office.

It has often been alleged by modern writers that the ancient mysteries were the conservatories of all occult science, and that those alone who became Heirophants therein, could arrive at a true understanding of Art Magic. It has lately become a received opinion, too, that a study of the ancient Caballah of the Hebrews and Orientals would supply this much desired information, and initiate any patient student of their pages into the arcanum of magic. Neither of these positions is correct. The mysteries indoctrinated their initiates into those theorems of speculative philosophy of which our former sections have given brief summaries.

The Caballah have been perused and studied with the most unwearied care by many a learned scholar, who at the last has utterly failed to enact one single rite of magic successfully.

Let the facts be plainly stated. In all the writings of true and highly endowed Mystics, whether ancient or modern, it is distinctly stated in the language of Cornelius Agrippa, that "a magician must be born so from his mother's womb," and that unless he is so gifted by nature, the processes by which real physiological changes are to be wrought in his system are slow, painful, and difficult of performance.

We have written to little purpose if we have failed to impress upon our readers that the source of all spiritual powers and functions resides in that mysterious combination of imponderable elements which we have termed the Astral spirit or spiritual body of man; that it is to the original and constitutional structure of that Astral spirit, that prophetic or mediumistic endowments are due, and that when these exist inherently in the organism, man is a prophet, a medium, and can readily exalt his powers into those of a magician. The reader may inquire wherein consists the difference between a medium and a magician? We answer, chiefly in degree. The medium is one through whose Astral spirit, other spirits can manifest, making their presence known by various kinds of phenomena. Whatever these consist in, the medium is only a passive agent in their hands. He can neither command their presence, nor will their absence - can never compel the performance of any special act, nor direct its nature. The magician on the contrary, can summon and dismiss spirits at will; can perform many feats of occult power through his own spirit; can compel the presence and assistance of spirits of lower grades of being than himself, and effect transformations in the realm of nature upon animate and inanimate bodies. He can control his fellow-men physically and mentally by will, irrespective of distance, and even cause changes in the destinies of individuals and societies. These powers seem in rehearsal fabulous, nevertheless they have been achieved, and we know that they are still attainable to man. The first great prerequisite, however, is as above stated, a prophetic or naturally mediumistic organization, and where this exists, culture will do the rest; where it is not bestowed by nature, the next step is to change the physique, and so modify its inherent tendencies, as to afford prepared conditions for the exercise of magical powers, and it is the recital of these conditions that will engage our attention during this and the following few sections.

In the first place let us disabuse the minds of those who have been informed that magical knowledge was to be procured only through initiation into the ancient mysteries, or certain modern branches of those orders that may still be found banded together in the Orient. This is emphatically a mistake, if not a willful perversion of the truth, on the part of those who may be still interested in throwing the halo of mystery around their cherished pursuits. There is absolutely nothing in the initiatory rites of any ancient order which can promote magical powers or spiritual afflatus. It is in the discipline enjoined upon initiates, and the effects of real physiological changes thus wrought in their systems, that the entire virtue of the initiation consists; furthermore, if such neophytes as entered upon the preparatory degrees of their initiation, did not manifest the well-known signs of innate magical power, or if after due preparation, they did not give evidence of the possession of magnetic or mediumistic faculties, they were never permitted to take rank as Hierophants, never elevated to that last degree which constituted them adepts.

To be an "Adept," was to be able to practice magic, and to do this was either to be a natural prophet, cultured to the strength of a magician, or an individual who had acquired this prophetic power and magical strength through discipline. The author has passed many years in India, Arabia, China and other Eastern lands, and has frequently practiced, as well as witnessed the rites of initiation in different societies, formed for the study of Magic.

From these, and opportunities suggested by the history of more remote times, we may confidently allege, that unless in the persons of naturally endowed mediums, or those whose organizations have been changed by long and persistent methods of discipline, magical rites have never successfully been enacted, neither have magical results been obtained by virtue of cabalistic words, fumigations, incantations, or other ceremonies alone. There are those now living, whose opinions are entitled to respect, who take other ground than this, and allege that the mere pronunciation of certain words, superstitiously termed "cabalistic," is sufficient to summon spirits of an inferior order to the speaker's presence, and that the possession of talismans and amulets will effect the same results. The author believes he shall be able to sustain his own fixed opinion to the contrary of these beliefs, by citing the teachings of the most authoritative Mystics of ancient and modern times.

For the present we shall argue from the standpoint assumed above, only adding that from early boyhood, the author has himself been both subject and operator in magical practices, and though often associated with noble minds fully skilled in the speculative philosophy of spiritual subjects, he has failed to find any operators in occult lore who depended upon knowledge alone, or who had not qualified themselves by preparatory discipline, or been prepared by inherent endowments, for the remarkable achievements which constitute the Magician.

Anticipating more detailed illustrations of the subject by a few general definitions, we proceed to say, that the first preparatory step for the elimination of magical power is abstinence. Abstinence not alone in food, but from the indulgence of all animal appetites. If, for instance, the student proposes to essay the performance of magical rites at any given period, he should set apart certain days during several months for total abstinence, and during a set period of probation observe the strictest laws of temperance and chastity. The Priests of antiquity were often married men, but, as we have before stated, they were not always prophetic men - on the other hand, the Prophets were almost invariably ascetics, and that of the strictest order - never indulging in the use of wine, seldom of meat, the society of the female sex, or the enjoyment of social and conjugal relations.

The more utterly ascetic they were, the more exalted became their spiritual powers, but without a certain amount of fasting and asceticism, let none expect to succeed in magical practices, for the physiological effects which fasting and asceticism produce, are unalterably essential alike to the male or female sex, in the development of the power under consideration.

The North American Indians, no less than the Charibs and South American tribes of poor, uneducated aborigines, compel their young men to undergo probationary fasts for a period of some eight or nine days, wandering meanwhile through the forests, and carefully avoiding contact with any of their fellow-men. These ascetic practices antedate their assumption of the duties of manhood, or the positions of power and trust, to which the red men deem their sons may become eligible, and it is claimed that this discipline is necessary to enkindle the noblest fires of manhood, quicken their powers of perception, accustom them to endurance, and above all, stimulate the latent spirituality of their Souls to perceive and commune with invisible Guardian Spirits. During these probationary states it is claimed that their Spirit Guides appear to them, reveal their destiny, instruct them in their choice of a mission, and establish a rapport between the spirit and mortal, which is continued through life.

Thus do these children of nature, these poor savages, as the proud Civilian contemptuously denominates them, instinctively perform those initiatory rites which it was the boast of the highest philosophy of antiquity to have instituted.

Every nation of antiquity practiced this species of discipline, previous to entering on a career of spiritual prowess.

The Sybils of Greece and Rome, the Hebrew prophets, the Indian Ecstatics and Egyptian mystics; the Chaldean soothsayers and Roman augurs, the Medes, Persians, Chinese and Japanese, all taught these necessary modes of preparation for prophetic offices.

All the mystics of the MIddle Ages exalt the practices of abstinence, and insist upon its necessity. Of all classes of religious thinkers, the Christians should be the most faithful in the observance of this rite, since it was charged upon them both by the example and precept of their founder, and prescribed as an essential of spiritual discipline, both in the Old and New Testament, and yet the Roman Catholics alone, of all the sects of

Christianity, observe abstinence as a part of their religious duty; and perhaps it is to this cause that we may attribute the greater prevalence of spiritual manifestations amongst them, than with any other religious thinkers of Christendom. Another mode of preparatory exercise for spiritual exaltation is prayer. Prayer, not in the mere routine form of verbal solicitation, but sincere aspiration of soul towards the great Source of all life, light and inspiration. And prayer must be supplemented by solitary communion with the inner consciousness, long periods of seclusion from the external world, and a complete abstraction of the senses from all outward observances; soul musings on the great I Am, and that deep absorption of the reflective powers upon the spirit within which constitutes the triumph of the Soul over matter and its belongings. Ablution, too, is another method of preparing the physique for the flow of the Astral fluid. By frequent ablutions the skin - the organ of the dual functions of evaporation and absorption - is prepared for a free transmission and reception of that Astral fluid which constitutes the magical element. During the intervals of fasting, the food should be very light, consisting chiefly of vegetables and fruits, whilst all stimulants or salacious substances calculated to excite the senses or pamper the appetites, should be carefully avoided. Tea and coffee have not only been deemed admissible, but taken in moderate quantities are recommended by some modern mystics, although the stricter order repudiate their use. It is quite evident that the ancients understood the uses of animal magnetism. The temples of the east are covered with representations of this practice in the treatment of the sick, and the constant allusion to it in ancient and classical writings leaves no doubt but that it was the universal method of therapeutic practice.

Animal magnetism was also the method by which the highest rites of initiation into the sacred mysteries were completed. Using this term in its modern sense, we find it was the special virtue by which both in ancient and modern mysticism the potential powers of the magical element in man is awakened.

The chief value of the initiatory rites of all secret societies, lies in the psychological effect they exert on the senses by the fumigations of incense, the presentation of scenic illusions, the performance of delightful music, no less than the effect which the rehearsal of high thoughts and sublime ideas must produce on the already over-wrought mind. When to all this is added the magnetic effect imparted by the presence and manipulations of powerful adepts, whose Astral fluid, charged with magical strength, is infused into the system of the Neophyte, it can hardly be wondered at that the final rites of initiation in such societies as are banded together for the purpose of discovering and practicing the highest and most occult laws of Nature, cannot fail to send forth Hierophants who feel as did Pythagoras when issuing from the crowning rites of Egyptian mysticism, "that he had been in the presence of the Gods, and drank the waters of life anew from divine chalices."

As a special illustration of our subject, we commend the following item of philosophy, extracted from "Ghost Land," to the reader's attention. It refers to the experiences of the most powerful order of magicians now in existence:

"They acknowledged that the realm of spiritual being was ordinarily invisible to the material, and only known through its effects, being the active and controlling principle of matter; but they had discovered, by repeated experiments, that spiritual forms could become visible to the material under certain conditions, the most favorable of which was somnambulism procured through the magnetic sleep. This state, they found, could be induced sometimes by drugs, vapors and aromal essences; sometimes by spells, or through music, intently staring into crystals, the eyes of snakes, running water, or other glittering substances; occasionally by intoxication caused by dancing, spinning around, or distracting clamors; but the best and most efficacious method of exalting the spirit into the superior world, and putting the body to sleep was, as they had proved, through animal magnetism."

After an experience of more than forty years subsequent to the period when the author learned the truth of the above quoted fragments of philosophy, he lives to confirm them in every iota, and especially the last sentence quoted, which, to his apprehension, contains the true gist of all magical experiences.

No methods ever have been found so potent for kindling up the most exalted fires of the soul, or transmuting its latent powers into active operation, as "the laying on of hands," or the magnetic manifestations of powerful, well-intentioned magnetizers, in a word, the infusion of the vital forces of a mighty and highly charged Adept into the organism of a susceptible and receptive subject.

All other modes are merely preparatory, but they can never equal the effect of that last, best magical charge, which can be wrought only by the infusion of the Astral fluid of one organism into another.

This is the last act of initiation in the highest temple rites of old. This is the potent spell by which Hindoo Fakeers obtain from their master minds the seal upon their magical studies. The Patriarchal act of blessing, the initiatory rites of the Jewish Priesthood, the Apostolic law of communicating virtue, was all wrought by "the laying on of hands."

The Pentecostal gatherings of the early Christians were simply means of magnetizing each other by accordance of a common will, and the focalization of ideas to a common subject.

Paracelsus, Van Helmont and most of the middle age mystics, well understood the virtue of magnetic relations, whether between animate or inanimate existences. In the citations we shall have occasion to make concerning their magical formulae and opinions, it will be seen that they recognized "magnetism and psychology as the two grand supports of the Temple of Spiritism."

Assuming that the Neophyte, who desires to exercise magical powers, has faithfully prepared himself by the methods prescribed above, that he has subjected his frame to fastings, ablutions and strict abstinence; observed periods of seclusion, and disciplined his spirit by silent communings with Deity, the spirit of nature, and his own inner consciousness, all that remains for him to do is to seek out a few harmoniously-disposed persons, who, with pure aims and high aspirations, shall join with him in the search for light and knowledge. Let these unite themselves into a select society, and, after the same order of preparation enjoined above, proceed to magnetize each other, selecting for the work the most powerful and well-composed of their number - in fact, the one who most nearly conforms to the Pythagorean type described in the last section as "No. 2." Should there be no chance to form such an association as is above suggested, let the Neophyte seek until he finds a magnetizer who corresponds as nearly as may be to the noble type of manhood required. Let such a one lay his hands, illuminated with the pure, invisible essence of Soul fire, on the Neophyte's head. let manipulations of magnetic power, accompanied by the infusion of strong, aspirational will, be practiced at given periods of time; let these exercises be conducted uninterruptedly, steadily, firmly and with high and noble intentions, and they cannot fail to perform the last best work of converting the Neophyte into the Adept, the passive subject into the active operator.

In the final formulae of evocation, the mind must be concentrated fully on the purpose and presence most desired. Thus, if the object be to summon the attendance of beloved spirit, friends, the ordinary methods of waiting, either alone or in a small harmonious gathering, now so popularly practiced amongst modern Spiritists in Europe and America, may be sufficient to ensure the desired results.

The performance of very good and spiritually inspired music should always precede, or rather form the invocatory process in such circles, the effect of good music producing as great a difference in the atmosphere as on the feelings and sensations of the listeners.

The light on such occasions should always be subdued, as light is motion in the atmosphere, and tends to promote an energy of action which is unfavorable to the influence of the Astral light, in which the spirits live and move and have their being.

Material light and Astral light are as antagonistic to each other as the north poles of separate magnets. They mutually repel each other; hence, avoid as much as possible the action of material light. For obvious reasons the custom of sitting in total darkness should be held equally objectionable, except under stringent test conditions, and where remarkable evidence of physical power is demanded.

The fumigations of aromatic and fragrant essences contribute greatly to promote the conditions under which Elementary Spirits can manifest, but retard the approach of human spirit visitants. "The introduction of streams of ozone into the apartment will be found a highly favorable condition to promote the communion between spirits and mortals and their friends in the form. Besides this, the action of a gentle current of electricity, evolved from an electro-magnetic battery, should be infused into the systems of the investigators, as it not only increases the strength and quantity of the Astral fluid present in each organism, but benefits the health, and prevents the depletion of vital force. The ethereal character of ozone, and the force of electro-magnetism, are also strongly in harmony with the Astral fluid which forms the bodies of spiritual beings, hence their use at spirit circles will be found effective and beneficial.

As the Spiritists of this age have enjoyed an extended experience in the constant intercourse, presence, and counsel of their "household Lares," it is needless for us to offer farther suggestions on this branch of our subject at present, save to add that the methods of intercourse with all spiritual existences will be found reduced to general principles in this volume, and may, therefore, be applied universally to all forms of communion between the invisible and visible worlds.

The means of awakening latent spiritual forces, or the processes of invoking and procuring the presence of spirits, may be conducted through any of the avenues to the material senses. For example: the magnetic sleep on the one hand, and the "mantic frenzy" on the other, may both be produced by appeals to the sense of hearing. The one is induced by soft and delightful strains of music, the other by noise and distracting clamor. Civilized nations are naturally most satisfactorily affected by the former mode; barbarous or semi-civilized peoples by the latter. Dull, monotonous, rhythmical intonations act an intermediate part between these two extremes, and are particularly favorable to the commencement of all magical ceremonials.

Appeals to the spirit can also be successfully made through the eye. The sight of frightful objects causes a revulsion in the entire circulatory system, lowers its tone, and may even suspend its functions to the point of swooning. The reverse of this action is produced by pleasing objects, beautiful colors, charming scenes or persons, all of which sights stimulate and quicken the circulation, tending to diffuse a soothing and healthful glow throughout the whole system.

Another very effective mode of acting upon the sense of vision results from gazing intently on mirrors, crystals, precious stones, shining bodies, or pure fluids. The magnetic rays which are reflected back into the eye from these objects pierce the brain, and charge it with Astral light, whilst the fixidity of the action induces that self-magnetization which is the first step in somnambulism, trance and ecstasy. Still another mode is in the inhalation of stimulating narcotics or aromatic vapors. As before remarked, these processes are essential to the control of Elementary Spirits, and produce no inconsiderable effect upon the senses of the magician.

Nitrous-oxide gas, either and other stimulating and anaesthetic vapors are powerful means of inducing either the trance state or "manic frenzy." For the evolution of the latter condition no method had proved so effective as violent gesticulations, dancing, jumping leaping, spinning around in circles, in a word, emulating the actions of the Oriental Ecstatics, in whom the "mantic frenzy" and the exhibition of the most astounding preternatural powers seem always to require these preparatory processes. And here we must strictly impress on the reader's mind the fact, that in describing these abnormal proceedings, we do not present them as examples for imitation, or commend them, as even possible for the execution of "well-to-do" ladies and gentlemen, moving in the first circles of London, Paris or America. We are simply answering the oft-repeated questions raised by the admires of Art Magic, "What can we do to perfect ourselves in its practice?"

We may have conclusions to draw ere we close this volume, which will induce the aspirants for magical powers to regard with more interest and reverence the pearls of spiritual beauty they are constantly treading under foot, whilst their eager gaze is directed longingly on some glittering bauble far away up the mountain heights, whose rugged paths their daintily slippered feet would essay in vain to climb; but these conclusions can only be understandingly arrived at when our work is done; to the act of present duty, therefore, we must now return.

The use of Hasheesh, Napellus, Opium, the Juice of the Indian Soma, or Egyptian Lotus plant, besides many other narcotics of special virtues, constitute a large portion of the preparatory exercises, by which Oriental Ecstatics produce their abnormal conditions; but when we name the last essential for the due performance of magical rites, we may confidently assure our readers we include all lesser means, and are about to disclose the true secret of the Philosopher's Stone, and the mystic Elixir Vitae, nay, we speak of an element more potent than either, for we point to the source and end of all Deific, no less than human capacity, the all-omnipotent and resistless power of will.

When the great Essenian Teacher, Jesus of Nazareth, assured his Disciples if they had faith as a grain of mustard seed, they could move mountains, and cast them into the sea, he uttered no myth, spoke in no parable, but enunciated a truth which the Adept of every country, and every age, will fully confirm.

The power of faith is the power of will, the essence of Soul, and Soul's action in producing forms and emulating the creative functions of the Divine Will.

Will is the purpose of the Eternal One, outwrought in existence and its operation in the outgrowth of more fully perfected ind ages, will elevate mankind to the functions of Deity by its triumphs.

Every Mystic, Sage, Magician and Psychologist, every student, ancient or modern, ranges the power of the human will in the category of all supreme intelligence, and attributes to its exercise the highest achievement of the true magician. Still it must be borne in mind that our present system of abject subservience to the opinions of our fellowmen, and our slavish dependence on popularity and custom, utterly neutralizes this all triumphant and magical power of will.

In our present condition of modern civilization the complete expansion of will power is simply impossible. We require several generations of culture, and patient experience ere it can attain to its true proportions, and become the executive power it ought to be in human life.

There are some abnormal existences that can subsist without food, and others in whom the processes of education are superseded by direct spirit teaching, so there are a few highly endowed minds who attain to their majority at birth, and who, like Jesus of Nazareth, Plato, or Pythagoras, live in the realm of spirit, from their first entrance upon the sphere of immortality, hence they can exercise spiritual functions with the same ease that others use the external senses; but these rarely-endowed minds form the exception, not the rule of human life.

We must not trust to the possibilities of miraculous changes in our own natures, but work for them, and industriously, scientifically and patiently pave the way for their achievement. The culture of the Will for the execution of abnormal acts of power is to be conducted by a regular series of mental processes, all tending to the subjugation of the senses and the exaltation of the spirit. Some of these have already been explained in this section, others will be elaborated as we proceed. The generalities of the process involve physiological and psychological changes, the methods of which have been briefly glanced at.

For the processes by which divination can be evolved, we refer the reader to future sections. All shall be told; but, for the present, we conclude with a tribute to the power of the human Will.

It is the Alpha and Omega of this mortal life, as the Divine Will is the Alpha and Omega of Being. It is the royal power by which matter bends before Spirit, as the leaf bends and sways in the rushing storm.

If the result seems to the student who has advanced thus far worth the cost, let him proceed. If his heart begins to fail him upon these, the first steps of the mystic threshold, how can he hope to succeed in ultimates which cost the sages of antiquity years of study, and half a life-time of faithful self-abnegation to achieve?

The discouragement which arrest the first steps in the path of discovery, are but the first trials of that stupendous will power, upon the full exercise of which the magician's triumphs depend.

Fail now, and you fail forever. Cherish but one spark of hope to light your way through the labyrinthine paths we are destined to trend together, and every mind of ordinary intelligence and indomitable purpose, may by the perusal of these pages become an Adept in Art Magic.

Section XI
Art Magic in India
--

The very name of Hindostan, with its long descended lines of Guroos, Brahmins, Yogees and Fakeers; initiates all into the highest and most potential of nature's occult powers, is itself suggestive of Magic, and few there are who have glanced superficially at the subject, or read the extracts from popular literature in the periodicals of the day relating to it, who do not regard India as the birthplace of all that is wild, weird and wonderful in the occult side of man's nature.

The immense antiquity of the Hindostanee dynasty, the invincible tendency of the Hindoo mind to regard the scheme of being as fixed and unchangeable, and the belief in "Yugs" or cycles of time, through which mankind must inevitably pass, in the fulfillment of a destiny as immutable as the Will of Deity, have paralyzed all effort at advancement, hence the basic principles of the Hindoo's belief, nay, most of their practices of a Theosophical character, are as much the stereotyped copies of what their ancestors believed and did five thousand years ago, as are their wonderful temples and colossal images the expression of the same far distant period of time. It is almost impossible to separate the magical practices of the Hindoos from the elements of their religion, and the changes which time has wrought in the aspect of nature and the political institutions which have been shattered by every description of national calamity, have failed to affect the deep metaphysical characteristics which soil, scenery, climate, and the doctrines of fatalism have engrafted on the Hindoo mind.

Since the tone of ancient metaphysics has changed but little then with the onward march of the ages, the following brief summary may be regarded as a transcript of Hindoo magic both in antique and modern times. Passing over the more sublime principles of Theism, the doctrines of the Trinity, Incarnation, Emanations, the Transmigration of the Soul, etc., etc., we come to the direct practices which the highest forms of religious belief imposed upon Hindoo Priests and Devotees.

The laws of Caste assigned to the ancient Brahmins the supreme control over all other classes, and the direction not only of spiritual ideas and teachings, but also gave them prerogative rights of succession, by which, through the assumed transmission of hereditary virtues, their sacred Caste was to be preserved in certain families and entailed upon long lines of posterity. There can be no doubt that the Brahminical order itself sprang from the natural endowments of those ancient Anchorites, who at the very edge of historic times, and perhaps long before, had retired from the busy hum of the cities, and in the depths of the wildest solitudes, held communion with Nature and Nature's God, and by the practice of excessive devotion and rigid asceticism, disciplined both soul and body into communion with the invisible worlds of being. The following graphic description of these ancient Forest priests is given in the charming and truthful language of Mrs. L. M. Child. This gifted authoress says:

"In times Ancient beyond conjecture, there were men who withdrew altogether from the labors and pleasures of the world and in solitary places devoted themselves to religious contemplation. This lonely existence on the silent mountains, or amid the darkness of immense forests, infested by serpents and wild beasts, and as they believed by evil spirits, also, greatly excited popular imagination. The human soul, unsatisfied in its cage of finite limitation, is always aspiring after the good and the true, always eagerly hoping for messengers from above, and therefore prone to believe in them. Thus these saintly hermits came to be objects of extreme veneration among the people. Men traveled far to inquire of them how sins might be expiated, or diseases cured, for it was believed that in thus devoting themselves to a life beyond the tumult of the passions occupied solely with penance and prayer, they approached very near to God, and received direct revelations of His divine wisdom."

"In the beginning, these anchorites were doubtless influenced by sincere devotion, and made honest efforts to attain what seemed to them the highest standard of purity and holiness. Their mode of life was simple and austere in the extreme. They lived in caverns, or under the shelter of a few boughs, which they twisted together in the shadow of some great tree. Their furniture consisted merely of an antelope skin to sleep on, a vase to receive alms, a pitcher for water, a basket to gather roots and wild berries, a hatchet to cut wood for sacrifices, a staff to help them through the forest, and a rosary made of lotus seeds, to assist in repeating their numerous prayers. The beard and nails were suffered to grow, and to avoid trouble with their hair, it was twisted into peculiar knots, resembling the close curls of an African."

"In later times they shaved their heads, probably from motives of cleanliness. However high might have been their caste in the society of the world, they retained no ornament or badge of distinction. They wore simply a coarse yellow-red garment made of the fiber of bark. Their food consisted of wild roots, fruit and grain; and of these they must eat merely enough to sustain life. They might receive food as alms, or even ask for it in cases of extreme necessity; but they must strive to attain such a state of indifference that they felt no regret if refused and no pleasure if they received it. They were bound to the most rigid chastity, in thought as well as deed. So far as they coveted the slightest pleasure from any of the senses, so far were they from their standard of perfect sanctity."

"Some made a vow of continual silence, and kept a skull before them to remind them constantly of death."

"In addition to this routine, they prescribed to themselves tasks more or less severe, according to the degree of holiness they wished to attain, or had courage to pursue. Some fasted to the very verge of dissolution. In summer they exposed themselves to the scorching sun, or surrounded themselves with fires. In winter they wore wet garments, or stood up to the chin in water. They went forth uncovered amid frightful tempests. They stood for hours and days on the point of their toes with arms stretched upward, motionless as a tree. They sat on their heels, closing their ears tight with their thumbs, their eyes with the forefingers, their nostrils with the middle fingers, and their lips with the little fingers; in this attitude they remained holding their breath til they often fell into a swoon."

"These terrible self-torments resulted from their belief that this life was merely intended for expiration; that the body was an incumbrance, and the senses entirely evil; that relations to outward things entangled the soul in temptation and sin; that man's great object should be to withdraw himself entirely from nature, and thus become completely absorbed in the eternal Soul of the Universe, from which his own soul originally emanated."

"Penances undertaken for sins committed were supposed to procure no other advantage than the remission of future punishment for those sins; but sufferings voluntarily incurred, merely to annihilate the body, and attain nearness to the divine nature, were believed to extort miraculous gifts from supernatural beings, and ultimately enable man to become God."

"Aiming at this state of perfection, they gradually attained complete indifference to all external things. They no longer experienced desire or disappointment, hope or fear, joy or sorrow. Some of them went entirely naked, and were reputed to subsist merely on water. The world was to them as though it did not exist. In this state the words they uttered were considered divine revelations. They were believed to know everything by intuition; to read the mysteries of past, present and future; to perceive the thoughts of whoever came into their presence; to move from one place to another by simply willing to do so; to cure diseases, and even raise the dead. Some of this marvelous power was supposed to be imparted even to the garments they wore, and the staffs with which they walked. The Hindoo Sacred Writings are filled with all manner of miracles performed by these saints. There are traditions that some of them were taken up alive to heaven; and impressions on the rocks are shown, said to be footprints they left when they ascended. By extraordinary purification and suffering, some were reputed to have attained such power, even over the Gods, that they could compel them to grant whatever they asked."

"Thus something resembling monasteries, or theological schools, was established in the forests of Hindostan, at a very remote period of antiquity. Seven of the most ancient of these hermits, peculiarly renowned for wisdom and holiness, transmitted their privileges to descendants, and thus became the germ of seven classes in an hereditary priesthood still existing under the name of Brahmins."

It has commonly been supposed that the strong temptation to assume unlimited power and acquire unlimited wealth which the reverence paid to these old anchorites opened up to them, induced the formation of a Priestly order, and the institution of the law of Caste, by which the immunities and privileges they enjoyed in their own persons might be secured to their posterity. Be this as it may, the result was that in process of time, the Priests, under the title of Brahmins (a name derived from Bramah, the first person of the Hindoo Trinity), exercised unlimited sway over the entire nation, not even exempting princes or rulers of armies.

The Brahmins are still the conservators of scientific lore, political influence and religious knowledge to those who have not protested from their form of belief. Many sects have arisen, however, dividing up the religious world of India into almost as many shades of opinion as Christianity itself; still it is a curious and significant fact that no class of the community, not even the famed Buddhist Priests, ever attained as an order, to such remarkable powers in the realm of magical achievements as the mighty Brahmins of India.

It is not that their creed teaches any special devotion to magical art, or aims to develop miraculous powers as an essential of Brahminical life. In this respect Brahminism differs from Christianity, whose Founder repeatedly demanded the performance of wonderful works as a sign of Christian faith.

No such charge is enforced in the education of the Brahmins; neither are all Brahmins wonder workers; but the truth is that the ascetic lives practiced by the strictest devotees of the order, their profound study of nature, and obedience to nature's laws; their contemplative habits, purity of diet, simplicity of dress, and perhaps the inherited tendencies bequeathed to them by a long line of spiritualized ancestors, all tend to endow this caste of men with the rare and peculiar gifts that distinguish so many amongst their ranks.

The sacred writings of the Hindoos, which are very numerous and rich in sublime ideality, contain many directions for invoking spirits, controlling the inferior orders, and soliciting the aid and protection of the superior.

Instructions also are given for the preparation of the body by fasting, chastity, ablutions and self-mortification. The spirit is to be disciplined by prayer, the singing of hymns, long periods of silent contemplation, solitary communion with God, nature, spirits and perfect soul abstraction from all external things. Seated in peculiar and far from luxurious attitudes, with the eyes fixed, and the very respiration regulated by abstract methods, the Atma, or soul within, is to be continually trained to complete absorption in Deific ideas to the exclusion of all worldly aims, desires, pursuits or scenes.

Directions are given in the sacred books for the use and preparation of the Soma drink, of napellus, hasheesh, opium and other narcotics by which ecstasy and trance are to be induced. Fumigations, also, and the use of spices, gums and aromatic herbs, are described; still a large portion of the initiatory rites by which magical powers are to be evolved, are not committed to writing; but from time immemorial have been orally communicated by Adepts to initiates and students.

Being versed in those oral traditions, and sufficiently informed upon the methods of initiation to know how far these rites can be disclosed without fear of misunderstanding, we may venture to state that every temple of ancient or modern India abounds with crypts and secret chambers, where devotees may pass their time absorbed in silent communication with God and Angels, or engaged in waging fierce mental warfare with the Evil Spirits who ever beset the path of the Neophyte, and strive to win him from the kingdom of light to the realms of darkness, in which their own unblest natures most delight.

To combat these subtle but ever-present enemies and guard their wandering thoughts against the intrusion of vain desires, also to regain that "internal respiration," which tradition teaches was once the privilege of humanity, enabling God to fill the interior man, and preserve the breath from pollution by admixture with the outer air, the devotee is required to suspend his respiration and inwardly repeat sixteen times the sacred syllable A U M - the ineffable word, which contains the name and attributes of Deity - and thus, by such methods of mental introversion, it is believed complete absorption in Divine things may be attained. Directions are often given for the attitude to be assumed in these exercises. Sometimes the vision is to be directed towards the end of the nose; sometimes to the region of the heart, liver or umbilicus. In each of these points it is assumed special virtues reside; these are under the government of certain planets, and the spirits who inhabit them.

By sitting square on four points, that is resting on the heels, and so fixing the thumbs and fingers as to exclude the action of external sight and hearing, the soul concentrated on these several centers of life and Astral influence, will call down the spirits of the planets who govern such regions of the body, and thus will be stimulated into supermundane force, the virtues which abound in those mystic centers of creative force.

Towards the middle ages, a strange, peaceful sect arose, who, from their methods of completely abstracting the senses from all external objects and concentrating their soul powers in certain regions of the body, were termed Hesychiasts. They took up their abode in the region of Mount Athos, where, under the direction of an Abbot, and laws founded upon the rigid discipline of monasticism, they devoted themselves to acts of charity, the curse of the sick, and the complete abstraction of all the senses from mundane things. Their mode of effecting this mental absorption is thus stated by one of their writer:

"Sitting alone in a corner, observe what I tell you. Lock your door, and raise your mind from every worldly thing. Then sink your beard upon your breast, and fix your eyes upon the center of your body. Contract the air passages, that breathing may be impeded. Strive mentally to find the position of the heart, where all the mind's powers reside. At first you will discover only darkness and unyielding density, but if you persevere night and day, you will miraculously enjoy unspeakable happiness, for the soul then perceives that which it never saw before, the radiance in which God resides; a great light dwelling between the heart and the soul."

The parity between these instructions and those which occupy a portion of the Hindoo sacred books, has suggested the idea that this order of ascetics drew their ideas from the Vedic writings, especially those directions communicated to the Neophytes aiming to attain to the exalted condition called Nirvana (the peace of God). The Hindoo teachers say:

"It is necessary, nay due to the soul, to free it from every human desire; to cut off all sources of delight save those which it finds in Nirvana."

"Avoid contact with those of an inferior caste, the indulgence of vain thoughts, or the ascendancy of any habit which draws the soul down to earth, and away from companionship with God. Obey without questioning thy teachers, and follow out each point in thine initiations, though they seem to lead thee to the feet of Siva. Abate not one moment of thine hours, nor let they sight wander from the points where they planet rules, or the beneficent spirits of the stars do dwell in thee."

Such exercises as these, with incessant periods of fasting, abstinence, self-mortification of every kind, the severest penances for the most trifling offenses, especially the least infraction of probationary discipline, lasted for years ere the devotee was deemed fit for admission to the higher rites of initiation. These, too, were communicated very gradually, and occupied months or years, according to the Neophyte's aptness and willingness to endure more personal suffering than the amount prescribed. in these, as in the preliminary rites, oral communication preserved the Temple secrets from the supposed dangers of entrusting them to writing. Amongst the higher methods of preparatory discipline, the scholar was required to listen to recitations from the most occult portions of the Vedas, to commit many of them to memory, and repeat them constantly. He was also instructed in the principles, as far as they were known, or algebra, geometry and mathematics, astronomy and astrology. The Hindoos, though not so expert or devoted to the latter science as the Chaldeans, taught the influence of the planets on certain days, months and periods of time. They reduced the configurations and constelled order of the sidereal heavens to a stupendous system, or at least laid the foundations of that belief in Astral and planetary order, which subsequently expanded into the magnificent astronomical religion. They were especially attentive to the phases of the moon, and attributed benign or malignant influences to the use of herbs, or the wearing of certain colors or precious stones during different phases of lunar increase or decrease.

All herbs gathered for magical purposes were to be prepared during the moon's increase. No great undertakings were deemed successful unless the order of the planetary bodies was consulted, and their configurations pronounced favorable. Another of the higher stages of study in Priestly discipline was instruction in the use and preparation of narcotics as means of procuring trance and divine ecstasy. Still another, the exercise of will in subjugating the lower order of spirits, and the occult forces in nature.

They were taught the magnetic virtues of plants, minerals, precious stones - especially the loadstone - the influence of colors, the methods of healing by touch, will, charms, amulets, and spells; the virtue of words, the methods of invoking spirits, and finally the form of manipulation called Tschamping, which imply signifies magnetism, or the infusion of "Akasa," the Astral Spirit of powerful Adepts, into their subject by passes, touches, and contact, exactly on the principles of modern mesmerism.

When the last rites of initiation were effected, it was found that the most stupendous physiological and psychological changes had been effected in the Hierophant's system.

He had commenced as a human being - he was now an Ecstatic; he had been a creature of parts, passions, emotions, he was now a machine, bearing about an emaciated frame and an organism in which the possessor moved, breathed, spoke, but only in a dream - yet he found himself endowed with a soul whose perceptions were as keenly alive to impressions from the invisible world, as his external senses had become blunted to all earthly things.

An Initiate of many years standing, just emancipated from training, having faithfully fulfilled all that is required of him, and elevated through powerful magnetism, into the position of an Adept, is less of a man than a monomaniac, one who deems himself dead, a Soul doomed to carry about with him a lifeless body. From this supreme condition of ecstasy, it is the duty of his teachers and leaders to arouse him far enough to confer upon him a special mission in life. If he is of the highest order of Ecstatics, he becomes a Yogee, a degree which excels all others in magical power. He may become a Brahmin admitted to the first order or Priesthood, and be permitted to marry, and rear offspring, entering into all the uses and duties which belong to the priestly class. If his choice inclines him to still higher realms of spiritual absorption, if he feels that the last stage of divine union with Deity, called "Nirvana" - is yet to be reached, he must continue his ascetic practices, nay double and treble their severity, retire to some dim forest solitude, deep cavern, or temple crypt, and there continue in the performance of the most terrible austerities, until his purified spirit is no longer of the earth, until he has elevated himself above the necessity or desire for food, the habitues of physical being, and then will the triumphant spirit spurn the dungeon walls of a material existence. The Angels of Siva will respond to the Soul's cry for liberty, the gates of the emaciated body will fly open, and let the purified Soul go free!

The narcotics chiefly used by Eastern Ecstatics, to elevate them to the highest conditions of somnambulism, are first, the Soma drink, or Asclepias acida.

The plant is prepared by expressing out the juice either between two stones, "braying it in a mortar," or pounding it in prepared vessels; - the liquid thus obtained is then carefully strained, mixed with clarified butter, laid for a season on fine fresh dewy grass, then gathered up and swallowed as occasion requires. In preparing this drink, many magical ceremonies are used, the value of which will be discussed in their appropriate place. Still it is deemed necessary to use exorcisms to evil spirits, invocations to good, and lunar and astral observation in the preparation of all materials employed in magical rites. The Soma juice, hasheesh, opium, the napellus, and distillations procured from two or three spirits of acrid fungi, are considered the most effective narcotics appropriate for inducing the trance condition. A great variety of anaethetics are now in use in the East, unknown to the ancients. The fumigations made use of were and are very numerous. Myrrh, cassia, frankincense, different preparations of lime, aloes, aromatic woods, gums and spices, as well as amber, ambergris, and other delicate perfumes, constituting a large portion of the medicaments used.

The "Law of Manu," one of the Hindoo sacred books, alleges that there are only three states in which human souls can exist whilst inhabiting the mortal tenement; these are alternations of "waking, sleeping and trance." The waking state of the body is the soul's period of darkness - material light always being deemed, in Oriental Theosophy, the opposite of Divine light.

In this condition, all the evils which belong to a material state are perceived and have power to operate. In sleep the soul oscillates between the attractions of matter produced by the relations it sustains to the body, and its natural tendency to ascend to its true home in a spiritual state of being.

The more perfectly the senses of the sleeper have been subdued by discipline, the more does the soul recede from the body and gravitate to the Divine light; hence arise those healthful slumbers from which so much strength and refreshment proceeds; but where the body is indisposed, or binds the soul in the chains of earthly attraction, unquiet dreams bear witness to the struggle between the opposing forces of matter and spirit, and unless guardian spirits induce the dream for purposes of their own, the sleeper awakes but little refreshed from the mental strife.

Much is written concerning the philosophy of sleep which we have not space to quote. Trance is considered to be the complete liberation of the soul from the chains of materialism, as - except a small portion of the Astral fluid, which inheres to the body, and maintains the action of instinctive life - the fetters of matter now become so loosened, that the soul can go forth, and wander abroad in space. Its spiritual senses have free exercise. It is all eye, all ear, all perception. It can ascend to the "third heavens," traverse the spheres, wander over the earth, read the hidden things of the heart, penetrate into all secrets behold the past, present and future outstretched as in a vast panorama, in short, Atma (the Soul), then becomes the true spark of Divinity, and enjoys unfettered powers and unlimited functions.

The full perfection of the trance state is very seldom reached until Death sets the soul at liberty; but even an approximation to this divine condition is eagerly coveted by illuminated minds.

Much stress is laid upon lunar influence in seeking to enter the trance state, and hence the real effects which the moon exerts on material bodies, especially in sleep, in lunacy, and in producing rapid growth in plants, and decomposition in dead matter, form the subject of much scientific speculation, and afford matter for highly suggestive thought.

Besides the processes necessary to prepare a true Brahmin, the Priesthood admitted other devotees to certain initiatory rites. There were many classes of ascetics in India, ranging from the High Priests or Gurooes, down to the begging Fakeers, who clamor for alms in every populous city.

The highest class of the Brahminical order, the princely Gurooes, are educated in all the learning the age can bestow, and besides being practiced in the rigid school of asceticism above described, are disciplined in the noblest of moral virtues.

The severe discipline and frightful self-mortifications inflicted by fanaticism upon the much-abused body, must not be understood as enjoined by the sacred writings of India. These, in many remarkable passages, deny the efficacy of such outward observances, sternly rebuke those who rely on them for salvation, and abound with beautiful hymns, admirable precepts and recommendations to the practice of deeds of charity, kindness, purity and truth. The excessive tendency to asceticism and self-mortification which has obtained for thousands of years in India, results from obedience to traditional law, and customs which have increased in stringency by the imitative habits of the people, and the examples of certain notable Saints and imaginary Avatars. Besides the Brahminical Priesthood, and often excelling them in Spiritualistic endowments, are classes of Saints and Ascetics known as Sanyassis, Nirvanys and Yogys, or Yogees.

These are emphatically the creme-de-la-creme of Indian Spiritism, and their wonder-working powers resulting from the most horrible self-inflicted tortures and probationary sufferings are almost beyond belief. In a free translation from the Dhammapada, the work of a Brahmin writer, who flourished in the first century B.C., the following description is given of the status of the Nirvany, or one of these ascetics who had attained to the inconceivable bliss and purity of Nirvana - the state of peace almost amounting to absorption in Deity.

"Patience is the highest Nirvana. This is the world of the Buddhas."

"If, like a trumpet when broken, thou art not roused to speech, thou art near Nirvana. Anger is not known in thee, or there is no noisy clamor in thee."

"He who has deepest insight - who knows all right and all wrong, who has attained to the highest - Him call I a Brahmana."

"He who has given up all pain, all pleasure, who is without ground for new birth, who has overcome matter and all worlds - Him call I a Brahmana."

Many writers are still more enthusiastic in praise of the Yogees than the Nirvanys. the latter are more speculative, the former the most accomplished in miraculous gifts of the Hindoo ascetics. The most exalted of the Yogees are selected as a council of Elders, and their decrees reverenced as the voice of Deity.

They form no inconsiderable portion of those fanatics, who like the Fakeers, wander over the east, subjecting their bodies to every description of unnatural torture, that their heated imaginations can devise.

It is claimed by Hindoo metaphysicians that there exists in the Universe, a pure, all-pervading fluid, invisible, fiery, radiant, wholly divine, free from the taint of matter, purer than ether, stronger than the loadstone, mightier than the thunderbolt, swifter than the winged lightning. It is heat, light, motion, force; the Soul principle of being - not Soul, but its power of life, being and motion. It connects Gods and Men, Heaven and Earth. It is the strength, that is, cohesive element, in minerals; the growing power of plants; the life of men and animals - it is Akasa, or, in other words, the Astral fluid, so frequently described in former sections, which is nature is Astral light, in animated bodies the Astral spirit - in substance, Astral fluid. The theory upon which asceticism is so largely practiced is, that the more the Soul isolates itself from sensuous habits and earthly surroundings, the greater becomes its power of freeing Akasa, and of attracting to itself this divine fluid from all things in nature. Thus the action of the Soul, using Akasa as its instrument, becomes freed from the entanglements of matter; whilst the quantity, power and quality of this mighty essence is increased until the Saint becomes all Akasa. He may, for a short period on earth, carry about with him a poor, emaciated body; but he only uses this as a vehicle to enable the Soul to come in contact with matter- it is the last end of the staff by which the divine hand of spirit touches earth.

"it is through the abundance, power and prevalence of Akasa over matter that the Bokt can rip up his abdomen, withdraw the intestines, and inspect them as calmly as the Priest examines the entrails of the sacrifice to discover oracular meanings. It is by Akasa that sensation in the slain body is made void, and wounds are instantaneously healed."

"This slain Bokt truly dies; but he feels nothing. Akasa is too potent. The senses are annihilated. He replaces the intestines in order to rebuild the body for another day's use. The Gods surround him. They infuse divine Akasa into his system. His hands stream with life fluid. His breath is all Akasa. he breathes on the blood; it is full of life; it instantly coheres; this severed parts re-unite. The Akasa, which has been displaced, is replaced. What more is needed? The body is whole again; it cannot be hurt, since Akasa makes, unmakes and remakes again."

In this philosophy be it remembered, Akasa, which is the Rosicrucian's Astral fluid, the Hebrew's Life, the modern magnetizer's Magnetism, plays the part of the creative principle.

It is pure force, cohesion, which divided by the knife can be replaced, causing the particles, fibers, and all the severed tissues to cohere again exactly as before they were severed.

It is the cause of growth in plants; hence if a heavy charge is poured out on a seed or germ, it can cause that growth in a few seconds, which a less quantity would cause in the slower processes called growth. A vast accumulation of Akasa can cause when projected by will, the heaviest bodies, even rocks, to move, transport them through the air, dissolve solids into fluids, fluids into airs, and recombine them again, for it is force. It can subdue the fiercest beasts by stupefying their senses; fascinate the serpent, charm the Boa, and palsy the Cobra de Capello. It can be diffused like a gauzy veil all through the atmosphere, and upon it, the will of a powerful magician can paint any images he pleases, and thus a whole assembly can see the objects created by that will at one and the same time. The magician can envelope himself in Akasa, and thus become invisible or visible at pleasure.

He can ride upon it, sail in it, stand upon it; use it as the chemist uses airs, fluids, solids; but these stupendous powers are only given to those who have utterly worn away all bodily impediments by the severest fasts and penances, who are freed from all entanglements of sense or sensuous attractions; whose souls can arise to ethereal spheres or sensuous attractions; whose souls can arise to ethereal spheres and communing with spirits, borrow their Akasa (spiritual bodies) to aid in those operations, strengthen their own powers by those of potent spirits, and thus become at once a man and a spirit.

A Soul having at command an earthly vehicle in which to approach matter, is yet, by the subjugation of matter and the exaltation of Soul, at once a man, a spirit - a God.

The reader will now understand the philosophy of the tremendous discipline enjoined and practiced by Hindoo wonder-workers, yet if they were not genuine wonder-workers, and the author of these pages had not for years proved them to be such, and partaken alike of their discipline and their powers, these enormous claims had never been made for them, and this exposition of their philosophy had never been written.

All Yogees, all Fakeers, all miracle workers of every age, country, and caste, summon to their aid the Pitris or spirits of ancestors. Bear this in mind, skeptics of every land, careless and unthinking Spiritists, who so lightly regard the privileges you have enjoyed, but will soon forfeit, if not more reverently used, and more intelligently appreciated. These Pitris are generally loving spirit friends, who delight to answer the summons of the Illuminee and aid him to ascend to their own divine height of beatitude, or to work those deeds of power which prove the ascendancy of spirit over matter.

The Fakeers, amongst whom are far more numerous grades than amongst the higher classes of ascetics, undergo like them, the most severe probationary discipline. Many of them, inspirited by ignorant rather than intelligent enthusiasm, far outlive the Yogees in the severity of their rites, the hideous and distorted attitudes they assume, and the life-long miseries to which they condemn themselves. Their revolting attitudes, mendicant habits, and disgusting appearance, have too often formed the theme of travelers' sketches to need description here. Still there are, as before intimated, many grades amongst them. Many perform years of initiatory services in the Temples, and accomplish themselves in the learning of the time, and speculative philosophy.

Many of them are intelligent and even handsome men, though most generally lean, emaciated and erratic. Some of these men become fire-eaters, serpent charmers, magicians, fortune tellers, star-gazers, strikers, dancers, thousand-eyed, finders of lost property, detectors of thieves - exhibitors of marvels, or mendicants. As to the wonders they perform, the greatest mistake in estimating them, is to attribute their acts to legerdemain. The true Indian juggler is a man of an entirely different class. A Fakeer in his most degraded condition may become a juggler, but jugglers are not necessarily Fakeers, and their marvelous powers are for the most part derived solely from the exaltation of their "mediumistic" or "magnetic" natures over their sensuous.

They perform by natural physical magic, marvels which make the myths of the Arabian tale-teller pale before them, from the act of burying themselves alive for weeks or months, to performing musical symphonies to an admiring audience of dancing Cobras and waltzing Boas.

These men, like the Yogees, perform their marvels through the abundance of the life fluid, their perfect control of it, and the aid of spirits whom they all insist they can summon at pleasure.

They emphatically allege this spiritual aid is always present when they perform. They deny that they can work without it, and though they are often urged by bigoted skeptics, pious missionaries, or puzzled materialists, to deny that they solicit or can obtain the aid of spirits, they one and all affirm and re-affirm it, and insist that without the Pitris (ancestral spirits) they can do little or nothing.

And now, reader, how like you the training necessary to become an accomplished East Indian magian? And which of our European or American aspirants for magical power will subject themselves to the discipline above described for half a life-time, in order that the other half may be spent performing deeds of glamour, deeds, too, that will wane in power, without a continual exercise of the same rigid asceticism by which the power has been procured? It will be urged that similar if not quite as powerful endowments exist in organisms that have not been thus trained, nor subjected to rightful processes of self-abuse and sensuous abnegation.

This is undoubtedly true of those in whom nature has already planted the seeds of "mediumistic" or magical powers. In those whom, as we have shown in earlier sections, nature has endowed with an abundance of the wonder-working Astral fluid, it only requires skill, some culture and intelligent direction, to turn its exercise to such account as the possessor desires. Still culture is needed, and where natural endowments utterly fail, or extra-mundane powers do not exist, art must supply the deficiency, and indicate the way.

We have only to add that in East Indian magic as in American spiritism, in ancient and in modern times, there are good and bad magicians, pure and impure media. These attract good and bad Pitris, high and low spirits. Magic no less than spiritism is divided into white and black, good and evil. The subjects always attract a class of spirits correspondential to the natures of the operators, and to the purposes designed.

The Hindoos, from the noble Gurooes, to the abject begging Fakeers, all believe in Elementaries, and all believe that they have special power to aid in such operations as their natures especially sympathize with.

There are spirits of the earth, air, fire and water. They vary in species, class and degrees of power just as mortals do; regard mankind as their Gods, and seek their aid as means of reaching higher spheres; desiring to serve them as opportunities of elevating them selves to the degree of immortality, which the souls of men alone enjoy. These poor embryonic beings range from the purely mischievous and evil, to the aspirational and good. They are the Ginn or Genii of the Orient, who serve mortals in proportion to their power to summon or command them, but we conclude with the assurance that - from the very heart of the secret crypts of initiation, from the lips of noble Gurooes, dreamy-eyed Purohitas, abstracted Nirvanys and tribes of Fakeers, the same tale is told.

The profoundest mysteries of initiation are the evocation of those called "dead," and the power of the magnetic touch, or the infusion of Astral fluid from one potent body to another. Both methods combined, form the keystone of the arch which unites the spiritism of ancient and modern India with that of the whole civilized world.

Supplement to Section XI
Art Magic in India – Continued
--

In the author's possession is an immense mass of testimony, sufficient indeed to fill many volumes, concerning the facts of extra mundane spiritism, kindred or similar to those recited in this section.

As many if not all of these, seem to draw too largely on the credulity of ordinary readers, it is our purpose with each narrative of personal experience, of more than common preternaturalism, to accompany it with a statement of similar character, verified by some historical personage, in whom the reader may have more confidence than in an anonymous writer.

If this method may burden our work with more illustrations than seems necessary, it will at least show how much more universal are these gigantic products of spiritual power than mankind has generally believed.

During the author's residence at Benares - the holy city of the Hindoos - in the years 1855 and '56, a party of English gentlemen, attracted by interest in Spiritualistic pursuits, frequently visited him, and assisted in experimenting with the swarms of Fakeers who crowd the city, and the numerous professing miracle workers who flock to Benares at certain seasons of periodical pilgrimage.

One of this English party, Capt. W., an officer of estimable character and high culture, experienced during his stay in Benares some family bereavements, which fixed his mind with painful solicitude on the condition of life in the hereafter. The Fakeers, lying on the banks of the sacred Ganges, or crouching in the city thoroughfares in every conceivable attitude of disgusting deformity, repelled this refined gentleman, and he refused to avail himself of their powers as the Ghost Seers, deeming the condition of the dead too sacred to be represented by such unhallowed interpreters. In vain his friends assured him these poor ascetics were merely instruments through whom the inhabitants of other worlds might announce their presence, as through the post-office or telegraph. The mourner required for the manifestation of an angelic presence, nothing short of an angelic instrument, and insisted that if the dead could return at all, it must be through means as holy as their own beatified condition.

One morning, Capt. W. entered his friend's apartment with a countenance beaming with excitement and exclaimed: "Eureka! the great object of my search is found. A mighty magician is coming to Benares who can solve all my doubts. Report speaks of him as the greatest of all wonder-workers; the city is alive with interest. A Sacred Bokt - a veritable Lama had indeed arrived, and would give exhibitions of his skill to whosoever desired his services. Without inquiring in what this skill consisted, the party, all too hastily, engaged the great Mystic, arranging that his first performance should be given in the private residence of one of their number in a large Bungalow, in the vicinity of the city. None but invited guests were to be present, but it was not until some few hours before the ceremonial was to take place, that the party of English gentlemen learned to what they had committed themselves, and the true nature of the horrible entertainment they had provided for a set of extremely refined and intelligent visitors. When the true state of the case was disclosed, the love of the marvelous prevailed over their disappointment. The Bokt was no necromancer, no seer or visionist, but a great ecstatic - a Lama of such stupendous sanctity that he was about to slay himself, die, and come to life again. Whatever he could or could not do, however, the engagement had been made and must be carried out.

The presence of seventy Fakeers of extraordinary power had been secured, an audience hall improvised, and altar erected, seats provided, all the arrangements made, and the Bokt now illuminating the sacred city with his presence, proposed in view of all beholders to rip up the abdomen, remove a portion of the intestines, read in them the decrees of fate, replace them again, and heal up the wound inflicted without damage to the person of the great performer. It must be confessed that when the full horror of this revolting rite was understood some of the party pleaded earnestly that the engagement might be cancelled and the scarcely human crowd of participants be dismissed with the promised fees; but the belief in some that the performance could not be real, but would end in an act of clever legerdemain, whilst the hope in the minds of others of witnessing a stupendous triumph of spirit over matter, determined them all to unite in suffering the ceremonial to proceed. When the hour of noon arrived, the Lama appeared and took his seat before the raised altar on which the candles had been lighted. Behind him was a radiant image of the sun, and on either side of the altar were grim idols which had been placed there by the attendants.

The Lama was in person a small spare man with fixed glittering eyes, an emaciated frame, and an immense mass of long black hair which floated over his shoulders. He appeared altogether like a walking corpse in whose head two blazing fires had been lighted, which gleamed in unnatural lustre through his long almond-shaped eyes.

He was about forty years of age, and report alleged that he had already performed the great sacrificial act he was now about to repeat some four times previously.

From the moment this skeleton figure had taken his seat, the seventy Fakeers who surrounded him, in a semi-circle, began to sway their bodies back and forth, singing meanwhile a loud, monotonous chant in rhythm with their movements. The party of spectators, twenty in number, were accommodated with seats in a little gallery opposite the Lama and so placed as to command his every motion.

In a few minutes the gesticulations of the Fakeers increased almost to frenzy; they tossed their arms on high, bent their bodies to earth, now forward, now backward, now swung them around as if thrown by the hands of others; meantime their monotonous chant rose into shrieks and yells so frightful that the ears of the listeners were deafened and their senses distracted by the clamor. On every side of the auditorium, braziers of incense were burning. Six Fakeers swung pots of Frankincense, filling the air with intoxicating vapors, whilst six others stood behind, beating metal drums or clashing cymbals, which they tossed on high with gestures of frantic exaltation. For some time the howls, shrieks and distracting actions of this maniac crew, produced no effect on the immovable Lama. He sat like one dead, his fixed and glassy eyes seeming to stare into illimitable distance, without heeding the pandemonium that was raging around him. "Can he be really living?" whispered one of the awe struck Englishmen to his neighbor, but this question was speedily answered by the series of convulsive shudderings which at length shook the Lama's frame. His dark eyes rolled wildly and finally nothing but their whites were to be seen, spasm after spasm threatening to shiver the frail tenement and expel its quivering life.

The teeth were set, and the features distorted as in the worst phases of epilepsy, when suddenly, and just as the tempest of horrible cries and distortions was at its height, the Lama seized the long glittering knife which was across his knees, drew it rapidly up the length of the abdomen, and then displayed in all their revolting horror, the proofs of the sacrifice in the protruding intestines.

The crowd of awe-struck ascetics bent their heads to the earth in mute worship; not a sound broke the stillness, but the deep breathings of the spectators. At length one of them who had witnessed such scenes before, addressing the living creature- for living he still was, though he uttered no sound, nor raised his drooping head from his breast - and said: "Man! can you tell us by what power this deed of blood is performed without destruction of life?" "The Lama is all Atma now," responded a thin shrill voice from the bleeding wreck before us. "Fo keeps the Manas (senses), until the work is done." "But why is that work necessary?" rejoined the querist. "Is it right?" "To show that life and death is his. Fo can withdraw the Atma (Soul) and give it back; it is his will to show his power." "Is the Lama then dead now?" "The City of Brahma (the body) is empty; Brahma Atma has retreated." "How long can the Atma remain absent?" "He returns even now. See he wings his way hither, and now he must re-enter the City's gate or it is closed against him forever." "Yet a moment; the Akasa (life principle) has it left the flesh that is severed - cut?" "Not yet - try it - it is warm - but soon the Akasa will ebb away, if your will detains the Pitris who guide home the Atma." The querist did not, as invited, examine the wound, nor even approach the ghastly figure, nearer than was requisite to observe the anatomy of the intestines laid bare. A dead silence ensued. The living corpse moves. It raises its quivering hands, and scoops up the blood from the wound, bears it to the lips, which breathe upon it; they then return to the wound, begin to press the severed parts together, and remake the mutilated body. The Fakeers shout, and send up praises to Brahma; the drums beat, the cymbals clash, shrieks, prayers, invocations resound on all sides. The fragrant incense ascends. The flute-players, planted on the outskirts of the estate, pour forth their shrill cadence.

The harps of some European servants, stationed in a distant apartment and previously-instructed, send forth strains of sweet melody among the frantic clamor.

The ecstatic makes a few more passes, and after wrapping a scarf, previously prepared, over the body as if to cleanse it from the gore in which he was steeped, suddenly he stands upright; casts all his upper garments from him, and displays a body unmarked by a single scar. Gesticulations, cries, shouts subside; low murmurs of admiration and worship pass through the breathless assembly, and then the Bokt, clasping his thin hands and elevating his glistening eyes to heaven, utters in a deep, low tone, far different to the shrill wail of the half-dead sacrifice, a short but fervent prayer of thankfulness - and all is done.

The man resumes his dress, accepts gravely the presents bestowed upon him, dismisses his admiring votaries, and walks away as calmly as if he had just parted from a gay festivity. Subsequently questioned concerning this strange and hideous rite, he declared he had fasted for six weeks pervious to its performance, partaking of no other sustenance than bread, water, and a few herbs. During the ceremonial he insisted that he felt nothing, heard nothing; stated that he had been lifted up to Paradise and beheld beauties ineffable, and partaken of joys which no other mortal could ever know. When asked to do so, he exhibited the parts that had been severed, which only retained a small ridgy white line about three inches in length. This the Bokt assured the investigators was unusual and might be attributed to the excess of Akasa or life fluid which the Fakeers dispensed. There were too many of them he thought. Had there been less, or those present had been less zealous, the parts would have cohered instantly. As it was, the life fluid bubbled up, and caused that seam by its excess. he expected to reduce it by manipulations. Wondering to hear this man use Hindoo phrases and speak the Tamul language with great purity, the inquirers found he had been born a Hindoo, graduated as a Fakeer, and finally embraced the doctrines of Buddha. It was doubtful whether he had been a Lama at all, but such was his performance.

We shall, according to promise, supplement this narrative with another on the same subject, published in a work entitled; Souvenirs D'un Voyage dans La Tartarie, et la Chine, par M. Hue Pretre Missionaire. Published at Paris, 1850. For the translation of this narrative we are indebted to an excellent periodical, published by Mr. Jas. Burns, of London in 1873, entitled "Human Nature." The date of the narrative is some twenty-five years earlier. M. Hue says:

"The fifteenth day of the new moon we encountered several caravans, following, as we did, the direction from east to west. The road was filled with men, women and children, mounted on camels or oxen. They told us they were all going to the lamasery of Rache-Tehurin. When they asked us if our object was the same as theirs, they appeared astonished at our negative response. Their surprise roused our curiosity. At a turning of the road we overtook an old lama who appeared to walk with difficulty, as he had a heavy package on his back. 'Brother,' we said, 'thou art old, thy white hairs are more numerous than the black; thou must be fatigued; place thy burden on the back of one of our camels.' After the pilgrim was relieved of his load, when his walk had become more elastic and his countenance brighter, we asked him why all these pilgrims were pacing the desert? 'We are all going to Rache-Tehurin,' they said, with accents full of devotion. 'Without doubt some great solemnity calls you to the lamasery?' 'Yes, to-morrow ought to be a grand day; a lama bokt will manifest his power; he will kill himself, but will not die.' ......We at once understood the kind of solemnity which had put all these Tartars and Ortous on the move. A lama was about to rip up his stomach, take out his entrails, place them before him, and then return to his normal state. This spectacle, atrocious and disgusting as it is, is nevertheless very common in the lamaseries of Tartary. The bokt who is 'to manifest his power,' as the Mongols express it, prepares himself for this formidable act by many days of prayer and fasting. During this time he must forego all communication with other men and keep in absolute silence. When the day arrives the multitude of pilgrims assemble in the large court of the lamasery, and an altar is raised in front of the doors of the temple. The bokt appears. He advances gravely, the people saluting him with loud acclamations. He moves to the altar and there he sits. He draws from his belt a long cutlass which he places on his knees. At his feet a number of lamas, arranged in a circle, raise loud invocations. As the prayers proceed the bokt is perceived to tremble in all his members, and then gradually to fall into phrenetical convulsions. The lamas become more and more excited; their voices are no longer measured; their chants become disorderly, til at length their recitations are changed into howlings. And it is now that the bokt suddenly casts off the scarf which envelopes him, detaches his belt, and, seizing the sacred cutlass, cuts up his stomach through all its length. While the blood is flowing from every part, the multitude falling before this horrible spectacle, interrogates the fanatic concerning hidden subjects, future events, or the destiny of certain persons. The bokt replies to all these questions by answers which are regarded as oracles by all.

"When the devout curiosity of the numerous pilgrims is satisfied, the lamas recommence the recitation of prayers with calmness and gravity. The bokt gathers up, with his right hand, some of the blood, carries it to his mouth, blows on it three times, and then casts it in the air with much clamor. He rapidly passes his hand over the wound and all returns to its primitive state, without leaving a trace of this diabolical operation beyond extreme languor. The bokt rolls his scarf again around his body, recites a short prayer with a low voice and all is over. And now the pilgrims dispense, with the exception of the most devout, who stay to contemplate and adore the blood-stained altar. These horrific ceremonies occur with sufficient frequency in the large lamaseries of Tartary and Thibet.

"All lamas have not the power to operate these prodigies. Those, for example, who have the horrible capacity of cutting themselves open are never found among the lamas of higher rank. They are ordinarily simple lamas of bad character, and held in small esteem by their colleagues. The lamas who are sensible, generally asseverate their horror of spectacles of this description. In their eyes all these operations are perverse and diabolical. The good lamas, they say; have it not in their power to execute things of this kind, and are careful to guard against seeking to acquire the impious talent.

"The above is one of the most notable sie-fa, that is, 'perverse powers' possessed by the lamas. Others of a like kind are less grandiose and more in vogue. These they practice at home and not on public solemnities. They will heat a piece of red hot iron and lick it with their tongues. They will make incisions in their bodies, and an instant after not a trace of the would remains, etc., etc. All these operations should be preceded by prayers.

In 1870, being on a visit to a friend residing near Paris, the author was informed that a party of Fakeers, otherwise called "Fire-eaters," who had been denied the opportunity of exhibiting their powers in London, might be seen and induced to give a private performance, by application to their leader, Lala Pokowra. These men being known to the author, had solicited him to procure them such patronage as would enable them to return to their own land. With this view several gentlemen united to arrange a series of private performances, the first of which we propose to give a brief transcript of, in the following narrative:

Three of the spectators had already become familiar with the performance expected; the rest were entirely skeptical as to the reality of what was described, especially Dr. L., a Corsican surgeon, who insisted that he should be able to detect the trick by his acumen and scientific knowledge.

It was evening before the party reached the chateau, and then Mons. de L., deeming they must be fatigued, desired that they might have refreshments served before commencing. This they all declined, however, explaining that in order to prepare for what was to follow, it was necessary to observe a strict fast.

It was near midnight before the arrangements were complete, and then all were assembled in a large hall, which in olden time had been used as a refectory. The floor was paved with black and white marble, and for this reason had been selected by the exhibitors in preference to other rooms where the waxed floors and carpets have been injured.

Several braziers exhaling incense and aromatic vapors were burning around the hall, which was only lighted by a bright fire, into which were stuck several iron bars, brands and other substances destined for the proposed exhibition. The spectators, amounting to about thirty gentlemen, took seats on a raised dais at one end of the apartment, while the Corsican surgeon, joined by two others of the French faculty, stationed themselves in the most convenient position for making their observations.

When all were seated the exhibitors entered, consisting of six men, four of whom were simply attired in a tunic belted around the waist and reaching nearly to the knees, their arms, necks and shoulders remaining bare. The two others were dressed in the ordinary coarse attire of the lower class of Fakeers. These men were all excessively emaciated, and the preternatural glare of their fierce black eyes was wild and repulsive. There was a seventh personage, not a Hindoo, but an European amateur, who became for the nonce their Adept, Lala Pokowra yielding up this post to him by request, and taking a seat with the spectators on the platform.

The four semi-nude men at first seated themselves on mats prepared for them, whilst the other two were busy in heating irons and attending to the braziers. The smoke ascending to the high-vaulted ceiling, and the fitful glare of the fires illuminating the half-savage figures of the reclining ecstatics, produced a weird and singular effect in this vast apartment. Branching antlers of stags' heads, torn old banners, and dim armorial bearings gleamed forth in the flickering light, contrasting strangely with the Oriental forms that lay stretched beneath them. For some time they remained motionless, the two assistants, however, stood together, chanting prayers in a low monotonous tone, and from time to time striking in rhythm a pair of silver cymbals. It was not until the Adept had sounded a few soft notes on the flageolet, that the ecstatics exhibited any signs of life.

At the first intonation they raised their heads like sleuth-hounds scenting game, then began swaying their bodies in time to the music. Shriller, louder, quicker, rang out the tones of the flageolet - fiercer sounded the clashing cymbals; louder and louder shouted the hoarse voices of the singers, and now upspringing from the ground the four Fakeers are seen whirling spinning, each as it were on his own pivot, arms outstretched, long hair flying in the circumference of each spinning human column like a fringe of black cloud around a water-spout at sea. Faster and faster screams the flageolet - faster and faster spin the human tee-to-tums, til now first one, then the second, at length the third sink down in rigid cataleptic swoons. The fourth still spins, when suddenly, tossing one hand aloft, with a whoop that would have thrilled the blood of a red Indian, he snatches with the other a keen knife from the girdle, and dashes it through the fleshy part of the other extended arm. A torrent of blood follows the wound, but another and another gash succeed in quick succession, until the hands, face, neck, breast, and arms are streaming from the open mouths of gaping wounds. One of the surgeons springs forth pale and trembling, and at a signal from the Adept, the ecstatic stops, and the man of science, with a face as white as the driven snow, examines the hideous gashes. "Great God! it is all true!" he cries. A few words in Hindostance from the Adept succeed, and now the bleeding creature stands motionless, whilst the Adept's hands rapidly pass from point to point, pressing the wounds together, manipulating them slightly, rubbing them over, making quick passes above them, and lo! the figure appears a man again.

All the surgeons come forward, even the spectators, those who have not fled sickened and fainting from the shocking spectacle, and gaze upon the exposed form now intact; not a gash left, not a wound unhealed, not a cicatrix remaining. A cup containing a stimulating drink of herbs is handed to the exhibitor who quietly wiping the still reeking gore from his person, subsides upon his mat with an air of stolid indifference.

Meantime, the voices of the chanters have sunk to a low monotonous cadence, yet never ceased. Now they increase in volume, again the cymbals clash, the flageolet gives out its piercing tones, when the falling Fakeers upspringing from their trance, commence to sway, dance, whirl, spin.

One darts to the blazing fire, and seizing a red hot iron, licks it with extended tongue; another gathers up a handful of burning coals and chews them as a precious morsel, then whirling the lighted brands above his head, he piles them, up in heaps, lays on them, hugs them, presses them to his naked breast, and dances with them till he appears a column of spinning fire. Again the knives flash, the blood springs from gaping wounds, but now appealing cries and even shrieks sound out from shivering spectators. Shouts of "Stop this hellish play!" ring from many voices. Some fall insensible, some stop their ears and close their eyes, and others stand like figures of stone, petrified by some Gorgon's head. All are unnerved, unmanned, and some weep like frightened children. The signal to suspend is given in haste and pity; pity not to the reeking victims, but to the shocked spectators.

Again the Adept and the two assistants busy themselves about the motionless figures. They stand as passive and unmoved as logs. The blood dries up; the wounds just breathed upon are pressed by busy hands, the bodies stroked and wiped, are healed and not a scar is left. Upright and motionless they stand, whilst the trembling spectators steal towards them, pass their hands about them, and turning to each other, exclaim: "This is the work of fiends and no mistake!" Aye, so it ever is. Any science which transcends the power of ignorance to explain, is always the devil's work, and horrible, revolting to humanity and every feeling of nature as such exhibitions are, it needs them to convince the material scientist that there is a realm of Spiritualism more tremendously potent than any that matter has yet revealed, and until this realm is explored, science will be driven to the ordinary expedient of ignorance and superstition, crying: "This is the work of fiends and no mistake!"

A narrative so appalling as the above demands like the former one additional testimony to strengthen it. Let the reader find this by perusing a sketch written by the Princess de Belgiojosa, in her charming work, entitled "Souvenirs de Voyage en Asie Mineure et en Syrie." This narrative was translated and published in the London Spiritual Magazine of 1868, from the pages of which we avail ourselves of an excellent translation.

"Amongst a variety of other wonders, the Count de Gobineau, the Ambassador of France to Persia, a rationalist, but a sincere and good observer, says that everybody in Persia, the Mussulmans as well as the rest, assured him that the Nossayris, one of the principal sects in Persia, perform the following marvels: They fill with fire a large brazier in the middle of the room, and whilst a musician plays the tar, a little drum, also called dombeck, the Nossayri approaches the fire. He is agitated, he is exalted, he lifts his arms and eyes towards heaven with violent contortions. Then when he is excited to such a pitch that the perspiration pours from his face and from every part of his body, he seizes a burning coal, and putting it in his mouth, blows it in such a manner that the flames issue from the nose. He receives no injury whatever from it. He then seats himself in the midst of the fire, the flames mount up and play in his beard, and caress without harming him. He is in the middle of the fire, and his dress does not burn; finally he lays himself down in the brazier, and receives no hurt from it. Others enter a baker's oven in full ignition, remain there as long as they like, and issue again without accident. What these people do with fire, others do with the air. They throw themselves from rocks with their wives and children, without receiving any damage, from whatsoever height they fall. This is the manner in which a Purzadeh, or descendant of a Pur, explained these extraordinary phenomena; 'Since," he said, 'everything in nature is God, so everything contains, secretly but plenarily, the omnipotence of God. Faith only is necessary to put in motion and make apparent this power. Therefore, the more intense and complete the faith, the more marvelous will be the effects produced. It is not merely from the air and the fire that we can draw prodigies, but from objects in appearance the most contemptible. If we wish to call our interior virtue, whatever it may be into action, we have only to apply the irresistible instrument of faith, and then , nothing is impossible.' such are the ideas of the Nossayris.

"One fine morning, as reclining on my divan, I endeavored, but in vain, to shake off the stupor and headache caused by the fumes of charcoal which issued from a metal stove, and circulated through my closed room, I saw enter a little old man in a white mantle, with a grey beard, a pointed cap of grey felt surrounded by a turban of green; he had a lively eye, and a countenance frank and good-natured. The old man announced himself as the chief of certain Dervishes, performers of miracles, whom the grand Muphti had sent to show me their operations. I offered him my warmest thanks, and expressed myself perfectly ready to witness the spectacle which they proposed. The old man opened the door, made a sign, and quickly reappeared, followed by his disciples.

"They were eight in number, and I must confess, that if I had met them on my journey, at the corner of a wood, their appearance would have given me little pleasure. Their clothes were in rags, their long beards untrimmed, their visages pale, their forms emaciated, a something indescribably ferocious and haggard in their eyes, all which contrasted singularly with the open smiling countenance and somewhat gay costume of their chief. These men on entering, prostrated themselves before him, made me a polite obeisance, and seated themselves at a distance, awaiting the orders of the old man, who, on his part, awaited mine. I experienced a degree of embarrassment, which would have been still more painful had the seance been of my own ordering. Happily I was perfectly innocent, and this consideration gave me a little self-composure, but I did not dare to make the sign for commencement of, I did not know what. I expected a scene of the grossest imposition, which I should be obliged to applaud out of politeness, and of which I must show myself a dupe of good breeding.

"I caused coffee to be served, to gain time, but the chief only accepted it. The disciples excused themselves, alleging the seriousness of the trials to which they were about to submit themselves. I gazed at them; they were serious as men who expected the visit of a host rather than a revered master. After a short silence, the old man asked me if these children might begin, and I replied that it rested entirely with themselves. Taking my answer as an encouragement, he made a sign, and one of the Dervishes arose; he then prostrated himself before his chief and kissed the earth; the chief placed his hands on his head as if to give his benediction and spoke some words in a low voice which I did not understand. Then arising, the Dervish put off his mantle, his goatskin fur, and receiving a long poignard from one of his companions, the handle of which was ornamented with little bells, he placed himself in the middle of the apartment. Calm and self-collected at first, he became animated by degrees from the force of an interior action. His breast swelled, his nostrils expanded, and his eyes rolled in their sockets with a singular rapidity. This transformation was accompanied and aided, without doubt, by the music and the songs of the other Dervishes, who, having commenced by a monotonous recitative, passed quickly into modulated cries and yells, to which the regular beating of a tambourine gave a certain measure. When the musical fever attained its paroxysm the first Dervish alternatively raised and let fall the arm which held the poignard, without being conscious of these movements, and as if moved by a foreign force. A convulsive twitching pervaded his limbs, and he united his voice with those of his confreres whom he soon reduced to the humble role of assistants, so much did his cries exceed theirs.

Dancing was then added to the music, and the protagonist Dervish executed such amazing leaps that the perspiration ran down his naked figure.

"It was the moment of inspiration. Brandishing the dagger, which he never abandoned, and every motion of which had made the little bells resound; then, extending his arm and suddenly retracting it, he plunged the dagger into his cheek so deep that the point appeared in the inside of his mouth. The blood rushed in torrents from both apertures of the wound, and I could not restrain a motion of my hand to put an end to this terrible scene.

"'Madame wishes to look a little closer?' said the old man, observing me attentively. Making a sign for the wounded man to draw near, he made me observe that the point of the dagger had really passed through the cheek, and he would not be satisfied til I had touched the point with my finger.

"'You are satisfied that the wound of this man is real?' he said to me. 'I have no doubt of it,' I replied emphatically.

"'That is enough. My son,' he added to the Dervish, who remained during the examination with is mouth open, filled with blood, and the dagger still in the wound, 'go, and be healed.'

"The Dervish bowed, drew out the dagger, and turning to one of his companions, knelt and presented his cheek, which this man washed within and without with his own saliva. The operation continued some seconds, but when the wounded man rose, and turned to one side, every trace of the wound had disappeared.

"Another Dervish made a wound in his arm, under the same ceremonies, which was healed in the same manner. A third terrified me. He was armed with a great crooked sabre, which he seized with his hands at the two extremities, and applying the edge of the concave side to his stomach caused it to enter as he executed a sea-saw motion. A purple line instantly showed itself on his brown and shining skin, and I entreated the old man to allow it to proceed no further. He smiled, assuring me that I had seen nothing, that this was only the prologue; that these children cut off their limbs with impunity - their heads, if necessary, without causing themselves any inconvenience. I believe he was contented with me, and judged me worthy to witness their miracles, by which I was not particularly flattered.

"But the fact is, I remained pensive and confused. What was that? My eyes, had they not seen them? My hands, had they not touched them? Had not the blood flowed? i called to mind all the tricks of our most celebrated prestidigitateurs, but I found nothing to be compared with what I had seen. I had had to do with men simple and ignorant to excess; their movements were made with the utmost simplicity, and displayed not a trace of artifice. I do not pretend to have seen a miracle, and I state faithfully a scene which I for my part know not how to explain. The next day, Dr. Petracchi, for many years the English Consul at ANgora, related many such marvels, and assured me that the Dervishes possessed natural or rather supernatural secrets, by which they had accomplished prodigies equal to those of the priests of Egypt."

M. Adalbert de Beaumont, who visited Asia Minor, in 1852, asserts the reality of the same wonders as the Countess de Belgiojoso. He says when the dancing Dervishes have reached the paroxysm of their excitement, they seize on iron red hot, bite it, hold it between their teeth, and extinguish it with their tongues. Others take knives and large needles, and pierce their sides, arms and legs, the wounds of which immediately heal and leave no trace.

It is time to bring these extravagant horrors to a close. We shall offer only one more example of East Indian spiritism, although our repertoire of similar facts, and that in personal experiences, would fill volumes.

At Bengal about the year 1860, there resided a Fakeer, who had obtained the name of Ali Achmet from a wealthy Arab, in whose service he had resided for many years. He had been a renegade to his faith and was little respected in a moral point of view, but his abilities as a wonder-worker had gained him a great reputation amongst foreigners who visited the city. At the death of his patron, Ali claimed that his "father's spirit" revisiting the scenes of earth he had loved all too well, and being bound to the performance of certain good deeds that he had left undone in earth-life, once more adopted his favorite, and informed him, speaking with a voice, that he would enable him to excel every Dervish in Arabia, every Fakeer in Hindoostan. This spirit kept his word. Ali achieved a great reputation wherever he went, and being the inheritor of his adopted father's wealth he gave his exhibitions freely, although his excessive vanity prompted him to tender them wherever he could find appreciative witnesses. Having conceived a whimsical friendship for the author, he spent much time exhibiting to him and his friend his wonder-working powers.

In the presence of this man many sprits of deceased persons had actually appeared to their friends. Their forms had been seen standing in the waning light of evening with perfect distinctness, and remaining long enough to be fully recognized. Spirit faces, distant scenes, and the presentment of living persons residing in foreign countries were frequently shown on the surface of a mirror which the author kept in his apartment devoted to that purpose. The ordinary expedient of calling in a boy from the street, pouring ink, walnut or fungus juice in his hand, and then "biologizing" him to see and describe the forms the inquirer wished to summon, were phases of power too petty to engage this Adept's attention.

After detecting thieves, discovering lost property, being raised in the air, carried through the grounds on several occasions, producing all manner of sights, sounds and strange phenomena familiar enough amongst modern spiritists, the Fakeer would often ask his audiences suddenly, if they would not like some object brought them from distant lands, and when an affirmative answer was given and the desired object named, a muttered prayer, a silent invocation to his beloved familiar, or perhaps a low chanted song, was sure to end in the production of what was required, though it had to be transported for a thousand miles or brought across the ocean.

Many persons residing at Benares will still remember the time, some thirty years ago, when this magician, exhibiting his power before the Temple of Siva in the presence of several thousand persons, caused three little half-naked Indian children to climb up a pole successively, one after the other, and when they had ascended about half the distance they suddenly disappeared. In two minutes after the last was lost to sight, a shout from the audience announced that the whole three were found on a plateau a hundred feet removed from the pole, and there they had appeared suddenly out of vacancy. The Fakeer explained the phenomenon by declaring that when the little climbers had ascended to a point where he had directed a circle of Akasa (life fluid) to gird the pole, the Pitris, headed by the spirit of his accommodating friend, had caught them up, concealed them in their own Akasa (spiritual atmosphere) and only put them out of it again when they placed them on the plateau above mentioned. The little ones were entranced and remembered nothing of their aerial flight.

By sticking a twig broken from a living tree into the ground, and extending his hand over it, or keeping his fingers pointed towards it, he could cause a fresh tree to spring up, bearing leaves, flowers and fruit, in less than twenty minutes.

This weird creature being one day alone with the author, was asked to show something which should prove to his friend, that he spoke with no double tongue, practiced with no double robe, that is, no concealed apparatus.

"What would my Brother chose to see?" inquired Ali.

"What can Ali do?"

"See! Ali wears no double robe, " cried the Fakeer, casting away his upper garment entirely.

"Tis well-proceed! Cause the Pitris to show their images in yon vase of water."

The vase indicated was a large stone tank which stood in a shady part of the outer court. Ali spoke not, but instantly pointing the staff he commonly carried towards the tank - it began visibly to oscillate. Its weight was immense. It could not have contained less than six gallons of water, yet as the Fakeer's knotted staff was pointed towards it - it began to slide along the court; reach the open glass doors which divided the apartment from without, to close which, a groove of metal intersected the floor.

Here the stone traveller paused like a thing of life, then as if reflection had ensued, it slowly but steadily floated up a foot above the ground, sailed in through the glass doors, then gently subsided to the ground, and still sliding on, stationed itself at the Fakeer's feet. "Will my Brother give the Pitris sweet air to breathe?" inquired the Fakeer. This remark referred to the use of Ozone, currents of which passed through an electric battery had frequently been used in that apartment in the evocation of spirits. There were several braziers, too, half burnt out, containing frankincense and aromatic perfumes. These were distributed in a circular form around the spot where the stone tank was held stationary.

The battery set in working order, and the braziers lighted, the Fakeer seemed satisfied, and this is what ensued. The fumes of the burning incense instead of as usual ascending to vents prepared to receive them, seemed to be bent by some outside power until the concentrated inwards towards the tank. The Fakeer now moved around this vessel several times, stretching both his hands towards it, and murmuring his low chant in subdued tones. Directing his single witness to stand on the north side of the vase, but outside the circle of braziers, he assumed a position exactly opposite to him, and then both perceived that every drop of the water in the tank had disappeared, the tank was empty!

Once more moving around the vessel in circles, stretching forth his hand which to the eye of clairvoyance streamed with Akasa (the life fluid) like the shells, crystals and fingers of Reichenbach's sensitives - and lo! the water came bubbling back, forming under the crystalizing process of spiritual life infused into the empty vessel, the gasses into which the fluid had been resolved, combining again, until the pool reached the surface, and seemed to attain the exact level it had before occupied. Again resuming his place to the south of the vessel, and beckoning his companion to approach nearer, one hand of each being laid on the edge of the tank, figures began to appear on the surface of the unruffled water. Seventeen presentations of forms known to the beholder appeared and disappeared in slow succession on the tranquil mirror of the water. Most of the apparitions represented spirits who had long been inhabitants of the silent land - some, however, were friends residing in distant lands, and these were surrounded with scenery appropriate to the position in which they might then most probably be residing.

Every picture was clear, distinct, life-like and highly characteristic of the individual presented, and the whole phantasmagoria strikingly illustrated those two spiritualistic aphorisms, which have lately become so popular: "There are no dead - and - "In spiritual existence there are neither time, space nor obstacles of matter." The last forms seen were those of the two witnesses themselves. Neither of them, however, represented the costumes that they wore, the one being arrayed in a uniform packed up in a distant wardrobe, the other - that of the Fakeer - appearing in the Arab dress he had long since cast aside. The unmistakable fidelity of the likenesses, but the singular change in the costumes thus presented, convinced the two observers that this manifestation was designed to show that the whole series of pictures were creations of the will - acts of attendant spirits, who, by exploring the minds of the mediums, shaped their representations in accordance with the images there impressed, or stereotyped in the memories of those they desired to serve.

The letter of European missionaries from India, China, and other eastern lands, popular accounts of snake-charmers, Indian magicians, etc., especially the writings of Messers. Salt, Lane, Wolff, Laborde, Mesdames Poole, Martineau and others, have so familiarized this age with the magical wonders wrought in the Orient, that the insertion even of the limited number of narratives this section contains, might be deemed supererogatory did we not feel the necessity, in a practical and affirmative work of this character, of saying, we, too, have seen and can testify of these things, nay more; let us add, we, too, can perform them; but again arises the question, can such things be done without all the efforts and initiatory processes above described, or those naturally occult endowments so rarely conferred? Once more we subjoin a fragment of philosophy on this subject given by a noble Brahmin, the father of the little Hindoo girl Sonoma, whose clairvoyance and extraordinary lucidity has been referred to an an earlier section.

The Brahmin of whom we now speak, a native of Malabar, was himself an ascetic and celibate up to the age of fifty years, when in the full exercise of his wonderful power, procured by fasting, abstinence and contemplation, he became a Yogee of the first degree, and one of the Council of elders.

At times he was not only levitated in the air, but during the performance of a solemn service on the banks of Orissa, he was floated above the heads of the multitude for a distance of over a hundred yards. The brahmin was moved in the direction of the river, and would doubtless have been carried across it, had not the great disturbance in the minds of the anxious spectators broken the currents of Astral fluid in which his spiritual conductors carried him, and compelled them to lay him gently down on the river's bank.

After this aerial flight, the Brahmin withdrew from public life and devoted himself to the duties of his calling as a healer of the sick, a work he performed solely by the laying on of hands. He frequently fasted for many hours, sometimes for days together, for the purpose of curing some notable case of disease, but these self-renunciations always produced their effect in the inevitable conquest the noble physician achieved over the malady, however severe.

Being present with the author on one occasion when a Fakeer who had been buried for eight weeks, was disinterred, and restored to life, in the perfection of health and good spirits, the Brahmin was pressed by a British officer whose soldiers had been appointed to keep guard over the grave, to address the party assembled, and render them some explanation of the phenomena they had witnessed. The Brahmin without hesitation answered: "Does not God effect all these magical deeds every day before your eyes and yet you marvel not at their occurrence? THe only difference between His procedure and that of the magician is, that God gives to everything its due share of life, sufficient for its growth or its maintenance in being. The magician imparts a greater share of life than originally belonged to the object, and calling upon the help of spirits good or bad, just as he may himself be, they, too, bring a share of their life principle.

"Thus the magician's art consists in accumulating and dispensing more of the life fluid than nature herself yields up without his aid. Whatever nature does slowly by process of growth and change, the magician does rapidly by aid of his larger stock of materials to work with." Here one of the missionaries present inquired whether such performances were not in direct opposition to the will of God, since he has designed them for the use of man, he would have himself effected them by processes of change as rapid as those which the magician effected.

"See yonder buildings," responded the Brahmin, pointing to the city with its glittering domes and Temple ornaments flashing in the sunlight. "God made the stones and the copper, the brass and silver, but He did not put them together, nor form them into a city. He gives the riches of the earth, and by inspiration poured into the intellect of man, points the way to achievement, but he leaves man to do the work, and whatever man can do, that is not hurtful to his fellow man, he ought to do, for the will of man is only a miniature reflection of the will of God."

"Look at these roses! They were once a small shoot, a mere pretty twig, placed in the ground. Left to the natural process of growth, they would slowly raise into the air, gather up nourishment from the earth, light and heat from the atmosphere. All this they do because their Akasa works within the shoot, and expands it into the tree, the tree into leaves, branches, flowers and seeds; but if that small twig, placed in the earth, is fed and irrigated by the Akasa which mean and spirits pour out upon it in vast abundance, then it waits not for the processes of nature, but springs up at once, shoots flowers, bears seed and dies, and all within the hour, instead of within the month, as the slower growth of nature would have ordered."

"But the buried Fakeer," questioned the officers.

"He is a man in whom the body, reduced by fasting and years of penance, scarcely inheres together. Nothing but bone, sinew and attenuated matter is there. He is all Akasa - all force, all life. When they laid him in the tomb, his Soul was freed by entrancement. His body was left alive, 'tis true, for a small portion of Akasa remained - enough to keep the particles of matter together.

"To prevent these from being excited to motion, the ears, nostrils and mouth were stopped with wax, no air could enter, and so the body remained intact; its functions were all suspended at a single point, and no attrition could take place between the atoms. It was as if a clock had been stopped and then placed in an exhausted receiver where no action of the outer air could reach it or cause its particles to wear; remove it from its encasement, and it resumes its action just where it was stopped.

"You saw the Fakeer exhumed, the wax removed, and the natural air admitted to the natural passages. The friction used, re-awoke the slumbering functions; the Akasa of those around poured in streams upon the receptive form. The Soul, warned of the body when it must return, is attracted back to the uninjured body, and so re-entering, the man resumes the machinery of life just where the clock was stopped." But the officers would know if they could be inhumed or any ordinary man, by such a process, and then resume their earthly life again.

The Brahmin smiled, and gazing upon their stalwart forms, replied: "Their souls inhered too closely to their bodies. Their souls were not half grown, their bodies overgrown. No; the trance with them could not be complete, and the life principle of their spiritual bodies was so closely interwoven with the particles of matter, that the soul could only be completely removed from the body by death, and anything that closed up the avenues of life in those bodies would os injure them as to crush out the soul altogether." "No! no! It was none but the half dead ascetic to whom such contempt of material law was possible"

Every feat of magic was the triumph of spirit over matter. But the spirit must be very strong and the hinderances of matter slight before those triumphs could be attained. The officers retired, but no tiding have ever been circulated concerning the fasts by which any of their number prepared themselves for living inhumation. This Brahmin teaches that for the performance of gross ponderous work, the more earthly and earth-bound spirits are in attendance, whilst to aid in illusory, magical or elementary feats of power, such as flying, walking on air, resisting fire, producing metals, causing plants to spring up suddenly, or transporting objects through the air; elementary spirits called in the East Ginn or Genii, are always ready to aid, and that the control which man exercises over them and the labors which they perform in his service, benefit and aid them to advance in the scale of being.

These being abound in the elements, are very strong, and prone to cling to man as a God and a great Ruler. If he delight in evil, the evil in nature flies to him as the needle springs to the magnet, whilst pure planetary spirits, good angels, or souls of the just and true, are equally repelled by the evil influences which evil men give off.

"Forsaken of God - abandoned by my good angel!" cries the evil doer. Never so! but evil causes man to flee from God and repels good angels from him. He shuts the door against them and retires into the citadel built up of his own bad purposes and strengthened by the sympathy of equally degraded natures. Man fear thyself! and tremble only before the Devil of thine own conception! All men, good and evil, can attain to high spiritual powers by the physical processes so elaborately described in this section, but few can attain to the highest good which may exist independently of spiritual power of all. Still, to those who desire it, the means are herein made plain. No item must be disregarded or thrown away as an idle superstition. Occult powers reside in planets, stars, suns, systems, inhere in atmospheres, plants, stones minerals, waters, vapors, and living beings. Nature ever demands an equilibrium. Matter or spirit will ever be in the ascendant in every human organism, and whichever prevails draws from all surrounding objects a quality of force to match its own.

Thus the gross man, the coarse feeder, the sensualist, the miser, find throughout nature the quality of element and the character of spiritual life that feed their specialty and pander to their tastes. The same law applies to the reverse of this position, and therefore it is, that a saint or the worst of sinners may each attain to magical powers; but magic is the sunbeam which gives life to the blooming rose when it falls on the rose germ, or quickens into being the noisome fungus when its radiance falls on heaps of corruption.

The forces of spirit are designed for good and use, or they could not be accessible to man. In ages yet to come, when the earth and its living freight are all spiritualized, that which is magic now will be ordinary practice then. The heavens will kiss the earth, and the thin veil which divides the inhabitants of either realm will become so transparent that every eye will pierce its mystery and rejoice in its holy revealments. Until then "knowledge is power," and all men by knowledge may achieve the power of practicing art magic.

Section XII
Magic Among the Mongolians
--

Few nations of the East exhibit a greater amount of devotion to magic than the Chinese, a people whose antiquity is the problem of history, whose priority of origin disputes the palm even with India, yet as far back as history can trace or tradition bear witness of, up to the present day, China, with all its surrounding Mongolian sister nationalities, has inseparably blended its religious belief with faith in spiritism. Mongolian spiritism divides itself into two kinds; the one is the performance of extra mundane acts or feats of magical power, the other, communion with spirits procured through what is now understood to be natural spiritual endowments. Although there is the closest resemblance between the magical practices of the Mongolians, and the East Indians, it would be impossible to overlook the spiritism of so vast a nation as that of China, and one in which its practices are so widely engrafted in the people's nature. The magic of the Mongolians, like that of the East Indians, is in a measure the results of their religious faith.

Buddhism, the ruling faith of the Mongolians, is said to be professed by over four hundred millions of the world's inhabitants, or about one-third of the human race, and to have been imported by Fo, from Thibet, some four thousand years ago. The doctrines of Buddhism differ widely from Brahminism. It teaches the total annihilation of Caste, the unity of the whole human family; it is kind, just, merciful - conservative of life-respecting the rights of every creature, from the highest man to the lowest worm - from the mammoth to the animalculae. It admits of no superiority except in morals, no difference, save in educational culture and degrees of civilization. Its sweet and gracious teachings divide the power with Brahminism in India where in all probability it originated, and spread over the territory inhabited by the Mongol tribes. The Buddhists allege that to those who in truth, purity and constancy, put in force the doctrines of Buddha, the following ten powers will be granted:

1. They know the thoughts of others.
2. Their sight, piercing as that of the celestials, beholds without mist all that happens in the earth.
3. They know the past and present.
4. They perceive the uninterrupted succession of the Kalpas or ages of the world.
5. Their hearing is so fine that they perceive and can interpret all the harmonies of the three worlds and the ten divisions of the universe.
6. They are not subject to bodily conditions, and can assume any appearance at will.
7. They distinguish the shadowings of lucky or unlucky words, whether they are near or far away.
8. They possess the knowledge of all forms, and knowing that form is void, they can assume every sort of form; and knowing that vacancy is form, they can annihilate and render nought all forms.
9. They possess a knowledge of all laws.
10. They possess the perfect science of contemplation.

With all this vast claim for occult power, their means of attaining it are chiefly moral, and will be found in the following transcript of their belief:

"From its birth to the present moment, true Buddhism stands alone as a religion without offerings. It is confined to good works, to prayers, to charity, to meditation, to the presentation of fruits and flowers in temples of the Most High. Buddhist priests perform few, if any functions that are sacredotal; they are confraternities of pious men who live on alms, who act as patterns of the sternest forms of self-renunciation, or as teachers of the highest and purest morality. They are celibates who devote themselves wholly to religion; who abstain from animal food, and who drink only water; who live in nervous fear lest they may destroy even the life of an insect."

It will thus be seen that the contemplative life, the practices of asceticism, chastity, purity and good works are made the foundation stones of the extraordinary powers attained to by numbers of the Buddhist priests, no less than subordinate personages in that beautiful system of belief.

The doctrine which assumes that the soul of the great founder, Fo, or Buddha, is not only re-incarnated in the great High Priest and Ruler of their nation, the grand Lama, but that his divine spirit may also be distributed through thousands and tens of thousands of such subordinates as devote themselves to a religious life, has flooded China, Japan, Tartary and Thibet with Lamas, who swarm in every district and city of Mongolian rule. Like the Fakeers of India, the Dervishes of Egypt, and the Christian Friars of the Middle Ages, these Lamas represent every grade of intelligence, every class, from the richest to the poorest, and every quality of character from the most pious to the most degraded and impious. Lamaeries are established all through the Mongolian territories, where the good and the true, no less than the ignorant and vicious, can receive their education and become fitted for the work, if not the duties of their semi-priestly office, and thus it is that thousands who are too lazy to devote themselves to mechanical toil, or others who are simply ambitious to excel in the arts of the magician, fortune-teller, or wonder-worker, enter these lamaseries and spend years in the routine of their discipline, for the sake of going forth with the coveted prestige of Lamaism. Many of these disciplinarians prove themselves to be excellent mediums and natural spiritists; a still larger number endure frightful penances, and pass years in self-mortification and abstinence, simply for the purpose of becoming great wonder-workers, and earning a miserable and precarious living in the arts described in our last section, namely in fire-eating, the mutilation of the body without ultimate injury to the tissues, the execution of great magical feats, even the power which many of these Lamas actually possess, of transporting themselves invisibly from place to place through the air. The capacity to work these marvels, like the most ponderable and astonishing feats of physical force effected in the presence of modern spirit media, are never enacted through the most refined, or philosophical of the great Brotherhood. They are assumed to be produced by strong and earth-bound spirits; also by the Ginn or evil Elementaries, who abound in the lower parts of the arth, and who delight to serve mortals as gross and physically inclined as themselves.

During the author's residence in Tartary, he witnessed feats of magic which could scarcely be credited, yet, though the media through whom they were produced, had led ascetic lives, and changed their physical systems by long years of self-inflicted tortures, they were never highly intellectual persons, and rarely endowed with qualities which entitled them to much respect.

In the magical practices of these lamas they generally use fumigations consisting of narcotic or stimulating vapors, and drinks of the same character. Also they induce ecstasy by loud noise, the beating of drums, crashing of cymbals, braying of wind instruments, shrieks, yells, prayers, and invocations, far more calculated as would suppose, to scare of the Gods than to attract them. Sometimes they dance in circles or spin around until they drop down in foaming epilepsy, or insensibility.

The Chinese sacred books abound with directions for the invocation of spirits, and the use of talismans, spells, amulets, fumigations, and other means of inducing trance, and spiritual vision.

A vast number of both males and females in China are natural mediums. Writing, rapping, seeing, trance, and even materializing mediums abound in the Mongol Empire, and in nearly all the exhibitions of spirit power, the media are more strongly gifted, more honest and far more reliable, than the professional spiritists of Europe and America.

Visitors in some parts of the "Celestial Empire" are invited to witness trials of strength between parties of spirits controlling rival practitioners.

The author was present on an occasion when a large eight-oared boat being brought into a public hall in broad daylight, where about a hundred spectators were ranged around the sides of the hall, leaving the central space free, four Lamas and their attendants followed the boat, and placed it at one end of the cleared space. One of the party then read aloud the names of eight spirits engraved on the oars, and as each name was pronounced, that one of the oars thus inscribed was tossed up in the air, and then returned to its appropriate place by invisible power.

Subsequently, certain spirits responding to the cries of the Lamas who invoked them by turns, began to move the boat; some sliding it the entire length of the hall, others moving it backwards or forwards a few feet; and others only an inch or two from its place. After these feats were ended, the four Lamas produced miniature pagodas beautifully carved and fitted up, in which, as they claimed four genii or familiar spirits had taken up their residences. These toy houses being placed each on a stand, and appropriate invocations having summoned the invisible tenants, one of them commenced by swiftly carrying his pagoda up to the ceiling, where it remained like a fly adhering to its roof and pinnacles for upwards of twenty minutes, when it was as swiftly and suddenly replaced. At this token of spiritual power, the other Lamas redoubled their songs and incantations, calling upon their familiars by name, to put their successful rival to shame by their superior power. Moved as it would seem by these representations, one of the invisibles slid his house along the floor, causing it to gyrate like a dancer; still another responded by jumping his house about in the air, mimicking the well-known movements of the grasshopper, after which creature the Ginn supposed to be operating was named. The fourth spirit who was called after the sacred Stork, caused his mansion to float majestically some six feet in the air; there it became balanced, then fluttering like the wings of a bird it swooped around in a circle, and lighted back again upon its stand.

At the conclusion of teach feat the spectators clapped, shrieked and uttered yells of commendation, at which the pagodas were moved to bend with all the grace and aplomb of a popular dancer receiving the plaudits of a fashionable assembly. During these performances, the Lamas stood apart, each chanting his prayer or invocation, whilst the space devoted to the exhibition was parted off with a rope, making it impossible for any one to intervene with, or disturb the operations of the invisible performers.

In the mountain regions of Burmah, reside a people called Karens, who dwell in small settlements, or villages, and live lives of singular temperance, purity and honesty. Their religious teachers are called Bokoos, or Prophets, and their office is to inculcate moral principles, predict the future, and interpret the will of the Great Spirit. Besides these are an inferior class called Wees, or Wizards, who cure the sick by spells and charms, fly through the air, bewitch cattle or exorcise the evil spirit out of them, besides performing, or professing to perform, other very wonderful things.

A Christian Missionary, who had long been a resident amongst these simple mountaineers, assured the author their faith in the presence and ministry of the spirits of their ancestors was immovable. They declared they saw them by night as well as day; they conversed freely with them by signal knockings, voices, the ringing of bells and sweet singing. They performed works of good service and warned their friends of danger, death and sickness. One of the Christian Missionaries, writing to the New York Examiner, a strictly religious paper, says:

"The Karens believe that the spirits of the dead are ever abroad on the earth. 'Children and great grandchildren!' said the elders, 'the dead are among us. Nothing separates us from them but a white veil. They are here, but we see them not.' Other genera of spiritual beings are supposed to dwell also on the earth; and a few gifted ones (mediums, in modern language), have eyes to see into the spiritual world, and power to hold converse with particular spirits. One man told my assistant - he professed to believe in Christianity, but was not a member of the church - that when going to Matah he saw on the way a company of evil spirits encamped on booths. The next year, when he passed the same way, he found they had built a village at their former encampment. They had a chief over them, and he had built himself a house, larger than the rest, precisely on the model of the teacher's without, but within, divided by seven white curtains into as many apartments. The whole village was encircled by a cheval de frise of dead men's bones. At another time, he saw an evil spirit that had built a dwelling near the chapel at Matah, and was engaged with a company of dependents in planting pointed stakes of dead men's bones all around it. The man called out to the spirit: 'What do you mean by setting down so many stakes here?' The Spirit was silent, but he made his followers pull up a part of the stakes.

'Another individual had a familiar spirit that he consulted and which which he conversed; but on hearing the Gospel, he professed to become converted, and had no more communication with his spirit. It had left him, he said; it spoke to him no more. After a protracted trial, I baptized him. I watched his case with much interest, and for several years he led an unimpeachable Christian life; but on losing his religious zeal, and disagreeing with some of the church members, he removed to a distant village, where he could not attend the services of the Sabbath; and it was soon after reported that he had communications with his familiar spirit again. I sent a native preacher to visit him. The man said he heard the voice which had conversed with him formerly, but it spoke very differently. Its language was exceedingly pleasant to hear, and produced great brokenness of heart. It said: 'Love each other. Act righteously; act uprightly,' with other exhortations such as he had heard from the teachers. An assistant was placed in the village near him, when the spirit left him again, and ever since he has maintained the character of a consistent Christian."

In a series of articles written for the North China Herald, by the celebrated eastern traveler, Dr. Macgowan, there occurs the following description of spirit writing - a mode let it be remembered, by now means rare in the present day in China, Japan and Thibet:

"The table is sprinkled with bran, flour, or other powder, and two persons sit down at opposite sides, with their hands placed upon the table. A basket, of about eight inches diameter, such as is commonly used for washing rice, is now reversed, and laid down with its edges resting upon the tips of one or two fingers of the media. this basket is to act as penholder; and a reed or style is fastened to the rim, or a chopstick thrust through the interstices, with the point touching the powdered table. The ghost in the meantime has been duly invoked with religious ceremonies, and the spectators stand around waiting the result in awe-struck silence. The result is not uniform. Sometimes the spirit summoned is unable to write, sometimes he is mischievously inclined, and the pen - for it always moves - will make a few senseless flourishes on a table, or fashion sentences that are without meaning, or with a meaning that only misleads. This, however, is comparatively rare. In general, the words traced are arranged in the best form of composition, and they communicate intelligence wholly unknown to the operators. These operators are said to be not only unconscious, but unwilling participators in the feat. Sometimes, by the exercise of a strong will, they are able to prevent the pencil from moving beyond the area it commands by its original position; but, in general, the fingers follow it in spit of themselves, till the whole table is covered with the ghostly message."

Numerous other modes of consulting spirits are in vogue amongst the Mongols. Where the Prophet, or Bokt, is good, pious or sincere, such an one works not for pay, and can scarcely be induced to accept the presents that are tendered to him. A faithful devotee of this character having been sent for to cure a case of obsession from an evil spirit that had befallen a favorite servant of the author's, commenced by practicing on him with prayers, invocations, and the usual methods of exorcism. Finding that the demon, who especially manifested his influence in violent and dangerous attacks of epilepsy, resisted all the good man's efforts to dismiss him in pious grounds, this true heathen (Christian, of course, we dare not call him) understood to fast for nine consecutive days, in order, as he said, that he might expel the demon by the spirits of power which Fo would only accord to the self-sacrificing.

For nine days this angel of mercy shut himself up in a remote chamber, subsisting on very small rations of bread, water and a little rice, carefully excluding the light of day, and spending nearly the whole time, except when sleeping from utter prostration, in long and endless repetition of prayers suitable for his purpose. On the ninth night after his voluntary incarceration, he came forth with a stern countenance, a sparkling glance, erect form, and a voice which sounded strangely sweet and mellow, as he chanted his sonorous litanies to his God. The unfortunate patient happened to be in one of his worst crises as the self-devoted physician made his appearance. Laying this hands on the man's head, with a voice of thunder he commanded the demon to depart from him and afflict him no more. Almost at the instant this rite commenced, the sufferer fell into a sound and tranquil slumber, from which he did not awake till twelve hours afterwards, when he arose refreshed and well, and never from that hour was troubled with his tormentor again.

When will our Christian physicians make similar sacrifices, and produce similar results to their suffering victims?

The processes by which the most stupendous powers are excited have been already sufficiently dilated on. They vary not in any land, although in India they become tinctured with the sublime and metaphysical nature of a great and elevated nation of thinkers, whilst amongst the Mongols, the more mechanical and even childlike characteristics of the people lend to their spiritism an air of superstition, or blemish it with an appearance of legerdemain. Jugglery and slight of hand are accomplishments peculiarly in accordance with the supple forms and imitative natures of these ingenious people, but none can remain long in their midst, or study their history and manners attentively, without perceiving that all the efforts of the Christians to quench the spirit that is amongst them, and teach them to despise prophesyings, have failed, and will fail evermore.

Spiritism ever has, ever will find its most fertile soil in the magical East. That land of Prophets, Saviors, Avatars, and Oriental Mystics - that land where matter bends and sways in the grasp of mind as a pigmy writhes in the clutch of a giant; a land where magic shoots up in every plant; gleams forth in many colored fires from lustrous gems and glittering minerals; where stars tell their tales of eternity undimmed by the thick vaporous airs of equatorial lands, and the sun and moon imprint their magical meanings and solemn glories in beams whose radiance goes direct to the inner consciousness of awe-struck worshipers.

Let the magic of the Orient combine with the magnetic spontaneity of Western Spiritism and we may have a religion whose foundations laid in science, and stretching away to the heavens for inspiration, will revolutionize the opinions, or ages, and establish on earth the reign of the true Spiritual Kingdom.

Section XIII
Magic in Egypt

--

The immense prestige acquired by ancient Egypt for unapproachable excellence in every department of art and science, has invested the name and history of this land with a reputation for magical wisdom which raises expectation to the very highest pitch. A general impression seems to prevail moreover, that Egyptian monuments, incomprehensible hieroglyphics. and buried crypts conceal treasure of magical lore unknown to other nationals and inaccessible to modern research. But assuming, as there is good reason to do so, that Hindostan preceded Egypt in the dynastic order of ancient civilization, India surviving, although Egypt is no more, still preserves the originals of those splendid myths which become the undertones of Egyptian sacerdotal science. And again, how many of the wisest and most philosophic minds of Greece visited the Egyptian priests, sat at their feet, and carried from thence those systems of esoteric knowledge which became the corner-stones of Grecian mysteries? Those mysteries are such to us no longer, and we lose nothing of Egyptian wisdom because we find it filtered through Greek philosophy. Neither must we forget that the founders of the Jewish nation were residents in Egypt during some portion at least of her most triumphant periods of civilization, and when this captive people were led forth my Moses, he carried with him as much of the far-famed wisdom of the Egyptians as a well instructed Hierophant could obtain.

Believing, as the best authenticated fragments of history would imply, that this same Moses claimed by the Jewish people as their own countryman was in reality an Egyptian priest, and an Adept of the famous school of Heliopolis, we marvel not to find every item of Jewish religious worship stamped with Egyptian characteristics; hence, too, we see little ground for the general belief that Egypt conserved within herself sacerdotal mysteries utterly unknown to contemporary nations of antiquity, or that those elements of mystic wisdom for which she became so famous, perished with her, and have been lost in the night of her antiquity. We believe that the veil of Isis concealed the mysteries of nature only from the vulgar who were unable to comprehend them, whilst the wisdom so hermetically sealed against all but the Initiates were preserved in the sum of Grecian philosophy, which is itself by no means inaccessible to the student of the nineteenth century.

As to the ornaments of which the Hebrews spoiled the Egyptians on the eve of their exodus, they are perfectly well understood to signify in Cabalistic language, the external rites and ceremonies of their religious worship. And all these are as fully revealed in the writings of the Hebrew prophets and the Book of Revelations, as they were, when breathed into the ears of trembling Neophytes by the Hierophants of Egypt,. Whilst therefore, we may admire, wonder, philosophize, and crown the land of the Nile with a mastery over arts and sciences unknown in any other country or time, whilst we gaze on her stupendous ruins with an awe and wonder that almost revives the belief that, the sons of God did take them wives of the daughters of men, and in those days there were giants; still, we cannot admit that the genius of great Egypt has perished, or that her understanding of nature's most occult laws lays buried in secret crypts of veiled hieroglyphics, forever remaining the unsolved problems of history.

The indisputable parity between Hindoo and Egyptian sacerdotalism, justifies the belief of many eminent scholars, that the famous books of Hermes, so pretentiously heralded forth to all subsequent ages as the writing of Thoth, "the secretary of the Gods," found their originals in the still existing four books of the Hindoo Vedas, and that those originals still exist, although the copies are said to have been lost, or only reproduced in fragments, treasured up as the most priceless gems of antiquity. The books of Hermes, like the Vedas, were divided into four parts, and subdivided into forty-two volumes.

They treated of the same subjects, were carried in procession in the same order, and by the same classes of Priests and Prophets. The treatises claimed from time to time to be reproduces as Hermetic wisdom, are direct paraphrases of Vedic writings, and the chief difference that exists between them is the value which posterity attaches to that which is unattainable, and the indifference with which it regards the treasures it still possesses. There can be no question that the Jewish Ark of the Covenant found its model in the Egyptian Oracleship; that the chest held so sacred as the repository of nameless treasures carried about in the celebration of Bacchic rites, is paraphrased from a similar instrument used in the Osiric mysteries, whilst the resemblance between the solar and phallic emblems, crosses, obelisks, pyramids, and temple services of india and Egypt, are too obvious to escape the notice of the most superficial observer. The sequence of descent from the rites performed at Benares to those of Heliopolis, and from thence to Eleuesis, may be clearly traced; in a word, whilst India may be regarded as the fatherland of myth and sacerdotal mystery, the entire East, including great Egypt, once splendid Babyionia, Palestine, Persia, Greece and Rome, all may be regarded as tributary nations, amongst whom the ages have parted the garments of the great Hindoo Messiah, the oft reincarnated original of all the worshiped Sun-gods of antiquity. We are aware that to many, these assertions will be deemed worthy only of an anonymous writer. "God understands!" And in that brief sentence is our recompense for all the misapprehension and wrong that our words may suffer at the hands of humanity.

The specialties of Egyptian magic were these. The priests of Egypt, who were the sole conservators of all the religious, spiritual, and metaphysical knowledge of their land - were perfect Adepts in the two great spiritual forces now called Magnetism and Psychology. In Egypt, as in India, the priestly caste included many grades, the highest of whom were the Prophets, a class who were obviously synonymous with the modern "Spirit mediums," that is persons in whom the gifts of the spirit were implanted by nature, and that without process of artistic culture.

Amongst the lower orders were those wonder workers who have obtained the name of magicians, and beneath them again, and not necessarily included in the priestly hierarchy at all, were itinerant ascetics, who performed marvelous feats by reason of natural magical endowments, quickened by culture and abstinent practices, called Dervishes, a class which finds an abundant representation throughout Egypt to this day.

The Egyptian priest, although an ascetic and rigid disciplinarian, did not practice the life-long and abnormal self-mortifications endured by the Fakeers of India and some of the Lamas of China. They were highly educated scientific men, and learned by experience that more potential virtues existed in nature, than were to be eliminated from the human body in a starved and mutilated condition. They understood the nature of the loadstone, the virtues of mineral and animal magnetism, which, together with the force of psychological impression, constituted a large portion of their theurgic practices. They perfectly understood the art of reading the inmost secrets of the Soul, of impressing the susceptible imagination by enchantment and fascination, of sending their own spirits forth from the body as clairvoyants, under the action of powerful will - in fact, they were masters of the arts now known as Mesmerism, Clairvoyance, Electro-biology, etc.

They also realized the virtues of magnets, gems, herbs, drugs and fumigations, and employed music to admirable effect. The sculptures, which so profusely adorn their temples, bear ample witness to their methods of theurgy and medical practice, for which their renown is immortal.

Their sacerdotal system was both exoteric and esoteric, and divided into speculative philosophy and practical magic.

The nature of their Theosophy we have already sketched out in earlier sections, treating of the astronomical religion and the worship of the powers of nature, especially of the generative functions.

In these systems the whole arcana of Egyptian wisdom was to be found. Their hierarchy of Gods, Goddesses, and intermediate spiritual agencies were derived from these systems of worship. All their grandest temples and priestly orders were devoted to the worship of the spiritual Sun, of whom the majestic god of day was but the external and physical type.

Every star, planet and element was impersonated in some form; hence, they found that immense range of correspondences in nature which impressed a sacred idea on so many animals, birds, insects, reptiles and plants.

The different powers and functions of Divinity that they imagined to be manifest in these objects, excited their reverential feelings, not the objects themselves.

The sacred triangle, representative throughout the East of the masculine principle of generation - the Yoni, circle, lozenge, or horizontal line, significant of the feminine principle, these, with crosses of every variety, indicative of the same generative functions, were esteemed by the Egyptians as most sacred symbols and will be found interspersed in all their sculptures.

Isis, the maternal principle in nature, was very commonly represented as a hawk-headed Deity, from the sacredness attached to the idea that the hawk was the bird of the Sun, could ascend to its resplendent heights and gaze with undimmed eye into its blazing beams. The serpent was esteemed in Egypt, as in other oriental lands, as an emblem alike of the Deific principles of good namely: immortality, rejuvenescence, wisdom and health, and of death, terror, destruction and evil.

The famous Anubis, whose emblem so often occurs in Egyptian sculptures, was derived from the Dog Star, whose sign in the ascendant gave notice of the rising of the sacred River Nile, worshiped for its beneficense in irrigating the land.

The Dog Star on this account was esteemed as the door-keeper of the house of life. He held the key of the portals of immortality. He was the invariable attendant of Osiris, the Sun-God and Judge of the Dead; hence, the dog-headed Deity Anubis is so constantly seen in connection with sculptures of religious significance.

The sum of Egyptian Theogony is too well known to send further description here; nor does it materially affect the magical practices of this great people. We shall only, therefore, allude to or describe it, inasmuch as it may throw light upon our special subject.

The belief in Gods, Goddesses, good and evil spirits, the immortality of the human soul, and its transmigrations for purposes of probation and purification, the magical union between the heavens and the earth, the influences of the sidereal heavens upon nature and human destiny, the fall of the spirit from a condition of innocence and bliss, and its ultimate restoration through long series of probationary states - the spiritual powers once enjoyed by the primeval man, now lost, or held latent, and in part only, restored by the practice of a divine life and initiation into the sacred mysteries; these were main ideas which underlaid Egyptian Theosophy, and connected its speculative science with its magical practices.

The history of the Sun-God, the worship of the powers of nature, the trials, discipline, probationary states, purification of the human soul and its ultimate restoration to Deity, were the doctrines taught through gorgeous dramatic representations in the famous mysteries of Isis and Osiris, to obtain a complete knowledge of which many a valuable life was vainly sacrificed. The full sum of magical knowledge was limited to the Kings and Priests, and the latter, according to their worthiness and different grades of rank, were instructed in all that appertained to the subject. The rite of circumcision was an absolute prerequisite to initiation, hence foreigners, who, having arrived at adult age, when this rite might, as it often did, prove fatal, feared to encounter its hazards, and were seldom admitted to the mysteries. The rite of circumcision was symbolized by a circle, and the Egyptian priests wore a consecrated ring in memory of its performance.

The ceremonies of initiation into these mysteries are not, as the would-be mystics of the present day imply, so entirely unknown to this generation. Those who really understand the esoteric meaning of Free Masonry, and the Apocalypse, might discover therein a clue to the ancient mysteries, which few merely exoteric or superficial thinkers dream of.

In the present limited treatise we can do no more than indicate the general tenor of their conduct. They were as follows:

The Neophyte upon being presented to the attendant priest, after having undergone a preliminary series of purifications by bathing, fasting and prayer, was conducted before a masked tribunal, each member of which was arrayed in funeral robes. On every side of the vast hall of assemblage were emblems of death, and sculptures representing the judgment through which departed spirits must pass ere they were permitted to quit the earth and enter upon the next stage of the soul's probation.

The Neophyte's conductor wore the Dog's head mask of Anubis. The chief Judge, representing Osiris, was surrounded with his bench of Assessors after the fashion of an actual judgment, such as was held upon deceased persons ere their remains were consigned to the sepulchre. After the usual funeral rites were ended, the Neophyte was advised that he must now consider himself as dead to the world. All its pursuits, pleasures and attractions must be renounced forever, and an embryotic life must be entered upon, preparatory to the expected new birth which he was to attain through a long series of painful, fatiguing and soul-distracting probations.

As an evidence of the power his Judges exerted over him, the Neophyte was astonished, and in some instances horror-struck to hear one after another - the Assessors starting forth as his accusers, each in turn rehearsing all the errors or shortcomings of his past life, dragging to light even his secret desires, and the hidden things of his inmost nature, thus proving the extraordinary facility with which these great Adepts could clairvoyantly perceive all secrets, and read the characters of men. After this, long list of penances and acts of severest discipline were imposed upon him. During this fearful trial the accused was not permitted the slightest opportunity of rebutting the charges brought against him, the strictest silence having been enjoined, all save the tremendous oaths and self-invoked penalties which he was called upon to pronounce, both on entering and quitting the sacred presence.

From this point the Neophyte was required to abide in certain crypts sculptured over with animals, typical of the criminal propensities to which the soul is addicted, and then instructed in the snares and temptations to which the passions were liable to seduce him. Thus he was taught how these passions might assail him, and in what manner to subdue them by penances, prayers and abstinence. Long hours were spent in total darkness, processes of discipline, and even sever scourgings, dramatic scenes representative of passages in the Sun-God's history, alternations of light and darkness, pleasure and pain, fasting and feasting; some scenes where the senses could be indulged, others where the means of gratification were presented, but the Initiate's strength of resistance was tested; all these were but preliminary exercises through which the emaciated body and tortured soul was required to pass ere he could become a Priest.

Frequent appearances before the awful Assessors of the Soul tested the actual progress he had made.

Sometimes the Neophyte was placed amongst the Judges, and required to pronounce upon the hidden secrets of others' souls, thus calling forth his intuitional powers, and strengthening his clairvoyant perceptions. Periods arrived when the severity of the discipline relaxed, and the tired spirit was magnetized to the somnambulic or trance sleep by powerful Adepts, who, by whispering in his slumbering ear, caused him to behold scenes of beatific beauty and prophetically pointed out the glory of the heavens to which conquerers in these fearful scenes of trail would ultimately attain.

Although gleams of hope, visions of beauty, and short, fitful periods of rest were thus permitted to the harassed spirits of aspirants for Priestly honors and magical knowledge, there were many who sank under the tremendous discipline, and passed to the higher life of the heavens ere its prototype was achieved on earth. Those who survived and triumphantly endured to the end were, as it was said, "often seen to weep, but never to smile." Their youth and all its blossoming fragrance was crushed out, and ever after they were stern, abstracted and isolated ascetics.

One stage of the initiation - probably its happiest phase - consisted in scientific schooling. The Neophyte having been previously prepared in the elements of rudimentary learning, was instructed in astronomy, astrology, medicine, mineralogy, mathematics, geometry and such arts and sciences as were known to that age. Magnetism and psychology were methods not only practiced on himself, but every Initiate was required to practice it on others, and it was during these processes that all the latent powers of the individual were expanded into stupendous growths. If the Neophyte was found to be possessed of natural prophetic endowments, much of the rigor of his probation was abated, and he was rapidly elevated to that higher rank amongst the Priests assigned to prophets, through whom the most transcendent spiritual powers were exhibited. Egyptian scholars have stated to the author that it was because Joseph, the Jew, was found to possess normally the spiritual powers which the Priests were compelled to acquire by art, that he was received into royal favor, and permitted to exercise such unlimited command; also, they alleged that MOses, or, in Egyptian phraseology, Mises (signifying law-giver), was a Priest of Heliopolis, and being naturally endowed with wonderful mediumistic, or spiritual gifts, he had excited the envy and jealousy of inferior orders of the Priesthood. A great feud existed, they said, between the Priests of different Temples and Moses, in his strong reliance on his invincible powers, revolted against the arbitrary authority of some of his oppressors, and hence was banished to the Lepers' quarter, a punishment so abhorrent, that, in revenge, he made his escape, joined the oppressed Israelitish captives, and retaliated upon his tyrannical countrymen by becoming the leader and deliverer of their unhappy bondmen.

One of the chief duties of the Egyptian priesthood was the cure of the sick, and for this purpose the Initiates were instructed in the simple arts of medicine then known and the routine of magnetic manipulations.

Loadstones were in constant use in temple service, and not a few of the most remarkable feats of magic were due to the knowledge of their use.

In therapeutic rites they were frequently held in the hands, applied to different parts of the person, and enclosed in metal balls held by the patients and connected by chains and rings. Thus they were formed into a kind of rude battery, in which the moisture of the body was deemed efficient in producing powerful magnetism. herbs, drugs, charms, amulets and sacred sentences inscribed on scraps of papyrus were often enclosed in metal balls, and applied to different portions of the body. Not unfrequently the unfortunate patients were treated to boluses made of sacred words and occult sentences.

Sometimes their afflicted members were bound up with these talismanic papyri or their foreheads were sealed with them after the fashion of the Pharisaic phylacteries.

Frequent bathings, the use of incense, spices, fragrant fumigations, herb drinks, simple medicaments, charms, amulets. spells, but above all, friction and magnetic manipulations, were the means by which the Egyptians acquired a skill in the mastery of disease, which has never been excelled, perhaps never equalled in any age or country of the earth. One of their most potential means of cure was to induce the famous Temple sleep practiced at a later day so successfully by the Greeks. In this condition - which was in fact somnambulic trance, procured through the magnetism of powerful Adepts - the sleepers were advised by whispers from the well-practiced watchers, to remember when they awoke that all the Gods communicated to them.

In this way dreams were procured or veritable visions seen, in which the patient received prescriptions, directions, and prophetic revelations which the priests never failed to apply, deeming this the most direct and infallible method of communicating with the Gods and insuring a certain cure.

We have said at the commencement of the second part of this volume, that Magnetism and Psychology were the two great columns that upheld the Temple of Spiritism.

Never was this sublime truth better understood and appreciated than by the Priests of Egypt. Their manipulations, knowledge of the occult virtues of stones, plants, vapors and magnets, their psychological powers cultivated up to the very verge where sanity ends and insanity begins, rendered them complete adepts in those noble sciences, of which we, in the nineteenth century, have but the slightest glimpses, but of which few save the inspired Mesmer have realized the full force since the ancient days of which we write. The chief process of initiation into the splendid mysteries depended on these arts. Appeals to the senses through delightful music, gorgeous scenery, dazzling lights, cimmerian darkness, the horrors of impending death, the appearances of frightful forms and ferocious beasts, the compulsion to ascend perilous heights, and descend into awful and interminable depths, the effects of solitude, fasting, scourgings, prayers, the sudden demand to explain the hidden thoughts of others, or execute deeds of daring and hardihood - all these terrible trials and soul disciplines, were means employed to evoke psychological powers of the mightiest kind. This was the far-famed wisdom of the Egyptians, these their mens of evoking all the latent powers of the mind, the triumphs of the spirit, the cure of the sick, and the mastery of the occult forces of nature. It must be admitted that in no nation of antiquity did such severe discipline and such intense intellectual culture precede the initiatory rites of Priesthood. In India the only methods required were the complete subjugation of the senses, and the annihilation of the passions, emotions, and attributes of matter; but the Egyptians were not only taught to elevate the spirit above the realm of matter, they were instructed how to call its highest powers into exercise. Their intellects were cultured by the acquisition of useful knowledge. The highest achievements of art were set before them. Science was hunted down, captured and forced to yield up its most occult revealments to the minds of these accomplished scholars.

Far deeper meanings than the multiplication or divisions of numbers were discovered in mathematics.

The Egyptians determined accurately the numbers which expressed men, Gods, the world and all things in the Universe. The occult principles in geometry were dragged from their lurking places beneath lines, circles and angles, and the true basic principles of world-building were revealed.

For thousands of years, the more than royal powers by which the Priests of Egypt ruled their land and held other nations tributaries to their mental achievements, continued in full force.

For thousands of years this noble Caste retained their integrity, maintained their justly acquired reputation for wisdom, and held their position as the guides of kings, the counsellors of warriors, the dictators of laws, the healers of the sick, Prophets of the future, wonder-workers and interpreters of the will of Deity and the ministrations of spirits.

Always ascetic, silent, true and faithful; their manners were reserved and taciturn. They never smiled nor partook of the amenities of social life and friendly intercourse. Cleanly active, pure and industrious; often tilling their own lands and taking the severest of exercise in sunshine and storm, they seemed to have completely ascended beyond the pains, penalties or interests of the world in their own persons, and only to be concerned for the weal, woe, or elevation of their fellow creatures. A more exalted race of men never won the secrets of eternity from the Gods, or more completely took the kingdom of heaven by storm through their own sublime powers.

Fascinating as are the researches connected with Egyptian magic, it would be useless to pursue them farther in regards their performance in ancient days. Those who pin their faith on Biblical accounts of the trial of magical power between Moses and the Egyptian magicians, perceiving in the recorded triumphs of the one, only the interference of their favorite God, and in the recorded failures of the others, the displeasure of the same partial Deity, will arrive at a very poor and imperfect conception of the truths which underlie the science of Egyptian magic. To the Priest, or in fact to any well-informed inhabitant of Egypt at this very day, the sudden visitation of lice, frogs, red rain colored by fine sand to the appearance of blood, boils, blains, murrain on cattle, or even the rapid approach and disappearance of thick darkness, will be no new phenomena nor require the miraculous intervention of a God to induce them. They may occur any day and at all hours, and they only require an accurate knowledge of atmospheric changes and the natural conditions of the land, to predict their appearance within any given space of time.

Those who have ever witnessed, as thy may do any day in the streets of Cairo, the marvels wrought by Egyptian serpent charmers, those who have seen these itinerant performers wandering through the cities, twining hissing snakes round their bare necks and arms, arranging them in dancing order and forming them into quadrille parties, will not question that Moses and Aaron learnt quite enough of serpent proclivities during a very long residence in ancient Egypt, to contend successfully with serpent charmers a little inferior perhaps to themselves - whilst for the story of the slaughter of the first born of Egypt! - Pshaw! the tale is too old and has been repeated too often to suit the purposes of rival sects, to be believed now of any nation in particular. One thing is certain. If the Pharaoh of the Jewish history did actually cause this hideous drama to be performed in his own land, he only paraphrased an old story long before imported into his nation by the Hindoos, on whose most ancient temple walls, sculptured representations of such a massacre may be found, dating back to periods long before the Jews were known as a people. The same remark applies to a similar tragedy said to have been enacted at a still later date in Judea under the reign of King Herod. If the writers of the New Testament had taken the trouble to acquaint themselves with the true origin of this fable, or had had skill and learning enough to have traced it from Egypt into India, and from most ancient Indian Sculptures into the realm of ancient mythical creations, it is doubtful if they would have permitted the same audacious fiction to have been twice repeated in the same volume.

Premising that we shall continue to write of Osiric mysteries in those of Eluesis; Egyptian Astrology in its succession from Chaldean Priests to Lilly and Dr. Dee; of Egyptian enchantments and fascinations in the magnetic passes of Paracelsus and Mesmer, and of their Priests' clairvoyant perceptions of heaven and earth, and all that in them is, in the equally grand and lucid revelations of a modern seer, whose name is all too little remembered and honored in his own country, but who will ere long be cited in evidence of the undying perpetuity of spiritual gifts, we take leave of a subject which the progress of ages and the diving economy of life assure us, we can never lose sight of in spirit, however the external form of its original may be buried beneath the super-incumbent masses of ruin and decay. The distinguishing feature of Egyptian magic, was the union of occult with natural science, the connection of super-mundane with mundane Spiritism. The specialities of the Egyptian magician were patience, devotion and self-sacrifice, in the acquirement of occult knowledge; skill in its use, purity of life, fidelity to his calling, and educational culture upreared on the foundation of natural gifts. These are the elements by which a true medium becomes an accomplished magician, and it was the Priests who rendered the name of Egypt famous through all time, and their land the synonym of all that is wise in intellect, stupendous in art, elevated in ideality and divine in spiritual science.

Supplement to Section XIII
The Great Pyramid of Egypt - Its Possible Use and Object
--

Amongst the intellectual triumphs achieved by the Egyptian mind, must be reckoned the knowledge of Astronomy, Astrology, Mathematics, Geometry, and a perception of that most profound of all sciences, namely, the universal law of correspondence existing between the four branches of knowledge above - named heaven, earth, man and all created things.

Those who search Egyptian records to their full depths, and can learn above all other examples, to read perfectly the meaning of the Great Pyramid, the object in its erection, the principles upon which it was built, and the use for which it was designed, will understand that man and his planet were fashioned in certain proportions represented alike in numbers, colors, sounds, forms and uses. Those who understand one department of natural science, possess a key which unlocks the whole. Therefore, this great Pyramid, built to illustrate the most perfect principles of astronomy, astrology, mathematics and geometry, ought to possess an interest in the eyes of the profound scholar, which removes it forever from the common-place idea that this wonderful structure was erected merely as a huge royal sepulchre. The tomb of its founder it undoubtedly became; for, in order to celebrate all the mysteries of life and being - the special object for which the great Pyramid was built - death must also take its place in the pageant, and the stupendous history of the Soul's progress through the section of eternity embraced by man's brief sojourn on this planet, could not be completed, unless the Angle of Death was assigned his niche in the splendid shrine.

It would be impossible, without entering into a labored and abstract description first, of mathematical principles, and next, of geometrical measurements, disquisitions which we are assured would not be acceptable to at least four hundred and ninety of our five hundred readers - to explain the methods by which the Egyptians obviously arrived at the idea, that the entire order of the Universe was based on a geometrical figure, and included in a mathematical sum - also that in all departments of being this figure would be found and this sum would exist. In this volume we can but vaguely hint at this sublime discover, but whilst a vast mass of Egyptian vestiges disclose its prevalence, the great Pyramid is in itself a complete illustration of the idea. As regards popular theories concerning the design of this vast monument, we must premise our own statements of belief by acknowledging that the number of wise and learned men who have devoted time, talent and indomitable effort to research in Egyptology, have justly earned the thanks of posterity, adn the respectful appreciation of all to whom their opinions have been rendered. It is not with a view of combatting the theories advanced by eminent Egyptian discoverers then, that we now write, but in view of the specialty of our subject we believe we have an interest in this great Pyramid which has not been sufficiently well considered by others, and therefore we venture to propound the subjoined opinions concerning the uses for which this marvelous structure was designed.

The most ancient Theosophists, amongst whom we include the Hindoos and Egyptians, taught that there existed throughout all being that universal law of correspondence to which we have before alluded.

All Eastern nations attributed the origin of life, light, motion and mind to the action of the Spiritual Sun, symbolized by the physical orb of day.

Character, destiny, physical form and external appearances of all kinds were determined principally by astral as well as solar influences.

Again it was argued that laws stern and immutable, principles strict and unvarying, must underlie a scheme in which millions of worlds are the actors, yet the whole drama is conducted in the most unbroken system of harmony and power. To arrive at any just idea of causation, it was believed that well defined mathematical quantities and geometrical proportions must be the underlying principles of this stupendous chain of being, all moving, living, and acting severally and singly in the most unbroken power and perfection.

Every sound in the universe must conform to the harmonic rule, every shade of color must combine to produce the totality of pure white light. Every creature must be a definite part, everything an organ belonging to the vast whole. Fanciful methods of interpreting this gigantic scheme by the laws of correspondence must ever remain fanciful, unless the keystone was found which should combine all the separated parts of the grand Temple of humanity by one mighty arch. This fair white stone would be neither oval nor square, yet its perfection would delight all eyes, its beauty excite the wonder of all beholders. In all mystic proportions would be found the square, the triangle, the circle and the line. In its combinations would be expressed the truths of Astronomy, or the science of Astral worlds; Astrology, or the science which connects the sum of worlds with the units, and teaches how the mass influences and disposes of the integral parts; Mathematics, or the science which assignes to each world its number, to each component part its unit, and finds in the whole sum the just relations which each unit sustains to the other, and to the whole. Fourthly and last is the science of Geometry, by which the universe is mapped out in lines, angles, squares and circles, in which all the component parts are arranged in just relations to each other, and united together in the grand circle of Infinity.

Let not our readers regard these words as meaningless, or deem them the mere rhapsody of a transcendental writer:

"The stone that the builders reject becomes the head of the corner."

For ages the great Pyramid has been this rejected stone.

The world has not known it, and the builders of science have thrown it away amidst the rubbish of speculative possibilities.

Long has it waited for recognition, and we deem we do not claim too much for it when we prophesy it will yet be read and understood, and take its place as the keystone in the lost art, which interprets the grand science of being as a Masonic Lodge. All creation, the Universe itself, is the Lodge of the Divine Mason, in which all the principles of science are found, from the smallest atom to an Astral system. All are arranged in the exact order of pure mathematics and geometry, and the great Pyramid was built to represent this sublime truth, to celebrate its mysteries and perpetuate its meaning from generation to generation.

We shall now present to the reader a few excerpts from various authoritative writers, whose opinions will strengthen the theory vaguely intimated above.

Bishop Russell, of St. John's College, Oxford, England - advancing the very just and reasonable hypothesis that the great Pyramid of Cheops was not built by a descendant of the ancient Egyptian dynasty, but rather by one who was determined to illustrate in its erection ideas imported from a still older and more advanced civilization - says in his fine treatise on "Ancient Egyptian Monuments:"

"It is manifest at first sight that the dynasty of princes to whom these stupendous works are ascribed were foreigners, and also that they professed a religion hostile to the animal worship of the Egyptians, for it is recorded by the historian (Herodotus) with emphatic distinctness, that during the whole period of their domination, the temples were shut, sacrifices prohibited, and the people subjected to every species of calamity and oppression. hence it follows that the date of the pyramids must synchronize with the epoch of the Shepherd Kings, those monarchs who were held as an abomination by the Egyptians, and who, we may confidently assert, occupied the throne of the Pharoahs during a part of the interval which elapsed between the birth of Abraham and the captivity of Joseph. The reasoning now advanced will receive additional confirmation when we consider that buildings of the pyramidal order were not uncommon amongst the nations of the East......At the present day there are pyramids in India, and more especially at Benares......An edifice of the same kind has been observed at Medun, in Egypt, constructed in different stories or platforms, diminishing in size as they rise in height until they terminate in a point the exact pattern of which was supplied by the followers of Buddha in the plan of their ancient pyramids, as these have been described by European travelers, on the banks of the Ganges and the Indus."

The author of this work has himself visited and examined these Hindoo structures, taking part in the rites of initiation still practiced in their ancient crypts, and that after a fashion, which clearly indicates that the great Pyramid of Cheops was designed upon the same model and for the same purpose. Bishop Russell adds:

"Such too, is understood to have been the form of the Tower of Babel, the object of which may have been to celebrate the mysteries of Sabaism (the astronomical religion), the purest superstition of the untaught mind. Mr. Wilford informs us that on his describing the great Pyramid to several very learned Brahmins they declared it at once to have been a Temple, and one of them asked if it had not a communication with the River

Nile. When answered that such a passage was said to have existed, and that a well was to be seen to this day, they unanimously agreed that it was a place appropriated to the worship of Padma Devi, and that the supposed tomb was a trough, which on certain festivals, her priests used to fill with water and the sacred lotus flowers.

"The most probable opinion respecting the object of this vast edifice is, that it combines the double use of the sepulchre and the temple, nothing being more common in all nations than to bury distinguished personages in places consecrated to the rites of worship. If Cheops intended it only for his tomb, what occasion was there for a well at the bottom, the lower chamber with a large niche in its eastern wall, the long narrow cavities in the sides of the large upper room, encrusted over with the finest marble, or for the ante-chambers and lofty gallery with benches on each side that introduce us into it? As the whole of Egyptian Theology was clothed in mysterious emblems and figures, it seems reasonable to suppose that ll these turnings, apartments and secrets in architecture were intended for some nobler purpose, for the catacombs are plain, vaulted chambers hewn out of the natural rock - and that the Deity rather, which was typified in the outward form of this pile, was to be worshipped within."

Always desirous of presenting the views of such writers as may prove more acceptable to our readers as authority than ourselves, we propose to render our own opinion on this recondite subject in another quotation from a curious little work put forth by an erudite American gentleman by the name of Stewart, on the subject of Solar worship. This author says:

"It is important not to lose sight of the fact, that formerly the history of the heavens, and particularly of the sun, was written under the form of the history of mean, and that the people almost universally received it as such, and looked upon the hero as a man. The tombs of the Gods were shown, as if they had really existed; feasts were celebrated, the object of which seemed to be to renew every year, the grief which had been occasioned by their loss. Such was the tomb of Osiris, covered under those enormous masses known by the name of the Pyramids, which the Egyptians raised to the star which gives us light. One of thse has its four sides facing the cardinal points of the world. Each of these fronts is one hundred and ten fathoms wide at the base, and the four form as many equilateral triangles. The perpendicular height is seventy-seven fathoms, according to the measurement given by Chazelles, of the Academy of Sciences. It results from these dimensions, and the latitude under which this pyramid is erected, that fourteen days before the Spring equinox, the precise period at which the Persians celebrated the revival of nature, the sun would cease to cast a shadow at midday, and would not again cast it until fourteen days after the autumnal equinox. Then the day, or the sun, would be found in the parallel or circle of the Southern declension, which answers to 5 deg. 15 minutes; this would happen twice a year - once before the spring, and once after the fall equinox. The sun would then appear exactly at mid-day upon the summit of this pyramid; then his majestic disk would appear for some moments, placed upon this immense pedestal, and seem to rest upon it, while his worshipers, on their knees at its base, extending their view along the inclined plane of the northern front, would contemplate the great Osiris - as well when he descended into the darkness of the tomb, as when he arose triumphant. The same might be said of the full moon of the equinoxes when it takes place in this parallel.

"It would seem that the Egyptians, always grand in their conceptions, had executed a project (the boldest that was ever imagined) of giving a pedestal to the sun and moon, or to Osiris and Isis; at midday for one, and at midnight for the other, when they arrived in that part of the heavens near to which passes the line which separates the northern from the southern hemisphere; the empire of good from that of evil; the region of light from that of darkness. They wished that the shade should disappear from all the fronts of the pyramid at midday, during the whole time that the sun sojourned in the luminous hemisphere; and that the northern front should be again covered with shade when night began to attain her supremacy in our hemisphere - that is, at the moment when Osiris descended into hell. The tomb of Osiris was covered with shade nearly six months, after which light surrounded it entirely at midday, as soon as he, returning from hell, regained his empire in passing into the luminous hemisphere. Then he had returned to Isis, and to the God of Spring, Orus, who had at length conquered the genius of darkness and winter. What a sublime idea!"

That this great Pyramid was built by those who transcended the ancient Egyptians in sacerdotal arts, sublimity of conception, and the knowledge of the exact sciences, none can question. That it was designed for a Temple as well as a tomb, all true Initiates of Oriental mysticism will affirm. Its external form is the purest example of mathematical rule and geometrical proportion in the world. The perfect square is obtained at its base; perfect triangles at each corner, and a perfect circle, when it becomes, as it was designed to be, the semi-annual pedestal of the Sun and Moon.

According to the hypothesis of Prof. Piazza Smythe, the object of this great Pyramid was to convert it into a granary in time of famine, and a storehouse for the preservation of treasures in the event of a general inundation, or other national calamity. Others imagine it to have been simply designed as the tomb of its founder, Cheops, and a monument to his memory. These and other opinions concerning its destined uses are supported with more or less plausibility. Prof. Smythe, the chief supporter of the first named hypothesis, triumphantly pointing to his wonderfully adjusted scales of measurement, and actually proving - at least to his own satisfaction - that the huge porphyritic coffer, found in the great upper chamber, lidless, open, empty, was designed for an universal standard of measurement, and that its division into certain nicely calculated parts, will coincide with the standard of dry measure now in common use throughout Europe and America! A better understanding of the profound heights of metaphysical speculation in which the Oriental mind employed itself would have shown the learned Edinburgh Professor that this vast edifice was designed as a sky and earth meter, not a mere standard by which farmers and market women could adjust their bargains during centuries after the great founder had ascended to his place of recompense and rest, and that the huge problem of scientific discoverers, the mystic, lidless, wholly unornamented, uninscribed coffer, in the midst of the vast unornamented and uninscribed chamber, was not intended as a model for all generations of succeeding corn and seedsmen, but as a sarcophagus for living men, for those Initiates who were there taught the solemn problems of life and death, and through the instrumentality of that very coffer attained to that glorious birth of the Spirit - that second birth so significantly described by the great Hierophant of Nazareth when he answered those who came to inquire of him by night, saying: "Except a man be born again he cannot see the kingdom of God."

Except a man be born of water and of the Spirit, he cannot enter the kingdom of God.

That which is born of the flesh is flesh, and that which is born of the spirit is spirit.

Marvel not that I said unto thee, ye must be born again ....

Nicodemus answered and said unto him, How can these things be?

Jesus answered and sid unto him, Art thou a Master in Israel and knowest not these things?

We might ask the same question of the learned Professors, but the succession of ideas revealing the sublime metaphysics of being, transmitted from God through nature to his first Priests, the ancient Priests of the Aryan tribes, from them to the Hindoos, on to the Egyptians, forward through Moses to the Hebrews, the "Masters in Israel," and chief of them all, to the Essences, of whom Jesus of Nazareth was the best type - these items of pure metaphysics, form no part of the learning of great Edinburgh professors, and so the huge sarcophagus of the might Temple of Cheops, in which Initiates were designed to by typically born again of water and of the Spirit, became a corn measurer in the eyes of the great British mathematician! When an angel spoke at the baptism of jesus, the by-standers said, "it thundered." Such by-standers are not all dead yet.

The time was when Egypt, the young untutored child of the desert, was not the Queen of arts and sciences, who sat enthroned over the intellectual world. Then did she become the prey of the spoiler. She was invaded and conquered by the "Pali" - Shepherd Kings of "Hyksos," who, according to Manetho, overran the land, put the inhabitants to chains and tributary service, and became for awhile the Rulers of Egypt. What this country was before the advent of these Shepherd Kings we can hardly conjecture, but after their rule, every monument, pyramid, and inscription, bore the stamp of Oriental ideality. It needs not that we particularize the details of these revolutionary changes; we only allude to them, to account for the wonderful parity which exists between the religious opinions which we have enlarged upon in our descriptions of Hindoo worship, and those which re-appear in Egyptian Theogony. Let us, as Solomon says, consider the conclusion of the whole matter. Cheops, a monarch of the invading line, caused a temple to be erected in conformance with those strict rules of science revealed to the ancient Hindoo metaphysicians, as the mode in which God worked.

The external of this gorgeous edifice was the symbolism of the world; built upon the purest principles of Astronomy, Astrology, Mathematics and Geometry.

The interior was a Temple designed to teach and illustrate those sciences, and as the soul of man was regarded as an emanation direct from Deity, so its progress through matter - its fall from spiritual purity to an alliance with gross matter - its transmigration through various forms for the purposes of probation and purification, its ultimate birth into manhood and - provided the animal prevailed in its nature - its descent again into animal forms, and provided the spiritual prevailed, its new birth and final transformation into a pure spiritual existence; these were the stages of the gorgeous drama which the Temples were built to display, and chiefest of all was the great Temple of Cheops, which by profound and correct astronomical calculations, the founders designed should be the physical centre of the world, so they also metaphysically designed it to be the great centre of all those sublime teachings which, in the form of sublime teachings which, in the form of mysteries too profound for the vulgar mind, they, the ancients organized into Free Masonry.

The base of this great building occupies something over thirteen acres of land. Its base line is 764 feet, and its vertical height 480. Descriptions of its bewildering passages, noble halls, chambers, galleries, sunken shafts, ending in secret crypts, blocked up by fallen stones and accumulations of sand, the descending passages invariably found leading to all sepulchral edifices, the ascending galleries and noble chambers which forbid the idea of its being a monument of death alone, its empty, lidless sarcophagus without any signs of attachment, whereby a lid could ever have been used, and the perfect absence in the upper chamber of all inscriptions which could declare the secrets of the rites performed within it, all speak in trumpet tones to the true and instructed masters in Israel, of the design and scope of this wonderful building and its actual nature as a veritable Lodge of Ancient Free Masonry.

We must add, that this dumb but most eloquent structure is full of revelation to the true mystic. its base is the perfect square which symbolizes in its four corners the sacred number 4, the union of the masculine and feminine principles. Its corners are the perfect triangle, the symbol so esteemed throughout the East as the masculine emblem, and significant of the mystic number 3. Its apex represents the Phallus, the sign ever deemed throughout the East the symbol of Deity, or the creative principle. The descent of the sun upon its apex at the two solemn epochs of the year, which signify life eternal, and death through the ever-constant adverse principle of evil, complete the series of allegorical ideas which this building was designed to celebrate.

The different stages of the mysteries celebrated within its crypts, tortuous passages, large halls and grand chambers, would not now avail to related, even if we did not feel bound in honorable promise to suppress them. But their spirit belongs to humanity. They are found in the grand law of universal correspondence - correspondence which makes Geometry the plan, and Mathematics the sum of all things that be; that knits up color and sound, form and function, matter and spirit, heaven and earth, man and his Creator, each planet with his solar system, and the solar system with the universe, in one stupendous scheme of harmony - harmony in which, a number, a sign, a color, a tone or a word will express the whole. The number is one - the color, white - the sound, the pure octave - the word, all the synonyms which relate to God - the sciences, Astronomy, Astrology,

Mathematics, Geometry - the parts, Infinity, the sum, Eternity. Fragments of this sublime philosophy have been obtained by all the capable minds who resorted to the Egyptian Priests for information concerning their occult wisdom. Parts of it are to be found in all the different philosophical systems of the Greeks and Romans, the Cabalism of the Jews, the mysticism of the mediaeval sects called Alchemists and Rosicrucians; the fullness of Ancient Masonry, and the effete exoteric puerilities of modern Free Masonry; the figure which typifies the perfection of this system in geometrical proportion is often passed by unnoticed in Egyptian monuments.

The world is spoken with cold, lifeless, unsanctified lips, and has no efect on the unresponsive air.

The magnificent unison that strikes from the lowest to the highest depths, including all the tones of Creation, sounds in vain in the harmony of choiring worlds upon ears that are dulled to every tone save the clink of money, the emblem of all materialism; but amidst this eclipse of the true faith - this total darkness on the subject of the scientific religion, and the religion of science, the grand old Pyramid of Cheops stands grimly mute - eloquently speechless, waiting for the hour when the builders of the new Temple of divine humanity, missing the keynote of the arch, which is neither oblong or square, shall search amid the rubbish of antiquity, and finding the stone that the builders rejected, place it as the keystone in the arch by which the heavens overshadow the earth, and constitute the universe the Divine Lodge of the Master Builder, God.

There is yet another fragment of metaphysical history to be given ere we feel free to close this section.

The Sun God, to whose honor this temple is dedicated, once in every year dies, and descends into the deepest portions of the earth.

So does death linger in the lowest crypts, in the ashes of the earthly founder of the building. The intricate passages, the narrow, rough and rugged paths, and the final openings into the great Temple Hall were only so many practical types of the Soul's progress to that of the Sun God through the constellated Zodiac of the skies. In the great Hall to which he at length arrives, the Neophyte was instructed in the last great lesson of life and eath. Slain by violence and laid in the coffer, with him is destroyed the Master's word on which the building of the Great Temple depends.

The aroma of death directs the searchers to the spot where he lies.

On the five points of human fellowship, he is raised to life again and elevated to the still higher degree of life eternal. Born again! - now he becomes the key-stone and is placed in the royal arch which completes the building of the Divine Temple. There the Sun of Heaven sits triumphant on the apex of the Pyramid -- the Pyramid which in itself is a symbol of generative life.

This temple was the work of those who lived 5,000 years ago. Its date is no uncertainty. Names and inscriptions ahve been found which justify this opinion inferred both by Manetho and Herodotus. The rites celebrated in this grand old fane at least 2,500 years ago, are not quite forgotten yet, nor are the principles upon which they were practices, blotted out. The moving phantasmagoria which which constituted the glory of ancient Egypt has disappeared from the scene, perhaps never again to be replaced, certainly never by a band of actors as sublimely perfect in the highest realms of life's melodramatic art as those who figured in the great Epic of antique Egypt's palmy splendors.

To-day tribes of wandering Arabs scarcely banded together, not ruled by some poor Sheik, who will perform magic for the value of a few English Shillings, or a set of Dervishes who will dance, whirl, howl, or throw themselves into epileptic trances, for a few dollars, represent the chief of what was once so wise, powerful, far-seeing, and sublime, in Egyptian Spiritism.

Notwithstanding this picture of external degradation, the spirit of ancient Egypt, filtered through the epics of classic Greece and the memories of stately Rome, still lives, still animates the earnest student and the patient scholar to fresh research in the letter of the dead Orient, and fresh discovery in the hidden meaning of its immortal Soul. The day will come when the magic of the ancients will be the Science of the moderns, and in that morning light of revelation the Great Pyramid of Cheops will be known for what it really is, the alphabet which spells out the signification of the Divine Drama of existence.

Section XIV
Spiritism and Magic Amongst the Jews
--

The Hindoos and Jews are almost the only ancient Oriental nations who have left any written records of their religious belief.

The Chaldeans and Egyptians, although disputing the palm of antiquity with India, have bequeathed to posterity on my monumental vestiges of their elaborate systems of worship, and the mysterious means by which they penetrated into the secrets of spiritual existence.

The sacred writings of the Hebrews have been so faithfully preserved, and they contain such a vast repertoire of Spiritualistic events, that they would have furnished an invaluable array of testimony on this subject, had not the excessive egotism of Jewish historians, and the unquestioning veneration with which all their statements were received by succeeding generations, intervened to throw doubts upon the credibility of much that they affirm.

It is now fully proved, that the enormous claims set up by the Jews themselves for the antiquity of their Scriptures, and the originality of many of the events related in them, are totally at variance with contemporaneous history.

The allegations of Hellenistic Jews also, that contain portions of Greek philosophy were derived from Hebrew writings have proved to be false; in fact, whilst candid students of the Bible will find in it an excellent transcript of the manners, customs, traditions and Spiritism of the Eastern nations generally, they will discover only a meagre account of the actual characteristics of the Jewish people, save in respect to their personal adventures, and their constant tendency to imitate the vices and idolatries of other nations.

Abraham, the father of the Jewish nation, was a Chaldean by birth, and though he protested against the idolatrous practices of his own land, and voluntarily quitted it, to found a purer and more monotheistic form of worship, still he impressed upon his descendants many ideas, derived from the astronomical religion of the Chaldeans, especially their reverence for fire, the custom of rearing altars to Deity of upright stones, their system of sacrificial offerings and direct communion with Tutelary Spirits, believed to have special charge over nations and peoples.

Josephus affirms that Abraham went into Egypt, and there became an auditor of the Priests, who greatly admired him for his wisdom. It was probably from Egypt that Abraham derived his ideas of the sacredness of circumcision, a rite which he enjoined as the most important of all religious obligations upon his posterity. His immediate descendants were only herdsmen, and far less instructed than himself, yet they openly communed with spiritual beings, and received counsel and direction through dreams and visions.

Making all due allowance for the necessity of interpreting much of the Bible by cabalistic methods, that is to say, by deeming the words written, designed to veil rather than to express their meaning, we must either treat the existence of the Jews and their whole history as mythical, or allow that they form one of the most remarkable specimens of Theocratic government as the world has ever known.

This people migrated and settled, directed their wanderings, even transacted their business, and governed their Tribes, under the direction of Angels and the inspiration received through dreams, visions or oracular communications. With the Jewish Scriptures so familiarly known to every child in Christendom, it would be useless to review its Spiritism in detail; it is enough to say then, that every page is a record of super-mundane signs, tokens, open intercourse with spiritual beings, and all those phases so familiarly known in the nineteenth century as "Spiritualism."

To judge of the origin and characteristics of Jewish Spiritism, it must be remembered that the people had been ruled over in turn by the Kings of Mesopotamia, Moab, Midian, Ammon, Egypt, Assyria, Babylon, Persia, Syria, Macedonia, and Rome.

The various forms of worship practiced in each of these nations, left their impress on Jewish Theogony, rendering it far more than a transcript of the beliefs then prevailing throughout the East, than a concrete system of any one nation's religion.

From the Jewish Scriptures may be gathered much information concerning those Priestly rites and sacerdotal ceremonies borrowed from Egypt, but of which that land preserves no written descriptions. The early chronicles of the Hebrews may be regarded as a complete representation of Egyptian Theosophy, the Jehovah being one of the Eloihim, or Tutelary Deities of Egypt, their Tabernacle, Ark, Priestly order, rites, ceremonials and sacred garments being all exact copies from Egyptian models.

During the prophetic dispensation, an interregnum occurs, marked by the struggle between a few inspired men to restore a pure form of Monotheistic worship, and the idolatrous tendencies of the people to imitate their neighbors, who throughout Arabia and Syria, practiced the lowest forms of Solar and Sex worship. The Babylonish captivity leaving its strong admixture of Chaldean ideas, follows, after which and during the Roman rule arises that sublime form of pure religion, so thoroughly identical with the doctrines of the Essenes, inaugurated by Jesus of Nazareth.

Under this inspired and holy teacher, the Spiritism of his wonderful works became united to the Spiritualism of his Divine life and doctrines, and so continued through the apostolic dispensation of his immediate followers, although it became modified by the commanding intellect of Paul, who, having been brought up in the sect of Pharisees, and instructed in the subtleties of Gnosticism, introduced into his otherwise kindly yet exalted Christianity, much of that ancient mysticism which distinguished the schools in which he had been educated.

Amongst the Jews, as with all other nations of antiquity, the line of demarcation was strongly drawn between the Priests and the Prophets. Abraham and his descendants, were evidently what would now be termed "Spirit Mediums," for their converse with spirits, their dreams, trances and visions are all described as of purely natural occurrence, yet they added to these gifts the practices of magic by building altars for burnt offerings and other sacrificial rites.

Moses was both Prophet and Priest. His extraordinary spiritual endowments might have been greatly exaggerated by the egotistical style employed throughout the Hebrew Scriptures, still the fact of his high inspiration and open communion with the Tutelary Deity Jehovah, can hardly be doubted, without questioning the fact of his agency in the Jewish history altogether.

This admitted, his power as a magician affords a stupendous picture of that esoteric wisdom, in which the Egyptian Priesthood were so well versed. His contest with the Magians of Egypt, his conclusion amidst the awful mysteries of Sinai, his establishment of Priestly laws, ordinances and rites; in a word, the whole order of his wonderful and sublime history, gives a strange insight into the almost God-like powers with which a Hierophant of the most ancient mysteries becomes endowed. Another, though a far inferior example of the dual powers of Prophet and Magian, is described in the person of Balaam, who, though an enchanter and diviner, one who was evidently familiar with the magical arts then so common in the East, who was hired both to curse and bless, or by strong psychological will to procure good or evil fortune for pay, was yet in modern phrase a Spirit Medium, subject to trance and vision, and when under the Divine Spiritual afflatus, one who was compelled to speak as the spirit gave him utterance, though gold and silver were offered as inducements to prophesy to a contrary effect.

The immense importance attached to psychological power is manifested in numerous instances throughout the pages of the Bible. The curse and blessing so solemnly pronounced by Moses on Mount Ebal and Mount Gerizim, were deemed as immutably prophetic as if they had been the utterances of the Deity in person. Curses and blessings were considered so potent in effect, that the trade of Balaam was commonly practiced, and Prophets were either solicited or hired to pronounce words of ban or blessing on enemies or friends, as was most desired. In the days of Samuel, schools of the Prophet were established, it being thought that young persons by mere association with these holy men, and by ministering to them as servitors, might partake of their Divine gift, and receive of their spirit by contact, or laying on of their hands. It was not considered derogatory in the days of Samuel, for Prophets to exercise their gifts of Seership for the recovery of lost property, and the custom of restoring to them for this purpose was considered just as legitimate as that of seeking oracular responses "from the Lord" through Urim and Thummim. On the Priestly modes of obtaining these responses, we shall speak in the concluding portion of this section; it is proper to notice, however, that whilst prophetic powers were evidently conferred upon certain individuals by natural endowment, and not by study or art, the Prophets of Israel led exceptional and devoted lives. They often retired into wilderness apart from the haunts of men; they observed long fasts, and subjected themselves to frequent penances, the latter more generally for the sins of others than themselves. They wore rough garments, most commonly a mantle composed of the skins of animals. Some amongst them were accustomed to wound their hands and rend their garments in prophetic frenzy. They spent much time in prayer, and were passionately addicted to the practice of music. Many indications appear throughout the Jewish Bible of the constant resort which the Prophets made to music, as a means of stimulating the prophetic afflatus, especially in the exorcism of evil spirits, and the rites of Temple worship.

There are many commentators on the Hebrew sacred writings who do not hesitate to affirm that such personages as Moses, Elijah, Elisha, and Jesus never existed, whilst Samson has been proved to be a mythical representation of the Greek Hercules, and Jeptha a paraphrase of the Greek Agamemnon.

The audacious transposition of ancient Heroes from their own lands into that of Judea by Jewish historians, and the bold plagiarisms of other nations' histories to sustain their own, does not alter the fact that at certain epochs of time, great and providential characters must have flourished and acted something of the parts set down for them. Moses, as we have already alleged, we believe to have been an Egyptian Priest - an opinion which is sustained by Manetho, a Greek historian who claims to have authentic knowledge on the subject. Still the part sustained by this remarkable man in the Jewish Exodus from Egypt, the enunciation of his noble code of laws, his establishment of the priestly ordinances, and the extraordinary spiritual influences which attended him, and enabled him to bring the Jews into direct and constant communion with their Tutelary Deity, are integral portions of history which cannot be blotted cut. Elijah, from his name signifying one of the houses of the sun, like his follower Elisha, has sometimes been deemed a mythical personage, a mere type of the Sun God. Even if the personality of both these exalted characters were to be resolved into allegory, it does not alter the fact that at certain periods of Jewish history, many wise, powerful, and spiritually endowed men arose, under whose scathing rebukes and sublime inspirations, the rebellious people were won back to the worship of one God, and the wise standards of government prescribed by Moses.

In the advent of Jesus of Nazareth a revolutionary change in Jewish history occurs, which could not have been effected without the intervention of just such a pure, high and holy teacher as he is represented to have been.

From the descriptions given by Philo and other contemporary historians of the Essenes, a sect of pure and holy men who arose about one hundred years before the advent of Jesus of Nazareth, it has often been supposed that he was one of their number. The doctrines, manners and customs of this sect conformed in almost every particular to those of Jesus and his Disciples. Even the famous Sermon on the Mount becomes little else than a transcript of Essenian aphorisms, when the two are carefully compared. The same extraordinary similarity of doctrine and practice has been traced between this sect and that of the Sage Pythagoras, and the universality of the idea which marks the great and inspired lives of the Jewish and Samian Teachers, naturally suggests that each of them drew their opinions from the same Essenian model.

As to the identity of the Jewish Christ with the popular myth of the Eastern Sun God - we have no opinion to offer in this place.

The truth that at least twenty different incarnate Gods were celebrated in the East, and taught of in Greece, to each of whom was attributed a history similar in general details to that of the Christian's Messiah, but the still more significant facts that these various incarnations were all supposed to have preceded Jesus in the point of chronology, and that the miracles attributed to him had been sculptured in Temples gray with age before the date assigned for his birth, bring their own comment to every mind not closed against the light of reason by bigotry, or incapable of appreciating the truths of history from blind superstition.

Notwithstanding the fact that the worshipers of the Sun God in the personality of the Jewish Messiah, destroy faith in his very existence by the willful perversity with which they insist upon maintaining for him an impossible biography, the origin, growth and specialties of the Christian faith in Jerusalem, demand the interposition of a human founder, and point, with conclusive testimony, to the influence of a noble Essenian of precisely the character attributed to the meek and gentle Nazarene.

The biographies of Jesus were compiled long after his decease, and were evidently the work of men who, in order that the Scriptures might be fulfilled in his person, interblended the records of his pure and holy ministry, with the miracles of that legend, which - as the history of the Sun God - had been so popularly engrafted into all religious systems throughout the East for thousands of years before the time of Jesus.

The true founder of Christian Theology was Paul. This indomitable Disciple was himself a Gnostic, and wrote in the true Cabalistic spirit of the mystery of the Lord Jesus Christ.

But to the immediate followers of the beloved Master, to those who had heard his voice, lived in his holy presence, shared his sufferings, and witnessed his exalted spiritual powers, Jesus was no mystery, his existence no myth. They had often marveled at his words, and failed to understand that when he spoke from the simple standpoint of his humanity, he was one of themselves, and represented himself only as an imperfect mortal; but when he was "in the spirit," as he doubtless often was, he spoke as if he had indeed lived before Abraham; as of the "Son of God," the mysterious and long-promised Messiah, who temporarily inspired, without being the actual personality of the man Jesus. The devotion which rose to enthusiasm, and subsequently to a faith which has survived the upheaval of dynasties, the rise and fall of empires, and the changes which have revolutionized the old earth and builded and rebuilded it again and again, was not founded on a myth, a mistake, or idle superstition.

When good, pure, divinely inspired and divinely acting men enter upon the scene, and this poor degraded humanity of ours can look up to such a one and feel his kind hands healing their sicknesses, and hear his tender tones compassioning them, and bringing them very near to the awful majesty of the unknown God, translating that majesty into the pitying and strictly human character of a Father, who can wonder that such a one was deemed of as a God, and invested with all the popular attributes of that mediatorial Deity, whose existence and occasional appearances on earth, incarnate in human form, had been taught and believed in for countless ages? The Jews were well acquainted with this popular idea, and their great theological teacher, Paul, obviously favored it; hence it cannot excite surprise that many of the early Christians were disposed to invest the memory of their beloved Master with the same divine attributes that had been assigned to many another great and good man before. Whatever the simple followers of Jesus may have deemed of his divinity, it was his gospel of love, his pure life, his divinely compassionate nature, that so endeared his memory to suffering human hearts, and sustained the faith of his disciples to preach his gospel amindst the fires of persecution and the tortures of martyrdom. But the simplicity and practical beauty of this gospel of love died out when it became entangled in the sophisms of learning, and identified with incomprehensible systems of metaphysical speculation.

The early Christian faith taught by the pure Essenian Jesus, perished about the time when Constantine the Great usurped its name and fame, in order to justify his own iniquities and atrocious murders. Its crucified remains were buried under the Athanasian Creed, and the ecclesiastical fables of the Council of Nice, and nothing of it was left but the name; the body without the soul, the letter without the spirit; the God without his humanity - the mystery without the meaning - nothing was left of the gospel of the loving Jesus, but the name.

We have made many allusions in this and former sections, to the Jewish Cabala, and it is now in order to give a brief notion of the origin and genius of this celebrated work.

Despite all the assertions of practical historians to the contrary, it is quite certain that the Jewish sacred writings, if not wholly lost or destroyed, were reduced to very few and scarce copies during the different seasons of captivity that so often overwhelmed the nation, despoiled the once glorious Temple of Solomon, and committed alike the books of the law and all the other sacred writings to the lames. This spirit of devastation was especially manifested before the Baylonish captivity. After the return of the exiles to their ruined City and desecrated Temple, the solemn duty of re-transcribing the Mosaic law devolved upon Ezra, a learned Priest, a most zealous Scribe, and one so highly esteemed in his generation, that he was commonly called the second founder of the law. Admiring Rabbis are still accustomed to say, "If Moses had not founded the law, Ezra was worthy to have done so."

In order to fulfill his difficult task with the most conscientious fidelity, Ezra not only transcribed the laws of which he had made a deep study during his period of captivity, but he gathered together the ancient men of his nation, consulted with them, carefully noted down the traditions which they had committed to memory, and sought in every direction to improve upon his own knowledge by the information thus acquired through oral tradition.

It was set from this circumstance that authoritative value came to be set on traditional records.

In process of time, as these traditions increased in number, and became easily stretched to suit the imagination of the narrators, or the temper of the times, the books of the law and the Prophets compiled by Ezra sank into insignificance compared to the superstitious veneration which to some minds clustered around these ever-growing traditions, and a sect of believers at length arose the Separatists or Pharisees, who absolutely pinned their faith and adjusted their lives, manners and actions entirely on the assumed authority of these traditions. This was the field in which Persian myths and Chaldean ideas where permitted to take root, until they almost supplanted the stern Monotheism of Abraham and Moses. Jesus frequently alludes to these traditions as making the law of Moses of no effect. It is from this source that the fantastic flights of Talmudic writers are drawn, and it is on the strength of these elastic oral teachings that the famous Cabala is founded. Cabalists and devoted admirers of these writings claim for them an antiquity ascending to Adam, and an origin stretching up to heaven. They trace the descent of this book to Seth, Enoch, Noah, Abraham, Moses, Joshua, the Judges, and with occasional flying visits back to Heaven from whence it came, straight on to the possession of a certain Hellenistic Jew, who, with a few followers, after having been banished for sedition to Alexandria, reappeared from exile about a century before the advent of Jesus of Nazareth.

One of the Cabalistic collections is called Zohar, or the Book of Light, and around this volume, the traditions cluster with immense enthusiasm.

The nature of Cabalistic writings we have already explained. They are for the most part, designed to mask, rather than reveal the true sense of the words, and this mystical style is assumed to be necessary in order to preserve sacred ideas from the vulgar, in short, not "to give pearls to swine," a favorite expression of the Cabalists.

A collection of Cabalistic writings was made in the second century, and some rare copies are still extant; from these we find that the writers enlarge much on the doctrines scattered throughout the East concerning Deity, the divine Trinity, which in its various phases, attributes powers and personalities, is exalted as the sublimest mystery of being. The Cabala discourses of the various emanations from Deity commencing with Adam Kadman, the Brahma of the Hindoos; the Osiris of the Egyptians; the Mithra of the Persians; the Logos, or Word, of the Greeks; the Divine Ensoph, or masculine Wisdom of Deity; and the Sophia, or Feminine principle of Creation. From thence it teaches of Hierarchies of celestial emanations, Angels, Archangels, Thrones, Dominions, Powers, Splendors; Fallen Angels, Planetary Spirits, Evil Angels, Demons, Elementaries, Men, Worlds, Spheres, and the entire order of that creative scheme, on which Hindoo Metaphysicians and speculated for thousands of years, and which the Egyptians had inscribed in colossal monuments, whose permanence will almost bid defiance to the destroying scythe of time.

The Cabalistic writings, besides the veiled mysticism with which they treat philosophical theories, contain directions for healing the sick, exorcising evil spirits, invoking good Angels and Planetary spirits; also, for the exercise of magical powers over winds, waves and elements generally. These powers are to be procured through purity of life, conduct and thought; strict attention to ablutions, purifications, prayers, the use of talismans, spells, charms, ceremonial rites, and other methods too familiar now to the reader to need further recital. The Cabalists put implicit faith in the use of sacred names, and the combination of certain numbers.

They rehearse seventy-two names of Deity, and affirm that according to the method in which they are written and pronounced, such will be the amount of virtue evolved from their use.

The system of numerals vaguely laid down in the Cabala is evidently a ray derived from the Egyptian figure before alluded to, as manifested in the building of the Great Pyramid, but still more lucidly defined in Pythagorean Philosophy, whilst the allusions so often made to the unity of design manifest throughout the universe, is a mixture of the ideas derived from Zoroaster, the Chaldean system of planetary correspondences, and a large infusion of Greek philosophy. The Cabala and Zohar are curious specimens of literature; compendiums of Eastern ideas, and fully sufficient examples of that style of writing justly termed Cabalistic, but when the full meaning of their obscure expressions is arrived at, the student will find broader, fairer, and more original fields of study in the elder nations, in their grand monuments, their most ancient writings, and above all, in the stately and inspired utterances of the Hebrew Prophets. One chapter of the sublime Isaiah, will convey a far higher conception of the relations between man and his God, than whole pages of the mystic Zohar, and the books of Ezekiel and Revelations, contain all the mysteries so elaborately concealed in Cabalistic writings; in short, we cannot promise our readers any higher results from their study, than such as many be attained by the perusal of other works on the antiquities of the East or initiation into the rites of modern Free Masonry. in the celebrated Rosicrucian diagram of Ezekial's wheel, the whole heart of the mystery is disclosed. Therein will be found the six ascending signs of the Zodiac representing Heaven, Good, the ascent of the human Soul, the Universe, or Macrocosm; in the six descending signs are all the opposite principles of evil, the fall of man, the descent of the Soul into matter, etc., etc., etc. in this consists all the mystery of Cabalism.

The succession of ideas representing the same primal thought in the varied but ever progressive intelligence of different nations, in different epochs of time, always present old truths in novel points of view. This is essentially illustrated in the history of Spiritism. The same fundamental principles underlie the whole structure of human and spiritual intercourse, and whether we study the relations that unite the two worlds from a Hindoo or European point of view, in the year 1 or our own time, we shall find that Magnetism and Psychology are the only keys which ever did or ever will unlock the gates of the Spiritual Kingdom, whilst the Spiritism or magic of different nationalities and times are only rife with examples of the various modes in which these two stupendous attributes of body and soul may be employed.

Learned men spend years in attempting to interpret the mystic raptures of Cabalism, whilst the stately old Jewish Bible lies open to their view, presenting an array of curious and varied literature, which far exceeds in valuable suggestion and breadth of information, every other ancient work extant save the Hindoo Vedas, or Persian

Zendavesta. The direct simplicity of Genesis, the elaborate details concerning Egyptian customs, manners, and modes of worship brought to light in the other books of the Pentateuch, the startling accounts of angelic ministry with which every page abounds - the sublime imagery of the Hebrew Prophets, and the curious insight which their denunciations afford into the nature and universality of the idolatrous practices they protest against; the exquisite pathos and beauty of the New Testament teachings, the mixture of high-toned morality and mystic Gnosticism of the Epistles, and the clue to all the ancient mysteries afforded by the writings of Ezekiel, Daniel and John in the Apocalypse, combine to render the Hebrew Bible one of the most remarkable and notable specimens of ancient literature now extant.

It is a book which must compel the skeptic either to pronounce the dictum of willful falsehood and causeless imposture against all ancient history, or else to acknowledge that there must in olden time, if not now, have been a substratum of truth, in the immense array of spiritual demonstrations claimed to have been rendered in the days of antiquity.

The Bible is a book of Spiritism; an Arbatel of Magic, a storehouse of Oriental knowledge, and as such, commands itself to the earnest seeker after magical lore and spiritualistic light.

There were periods in the history of the Jews, when the prophetic afflatus was lost, quenched, as it would seem, by the idolatrous perversity of the people and their devotion to other rites than those enjoined by their Priests and Prophets.

Such was the interregnum that occurred after the death of Samuel; and again after the closing up of the Prophetic era in the person of Malachi, called from thence "the seal of Prophecy." With the advent of Jesus of Nazareth, a new era dawned upon the world, not only in relation to the sublime teachings which he inculcated, and the good words by which he sealed his commission, but by the strictly human evidences of magnetic and psychologic power which resulted from his mission.

All history proves that there are mental as well as physical epidemics; contagious affections of the mind as well as of the body.

When a great reformatory thinker appears in the arena of human life - when such a one is endowed moreover with that mysterious charge of Astral fluid which effects cures of disease, and produces other magnetic phenomena on all who come within his influence - look to see that combination of mental and physical power diffusing itself far beyond the sphere of its immediate source.

From such magnetic and psychologic influences arose that irresistible tide of religious opinion which spread throughout the East from the minds of inspired teachers like Confucius, Zoroaster, Buddha and Christ. Such was the source of those mental and physical epidemics which imparted belief in, and power to effect, the practices of witchcraft in the middle ages; which influenced the French Prophets of the Cevennois with a mighty enthusiasm equal in effect to the ecstasies of Indian Fakeers; which animated the Ecstatics at the tomb of the Abbe Paris, and rendered the "Convulsionaires" insensible to pain; which exhibited itself in demoniacal possessions in the multitudes who made up the ghastly records of Witches and Wizards in Scotland, New England, Sweden, and in later times, in the Valley of Morzine - in short, in all cases of mental epidemic, whether it take the shape of that enthusiasm which enabled frail women, young children and feeble old men to court the agonies of martyrdom during the first centuries of the Christian era, or that subjugation of sense and reason to the control of evil spirits, which marked the madness of witchcraft.

We shall conclude this section by a supplement giving extracts from an old work, entitled "Moses and Aaron," or an account of the civil and ecclesiastical rites of the ancient Hebrews, by Thos. Godwyn, B.D., published at London in 1628.

In these curious excerpts the reader will find correct and graphic descriptions of the various kinds of divination, etc.l, whether lawful or forbidden, practiced by the Jews of all.

Supplement to Section XIV
Idolatry and Ancient Scripture
--

This section is typed in exactly as in the book, including the really awful supposedly old spelling, the inconsistencies, and the improper punctuation and grammar. Proofreading this would be a waste of time. - ed.

"As Idolatrie originally sprang from mistaking of Scripture, so witchcraft and sorcery seemeth to have had its first beginning from an imitation of God's oracles. God spake in divers manners (Heb. i., 1); but the chief means of revealing himselfe observed by the Hebrew writers are foure, which they term foure degrees of prophecie or divine revelation.

The first degree was nebuah, which was, when God did by certaine visions and apparitions reveale his will.

The second was Ruach Hacodesch, or inspiration of the Holy Ghost, whereby the partie was enabled, without visions or apparitions, to prophecie. Some, shewing the difference between these two, adde, that the gift of prophecie did cast a man into a trance or extasie, all his senses being taken from him; but the inspiration of the Holy Ghost was without any such extasie or abolition of the senses, as appeareth in David and Daniel. Both these degrees, as likewise Urim and Thummim, ceased in the second Temple, whence their ancient Doctors say, that after the latter Prophets Haggai and Malachy were dead, the Holy Ghost went up, or departed from Israel. Howbeit they had the use of a voice or eccho from Heaven. In which speech we are not to understand that the Holy Ghost wrought not at all the sanctification of men, but that this extraordinary voice, enabling men to prophecie by the inspiration of the Holy Ghost then ceased; and in this sense the Holy Ghost was said to have departed from Israel.

The third degree was Urim and Thummim. Urim signifieth light, and Thummin perfection. That they were two ornaments in the High Priest's brest-plate, is generally agreed upon; but what manner of ornaments, or how they gave answer, is hard to resolve. Some thinke them to be the foure rowes of stones in the brest-plate, the splendor and brightnesse of which foreshewed victory, and by the rule of contraries, we may gather, that the darknesse of the stones not shining presaged evil. Others say it was the name Johovah, put in the doubling of the brest-plate, for that was double. Others declare the manner of consulting with Urim and Thummim consisted of all the Tribes' names, and likewise of the Patriarchs, Abraham, Isaak and Jacob, so that no letter of the Alphabet was wanting. The question being proposed, some say that the letters which gave the answer did arise and eminently appear above the others. An example they take from the 2nd Sam, 2: 1. When David asked the Lord, "Shall I goe up into any of the Cities of Judah?" the Lord answered, "Goe up." herre did they, that the letters which represented the Oracle, did, after a strange manner, joyne themselves into perfect syllables and intire words, and made the answer compleat. The fourth degree was Bath Kol, "the daughter of a voice" or an echo; by it is meant a voice from heaven, declaring the will of God; it tooke place in the second Temple, when the three former degrees of prophecie ceased.

"THE SEVERAL SORTS OF DIVINATION FORBIDDEN

Wee shall find, Deut. 18: 10, 11, those Diviners which are by the law forbidden, distinguished into seven kindes, not because there were no others, but they were the most usual. 1st, An observer of times. 2d, An inchanter. 3d, A witch. 4th, A charmer. 5th, A consulter with familiar spirits. 6th, a wizard. 7th, A necromancer. To these we may adde an eighth, Consulting with the staffe. And a ninth, A consulter with intralls. The first is: An observer of times, one that distinguisheth times and seasons, saying , such a day is good, or such a day is naught, such an houre, such a month is luckie, and such and such unluckie, for such and such business......The second sort of unlawful Diviner is also an observer of times; the first, drawing his conclusions from the colour or motion of the clouds; The second, from his owne superstitious observation of good and evil events, happening upon such and such dayes, such and such times; the first seemeth to have drawne his conclusions a priori, from the clouds or planets, causing good and bad events; the second, a posteriori, from the events themselves, happening upon such and such times. This planetary observer when he watched the clouds, seemeth to have stood with his face Eastward, his backe Westward, his right hand towards the South and his left hand towards the North.

2. The second is Menachesch, rendered an Inchanter; it importeth rather an Augur, or Soothsayer. The originall signifieth such a one who out of his owne experience draweth observations, to foretell good or evil to come, as soothsayers doe by observing such and such events, by such and such flying of birds, screechings, or kawings. The Rabbines speake in this wise. He is Menachesch, a Soothsayer, who will say, because a morsell of Bread is fallen out of his mouth, or his staffe out of his hand, or his sonne called him backe, or a Crow kawed unto him, or a Goat passed by him, or a Serpent was on his right hand, or a Fox on his left hand, therefore he will say, doe not this or that to-day. This word is used in Gen. 30: 27. "I have learned by experience saith Laban, that the Lord hath blessed mee for they sake." Againe, Gen. 44: 5. "Is not this the cup in which my Lord drinketh? and whereby indeed hee divineth?" That is, proveth or maketh triall or experience what manner of men yee are; the Heathen people were very superstitious in these observations; some days were unluckie, others luckie; on some dayes they counted it unfortunate to begin battaile, on some months unfortunate to marry.

And as they were superstitious in observing unluckie signes, so likewise in the meanes used to avert the evil portended; the meanes were either words or deeds. Deeds; if an unluckie bird, or such like came in their way, they would fling stones at it; and of this sort is the scratching of a suspected witch, which amongst the simpler sort of people is thought to bee a meanes to cure Witchcraft. By words, they thought to elude the evill, signified by such signes, when they say:

"This evil light on thine owne head."

The third is Mecascheph, A Witch, properly a Jugler. Th originall signifieth such a kinde of Sorcerer who bewitcheth the senses and mindes of men, by changing the formes of things, making them appeare otherwise than indeed they are. The same word is applied to the Sorcerers in Egypt, who resisted Moses, Exod. 7: 11. Then Pharoh also called Mecaschphim, the Sorcerers. Now the magicians in Egypt, they also did in like manner with their Inchantments. This latter part of the text explaineth what those sorcerers were. In that they are called magicians, it implieth their learning, that they were wise men, and great philosophers; the word inchantments declareth the manner of the delusion, and it hath the signification of such a slight, whereby the eyes are deluded, for Lahatim, there translated inchantments, importeth the glistening flame of a fire, or sword, where-with the eyes of men are dazled.

The Greeke version doth not unfitly terme them compounders of medicines, or if you please, complexion-makers, such artisens who make men and women false complexions. hence it is that the Apostle compareth such false teachers, who under a forme and shew of godlinesse, leade captive silly women, to the Egyptian Sorcerers, Zannes and Zambres, who assisted Moses, 2 Tim. 3:8. These two were of chief note. In the Talmud they are called Johanne and Mamre.

The fourth is Chober, a Charmer. The Hebrew word signifieth conoining or consociating; either from the league and fellowship which such persons have with the Devill, or as Bodine thinketh, because such kinde of witches have frequent meetings, in which they dance and make merrie together.

Onkelos translateth such a charmer Raten, a Mutterer, intimating the manner of these Witcheries to be by muttering or soft speaking of some spelle or charme. The description of a charmer is thus: Hee is a charmer who speaketh words of a strange language, and without sense, and he, in his foolishnesse, thinketh that these words are profitable; that if one say so, or so, unto a Serpent or Scorpion, it cannot hurt a man, and he that saith so, or so, unto a man, he cannot be hurt. Hee that whispereth over a wound, or readeth a verse out of the Bible, likewise he that readeth over an infant, that it may not bee frighted, or that layeth the Booke of the Law, or the Philacteries, upon a child that it may sleepe, such are not only among Inchanters, or Charmers, but of those that generally deny the Law of God, because they make the words of the Scripture medicines for the body, whereas they are not, but medicine for the Soule. Of this sort was that, whereof Bodinus speaketh. That a childe by saying a certain verse out of the Psalmes, hindered a woman that shee could not make her butter; by reciting the same verse backwards, hee made her butter come presently.

The fifth Schoel Ob, a consulter with Ob, or with familiar spirits. Ob signifieth properly a Bottle, and is applied in divers places of Scripture to Magicians, because they being possessed with an evil spirit, speake with a soft and hollow voice, as out of a bottle. The Greek calleth them Ventriloquos, such whose voice seemeth to proceed out of their belly. Such a Diviner was the Damosell, Acts 16: 16, in Staine Augustin's judgement, and is probably thought so by most Expositors, who are of opinion, that the spirit of Python, with which this Damosell was possessed, is the same which the spirit of Ob was, amongst the Hebrews. Hence the Witch of Endor, whomo Saul requested to raise up Samuel, is said in Hebrew to have consulted with Ob; but among the Latine Expositors, she is commonly translated Pythonissa, one possessed with the spirit of a Python.

The sixth is Jiddegoni, a Wizard; he is translated sometimes a cunning man. hee had his name from knowledge, whcih either the wizard professed himself to have, or the common people thought him to have. The Rabbies say hee was called in Hebrew from a certain beast, in shape resembling a man, because these wizards, when they did utter their prophecies, held a bone of this beast between their teeth. This haply might bee some diabolicall sacrament or ceremonie, used for the confirmation of the league betweene Satan and the Wizard. Prophane history mentioneth diinations of the like kinde, as that Magicians were wont to eat the principall parts and members of such beasts, which they deemed propheticall, thinking thereby that the soule of such beasts would be conveyed into their bodies, whereby they might be enabled for prophecy.

The seventh is Doresch el hammethim; the Greeke answereth word for word - an enquirer of the dead, a Necromancer. Such diviners consulted with Satan in the shape of a dead man. A memorable example wee finde recorded; 1 Sam. :29. There King Saul, about to warre with the Philistins, (God denying to answer him either by dreames, or by Urim, or by Prophets,) upon the fame of the Witch of endor, he repaired to her, demanding that Samuel might bee raised up from the dead, to tell him the issue of the warre. Now that this was not in truth Samuel, is easily evinced, both by testamonies of the learned, and reasons: First, it is improbable that God, who had denied to answer him by any ordinary meanes, should now deigne him an answer so extraordinary. Secondly, no Witch or Devil can disturbe the bodies or soules of such as die in the Lord, because they rest from their labors; Rev. 14: 14. Thirdly, if it had beene Samuel, he would doubtless have reproved Saul for consulting with Witches.

The eighth is Scoelmakle, a consulter with his staffe. Jerome saith the manner of this divination was thus: That if the doubt were betweene two or three cities, which first should be assaulted; to determine this, they wrote the names of the cities upon certain staves or arrowes, which being shaked in a wuiver together, the first that was pulled out determined the citie.

Others deliver the manner of this consultation to have been thus: The consulter measured his staffe by spans, or by the length of his finger, saying as he measured, I will goe, I will not goe, I will doe such a thing, I will not doe it, and as the last spanne fell out, so he determined. This was termed by the Heathen, Divination by rods or arrowes.

The ninth was Roebaccabed, a diviner by intralls. Nebucadnezar being to make warre both with the Jews and the Ammonites, and doubting in the way against whether of these he should make his first onset: First he consulted with his arrowes and staves, of which hath beene spoken of immediately before; Secondly, he consulted with the entralls of beasts. This practice was generally received among the Heathens, and because the liver was the principall member observed, it was called Consultation with the liver. Three things were observed in this kind of divination. First, the colour of the intralls, whether

165

they were all well-colored; Secondly, their place, whether none were displaced; Thirdly, the number, whether none were wanting. Among those that were wanting, the want of the liver or the heart chiefly presaged ill. That day when Julius Caesar was slaine, it is storied, that in two fat oxen then sacrificed, the heart was wanting in them both.

Section XV
Magic and Spiritism Amongst the Chaldeans

--

The religious doctrines of the Chaldeans, varied from those of the Hindoos and Egyptians chiefly, in their different modes of expression, in the name appropriated to different Deities, and the functions which these mythical personages were supposed to be endowed with. The basic idea of Solar and Astral worship however prevailed in all nations alike, but the absence of sexual emblems on Chaldean monumental remains, seems to imply that this people adhered to the astronomical religion, without engrafting its popular successor, Sex worship, upon its purer Theosophy. Although our only information concerning the Spiritism of Chaldea is derived from monumental records, oral traditions, and contemporaneous history, these sources are abundantly sufficient to testify to the fact that Balylon the great and the Priests of Chaldea, so widely renowned for occult wisdom, acquired this vast reputation princiapply for transcendent skill in the arts of divination, and the methods of reading the future by Astrology. The Chaldeans were also celebrated for certain branches of chemical knowledge, especially for the means whereby they learned to resist the action of fire and poisons.

Schools of the Magi were established at Babylon, and as magic was deemed an essential item in the art of governing the nation, and conducting armies to victory, even Kings, Statesmen, and warriors, no less than the Sons of he Nobles and wealthy Citizens, resorted to these famous seminaries of occult learning, or sat at the feet of the magi to drink in the elements of their profound wisdom. It was in these schools that Daniel and some of the handsomest and most intelligent of the Hebrew captives were placed for education after the conquest of Judea by the Babylonians. It was from thence that the remarkable admixture of Chaldean and Persian philosophy was derived, which marks the literature of the Jews after the Babylonish captivity. There are many scholars who believe - and that upon good foundation - the writings of the Pentateuch, the composition of the Cabala, and the fables of the Talmud, owe so much of their peculiar spirit to the Caldean Magi, that those who are well acquainted with these Hebrew writings, lose nothing by the total lack of Chaldean Scriptures.

In Chaldea, as in other Asiatic and Eastern nations, the connection between religious rites and the art of magic was inseparable. The highest class of the Priesthood - those set apart for Temple service - were "Star Gazers" or Astrologers, healers of the sick, by magnetism (i.e.,), the laying on of hands - and even the High Priest himself - the functionary who virtually ruled the land through his influence over the reigning monarch - delivered oracles, and often practiced the highest form of magical rites. So great was the skill of the Chaldean Magi in Astrology, that it has become proverbial in all ages to attribute the invention of this art to the Chaldeans, and in some lands the term Astrologer and Chaldean were held to be synonymous.

The Babylonish Priests were reputed to be thoroughly well acquainted with the occult virtue of stones, plants, herbs, vapors and narcotics. They claimed to be able to cast spells on whole armies, arresting their progress, or paralyzing their power of action. They could even cause the downfall of nations, though it is obvious they had no such power in the preservation of their own once splendid dynasty. Their achievements during the flush of their splendor and magnificence, caused their vast claims for magical knowledge to be feared and quoted through all contemporaneous nationalities.

Their methods of interpreting dreams and visions, of prophesying or soothsaying, and resisting the action of fire, are significantly alluded to in the book of Daniel, wherein it clearly appears that the natural endowments, or in modern phraseology, the normal mediumship of the young Hebrew Captives, were found superior in truthful results to the arts of the instructed Magians, and it is quite probable that if many of the stupendous claims set up for the magical practices of antiquity could be brought to a similar test, they would be found inferior to the true prophetic gifts which spring from natural endowments. It is well to notice, however, that Danies and his companions practiced that strict regimen and remarkable abstinence which has been so universally found efficacious in promoting spiritual afflatus. Let not those who rely solely on their mediumship without culture, mistake this important suggestion.

In Chaldea as amongst all other ancient nations, the most honored class of the Priests were true prophets, persons naturally endowed, but these fortunate individuals, like the Hebrews, often arose outside the priestly ranks, and even when within them, seldom accepted office, preferring - as those gifted by the power of the spirit invariably do - to act independently of priestly organizations. Amongst the priests there were three distinct classes. The first were the Singers, Musicians, or Exorcists, who were commonly employed in exorcising demons and ministering to the sick. These by their admirable performances on instruments or in solemn chants stimulated the minds of worshipers to devotion, enchanted the listeners, even serpent becoming obedient, and ferocious beasts yielding themselves up to the spell of their delicious melodies. The second class were the magicians or wonder-workers, through whom all manner of soothsaying was effected, also ordeals by fire were shown, elements stilled, or storms raised; spells and enchantment procured, and divination or auguries from entrails, burnt offerings, flights of birds or other natural object obtained. The third and highest class were the "Star Gazers," for whom were erected those gigantic temples of which the famous tower of Babel or Belus forms an example. The exterior and apex of these wonderful monuments were used for astronomical observations, the interior for those mysterious rites through which Initiates were taught, and Priestly Hierophants received their education. As these famous mysteries were subsequently inaugurated in Persia under the name of Mithraic rites, we learn from them that the Chaldean originals were simply designed to teach the fundamental principles of Sabaeism, or the most ancient astronomical religion.

Cicero, in his treatises on Soothsaying and Divination, attributes paramount excellence to the Chaldeans, intimating in fact that to these most ancient priests the origin of Astrological Science and Magical art is due. Their modes of initiation and study were very severe. Lives of purity and asceticism were demanded, but though they were required to abstain from wine and the flesh of animals, they never practiced the rigid discipline enforced upon the Hindoo Fakeers, on the contrary, they maintained that emaciated bodies and enfeebled frames were more subject to the attacks of evils spirits, and less capable of resisting them, then healthy, pure, and well-balanced organisms.

ALthough a vast number of the engraved tablets found amongst the ruins of ancient Chaldea, exhibit zodiacs and astronomical signs in abundance, there is no authentic record of the exact system of calculation upon which these great Adepts based their methods of Astrology. The Persians, Chinese and Mediaeval Professors of the art, claim to be in possession of correct Chaldean schemes, but whether this be true or false, the scientific astrologer is aware that the system of calculation by which successful results are to be obtained, is as exact and unvarying a science as astronomy, and does not change with country or clime. Those who can obtain successful results then, even in the nineteenth century, may assure themselves they are in possession of the same rules by which the Chaldean Adepts achieved their vast renown. As the methods of Astrology are very elaborate, and require much more space than we could assign them in this volume, we refer those who may be disposed to study this curious science, to the many treatises on the subject that are now extant. Those who desire to acquaint themselves with the most approved rules of the art, should study Lilly's Astrology, published in 1647. Students well versed in this branch of occultism, claim the work in question to be the most reliable and authentic now in print.

It would be useless to pursue our investigation into ancient Asiatic or African researches farther.

The spiritism of the Jews, Medes, Persians, Gnostics, Neo-Platonists and early Christians, with the modifications which we so often insist on, as the result of growth through different epochs of time, and changes induced by varied climes and scenes - all proclaim the steady and unbroken succession of ideas springing up from one original source, namely, an observance and worship of the powers of nature. Now, as heretofore, we claim that nothing is lost in history or in nature.

However limited the intercourse between ancient nationalities might have been, their frequent irruptions into each other's territories, the transmission of opinions through mutual captivities, through commerce, oral tradition and the contagion of thought, render it certain, that the utter obliteration of ideas from any one land by the destruction of their scriptures, or the loss of a key to their hieroglyphical inscriptions is simply impossible. It is the favorite opinion of modern students, especially those of a romantic and naturally mystical turn of mind, that Egypt and Chaldea, the two most antique nations of civilization, Hindostan excepted, conceal beneath their cuniform characters, profuse hieroglyphics and singular tablets, profound revelations in occultism that are forever lost to mankind, unless, indeed, some spiritual "Edipus" of these ruined lands, should disclose their mysteries through the entranced lips of a modern Somnambule.

With these attempts to repair the breaches in that tremendous veil of mystery which once shrouded the sacerdotal power of Babylon the great, hushed the voice of musical Memnon, and put the finger of eternal silence on the stony lips of the Sphinx, we have no sympathy, nor do we offer any plea for belief in such directions.

We claim now, as heretofore, that we have more of the real spirit of antiquity in our midst, than the race in this utilitarian and materialistic age understands; besides, the same imperishable sources of knowledge from which the ancients derived their opinions and framed their system of Theosophy, are open to the students of the nineteenth century in all their fullness. The starry Scriptures of the skies still unfold their pages of light for the perusal of the patient Astrologer. The plants dispense their fragrance, the herbs their virtues, the gums and spices stimulate the senses with aromatic odor now, as in olden times. The wonderful loadstone and the subtle amber have yielded up mysteries to the researchers of modern Science, of which the ancients scarcely dreamed. What oracular responses could now be given by the telegraph, which would put the magic of Dodona to shame! What miracles of necromancy are daily effected by the magic of the photographer, by aid of the Egyptian's Sun God! The five hundred thousand men that were required to drag stones over a made road, and then upheave them by clumsy levers to build the pyramid of Cheops, might now stand by with their hands in their pockets, watching labor-saving machinery, propelled by that mightiest of all magicians, the noble steam engine, doing the work a thousand times quicker, and a thousand times better, than even the poor bruised hands of unwilling captives could have done! It is not in executive power in any single direction that the ages of antiquity can successfully compete with the scientific triumphs of the nineteenth century, when man's knowledge of how to control the elements, and his perfect comprehension of imponderable forces as applied to mechanical uses, produce results in physical science, which would make all the Magicians of the East, and all the wonder-workers of antiquity, give up the ghost in envy and amazement. But it is not in materialistic acquirements or physical science, that the ancients transcended us or even begin to equal the magical marvels, which the building and furnishing of one single modern mansion displays. It is in the realm of metaphysical speculation and the utilization of Soul powers, that the ancients were our masters, and that the moderns are willfully blind, and contemptuously determine to remain so --nay more: when the mere suggestion is thrown out that spiritual science may correlate those of physics, the scoff, sneer and jeer of Scientists, and the anathema maranatha of Priests, effectually stifles all attempts at research save on the part of those who are bold enough to face the rack and thumb and screw of moral martyrdom. Take, for instance, the correlation of astronomy and astrology. Whilst astronomy declares the mathematics and geometry of the sidereal heavens, astrology defines the executive forces which suns, planets and systems mutually exercise upon each other, and the influence which each atom of matter exercises upon every other atom. Physicists allow that light and heat are the two great motor powers of form and being; yet, whilst admitting that man is the creature of physical organization, that his character and physique are determined by the place where he is born, the ante-natal influences which create his special tendencies, he shoots out the lip of scorn when Astrology claims that the configuration of the heavenly bodies, the original sources of light, heat, and therefore of all subordinate effects, have aught to do with shaping man's destiny, or determining the career he has to run. Nothing is so thankless and unprofitable as the attempt to pit spiritual phenomena against physical formulae, or argue inductively against bigotry and materialism; but we venture to assert, that if one score of thoroughly well-instructed astrologers who are both astronomers and mathematicians, shall undertake to set up the figure of one life submitted to their methods for analysis, the results in each instance shall be precisely the same, and every leading feature of the physical form, mental tendency and leading events of the human pilgrimage, shall closely correspond, every one of the twenty with the other.

If such a possibility as the above does not indicate the elements of "exact science," we are at a loss to know the application of the words. Meantime, the modern spirit medium of Europe and America, has within the last quarter of a century exhibited natural gifts and spontaneous powers, which put the acquired arts of ancient Magians into the shade. Why they are not as great as the mediums of India, Arabia, and Asia Minor, is, because the Western medium depends entirely on the spirits to do the work for him, and offers no prepared conditions, either physically, mentally, or in circumstantial surrounding, to aid the spirits, whilst the Asiatic and African medium fasts, prays, thinks, dresses, washes, and practices the spiritualistic conditions necessary for the highest gifts, through years of discipline. Spiritual bigotry, scientific prejudice and popular indifference on religious subjects, are the underlying causes which have cast their blight on Spiritism and Magic in the nineteenth century, and cause these wonderful elements of knowledge to loom up from the antique ages, in proportions as stupendous and overwhelming as the Pyramid of Cheops compared to a modern church, or the cave Temples of Elephanta and Ellora, gauged by the proportions of a London museum or a Parisian gallery of art.

The absence of magical art is not the lack of magical knowledge. The spirit world will not confer its prizes upon dunces and idlers. The natural world is the open page, the heaven, earth, and all that in them is, are the letters of the magical alphabet, and until man learns these, and enters upon the spelling-book of magnetism, and the grammar of psychology, this pen of ours may point the way, but every pilgrim foot must tread the path for himself. Thus, and thus only, may we rival the ancient man in the goal of magical achievements to which he ascended.

We shall conclude this section by a few quotations, the first of which we take from Ennemoser's History of Magic, in which he gives an appropriate sketch of the characteristics of the Lapps and Finlanders, whose spiritism strongly illustrates our opinion, that climate, soil, scenery and surroundings, exert remarkable effect in modifying natural spiritualistic endowments, also that these are communicated by the contagion of thought in communities already predisposed to such affections.

"The present nations of Asia, among whom ecstatic states and visions are to be met with, are worthy of mention. Among them are the Siberian Schamans, the Arabian Dervishes, and the Samozedes and Lapps. Among all these nations a species of somnambulism is common, into which they fall, either by means of natural susceptibility, or by peculiar movements and exercises of the body, and rarely by the use of narcotic substances. Among the northern nations, the phenomenon of second-sight is said to be frequent.

"Among the many Mongolian tribes, and also the Lapps, particularly excitable and susceptible persons are chosen as ghost-seers and sorcerers; in India as Jongleurs, in Siberia as Schamans. With much natural disposition, strengthened by practice and mode of life, the majority require nothing more than to shout violently, to storm, to dance and to drum, to turn round in a circle to induce insensibility and convulsive rigidity. Among the Siberian Schamans, as we learn from Georgi, narcotic substances are used, such as a decoction of fungus or other exciting vegetable substances to produce visions, in which they see and communicate with spirits, learning from them future and distant events. They also see distant countries and the souls of the dead, to whom they ascend from the body through the air to the seats of the gods, which Hoegstrom especially relates of the Lapps, among whom, such a high degree of susceptibility exists, that the most remarkable phenomena are witnessed. If any one opens his mouth or closes it, or points to anything with his fingers, or dances, or makes other gesticulations, there are many who will imitate all this, and when they have done so, inquire whether they have done anything improper, as they knew nothing of what they did. These Lapps are excitable to such a degree, that they are thrown into insensibility and convulsions, by the most trifling and unexpected occurrence, such as a sound, or a spark of fire. In the church they often fall into insensibility when the preacher speaks too loud or gesticulates too much; while others, on the contrary, jump up as if mad, rush out of the church, knock down all who oppose them, and even strike their friends and neighbors."

"Pallas relates that the Schamans, the Samozedes, the Katschinzes and other north Asiatic nations, are so extremely excitable, that it is only requisite to touch them unexpectedly to disturb their whole organization, to excite their imagination and make them lose all self command. Each one infects the person next to him sympathetically, so that in this manner, whole neighborhoods fall into fear, uneasiness and confusion. Pallas relates of some girls among the Katschinzes, that they fell simultaneous suffering as soon as one of their number becomes ill. 'For the last few years,' says he, 'a species of insanity has made its appearance among the young girls of the Katschinzes as if by infection. When they have these fits, they run out of the village, scream, and behave with the greatest wildness, tear their hair, and endeavor to hang and drown themselves. These attacks last usually some hours, and occur when their sympathy has been excited by the sight of other girls in similar condition, without any certain order - sometimes weekly, at other times not appearing for months.' All these and similar phenomena are related by Georgi of the Mongol and Tartar races, who all have the same common origin."

Our next quotation will be from a series of autobiographical sketches, entitled "Ghost Land," written by the author of this work, published by Emma Hardinge Britten in her admirable American periodical, "The Western Star."

"In Lapland, Finland, and the northeastern part of Russia, our new acquaintances had beheld so many evidences of inborn occult powers amongst the natives, that they had come to a conclusion which the well informed Spiritualist of modern times will no doubt be ready to endorse, that is, that certain individuals of the race are so peculiarly endowed, that they live, as it were, on the borders of the invisible world, and from time to time see, hear, act, and think under the influence, as naturally as other individuals do who are only capable of sensing material and external things.

"Moreover, our friends had arrived at the opinion that certain localities and climactric influences were favorable or otherwise to the development of these innate occult endowments.

"Experience had shown them that mountainous regions, or highly rarefied atmospheres, constituted the best physical conditions for the evolvement of magical powers, and they therefore argued that the great prevalence of supermundane beliefs and legendary lore in those latitudes arises from the fact, that intercourse with the interior realms of being are the universal experience of the people, not that they are more ignorant or superstitious than other races. Lord D----- had brought to England with him a 'Schaman,' or priest, of a certain district in Russia, where he had given extraordinary evidence of his powers. This man's custom was to array himself in a robe of state, trimmed with the finest furs and loaded with precious stones, amongst which clear crystals were the most esteemed.

"In this costume, with head, arms, and feet bare, the Schaman would proceed to beat a magical drum, made after a peculiar fashion, and adorned with a variety of symbolical and fantastic paintings.

"Commencing his exercises by simply standing within a circle traced on the ground, and beating his drum in low, rhythmical cadence to his muttered chantings, the Schaman would gradually rise to a condition of uncontrollable frenzy; his hands would acquire a muscular power and rapidity which caused the drum to resound with the wildest clamor, and strokes which defied the power of man to count.

"His body, meantime, would sway to and fro, spin round, and finally be elevated and even suspended several feet in the air, by a power wholly unknown to the witnesses. His cries and gesticulations were frightful, and the whole scene of 'manticism' would end by the performer's sinking on the earth in a rigid cataleptic state, during which he spoke oracular sentences, or gave answers to questions with a voice which seemed to proceed from the air some feet above his prostrate form. During my stay in England I was present at several experimental performances with this Schaman, and thought he could unquestionably predict the future and describe correctly distant places and persons, Professor M--- and myself were both disappointed in the results which we expected to proceed from his very elaborate modes of inducing the 'mantic' frenzy. Lord D--- accounted for the inferiority of his protege's powers by stating that the atmosphere was prejudicial to his peculiar temperament, and though he had striven to surround him with favorable conditions, it was obvious he needed the specialties of his native soil and climate for the complete evolvement of the phenomena he had been accustomed to exhibit.....

We found another class, who seemed to have no extraordinary endowments of a spiritual nature, yet in whom the most wonderful powers of inner light, curative virtue, and prophetic vision could be awakened through artificial means, the most potent of which were the inhalation of mephitic vapors, pungent essences, or narcotics; the action of clamorous noise, or soothing music; the process of looking into glittering stones and crystals; excessive and violent action, especially in a circular direction, and lastly, through the exhalations proceeding from the warm blood of animated beings. All these influences, together with an array of forms, rites and ceremonials which involve mental action, and captivate the senses, I now affirm to constitute the art of ancient magic, and I moreover believe that wherever these processes are systematically resorted to, they will,

173

in more or less force, according to the susceptibility of the subject, evoke all these occult powers known as ecstasy, somnambulism, clairvoyance, the gifts of prophecy, healing, etc.

"We derived another item of philosophy from our researches, which was, that under the influence of magical processes, the human organism can not only be rendered insensible to pain, but that wounds, bruises, and even mutilation can be inflicted upon it, without permanent injury; also, that it can be rendered positive to the law of gravitation, and ascend into the air with perfect ease.

"Also, the body can be so saturated with magnetism, or charged with spiritual essence, that fire cannot burn it; in a word, when the body becomes enveloped in the indestructible essence of spirit, or the soul element, it can be made wholly positive to all material laws, transcending them in a way astonishing and inexplicable to uninterested beholders. Of this class of phenomena, let me refer to the 'Convulsionaires of St. Medard'; the history of the 'French Prophets of Avignon'; the still more recent accounts of the frightful mental epidemic which prevailed in the district of Morzine in 1864; the now well attested facts of supermundane power enacted by the Fakeers, Brahmins, and ecstatics of the East, and many of the inexplicable physical and mental phenomena attributed to monastic ecstatics.

"Amongst the 'Convulsionaires of st. Medard' and the possessed peasants of Morzine, one of the most familiar demonstrations of an extra-mundane condition was the delight and apparent relief which the sufferers represented themselves as experiences, when blows violent enough, as would seem, to have crushed them bone by bone were administered to them. At the tomb of the Abbie Paris, and amongst the frenzied patients of Morzine, the most pathetic appeals would be made that powerful men would pound their bodies with huge mallets, and the cries of 'Heavier yet, good brother! heavier yet, for the love of Heaven!' were amongst the words most constantly uttered ......

"During the fearful struggle maintained by the brave and devoted prophets of the Cevennes against their oppressors, every history, whether favorable or antagonistic, makes mention of the exhibitions by which Cavillac and others of 'the inspired,' proved their ability, under the afflatus of ecstasy, to resist the action of fire."

The ancient Chaldeans acquired this art not by any magical process, but by the knowledge of such chemicals as asbestos, and other substances which would render the body fire-proof. The French Prophets, and many spirit mediums of the nineteenth century, have proved their power to resist the action of fire under spiritual afflatus. Another example, if more were wanting, of the superiority of natural spiritualistic endowments, over the most occult methods of magical art.

Section XVI
The Poetry of Life's Sterner Prose
--

Magic in the classical lands of Greece and Rome becomes so thoroughly transformed from the solemn metaphysics of India, the semi-savagism of Arabia, and the profound mysticism of Egypt, by the young life, blossoming intellect, and love of the beautiful which characterized Grecian genius, and in a measure imparted its grace to the sterner spirit of Rome, that no attempt to condense descriptions of their spiritism could do justice to the subject. On the other hand our available space has been too much taken up with analyses of the underlying principles of magical history in the Orient - the true fatherland of magic - either to permit of, or to need our dwelling at any length upon these fascinating themes, so clearly defined as the poetry of life's sterner prose.

Magic, sorcery and the correspondingly dark shades of Spiritism, were not in harmony with the graceful and elastic character of classic lands. Their peoples loved philosophy, and revealed in the subtleties of thought, as portrayed through the brilliant ideality of Greek and Roman history with stars of immortal lustre.

Strictly speaking, no well marked systems of religious belief prevailed in Greece and Rome. Their Pantheon of countless Gods and Goddesses were too closely allied with humanity to impress their votaries with the awe and majesty appropriate to the idea of Deity, and even their most exalted flights of imagination could not embody the creative principle in aught beyond an impersonated Demiurgus.

As we have already premised that we are not prepared in this place to render any justice to the abundant and mobile shapes in which spiritism was represented in classic lands, we shall limit the present notice to a brief account of certain specialties not found in former sections, illustrated by the famous mysteries of Eleusis, and the Sybilline women of Greece.

The Samothracian mysteries date back to the earliest periods of Grecian history, and attempts have been made to show, that in these veiled rites the use of the loadstone, the secret powers of electricity, and the twin fires of magnetism were brought into play, and hence arose the worship of the constellated Deities Castor and Pollux.

There is little contemporaneous evidence, however, to show that the Samothracians possessed any practical knowledge of mineral magnetism, or understood the use of the loadstone, although they cherished a deep and superstitious reverence for its mysterious properties of attraction and repulsion.

The highest and most elaborite rites, and knowledge of which has descended to us from the days of antiquity, were those of Eleusis and Bacchus in Greece, and the Saturnalia of Rome. These, no less than the Samothracian rites, were unquestionably derived from Egypt, and as the Eleusinian mysteries probably afford the best representation of their famous Egyptian model, the Isic and Osiric mysteries it is to a brief account of this famous pageant that we shall call our readers' attention. So much has been written in fragments concerning these great mysteries, and the general tone of every description so invariably pre-supposes that the reader is already acquainted with the basic ideas upon which it discourses, that we deem it not out of place to present a consecutive statement of the myth, as well as the underlying principles upon which these mysteries were founded. For this purpose we avail ourselves of an admirable edition of Taylor's Eleusian and Bacchic rites, published by Dr. Alexander Wilder, of New York, in 1875. We quote an abridged account of the legend rendered by Minutius Felix. in Thomas Taylor's translation. This author says:

"Proserpina, the daughter of Ceres by Jupiter, as she was gathering tender flowers in the new spring, was ravished from her delightful abodes by Pluto, and being carried from thence through thick woods, and over a length of sea, was brought by Pluto into a cavern, the residence of departed spirits, over whom she afterwards ruled with absolute sway. But Ceres, upon discovering the loss of her daughter, with lighted torches, and begirt with a serpent, wandered over the whole earth for the purpose of finding her, til she came to Eleusis; there she found her daughter, and also taught to the Eleusinians the cultivation of corn.' Now in this fable, Ceres represents the evolution of that intuitional past of our nature which we properly denominate intellect, and Proserpina that living, self-moving, and animating part which we call soul. But in order to understand the secret meaning of this fable, it will be necessary to give a more explicit detail of the particulars attending the abduction, from the beautiful poem of Claudian on the subject. From this elegant production we learn that Ceres, who was afraid lest some violence should be offered to Proserpina, on account of her inimitable beauty, conveyed her privately to Sicily, and concealed her in a house built on purpose by the Cyclopes, while she herself directed her course to the temple of Cybele, the mother of the Gods. Here then we see the first cause of the soul's descent, namely the abandoning of a life wholly according to the higher intellect, which is occultly signified by the separation of Proserpina from Ceres. Afterward, we are told that Jupiter instructs Venus to go to this abode, and betray Proserpina from her retirement, that Pluto may be enabled to carry her away; and to prevent any suspicion in the virgin's mind, he commands Diana and Pallas to go in company. The three goddesses arriving, find Proserpina at work on a scarf for her mother; in which she had embroidered the primitive chaos, and the formation of the world. Now by Venus in this part of the narration we must understand desire, which, even in the celestial regions (for such is the residence of Proserpina till she is ravaged by Pluto), begins silently and stealthily to creep into the recesses of the soul. By Minerva we must conceive the rational power of the soul, and by Diana, nature, or the merely natural and vegetable part of our composition; both which are now ensnared through the allurement of desire. And lastly, the web in which Proserpina had displayed all the fair variety of the material world, beautifully represents the commencement of the illusive operations through which the soul becomes ensnared with the beauty of imaginative forms.

"Proserpina, forgetful of her parent's commands, is presented as venturing from her retreat, through the treacherous persuasions of Venus.

"After this we behold her issuing on the plain with Minerva and Diana, and attended by a beauteous train of nymphs, who are eviden symbols of the world of generations, and are, therefore, the proper companions of the soul about to fall into its fluctuating realms.

"But the design of Proserpina, in venturing from her retreat, is beautifully significant of her approaching descent; for she rambles from home for the purpose of gathering flowers; and this in a lawn replete with the most enchanting variety, and exhaling the most delicious odors. This is a manifest image of the soul operating principally according to the natural and external life, and so becoming effeminated and ensnared through the delusive attractions of sensible form. Minerva (the rational faculty in this case), likewise gives herself wholly to the dangerous employment, and abandons the proper characteristics of her nature for the destructive revels of desire.

"After this, Pluto, forcing his passage through the earth, seizes on Proserpina, and carries her away with him, notwithstanding the resistance of Minerva and Diana. They, indeed, are forbid by Jupiter, who in this place signifies Fate, to attempt her deliverance.

"Pluto hurries Proserpina into the infernal regions; in other words, the soul is sunk into the profound depth and darkness of a material nature. A description of her marriage next succeeds her union with the dark tenement of the body.

"Night is with great beauty and propriety introduced as standing by the nuptial couch, and confirming the oblivious league. For the soul through her union with a material body becomes an inhabitant of darkness, and subject to the empire of night; in consequence of which she dwells wholly with delusive phantoms, and till she breaks her fetters is deprived of the intuitive perception of that which is real and true.

"The reader may observe how Proserpina, being represented as confirmed in the dark recess of a prison, and bound with fetters, confirms the explanation of the fable here given as symbolical of the descent of the soul; for such, as we have already largely proved, is the condition of the soul from its union with the body, according to the uniform testimony of the most ancient philosophers and priests.

"After this, the wanderings of Ceres for the discovery of Proserpina commence. Begirt with a serpent, and bearing two lighted torches in her hands, she commences her search by night in a car drawn by dragons. The tears and lamentations of Ceres, in her course, are symbolical both of the providential operations of intellect about a mortal nature, and the miseries with which such operations are attended.

"These sacred rites occupied the space of nine days in their celebration; and, this, doubtless, because, according to Homer* this Goddess did not discover the residence of her daughter til the expiration of that period. Hence the first day of initiation into these mystic rites was called agurmos, i.e., according to Hesychius, an assembly, and all collecting together.

*Hymn to Ceres. "For nine days did holy Demeter perambulate the earth .. and when the ninth shining morn had come, Hecate met her, bringing news." Aphuleius also explains that at the initiation into the Mysteries of Isis, the candidate was enjoined to abstain from luxurious foods for ten days, from the flesh of animals, and from wine

"After this, the soul falls from the tropic of Cancer into the planet Saturn; and to this the second day of initiation was consecrated when they called ' to the sea, ye initiated ones!' because, says Meursius, on that day the crier was accustomed to admonish the mystae to betake themselves to the sea. Now the meaning of this will be easily understood, by considering that, according to the arcana of the ancient theology, as may be learned from Proclus, the whole planetary system is under the dominion of Neptune. hence when the soul falls into the planet Saturn, which Capella compares to a river voluminous, sluggish, and cold, she then first merges herself into fluctuating matter, of which water in an ancient and significant symbol. But the eighth day of initiation, which is symbolical of the falling of the soul into the lunar orb, was celebrated by the candidates by a repeated initiation and second sacred rites; because the soul in this situation is about to bid adieu to everything of a celestial nature; to sink into a perfect oblivion of her divine origin and pristine felicity; and to rush profoundly into the region of ignorance and error.* And lastly, on the ninth day, when the soul falls into the sublunary world and becomes united with a terrestrial body, a libation was performed, such as is usual in sacred rites. Here the Initiates, filling two earthen vessels sacred to Bacchus, they placed one toward the east and the other toward the west. And the first of these was doubtless, according to the interpretation of Proclus, sacred to the earth, and symbolical of the soul proceeding from an orbicular figure, or divine form, into a conical defluxion and terrene situation;** but the other was sacred to the soul, and symbolical of its celestial origin; since our intellect is the legitimate progeny of Bacchus. And this, too, was occultly signified by the position of the earthen vessels; for, according to a mundane distribution of the divinities, the eastern centre of the universe, which is analogous to fire, belongs to Jupiter, and the western to Pluto, who governs the earth, because the west is allied to earth on account of its dark and nocturnal nature.

* The condition most unlike the former divine estate.
** An orbicular figure symbolized the material, and a cone the masculine divine Energy.

"Again, according to Clemens Alexandrinus, the following confession waas made by the Initiate in these sacred rites, in answer to the interrogations of the Hierophant: 'I have fasted; I have drank the Cyceon; I have taken out of the Cista, and placed what I have taken out into the Calathus; and alternately I have taken out of the Calathus and put into the Cista.'

"We may easily perceive the meaning of the mystic confession, I have fasted; I have drank a mingled potion, etc.; for by the former part of the assertion, no more is meant than that the highest intellect, previous to imbibing of oblivion through the deceptive arts of a corporeal life, abstains from all material concerns, and does not mingle itself with even the necessary delights of the body. And as to the latter, it alludes to the descent of Proserpina to Hades, and her re-ascent to the abodes of her mother Ceres; that is, to the outgoing and return of the Soul, alternately falling into generation, and ascending thence into the intelligible world, and becoming perfectly restored to her divine and intellectual nature. For the Cista contained the most arcane symbols of the Mysteries, into which it was unlawful for the profane to look. As to its contents,* we learn from the hymn of Callimachus to Ceres, that they were formed from gold, which, from its incorruptibility, is an evident symbol of an immaterial nature. And as to the Calathus, or basket, this, as we are told by Claudian, was filled with the spoils or fruit of the field, which are manifest symbols of a life corporeal and earthly. So that the candidate, by confessing that he had taken from the Cista, and placed what he had taken into the Calathus, and the contrary, occultly acknowledged the descent of his soul from a condition of being supra-material and immortal, into one material and mortal; and that, on the contrary, by living according to the purity which the Mysteries inculcated, he should re-ascend to that perfection of his nature, from which he had unhappily fallen."

*A golden serpent, an egg and the phallus. The epopt looking upon these, was rapt with awe as contemplating in the symbols the deeper mysteries of all life or being of a grosser temper, took a lascivious impression. Thus, as a seer, he beheld with the eyes of sense or sentiment; and the real apocalypse was therefore that made to himself of his own moral life and character.

Throughout this curious fable it must be borne in mind that the Egyptians, Greeks, and all ancient as well as classic nations, believed in the doctrines recited in the earlier sections of this work, namely: that the Soul had once existed in a purely spiritual state; that, tempted by the demands of sense, it had yearned for mortal birth - descended or fallen into an earthly condition, and by its probationary sufferings and trials on earth, regained the Paradisaical bliss from which it had fallen (vide sections 2 and 3). These ideas are represented in the myth of Proserpinie, and constituted the chief legend of all the ancient mysteries. At the point, however, where our quotations cease, it is proper to state that the drama proceeds after a fashion, the direct simplicity of which is a part of that arcanum wherein the ancients represented the Soul's alliance with and birth into material form through earthly generation.

The plainness of speech and characteristic nature of the symbols employed, would prove revolting to our modern sense of propriety; but most learned commentators admit that the ancients sought to strengthen the Soul against sensual indulgence by familiarizing the mind with ideas and forms connected with sensual rites.

Jamblichus excuses this part of the mysteries, and especially the dramatic scenes which depict the descent of the Soul into earth through human generation by saying:

"Exhibitions of this kind in the Mysteries were designed to free us from licentious passions, by gratifying the sight, and at the same time vanquishing desire, through the awful sanctity with which these rites were accompanied; for the proper way of freeing ourselves from the passions is: first, to indulge them with moderation, by which means they become satisfied; listen, as it were, to persuasion, and passion may thus be entirely removed."

The mysteries were divided into two sections, of which the first or lesser mysteries were mere rudimentary states, during which the Neophyte was supposed to undergo those embryonic conditions necessary to prepare him for the higher revelations of the great mysteries. In the first, the candidate was called a Mysta, or "veiled one;" in the second, he became an Epopta, or Seer, and was henceforth deemed exalted to the highest attainable knowledge of human life and destiny, and the highest condition of purity which ceremonial rites could typify.

The chief aim in these celebrations was to impress the Neophyte throughout with the sacredness and divine significance of life, generation, the generative functions, and all the rites and symbols thereto belonging.

The ministering priests were all persons of the purest lives and most ascetic habits. Their garments and vessels were consecrated, their ornaments of the most splendid character, and "their performances dignified with a lofty bearing impossible to be described." All who took part in these rites were required to be of pure life and unspotted name. No notoriously evil-doer could be admitted even to the lesser mysteries, and every candidate was required to observe long fasts, strict asceticism, prepare for the ceremonies by ablutions, and many purifications, and present themselves unspotted in mind, body and garments, and crowned with freshly gathered wreaths of myrtle.

The Temple devoted to this purpose was vast and gorgeous. It was full of magnificent halls, solemn crypts, long galleries, winding passages ascending and descending fearful precipices, steep rocks and gloomy caverns.

The whole order of these wonderful buildings was designed to typify the procession of the Soul's spiritual origin, descent into matter, its struggles, trials, temptations, new birth, final regeneration, and re-ascent to the supernal glories of the Elysian realms, from which it was assumed to have fallen. During the rites, the Neophyte was conducted through scenes most terrible to endure, most trying in all senses. Sometimes he was enveloped in thick darkness, and assailed with shrieks, groans, wails and lamentations, symbolical of the despairing condition of the lost Souls peering through flames and torments in the realms of Pluto.

Peals of crashing thunder distracted him with terror; forked lightnings gleamed fitfully through darksome abodes, revealing the forms of hissing serpents, ferocious beasts, and sheeted spectres, doomed to perdition. One of the final scenes of this tremendous Drama, was the descent of the appalled Neophyte through a rifted rock designed to typify the Yoni, and thence through a rough and narrow cleft, the struggling victim emerged into a fearful and unknown realm, the perils of which he could only surmise by the awful stillness around him, broken by low groans and convulsive sobs, designed to signify the agonies of new birth, and a physical process of regeneration. Drawn through the sacred waters of a new baptism, and borne onward by invisible conductors, the half dead Initiate was left for awhile to repose after the tremendous struggle of final emergement through the stony matrix. It was unquestionably from this great central idea of the ancient mysteries that the Christians have derived their doctrines of new birth and regeneration;

words which, to all but true Initiates, are merely words, and significant of nothing more than a senseless mystery.

After the great final trial, the Soul, by passing through the allegorical new birth, was deemed to have become spotless and innocent as a babe. Holy hymns were chanted, eloquent appeals to the Initiate's constancy and virtue were uttered; and he was ushered into a magnificent Temple, where a colossal image of the glorious Maternal Goddess burst upon his sight, surrounded with all the pageantry and pomp of Grecian luxury, art and splendor. Scenes of dazzling beauty and supernal glory opened upon his ravished vision. Exquisite representations of the Elysian fields allured him to ramble amidst their flowery glades. Forms of unearthly loveliness surrounded him; strains of delicious music and songs of penetrating sweetness filled his soul with rapture, and lifted him up to ecstasy.

Many of the noblest sages of antiquity passing through these stupendous rites, have affirmed that their eyes beheld the forms of the Gods, looked upon heavenly scenes, dazzling suns, blazing stars, and figures of resplendent glory that were not of this earth. Visions of the blest in their abodes of Paradise glanced before them, and triumphant lyrics were heard chanted by no mortal lips. Why should we doubt these repeated assertions of the great, the wise, and the inspired ones of old? On the contrary, it is possible to imagine that any truly sensitive nature could partake of such scenes without unfolding to a higher life and more exalted powers than they had ever enjoyed before?

The physical nature was under complete subjection. The magnetic life of powerful Adepts permeated the air and filled the Temple with astral light and life.

The invocations, prayers and fervent aspirations poured forth by the Neophytes must have charged the Temple spaces with Soul aura, and transformed it into a spirit sphere. If there was a spark of luminosity in the souls of those who toiled through these tremendous initiatory processes, they must have been enkindled into celestial flame then or never, and it is equally impossible to conceive of the existence of spiritual realms, and suppose their inhabitants were not attracted to their earthly loves, and the subjects of their tenderest care and ministry in these hours of exhaltation and trial. The Soul's powers must have been quickened, the spiritual senses must have been awakened, and it could not be otherwise than a true season of new birth or regeneration.

And thus it was that so many Initiates came forth from these mysteries changed both in body and mind; hence that so many regarded them with a reverence unspeakable, and memories so hallowed, that it left an impress on the entire of their after lives. Neither can we wonder that it was the policy of governments to uphold these sacred mysteries; of legislators to constitute them one of the most essential portions of ancient theocratic institutions.

Amidst all the temptations to linger in description which the graceful imagery, sparkling fancy and abundant Mythology of Greek Spiritism abounds with, we are only privileged to pause for one more notice, and that is of the famous Sibylline women by whom the

Oracles of Greece were delivered for so many centuries, and for this purpose we select a few excerpts from a comprehensive and authentic sketch, taken from the Western Star, before quoted, and written by the fluent pen of Emma Hardinge Britten:

THE CUMAEAN SIBYL AND THE PYTHIA OF DELPHI.

Some classical authors have limited the number of Sibyls to four, but the generality of ancient writers give a list of ten, to whom they assign names according to the countries of their birth. Varro thus enumerates them:

"The Delphian - elder and younger; the Cimerian, and two Sibyls, both named Erythraen; the Samian, the Cumaen, the Hellespontian, the Phrygian, and the Tiburtine. Of all these, the Cumaean and the Delphian have been the most renowned. It is to the Cumaean Sibyl that is attributed the authorship of the famous Sibylline books, the sale of which to King Tarquinius, by an unknown old woman (supposed to have been the Sibyl herself) all classical historians have frequently mentioned. These books were nine in number when first tendered for sale to the king. When he refused to purchase them, the old woman threw three of them into the fire, and returning to the king, demanded the same price as before for the remaining six. The offer being still refused, the unknown destroyed three more of her singular wares, and again returning, demanded the same price for the three, which she had asked in the first instance for the whole nine. Struck with the oddity of this proceeding, Tarquinius paid the price demanded, but no sooner became possessed of the books, than the old woman who had sold them disappeared.

On examination, the contents of the volumes proved to be the vaticinations of the renowned Sibyls, and so great was the value set upon these writings, that Tarquinius appointed two officials, especially charged with the duty of guarding them, and only permitting them to be inspected and consulted by duly constituted authorities, in seasons of great national emergency. Notwithstanding this, several succeeding collections shared the fate of their predecessor; so it is fair to conclude that the voluminous mass of books attributed to the Sibyls, and quoted by the early Christian, as well as heathen authors, in support of their favorite dogmas, contained as many interpolations as genuine writings; indeed, it is questionable whether any of the original Sibylline vaticinations survived the wreck of fire and revolution, which consumed the most valuable records of those stormy times. On the question of the number of those whom history had designated the Sibyls, there can be no doubt but that many prophetic women, who succeeded each other in the temple services of different districts, were called by the same name, so that, in fact, the classification of Varro, given above, applies rather to the places with which they were associated, than to the actual limitation of their numbers. There seems to have been some points of difference between the Priestesses, the Pythia of Delphi, wandering Prophetesses, and the personages mentioned as Sibyls. The fact that so many women of antiquity manifested prophetic powers, and were so frequently endowed with the faculty of rendering oracular responses under the afflatus of what was deemed 'Divine inspiration,' renders it a task of some difficulty to discriminate amongst the variety of powers from which they derived celebrity.

Virgil, in describing the Cumaean Sibyl, says she was born in the district of Troy, but went to Italy, where for a time she dwelt in a cavern in the vicinity of the Avernian lake.

"She sometimes wrote her oracles upon palm leaves, which she laid at the entrance of her cave, suffering the winds to scatter them and bear them whither the Gods directed. At other times, she gave responses orally to those who came to consult her, and many chapters could be written on the marvelous accuracy of her prophecies, and the remarkable lucidity with which she delivered her descriptions of distant persons and things. In writing of this 'Sacred Maid,' as he styles her, Virgil gives the following well-known delineation of her "Corybantic' modes of prophesying:

"Aloud she cries,
'This is the time! inquire your destinies!
He comes! Behold the god!' Thus while she said,
And shiv'ring at the sacred entry staid,
Her color changed, her face was not the same,
And hollow groans from her deep spirit came;
Her hair stood up, convulsive rage possessed
Her trembling limbs, and heaved her laboring breast.
Greater than human kind she seemed to look,
And with an accent more than mortal spoke.
her staring eyes with startling fury roll
And all the God came rushing on her soul.
Struggling in vain, impatient of her load,
And laboring underneath the ponderous God,
The more she strove to shake him from her breast,
With more and far superior force he pressed,
Commands his entrance, and without contest
Usurps her organs, and inspires her soul."
Dryden's Translation of Aeneis, Book VI.

"This Cumaean Sibyl declares of herself:

"I am entirely on the stretch, and my body is so stupefied that I do not know what I say, but the God commands me to speak: Why must I publish my song to every one? and when my spirit rests, after the divine hymn, the God commands me to vaticinate (prophesy) again. I know the number of the grains of sand, and the measure of the sun. I know the height of the earth, and the number of men, stars, trees and beasts."

The Cumaean Sibyl, amongst other very important prophecies, foretold that terrific eruption of Vesuvins, in which Pliny, the naturalist, is said to have perished and so many cities were destroyed. She wrote, besides, many books which were held in the highest veneration by the Romans, and is supposed to have been the original of the fine statue which was placed in the temple of Jupiter Capitolinus, representing her holding one of her famous Sibylline books in her hand.

"Passing over the vivid descriptions rendered by Plutarch, Varro, Heraclides, and others, of the various Sibyls of other names, we must now draw a slight sketch of the famous Pythia of Delphi, who, whether one or many, has been more widely renowned for demonstrating the fact of prophetic power than any other name in history, the Cumaean Sibyl alone excepted.

"The small town of Delphi, in Phocis, would never have attained any celebrity from its situation or commercial importance had it not been the site of one of the most renowned of all the Grecian oracles - that of the Apollo of Delphi.

"The site of the once magnificent temple, so famed for its Pythian oracle, is at the northwestern extremity of the town, built on the slope of the beautiful mountain called Parnassus.

"Shutting in the crescent-like inclosure which comprises the ancient site of Delphi, is a vast mountain, split asunder, apparently by volcanic action, and presenting two high peaks or cliffs, which the Greeks called 'The Brothers,' It is from this circumstance that the town is supposed to have derived the name of Delphi or Adelphus. From the cleft which divides these two gigantic peaks, flows out the far-famed Castalian Spring; and here tradition asserts that Apollo and the nime Muses, to whom the spring was dedicated, endowed those who drank of, or bathed in its cool, translucent waters, with the gifts of prophecy, musical and poetical inspiration.

"On the spot which subsequently became the centre of the gorgeous temple of Apollo, formerly yawned a deep cavern, from which issued those strange mephitic vapors which were supposed to exercise so powerful an influence in preparing the Pythia for the possession of the oracular god. All authors of the time declare that the cavern was charged with vapors of that peculiar quality which excited a species of frenzy in animals, and delirious ecstasy in the human beings who inhaled it.

"The discovery of these remarkable properties in the cavern was due, it is alleged, to a goat-herd, who noticing how wild and frantically his flock leaped about after straying into the entrance, made his way into its recesses, and was afterward found in the frenzied condition common to all who ventured within its charmed precincts. After the spot had attracted general attention and become in that superstitious age venerated for its mysterious power of evoking the spirit of 'vaticination' or prophecy, it was set apart as a hallowed place. The priests of Apollo declared it was the choice dwelling-place of the God, and that the utterance of those who resorted thither, and came under the influence of 'the divine fury,' were henceforth to be regarded as prophetic, and their ravings received as oracular.

"It must be remembered that it was the universal belief of the time, that the ravings of lunacy were prophetic, and denoted the possession of some God' hence it is not surprising that a place capable of producing upon all comers the afflatus so highly reverenced should be regarded as holy, and become the scene of those superstitious rites common to the time and country. As it was found that little else than wild confusion and unintelligible ravings resulted from permitting the cavern to become a place of universal resort, the Phocian authorities commanded that a maiden of pure life and unspotted character should be selected, who was brought to the sacred spot, immersed in the waters of the Castalian Spring, arrayed in white, crowned with laurels, and required to perform divers other ceremonies of purification and preparation. When this was done, the priests of Apollo held the 'Pythia,' as she was termed, over the entrance of the cavern, and, provided she could endure the inhalation of the exhalations without permanent loss of reason, or, as it more than once happened, without yielding up life itself in the frantic convulsions which sometimes ensued, the noviate was deemed the elect of the God and duly installed as his priestess, by taking her seat on a tripod or basis with three ears of gold, placed at the entrance to the cavern.

Plutarch alleges that the first and most celebrated Pythia who served the Delphic oracle was a beautiful young country girl named Sibylla, from the district of Libya. It is probable that from this ancient prophetess was derived the name of Sibyl, afterwards conferred on all her class. In later years it was found necessary to select women of mature, and sometimes of advanced age, to serve the oracle, the sacred character of their profession having been found insufficient to protect the Pythia from the licentiousness of the age. Plutarch, writing of this inspired woman, says:

'We derive immense advantages from the favor the Gods have conceded to her. She and the priestess of Dodona confer on mankind the greatest benefits, both public and private.

"It would be impossible to enumerate all the instances in which the Pythia proved her power of foretelling events, and the facts themselves are so well and generally known, that it would be useless to bring forth new evidences. She is second to no one in purity of morals and chastity of conduct. Brought up by her poor parents in the country, she brings with her neither art nor experience, nor any talent whatever, when she arrives at Delphi, to be the interpreter of the God. She is consulted on all accounts - marriage, travels, harvest, disease, etc., etc. Her answers, though submitted to the severest scrutiny, have never proved false or incorrect. On the contrary, the verification of them has filled the temples with gifts from all parts of Greece and foreign countries."

"A gentleman, who once resided at the spot (the author of Art Magic) so venerated as the seat of divine inspiration, furnishes us with some descriptions of the wild region which was the scene of the Cumaean Sibyl's vaticinations. He says:

"The Lake of Avernus was once the extinct center of a mighty volcano, and the whole region, though now fertilized by its waters, bears the marks of being fire-scarred, and presents a most gloomy and repulsive appearance. The clefts in the savage rocks abound with caverns exhaling mephitic vapors and bituminous odors. it was in one of the wildest, grandest, yet most awe-inspiring gorges of these mountains, that the cavern existed which tradition affirms to have been the dwelling of the Cumaean Sibyl. The scattered inhabitants of the surrounding district believed that this gloomy grotto was the entrance to the nether world; that the hammers of the Titans, working in the mighty laboratories of the Platonic realms, might be heard, ever and anon, reverberating through the thick and sullen air. THe dark waters of the gloomy lake were supposed to communicate directly with the silent flow of the river of death, the Lethean stream, made dreadful by the apparitions of unblest spirits who floated from the Avernian shores to the realms of eternal night and torture. Here dwelt the famous Cumaean Sibyl, and from the exhalations of those poisonous regions, fatal to the birds that attempted to wing their way through its burdened airs, or the living creatures that strayed amidst its savage wilds, this weird woman derived that fierce ecstasy in which she wrote and raved of the destiny of nations, the fate of armies, the downfall of kingdoms, and the decay of dynasties.

"Monarchs and statesmen shaped their acts by her sublime counsels. The secrets of the unwritten future were mapped out to her far-seeing eyes, as on an open page.

"The purposes of the Gods were made known to her as if she had been their counsellor, and the inexorable fates revealed, through her lips, the decrees in which thrones and empires crumbled into dust, as though she had been the mouthpiece of the Eternal One.

"The mournful regions of the Avernian Lake were in strange contrast to the equally celebrated, but far more attractive scenes consecrated to the oracle of the Sun-God, in the delightful country of the Delphian Pythia.

"All travelers agree that the neighborhood of Mount Parnassus and the beautiful Castalian Spring is of much more genial character, sparkling, as it is, with the sunlight, and fragrant with blood, yet there is, to my mind, an evident connection between the influences of the exhalations derived from the Avernian and Delphic caverns. The chasm, so famed as the scene of the Pythia's utterances, is now no longer to be seen. The superb temple of Apollo was so built as to inclose, and secure it from the approach of the vulgar, and at this day no sign of such a chasm is visible; but there are many clefts in the rocks, and one in special, which forms a deep cavern, into which I have myself penetrated as far as I dared; but as I descended, clinging to its rugged sides, with the intention of exploring it, I noticed the exhalations which arose from it, and soon found that they were beginning to produce upon me the same effect as the inhalation of nitrous oxide (laughing) gas. The following day I visited that and two other caverns piercing the mountains in the same direction, and by applying chemical tests to the vapors exhaling from within, I found my suspicions confirmed, and am convinced there are chemicals in these regions which continually generate nitrous oxide gas."

"The stately forms of the Sibyls have vanished from the earth. The white-robed priest and the vestal virgin no longer float through multitudes of adoring votaries, as mediums between a race of Gods and men. The altar fires of the temples are quenched, the colossal forms of marble deities overthrown; the oracles are dumb, and the books of the Sibyls all consumed in the whelming flames of time and change.

"The bowers of Grecian myrtle and rose are choked up with trailing weeds, and the voluptuous shade of the laurel groves are deepened into an unbroken night of rank vegetation. Faded beauty, and living ugliness, death, ruin, and decay, occupy the stately seats of ancient devotion, and the sunlight of inspiration seems to have gilded the purple and gold peaks of Parnassus for the last time; but the cup of inspiration, run dry in classic Greece, is flowing full and abundantly in newer, happier lands.

"The links which bind the mortal and immortal, torn asunder by the catastrophies of war and desolation, in ancient lands, have stretched out into telegraphic lines between the worlds of spirit and humanity; and though the modern medium can never fill the place which Sibyl of antiquity occupied in sublimity of inspiration, in romantic lore and heathen splendor, she is sufficient for the age she lives in; sufficient to bring to a cold and materialistic world the undoubted proofs of the soul's immortality, and the fatherhood of one universal God who is a spirit."

Section XVII
Medieval Theosophy - Elves or Fairies
--

Elementary and Planetary Spirits, or Sub-Mundane and Super-Mundane Spiritism - The Jewish Cabala - Schedim - The Intermediary Spirits - Their Four Orders.

In entering upon the third and concluding portion of this volume, it becomes necessary that we should explain to our readers what were the opinions cherished by the mystics of all ages, concerning the existence and influence upon earth of other than human spirits.

Ancient Theosophy in every land taught the existence of Spirits, both higher and lower than those of earth's inhabitants.

The Jewish Cabala, which, as we have before alleged, contain the sum of the opinions derived from Persia and Chaldea, and in all probability, from still older lands, teaches that besides the Angels and Archangels, who include many celestial orders, there are between men and the lowest condition of fallen or evil angels intermediary Spirits termed Schedim, who live in the elements, and were divided into four orders corresponding to Fire, Air, Earth and Water.

The first class belonged to the Fire, and in German Theosophy were termed "Salamanders." They were supposed to be wise, powerful and prophetic, partaking very nearly of the angelic nature, yet not sufficiently advanced in the scale of being, to become immortal. It was deemed that they knew many of the secrets of nature, and to those toward whom they were beneficently inclined, they would impart their knowledge freely. They were sometimes said to be fierce and even terrible in their wrath, and hence were as much dreaded as courted by the ancient Magians. The second class were spirits who partook of the fiery quality of the first order, but were more properly spirits of the air. The Scandinavian and Teutonic traditions simply define them as spirits of the earth, but give them a wide range of class and function, and represent them generally as dangerous and very capricious.

It is in this order that mediaeval Theosophists ranged the sweetest and most popular of all the Elementaries, those of whom so many poets have sung, and traditions celebrated - the Elves or Fairies - those moonlight loving Sprites whose tiny feet leave their imprint on the green sward in magic rings - those impersonated blossoms of the earth and air, on whose fantastic and half mythical existence so many thousands of epics have been founded, so many charming legends written. For ages these fascinating spirits have served as the inspiration of the musician's sweetest strains, the sculptor's fairest ideals, and the painter's chef-d'oeuvres. Even the royal mind of Shakespeare stooped to revel amidst the flowers and bloom, the merry Puck-like tricks and pretty vagaries of these moonlight haunting phantoms, and the world of poetry and imaginative literature will miss a rare streak of sunshine from the dreary paths of dry matter-of-fact narrative, when plain common sense shall begin to realize the duty of extinguishing "the idle superstition" of Fairy love.

Besides these charming "little people," whole nations of half-aerial, half-earthly beings, of a kindred character, have been ranked in the third class of Elementaries, especially by the Scots, North Britons and Scandinavians. Such are the Trolls, Nixies and Brownies, to say nothing of the Pigmies, who inhabit the lowest parts of the earth; also the Gnomes and Kobolds, a good-natured but very low type of being who are said to dwell in mines, caverns, crypts where hidden treasures abound, and places where metals are hid. These dwarfish being were always represented as kindly-disposed toward humanity, and especially prompt to aid miners and other treasure-seekers in discovering the object of their search. Sometimes they were malign, and strove to hinder rather than assist humanity, guarding their earthy treasures with jealous care, and using mysterious arts to baffle the seekers for buried wealth; but, as a general rule, all miners who were not too strong-minded to reject the idea of such spirits, unite in declaring that these sub-mundane dwarfs actually exist; that the workmen often encounter them, and that many of them have been guided by their friendly lights, or directed by the sounds of their invisible hammers to the best mineral "leads." The author is in possession of a vast mass of testimony on this subject, some collected from experiences in Hungarian, Bohemian and Cornish mines, in which he has himself partaken; others gathered from reliable sources, containing narratives of the many kind acts of warning against danger, and guidance for good, miners have received from these subterranean Elementaries.

There are several still lower classes of impish beings, who correspond to various species of animals and reptiles, and these, though possessing hardly any traits of intelligence - except such as are peculiar to the creatures of whom they are the spiritual types - for the most part delight in mischief, and are ready when summoned to aid human beings, as low in the scale as themselves, in working ill to others.

In the ghastly records of mediaeval witchcraft, this class of Elementaries were known as Vampires, Incubi and Succubi.

They were supposed to parasite on the bodies of the Witches whom they served, acting as their "Imps or Familiars," in return for the nourishment afforded them, and the caresses they received. There can be no doubt that the most absurd and wild exaggerations have arisen, concerning the supposed communion between Demons, and poor, degraded mortals, whose ignorance, helplessness and perhaps the involuntary exercise of these occult powers, which often manifest themselves in low types of humanity,l have rendered them obnoxious to the charge of witchcraft.

To accept the literal truth, of all the revolting tales of such demonic intercourse, would be a libel upon human nature, but to deny that strong and irresistible sympathies exist between the visible and invisible realms, united alike the spirits of the lower as well as the higher orders of being with man, would be to accept the truth so flattering to pious egotism, of angelic ministry, and blind our eyes to that unpleasing correlative, which binds up man with the lower grades of being, and thus combines the whole scale in one interblended chain of harmonic dependency.

As it is above, so it is below - on earth as in the skies. The Universe is an endless chain of worlds in which spiritual spheres above, and semi-spiritual spheres below, stretch away from the lowest tones of being to the highest, in which embryonic life is swarming upwards to manhood, as man himself aspires to spiritual existence beyond. In this wonderful Oratorio of Creation, every keynote struck by man finds an echo in the cavernous depths below, and awakens vibratory harmonies in the corridors of heaven above.

Spirits and angels are attracted to the necessities of humanity; elementaries reach up to sustain themselves by man's superior endowments. If on the other hand he descends by the indulgence of animal passions, or sensual tendencies, to the lower realms of being, can it be questioned that the creatures who derive influence and influx from man, should be ready to respond to him in those particular directions, to which their own instincts and impulses point? The only questions that can legitimately arise in this connection are these: Do such beings as Elementaries exist at all? and can they communicate and hold intercourse with man? If the reiterated assertions of Sages, Seers, Prophets, and Philosophers, in the antique and Middle ages, be worth acceptance as testimony - if the experience of modern Mystics and Seers, whose prejudices do not interfere to prevent their reception of any form of truth, deserve credit, then do these Elementaries exist - swarm through all departments of nature, manifest their presence, and become the willing subjects of human beings when the conditions for intercourse are open to them. The gradations of elementary existence extend, as we have before intimated, down to the very lowest depths. There are beings whose rude embryonic life corresponds to the lowest species of plants, earth, stones, metals and minerals.

There are also two classes of watery spirits, namely; those who inhabit marshy lands, stagnant pools, ditches, and still water; and another of a higher type who govern rivers, fountains, seas, ocean depths, and all kinds of running waters. These were anciently called "tritons, Mermaids, Mermen, and Undines." The Earthly and Watery Elementaries were assumed by the Cabala to be governed by a powerful Chief termed Asmodi. They were taught of in all lands and in all times and though different nations assign to them varieties of names, and functions as numerous as the varieties of matter, there is in all the legendary accounts rendered of them, a generic similitude, which leaves no doubt that one basic idea prevails through all.

As the Author emphatically renders in his testimony of belief to the existence of an intermediary class of beings, termed with great propriety Elementaries, we shall drop the tone of traditionary description, and enter upon that more suited to convey an idea of actual realities.

The Elementaries are neither wholly spiritual, nor entirely material in substance. The corporeity of their bodies is too dense to inhabit the spirit spheres, or consort with purely spiritual existences, yet not sufficiently palpable to become visible to material eyes, or the external senses of man. They inhabit strata of atmospheres infinitely more sublimated than gases, yet far less refined than pure Astral light. They correspond in the infinitude of their states and functions to every particle of matter that exists, from the most solid

190

crystal to the most rarefied gas. We claim in short, that for every material body, animate or inanimate, organized or inorganic, there is a correspondential realm of spiritual existence 0 a counterpart in every stage of being. The disembodied Souls of men are the counterparts to man himself - the Elementaries to the world of matter, including the animal, vegetable and mineral kingdoms. The two highest classes of these beings, possess a fine ethereal sensitive spirit, yet not one whose organization is sufficiently perfected to become self-conscious, after the span of their earthly lives terminates, hence they are not, strictly speaking, immortal. The same remarks apply in a measure to the two lower classes, although their vital or animating principle is inferior to the "Sylphs and Salamanders"; in fact, they are little more than animal, vegetable and mineral existences, with strong and powerful instincts in the special realms of nature to which they belong, but incapable of reason, reflection or self-knowledge. From the highest to the lowest these beings are aware of the existence of man; they honor and even reverence him as a God, and are drawn by a mysterious instinct to desire contact and association with him. The highest orders understand the nature of continued existence, passionately long for it, intuitively hope for it in some distant realms of being, and closely connect the idea of immortality with man, hence their yearning for intercourse with him, and their general desire to serve and oblige him. There seems to be a descending scale of moral as well as mental and physical inferiority amongst these intermediary existences, for the finer purer and more kindly traits of character diminish, and at last utterly merge into ferocity, mischief and soulless animation, as we descend through the various grades of Elementary life.

These beings are all embryotic and rudimentary, but whilst the highest grades obviously prophesy of man - modeling after him, though lacking his completeness, and always deficient in some part, organ, or function - the lower we descend the more rudimental becomes each type. It would be difficult to convey an idea of the localities occupied by this wonderful realm of existence, to those Scientists who are accustomed to divide the world of matter into solids, fluids, gases, ether, and perhaps the still finer element so vaguely termed "Electricity"; but supposing we were to add to these subdivisions one hundred, then one thousand more, and then multiply that number by the largest sum in mathematics, we might conclude by affirming, that Science had still failed to find the two extremes of solidity and rarefaction any more than the largest telescope and the most powerful microscope now in existence, have traced the finalities of this infinitely large, and the infinitely little, or the gold-beater with all the tenuity of his finest work has arrived at the last point of divisibility in the atom.

Permeating all space, interpenetrating even man's dense world of solids, fluids, and gases, is a realm whose ethereal sublimations, the explorations of science have never yet mastered. Vitalizing this material world of ours as the Soul animates the body, this substantial yet invisible spiritual kingdom sustains all the countless generations of human souls, that have been liberated by death from the encasements of mortal structure. Between this realm of pure Astral light, with all its fright of living spirits, clothed in bodies of the same imperishable element, is a still denser realm, neither as gross as the earth's atmosphere, nor as sublimated as the spirit land, and yet it partakes of the quality and essence of both, for between the rarefactions of the one, and the density of the other, float those strata of element which form the world of the embryotic beings of whom we have been writing.

Away up beyond the sunny paths cleft by the wing of the soaring eagle; deep down amidst the cities of perl and kingdoms of coral that pave the ocean floor; burrowing in the unexploded depths of the cavernous rocks where mile upon mile of mountain limestone and crystalline granite combine to form the overarching roof of the fire king's castle; in all, through all, everywhere, in every unit of space, there roll the waves, and float the winds of the country inhabited by the Elementaries, so that could the eyes of mortality be opened as were those of the Jewish boy of old, in response to the prayer of Elisha, they would gaze upon oceans and seas of living creatures, finer than the Infusoria, larger than the fabled giants - each in his place, in his town, city, nation, divided off into his peculiar realm, inhabiting each his special portion of the kingdom to which he belongs, the whole constituting the realm of the Elementaries.

These creatures cannot ordinarily see mortals, any more than they can in turn be seen. Some amongst them, endowed with finer instincts than others, can peer into the rifts and rents of matter, and looking through, behold the God-like world of humanity, just as prophetic clear-eyed men can - at special moments of lucidity - gaze upon spirit land. Also they can be invoked, much after the fashion that mortals employ in summoning human spirits. Magicians - especially those who have prepared themselves for the control of spirits - can summon the Elementaries and cause them to appear as readily as human spirits. The powers of the Elementaries are limited to the peculiar departments of nature to which they belong. The beings who inhabit woods, forests, and rural scenes, attach themselves to huntsmen, charcoal burners, and others similarly employed.

Miners, fishermen, sailors, florists, metallurgists, all individuals who find their spheres of labor, in special departments of nature, are surrounded by Elementary Spirits of a correspondential character. Persons of peculiar temperament too, attract different grades of Elementaries, and thus, some are specially attractive to spirits of the fire, others to the aerial, earthly, or watery spirits, just as the idiosyncrasies of their organisms dispose them. It may be asked, how these beings are attracted to mortals, if there is no sensuous perception between the two worlds. Again we are at a loss to find analogies by which to explain to an age, totally insensible to metaphysical laws, the intense and irresistable sympathies which bind up the different objects in nature, prevailing between man and all lower as well as higher existences, diffusing a kind of blind consciousness even through the lowest classes of inorganic matter. How tenderly does the blossom turn to the light. How will the atoms of matter seek their chemical affinities, exhibiting even their preferences, dropping one class of metal, and rushing to another as soon as their favorite approaches!

Who instructs the sea-gull of the impending storm? Who apprizes the terrified animals and fluttering birds, that an earthquake is at hand, and what kind hand closes up the cups of the flowers when the last sunbeam has disappeared, or warns them to open their shining petals to its return? Consider above all, the nameless and indescribable realm of antipathies and attractions, between which our whole system of society and companionship oscillates, and then we may begin to comprehend how the half spiritual, half corporeal creatures of the elements apprehend the presence of man; are drawn to the kindred natures, or repelled from antagonistic ones; revel in the atmosphere of special temperaments, and are driven off from others, as men shrink from contact with uncongenial companions. in the higher teachings of wise spirits, we learn that these Elementaries are born, and die, marry, propagate their species and rear their young, even as mortals do. As they die out of earth they are born into some other spheres, alternating between spirit spheres and earths, until they arrive at that state of perfect self-consciousness which antedates their birth into those fully completed organisms capable of maintaining an immortal existence. Many of the higher orders of Elementaries attracted in the first instance by sympathy, have become the tutelary spirits of certain distinguished families, and continue their protective care for succeeding generations. This is the origin of what has so generally been deemed an idle superstition - like the "Banshee" of Ireland, the vision of an armed knight, a weeping woman, a white spectre, the unlooked for appearance of white pigeons, lambs, or other unaccountable apparitions, preceding death, sickness, or calamity, the traditions of which have been handed down through all time, although it has become the fashion to sneer the actualities out of orthodox acceptance.

The Red Indians of North America are especially distinguished for guardianship of this character.

Before entering upon the duties of leadership to their tribes, their young men retire into the wilderness to fast and pray. For the space of nine days the bravest and best of these wild races have been accustomed thus to await in solemn preparation, the visits of their tutelary spirits, and the direction of their future path in life. The author has conversed with many of the ancient men of these Indian tribes, and they have invariably confirmed the report which all tradition alleges namely; that the spirits who appear to the young men during, or after the probationary days of their long fast, are seldom human, but though they communicate after the fashion of human speech, or else infuse thoughts into the mind by the process of inspiration, their forms are generally those of birds, beast, or some member of the lower kingdoms. During several of their ceremonial rites at which the author has been present, their "Jokassids" or Prophets have succeeded in summoning around them powerful spirits who could play instruments, shake their lodges, beat drums, and create the wildest clamor of unearthly voices; and in all such scenes the spiritual performers were scarcely ever seen by clairvoyants, or known by mediums, to wear a human form. They were often wise in counsel, always prophetic, and very mighty - good to their prophets, subtle in knowledge of healing, and always faithful to those whom they chose to protect, but still these children of the forest see them, hear their voices, and hold inspirational communion with them, not as with spirits of their friends and kindred, whom they also profess to see and converse with, but as tutelary spirits --"spirits of nature"--or as we prefer to call them, Elementaries.

Another marked and distinctive sphere in which these Elementaries have played their part, has been in the scenes of mingled ignorance, superstition and spiritual afflatus, termed "Obsession."

During some of those periods of moral and mental epidemic in which vast waves of Astral fluid swept over certain districts, kindling up into abnormal prominence the latent powers of mediumistic persons, and by sympathetic contagion communicating their influence to whole communities, the Elementaries, like the spirits of Earth, have found themselves brought into direct and open rapport with human beings.

Conditions already prepared broke down the barriers between the three worlds.

The Elementaries, Mortals, and Spirits, steeped in cyclones of Astral light, blowing over the Earth just as storms, tempests, and contagious airs traverse its surface, have become at times so curiously interblended, that they could neither one nor the other resist the attractions that involved them. These were the periods marked as the eras of witchcraft, ecstasy, great religious revivals, or moral revolutions. As the aim of the Elementaries is ever to tend upwards towards man, so that of man gravitates to the spirit world, and aspires to the companionship of Gods and Angels.

In these great seasons of mental unfoldment and spiritual trial, kindred natures attract each other, and dissimilar ones are violently repelled; yet out of the frenzy of these stupendous mental epidemics the races emerge, disciplined, and informed of many of the most occult mysteries of being that would otherwise remain profound secrets, and utterly unknown.

In the early periods of the celebrated New England Witchcraft, the afflicted children first attacked, manifested the most marked tendency to imitate the actions of animals, crawling around the walls and cornices of houses, climbing like squirrels up high trees, barking, crying and mimicking the voices of animals, with a fidelity as shocking as it was unaccountable.

Similar tendencies to imitate animals and mimic their actions have marked many other great popular outbreaks of spiritual contagion. In Mora, Sweden, and Scotland, during the seventeenth century; at Morzine, during the nineteenth, these same perplexing features occurred in the tremendous fever of obsession that spread over whole districts, causing many of the unhappy victims to conduct themselves more like animals than human beings, during their paroxysms. Many of the features of Fetichism and Vaudooism, partake of these dark characteristics, and though the author is of opinion - founded upon deep study of the facts - that the majority of the demonstrations produced in Europe and America during the great dispensation termed "Modern Spiritualism," are produced by human spirits, though the maximum of all testimony inclines to prove that the spirits of humanity are the nearest to mortals, the most ready to serve and influence, and the most efficient to control, in fact that, wherever intelligence is rendered, it is strictly human, and implies human spiritual agency, still there are some features of mediumship, especially amongst those persons known as physical force mediums, which long since should have awakened the attention of philosophical Spiritualists to the fact, that there were influences kindred only with animal natures at work somewhere, and unless the agency of certain classes of Elementary spirits was admitted into the category of occasional control, humanity has at times assumed darker shades than we should be willing to assign to it.

Unfortunately in discussing these subjects, there are many barriers to the attainment of truth on this subject. Courtesy and compassion alike protest against pointing to illustrations in our own time, whilst prejudice and ignorance intervene to stifle enquiry respecting phenomena which a long lapse of time, has left us free to investigate.

The Judges whose ignorance and superstition disgraced the Witchcraft trials of the sixteenth and seventeenth centuries, found a solvent for all occult or even suspicious circumstances, in the control of "Satan and his Imps." The modern Spirtualists with few exceptions, are equally stubborn in attributing everything that transpires in Spiritualistic circles, even to the willful and cunningly contrived preparations for deception on the part of pretended Media, to the influence of disembodied human spirits, good, bad, or indifferent; but the author's own experience, confirmed by the assurances of wise-teaching spirits, impels him to assert that the tendencies to exhibit animal proclivities, whether mental, passional, or phenomenal, are most generally produced by Elementaries.

The rapport with this realm of being is generally due to certain proclivities in the individual, or when whole communities are affected, the cause proceeds from revolutionary movements, in the realms of Astral fluid; these contingently affect the Elementaries, who in combination with low developed spirits of humanity, avail themselves of magnetic epidemics to obsess susceptible individuals, and sympathetically affect communities.

From afflictions of this character, the only successful method of exorcism is through the magnetic passes of strong, healthful, and well-disposed magnetizers.

Although as we have before stated, the means of summoning Elementaries are similar to those employed in the evocation of spirits, the aims for which their services are solicited entirely determine the class of respondents. Whether the spirits invoked become visible or not, the presence is surely there. The call is always heard and obeyed. Man rules potentially over all lower existences than himself; but woe to him, who by seeking aid, counsel or assistance from lower grades of being, binds himself to them; henceforth he may rest assured they will become his parasites and associates, and as their instincts - like those of the animal kingdom - are strong in the particular direction of their nature, they are powerful to disturb, annoy, prompt to evil, and avail themselves of the contact induced by man's invitation to drag him down to their own level.

The legendary idea of evil compact between man and the "Adversary," is not wholly mythical. Every wrongdoer signs that compact with spirits who have sympathy with his evil actions.

Many and many a hapless soul which has "shuffled off the mortal coil," finds to his cost that his evil deeds on earth have been performed in obedience to evil promptings, and that when he deemed he was procuring gratification to himself alone by the indulgence of his passions, he was actually doing the bidding of Elementaries, and undeveloped human Souls, who by virtue of his subjection to their will, or by reasons of obligations conferred upon him, now become his rulers, and enact in reality the fabled myth of Satanic compacts and Satanic possessions.

Except for the purpose of scientific investigation, or with a view of strengthening ourselves against the silent and mysterious promptings to evil that beset us on every side, we warn mere curiosity seekers, or persons ambitions to attach the legions of an unknown world to their service, against any attempts to seek communion with Elementary spirits, or beings of any grade lower than man.

Bring below mortality can grant nothing that mortality ought to ask. They can only serve man in some embryonic department of nature, and man must stoop to their state before they can thus reach him.

The author has in vision, and guided by spirit friends and radiant Planetary Angels, visited many spheres of these Elementary races. He has seen them in every stage of degradation and progression, some almost ready to burst the chrysolitic shell of their caterpillar condition, and emerge into the spiritual realm, from which they would be attracted back to matter, and be born as men. Others, scarcely conscious of any higher existence than their own, rudimentary beings who would have to undergo ages of progressive transition ere they could attain the coveted boon of immortality.

In some of these embryonic spheres, the dwellers, conscious of their superior existence and potential influence of man, and informed by their quick intuitions of the approach of spiritual visitants, made great preparations for their reception, and offered oblations and homage to them, after the fashion of deific worship. It will be asked why we allude to experiences so recondite ad from which we would warn others back, as we would guard them from the unrest which attends too wide a perception of the mysteries of nature. We answer, knowledge is only good for us when we can apply it judiciously. Those who investigate for the sake of science, or with a view of enlarging the narrow boundaries of man's egotistical opinions, may venture much farther into the realms of the unknown, than mere curiosity seekers, or persons who desire to apply the secrets of being to selfish purposes. It may be as well also for many to remember that he had his planet are not the all of being, and that besides the revelations included in the stupendous outpouring called "Modern Spiritualism," there are many problems yet to be solved in human life and planetary existence, which "Spiritualism" does not cover, nor ignorance and prejudice dream of.

Besides these considerations, we would warn man of the many subtle though invisible enemies which surround him, and rather by the instinct of their embryotic natures, than through malice prepense, seek to lay siege to the garrison of the human heart. We would advise him, moreover that into that sacred entrenchment, no power can enter, save by invitation of the Soul itself. Angels may solicit, or demons may tempt, but none can compel the spirit within to action, unless it first surrenders the will to the investing power.

After the weird clairvoyant pilgrimages into the secret crypts or aerial kingdoms of the Elementaries alluded to above, the author has speculated curiously upon the unborn triumphs which Science will yet achieve, when her indomitable researches shall have advanced from the realms of invisible gases, into those of the countless strata, which make up the imponderable element of FORCE, the lowest of which is the realm of the Elementaries, the highest, that of Astral Light or Spirit Land. If the telescope can gauge the infinite realms of space, and bring to the Astronomer's view whole hemispheres of blazing suns, where the naked eye could discern only darkness impenetrable; if the microscope can reveal a kingdom of animalculae, where the unassisted vision beholds only a drop of water, why may we not hope that the realms of the imponderable will yet be gauged by scientific instruments, and the blank and non-intelligent element of Force, yield up to view a Soul Universe, consisting of Kingdoms and Empires, before whose magnitude, power and beauty, the worlds of matter will shrink into atomic littleness! When Science stands still or goes back, we shall see the gates of future possibilities shut against her; until then, the conquest of two new worlds await her discovery, those inhabited by the enfranchised souls of men and the Elementaries.

Of the radiant and exalted realms of being termed Planetary Spirits, who with the countless orders of Angels and Archangels come under the category of Super-mundane Spiritism, it seems impossible to convey any adequate conception, save to those who have enjoyed the glorious privilege of communion with them.

All nations of antiquity believed in and taught of them, yet even as "tutelary spirits," they rarely communicate openly with earth, and except to such Mystics as have by years of preparation fitted themselves for such high communion, their natures and functions are but little known.

Still we feel impelled to speak of their existence not alone for the truth's sake, but also because we would enlarge that narrow and limited view of God's universe, which in so many minds can never expand beyond the idea of a mortal pilgrimage and immortal existence for the inhabitants of this visible earth only. Every planet, sun, and system, is teeming with life, and life both material and spiritual appropriate to each particular orb in space. The higher minds of every spirit sphere, interchange communion with others in the same system of the Universe as their own. Clairvoyants, Seers, and instructed Magicians, can, if they will, invoke planetary spirits, in preference to those of their own natures; but here as throughout this volume, we affirm that the most direct, normal, and harmonious spheres of communion, are those which connect man and the spirits of ancestors, those whose impelling motives in each case are love, kindness, desire for spiritual light and progress on the one side, and the undying affection which survives the shock of death, and urges kind spirit friends to minister tenderly to those they have left behind, on the other.

The ties which unite in bonds of natural affinity the inhabitants of earth and their spirit friends and kindred, are those of root and branch, parents and offspring, and can never be broken, or superseded in the scale of natural harmony.

For the names and offices of the Planetary Spirits who are chiefly instrumental in communicating with mortals, as well as the method of invoking them, we refer the reader to the Magical Elements of Peter D'Abano, to be found in a future section, and for a concluding notice concerning Elementary Spirits, we point to the following excerpts, taken from the Author's Autobiography, entitled "Ghost Land."

"They (the Brotherhood) alleged that every fragment of matter in the universe represented a corresponding atom of Spiritual existence, hence they claimed there were earthly spirits; spirits of the flood, the fire, the air; spirits of various animals; spirits of plant life, in all its varieties; spirits of the atmosphere; and planetary spirits, without limit or number. The spirits of the planets, and higher worlds than earth, take rank far above any of those that dwelt upon, or in its interior. These spirits are far more powerful, wise, and far-seeing than the earth spirit. They assumed that as man's soul was composed of all the elements which were represented in his body, so his spirit was, as a whole, far superior to the spirits of earth, water, plants, minerals, etc. To hold communion with them, however, was deemed by the Brotherhood legitimate and necessary to those who would obtain a full understanding of the special departments of Nature in which these embryotic existences were to be found. Thus they invoked their presence by magical rites, and sought to obtain control over them, for the purpose of wresting from them the complete understanding of, and power over the secrets of Nature. They believed that the soul's essence became progressed by entering into organic forms, and ultimately formed portions of that exalted race of beings, who ruled the fate of nations, and from time to time communicated with the soul of man as planetary spirits. They taught that the elementary spirits were dissipated into space by the action of death, but were taken up in higher organisms, and ultimately entered into the composition of human spirits....Professor M. was exceedingly generous and distributed his abundant means with an unstinted hand. One day, discoursing with me on the subject of his lavish expenditure, he remarked carelessly:

"There is that mineral quality in my organism, Louis, which attracts to me, and easily subjects to my control, the elementary spirits who rule in the mineral kingdoms. Have I not informed you how invariably I can tell the quality of mines, however distant? how often I have stumbled, as if by accident, upon buried treasures? and how constantly my investments and speculations have resulted in financial successes? Louis, I attract money, because I attract mineral elements, and the spirits who rule in that realm of Nature.

"'I neither seek for, nor covet wealth. I love precious stones for their beauty and magnetic virtues, but money, as a mere possession, I despise. Were I as mercenary in my disposition, as I am powerful in the means of gaining wealth, I could be richer than Croesus, and command a longer purse than Fortunatus. Nevertheless the magnetic attractions which draw unto me the metallic treasures of the earth, fail to find any response in the attractions of my spirit; whereas, were I so constituted as to lack the force which attracts the service of the spirits of the metals, my whole soul would feel and yearn for a supply to the deficiency, in constant aspiration for money and treasure.'

"And that is why Professor M. was rich, but did not care for, or value his wealth, whilst so many millions, who do not possess in their organisms that peculiar mineral quality, which, as the Brotherhood taught, was necessary to attract wealth, pine for its possession, yet spend their lives vainly in its pursuit.

"Thus it is, that moral, mental, and physical equilibrium is sustained throughout the grand machinery of the universe."

....."I must close this chapter by pointing out to the reader how naturally a careful analysis of the human spirit throws light upon all the psychological problems that have confused the race, and perplexed the philosopher. One individual becomes rich without effort, inherits wealth, finds wealth, acquires it in a thousand ways, and that without needing or laboring for it. Another spends his life in toiling to acquire it, and yet can never succeed. No one leaves him an inheritance, he never purchases the successful number in a lottery, never succeeds in financial speculation.

"May there not be truth in the theory of the Brotherhood, to wit, that beings potent in the realms of mineral treasure, are magnetically attracted to such organisms, as assimilate with their own?

"I have known one of the Brothers, who passed through nine battles unharmed, whilst more than fifty of his acquaintances, who had just entered the field of carnage, fell at the first or second shot.

"Our philosophers alleged, that spirits of the fiery elements could avert swift blows (especially such as struck fire) from those who had a preponderance of a similar element in them, whilst others, deficient in that quality of being, attracted all such blows as produced fire. They carried this theory forward into the tendency to be drowned, or to avoid the action of the watery element - to become subject to a certain class of accidents, to be in danger from cattle, serpents, falling bodies, and indeed to all the events of life, asserting that as spirits pervaded every atom of space, and man's being was made up of all the elements, so when certain elements prevailed, corresponding spiritual influences were attracted and became favorable to him; whereas the reverse of this position obtained, in organisms deficient in special elementary forces. It was to this cause that they attributed the good and bad luck of different individuals, and special successes and failures in all. I was introduced by one of the Brotherhood, to two young girls, one of whom was passionately fond of flowers, and the other of birds. In the clairvoyant condition, I was subsequently shown by our ruling spirit, 'the crowned angel,' and the attendant spirits who were attracted to these young creature; and I now affirm, that all the fairy tales and legends of Supernaturalism, which have been written on the subject of Sylphs, Undines, etc., pale and grow cold before the divine beauty, exquisite purity, and aspirational grace, which shines out through the fleeting fragrance of those spirits that correspond to flowers and birds."

"In a conversation with a beautiful Mystic, one of the author's earliest friends and associates in the realms of spiritual research, now herself a glorified angel, the following items of philosophy were suggested:

"'Constance,' I asked, 'is it given you to know what new form you will inhabit? Surely, one so good and beautiful can become nothing less than a radiant planetary spirit?'

"'I shall be the same Constance I ever was,' she replied. 'I am an immortal spirit now, although bound in material chains within this frail body.'

"'Constance, you dream. Death is the end of individuality. Your spirit may be, must be, taken up by the bright realms of starry being, but never as the Constance you are now.'

"'Forever and forever, Louis, I shall be ever the same! I have seen worlds of being, these Magians do not dream of. Worlds of bright resurrected human souls upon whom death has had no power, save to dissolve the earthly chains that held them in tenements of clay. I have seen the soul world; I have seen that it is imperishable.

"'Louis, there are in these grasses beneath our feet spiritual essences that never die. In my moments of happiest lucidity, my soul winged through space and pierced into a brighter interior than they ever realized - aye, even into the real soul of the universe, not the mere magnetic envelope which binds spirit and body together. Louis, in the first or inner recesses or nature is the realm of force - comprising light, heat, magnetism, life, nerve-aura, essence and all the imponderables that make up motion, for motion is force, composed of many subdivisible parts. Here inhere those worlds of half-formed embryotic existences with which our teachers hold intercourse. They are the spiritual parts of matter, and supply to matter the qualities of force; but they are all embryotic, transitory, and only partially intelligent existences. Nothing which is imperfect is permanent, hence these elementary spirits have no real or permanent existence, they are fragments of being; organs, but not organisms, hence they perish - die, that we may gather up their progressed atoms, and incarnate their separate organs into the perfected man.'

"'And man himself, Constance?'

"'Man as a perfected organism cannot die, Louis. the mould in which he is formed must perish, in order that the soul may go free. The envelope, or magnetic body that binds body and soul together, is formed of Force and Elementary Spirit; hence this stays for a time with the soul after death, and enables it to return to, or linger around the earth for providential purposes, until it has become purified from sin; but even this at length drops off, and then the soul lives as pure spirit, in spirit realms, gloriously bright, radiantly happy, strong, powerful, eternal, infinite. That is heaven; that is to dwell with God; such souls are His angels.

"'The hand is not the body; the eye is not the head; neither are the thin, vapory essences that constitute the separate organs, of which the world of force is composed, the soul. Mark me, Louis! Priests dream of the existence of soul worlds; the Brotherhood of the beings in the world of force. The priests call the Elementary spirits of the mid-region mere creations of human fancy and superstition. The Brothers charge the same hallucination upon the priests. Both are partly right and partly wrong, for the actual experiences of the soul will prove, that beings exist of both natures, and that both realms are verities; only the Elementary spirits in the realms of force are like the earth, perishable and transitory, and the perfected spirits in the realm of soul are immortal and never die.'"

Section XVIII
Spiritism and Magic in Transitional Eras

--

The history of Spiritism and Magic recedes from view and becomes dim to the eye of the superficial observer, as the night of ruin and decay deepens into impenetrable gloom, and settles over the splendid Orient and the classic beauty of Greece and Rome.

With the extinction of national life and glory in these once powerful dynasties, the spiritualistic influences they diffused throughout the world seem to wane, and finally vanish from the page of history, becoming only a memory, a tradition, or a sacred myth.

But this absence of metaphysical life from physical history is more apparent than real. Many causes combined to prejudice public opinion against the belief in Spiritism, yet Spiritism stretching forward in one unbroken chain of influence from ancient to modern times, has never ceased to exist, and the changes effected by altered conditions, altered opinions, and the rise and fall of dynasties, have no more succeeded in obliterating spirit manifestations from the page of human destiny, than the overshadowing pall of midnight crushes out the fragrance and bloom of the flowers it effectually conceals.

The early Christian Fathers not only retained their faith in the power and ministry of Angels and Spirits, on earth, but they proved that faith by the works of the Spirit, which they performed as their Master commanded them, and for some centuries after His death they looked with suspicion on those who failed to render this important testimony to their belief in Christianity.

Tertullian, one of the most zealous of the second century converts to Christianity, sternly advised that, "any persons calling themselves Christians, who could not even expel demons, or heal the sick, should be put to death as impostors."

The celebrated Bishops Montanus and Gregory, Origen, St. Martin, Theophilus, and numerous other eminent Christian Fathers, urged that the same tests suggested by Tertullian should be required of professing Christians. They alleged their own willingness to submit to such an ordeal, and report affirms that they gave continual evidence of their ability to sustain their claims.

So long as Greece and Rome maintained an independent nationality, spiritual influences ruled their councils, and interpreted every phase of their history. In China, Thibet, India and amongst the Northern Asiatic nations, Spiritism has never died out, and continues in force, subject only to modifications in the decadence of religious zeal and fervor to this day.

In every land where gregarious man yet resolves himself into national communities, the exceptional gifts of Seers and Prophets have furnished means by which spirit visitants glance athwart the darkened paths of mortality. Spirit voices have resounded in the air. The semblances of the buried dead have glided through the open door, mounted the stair, and flashed upon our sight like glimpses of moonlight breaking through thick banks of clouds. Luminous forms radiant with the glory of the better land; shapes of woe, shipwrecked waifs from the shores of a retributive hereafter, have come and gone, forming a perpetual chain of spiritual revelation, which time and change have never had power to break. The realms of spiritual existence have never been without some witness in human consciousness. Bland materialism or bigoted ecclesiasticism have never had the excuse to say, in any decade of time, "The vision is closed;" "the gates of the eternal city are shut;" "the canon of revelation is ended."

Magic as an art may have been pursued in the middle ages, only at spasmodic intervals, and that under the ban of the church, and the prohibitory frown of the State.

We are not writing the history of Spiritism and Magic, otherwise we could assign reasons in abundance for this decadence in the faith of old; a few suggestions, however, we feel compelled to make in this direction, and commence by claiming that the brand of reprobation first launched against the name and fame of Spiritism was cast by the hands of Christian Ecclesiastics.

By internal luxury and external pride, the aristocratic rulers of the Christian churches in the sixth and seventh centuries succeeded in driving spirit influence from their midst, and finding themselves deprived of spiritual gifts, and rebuked by the sight of laymen performing those apostolic works required of them in proof of their faith, they resolved in solemn council that henceforth it should be unlawful for any layman to attempt the rites of exorcism, or the cure of disease, by the laying on of hands. PUblic opinion once impelled in this direction soon gained force by momentum.

In Great Britain the ignorant and prejudiced missionaries who were sent to convert the poor natives to Christianity, commenced their work by leveling their bitterest diatribes against the prevailing worship of Druidisim.

The ancient rites of the Druids consisted of solar and sex worship interblended. The heaps of stones sometimes piled in single cairns, sometimes arranged in circles, but above all, these gigantic rings formed of upright unhewn stones, with others horizontally laid across them, were all symbolical of the ancient faith of the Sun worshipper, blending with those emblems significant of the Eastern Phallus and Yoni. The upright unhewn pillars of Lithoi were Phallic emblems, the horizontal slabs formed the mystic Gate or Tau, both important symbols of Phallic worship. Other Druidical altars formed of stones there were, which, either under the subtle influences communicated to them by powerful Priests and Priestesses, or from another peculiar virtue in the stone itself, when balanced one mass on another, could be caused to rock and thus give responses to inquiring worshipers, just as the modern Spiritists obtain communications through the movements of inanimate bodies.

The curious investigator of Druidical remains and ancient faiths will find abundant evidence to show that these "Cromlechs" or rocking stones were nothing less than oracular tables used by the Priestly orders to obtain responses from the invisible world.

The nature of these weird rites was known to the ancient Britons, and when they became converts to Christianity, the Prophetic powers of the Priests and Priestesses, connected, as they were, with dreadful sacrificial offerings, in which the sacred human form was not always exempt, left such impressions of mystery and awe upon their untaught minds, that it was not difficult for their Christian Teachers to convince them that this powerful Priesthood wrought their marvels and obtain responses through the devils whom they propitiated with human sacrifices.

Thus the early Christians in Great Britain grew up with an instinctive horror of Spiritualistic rites, and never failed to connect them with the influence of evil spirits and Satanic worship.

In Continental Europe whenever spiritual gifts were manifested in the Convents or Monasteries, they were deemed evidences of the special favor of God, and signs of extraordinary sanctity. The individuals thus highly favored were canonized after death as saints, and vast revenues accrued to the shrines, which enclosed their ashes, from the miracles they were assumed to work.

That the lives of the saints, and holy ascetics of the Christian Monasteries should be full of spiritual works, was naturally to be expected. The conditions for the unfoldment of latent spiritual powers were as rigidly enforced in monastic rule as they were voluntarily endured by Hindoo Fakeers. The severe discipline, numerous fasts, vigils, and penances of these gloomy recluses, produced the same physiological and psychological changes which have been indicated as resulting from Hindoo and Egyptian methods of Initiation. By the same law, the fires of persecution and continual prospects of martyrdom only served to quicken the zeal and stimulate the devotion of the early Christians, until they actually attained to those degrees of exalted insensibility to pain, that mark even now the self-inflicted mutilations of Eastern Ecstatics.

The rack and the thumb-screw, the convent and the monastery, each produced their legitimate fruits in legions of wonder-working saints and inspired martyrs, and these sufficed to supply the Christian church with all the spiritism it was either safe or politic to encourage.

As it became the interest of the Christianity Hierarchy to attribute all marvels wrought in Monastic Institutions to the special favor of God, and the incomparable sanctity of Catholic devotees, so it was also necessary to reserve such vast auxiliaries to Clerical power within clerical boundaries, and hence, all who presumed to manifest miraculous powers outside the privileged pale of the church and its dependencies, were at once branded with the odious charge of witchcraft, necromancy and black magic.

The more vague these charges were, and the more difficult of definition, the more they struck terror into the mind of an ignorant populace, until it was deemed the highest act of piety on the part of laymen to accuse, and churchmen to destroy, every hapless creature whom the superstition of the time, or the possession of actual spiritual endowments, furnished excuses to brand with the fearful charge of witchcraft.

It must be remembered that whilst the power of life and death was vested in the hands of civil governments, the power of conferring eternal life or eternal torments, was claimed by the Ecclesiastical Hierarchy of the middle ages.

The Church, usurping the name and authority of Christ, claimed not only to be god's vicegerent on earth, and to hold the keys to the kingdom, but to be the very porter and door-keeper of heaven, peddling out passports and selling seats for the divine amphitheatres of eternity, to those who could pay best, or confer the richest benefits on its luxurious orders.

If Spiritual gifts had passed away from such a Church, if its well-fed, pampered and ambitious disciples could no longer perform the works enjoined on them by the houseless and wandering Nazarene, was not that sufficient reason why no one else should presume to do more than themselves? - that is no one outside of ecclesiastical dependencies - for it was as much the policy of such a Church to encourage the prestige of miraculous gifts within the limits of its own holy "ring" as it was to burn, crush, torture, hang, drown, and slay generally, all who made profession of the same stupendous powers, outside their special jurisdiction.

Every layman who could perform the works which Christian ecclesiastics ought to have done, was a living rebuke to them for their lack of faith, and so there was but one remedy, and that the all potential one of death. Thus perished to the number of nine thousand, the brave and devoted Stedinger, a section of the Frieslanders, who fired with the love of freedom, protested against the insolent autocracy of the church, and so under letter of authority from the Pope and their Catholic Majesties of Germany, they were exterminated root and branch. Thus died the noble Waldenses, a sect of early Protestants, whose death warrant was sealed for the same cause and by the same murderous hands.

Thus, in the fourteenth century perished miserably, fifty-nine of the celebrated military knights of the Holy Temple with their brave and noble Commanders Jaques de Molay and Guy of Normandy, all roasted alive before slow fires by Christian Priests, and that under the accusation of excelling in those very arts for which the model man of the Christian Bible, the great law-giver of the Jews - Moses - has proved himself to be so accomplished an adept, namely, magic. According to the most authentic records of the times, and from transcripts of the very trials themselves, we learn that between the twelfth and eighteenth centuries, thus perished amidst tortures too shocking for recital, and under circumstances that curdle the blood to remember, over 200,000 persons of both sexes and all ages, and that in Continental Europe alone! These murders were perpetrated by roasting alive, hanging, burning, slaying and crushing. They included the destruction of the pure, pious, self-devoted and Angel-led Joan of Arc, the Savior of her country, and the ungrateful monsters who publicly burned her, and all thus perished, either being totally guiltless of any crime, or charged only with the possession of those spiritual gifts which the founder of Christianity demanded as the evidence of Christian faith.

In all lands but those dominated by Christianity, Spiritism has not only prevailed, but it still exists; has been, and is openly taught as an art, engrafted on the services of religion and cultured as a science. Under Christian rule alone have its hapless votaries' powers been crushed out by torture, or silenced by death; and thus it is that so strange and sudden a decadence appears on the page of history to have fallen upon the once popular and universal methods of intercourse which prevailed between spirits and mortals in the early ages. The attitude of the Christian Ministry towards the spiritual side of man's nature has been that of unceasing hostility and presumptuous denunciation; can we wonder then, that a final eclipse of faith has fallen upon the people thus materialized by the very power to whom they have entrusted the charge of their spiritual relations, or that the soul of Christian humanity has become secularized, and its spiritual functions dwarfed almost to annihilation by such a process of training?

To gather up the scattered fragments of spiritual life and phenomena which have burst forth like pent-up fires from every hamlet, city, or nation, of civilization, during the bitter clerical proscriptions of the middle ages, would be impossible in a book of this character. Nothing less than a consecutive and all-embracing history could do justice to so vast a theme; our part, therefore, must now be limited to a few brief notices, and for this purpose we select five classes of representative Spiritists, who figured most prominently during the middle ages, and connected the first or ancient era of spiritual history with the present time.

The three first of these are the Alchemists, Rosicrucians, and Mesmerizers; a noble triad of scholarly men, who, inspired with the belief that spiritual powers and forces must be based upon scientific laws, endeavored to discover and practicalize these, by occult researches into nature, and the revival of magical rites and ceremonials.

The two remaining classes included all those unfortunates branded with the crime of witchcraft, and unquestionably in many instances endowed with true prophetic powers, and finally the Modern Spiritualists.

Of the Alchemists, as a class, we have but little now to say. Although they professed to be engaged in seeking that mysterious stone, which would enable them to transmute base metals into gold, and by expressing the virtues of certain drugs and herbs compound an elixir which should prolong life indefinitely, it is well known to modern scholars that the prestige of these pursuits was designed in many instances to conceal a more occult and spiritual idea. Alchemy owed its introduction into Europe to the to the Arabians, amongst whom Alfarabi and Avicenna were the most celebrated.

These men were no idle pretenders to the Hermetic philosophy. They were both instructed Physicians, wise Magnetists, and profound Psychologists. Some of their cures effected by the laying on of hands and inimitable performances on the lute and other instruments of music, proved them to be adepts, if not in magical art, at least in the powers of magnetism and psychology. The first Alchemist of any repute, whose writings are preserved, was Geber, supposed to have been an Arabian, but historically proved to have been a German. This philosopher claimed that Alchemy was first practices by Noah, and transmitted to his son Shem, from whom the derivation of the word Alchemy was traces. He proved that which the Jesuit Father Martini and Lenglet du Fresnoi, in their several histories of the Hermetic philosophy, have clearly shown, namely; that Alchemy was believed in, and its principles attempted, if not successfully practiced, in most early periods of time. The Chinese taught of its possibility more than two thousand years before the birth of Christ, and many learned Alchemists claimed both Abraham and Moses as brothers of their craft.

The facts were, that the bitter persecutions heaped upon all dissenters from the stereotyped doctrines of Christianity, as enunciated by the Roman Catholic Hierarchy, compelled the concealment of heretical opinions beneath some external form of science, whose semblance could give no offense to the ruling powers.

The Arabian Alchemists and their philosophic successors - the German Rosicrucians - were all waifs drifted off from the great ocean of natural Theosophy, whose source was to be found in the East, and whose origin dates back to the foundations of Sabaism and Ancient Masonry, in Chaldea, India and Egypt.

These men were essentially the "Fire Philosophers" of the middle ages, and their doctrines and practices were derived from a profound study of the truths discoverable only in the powers of nature.

They assumed that matter was resolvable back into two, three, or at most, four primordial conditions. That by various combinations of these original elements all the varieties of material form and substance were produced, hence gold (in these philosophers' opinion) was but a result of the highest combination of elements, and the most perfect experiments of nature.

If them, they argued, they could reduce matter back to its primordial states and then recombine, leaving out the subsidence or flux, and preserving only the finer particles, they could make gold at will, and that form the very same substances that produced iron, lead, and all the baser metals, which were really gold in embryonic condition.

To find the great factor by whose universal agency these natural transmutations proceeded in the bowels of the earth, they had only to resort to the Rosicrucian theory of latent, divine, invisible fire, permeating every portion of matter, theories of which we have written in former sections. Time, experience, and deep study discovered to many ancient philosophers a resemblance between the virtues which proceeded from certain stones, crystals, minerals, drugs, herbs, and plants; astral, solar and lunar influences and the touch of the human hand, or even the contact of any object which had been worn by human beings.

These, together with the mysterious powers of the loadstone, and the universal correspondence which the realms of nature and the sidereal heavens disclosed, convinced these fire philosophers that the great hidden virtue, the universal motor of being, was this all-pervading latent fire, or that which we call magnetism in the earth and minerals; attraction and repulsion in the loadstone; electricity in the clouds and plants, and sparks evolved from batteries; life in animated bodies; and force throughout the Universe of moving forms. In recondite treatises elaborating the ideas which we have thus briefly summed up, the ancient Fire Worshipers, Mediavel Alchemists and Rosicrucians, dilated on the Universal Force of being, as the "Philosopher's Stone," which applied to chemical lore could make and unmake worlds - dissolve all bodies, and recombine them in whatever proportions the accomplished chemist desired, or if expressed into juices and mixed in such degrees as would preserve the largest amount of this force in a liquid form, it would be the "Elixir Vitae" of which those who partook, drinking in the true element of life, might prolong it at will, or if supplied with a sufficient quantity from time to time, live forever!

Had Albertus Magnus, Thomas Aquinas, Geber, Artephius, Friar Roger Bacon, and other great and truly learned students of these occult ideas, once beheld a Voltaic pile reducing huge bars of metal into a few particles of ash in a single lash, could they have seen similar lightning sparks passing through invisible airs, crystallizing them into drops of water, or acting upon water, solidifying it into hard crystals - could they have witnessed processes now so simple then so stupendously magical, and beheld as the only visible agent of these wonderful transmutations, nothing but a flash of lightning, who can question that their faith in the philosopher's stone would have been sealed into certainty, and that they would have joined in the choral cry "Eureka! The grand Hermetic secret is revealed!"

Again, had these Adepts beheld, as the author has, a frail, wasted, dying creature, extending its emaciated frame on the couch over which the shadows of impending death were falling fast, and watched, as the author has, a simple, untaught countryman waving his rough warm hands over the helpless sufferer, until, without an atom of visible matter used, a single particle of sensuous cause discoverable, the color returned to the wan cheek, light to the glazing eye, the crimson glow of life to the pallid lip, and strength to the wasted form, until upspringing from the couch of death and agony, the sufferer becomes a man again quite restored to life, strength, and health, would not the watching Sages have pertinently asked, "Do you now question the potency of the Elixir Vitae, or doubt that under its influence the mortal might become immortal and live forever?"

With every day's experience in marvels of transformation, transmutation and chemical change wrought by the all-potential magician Electricity, with an equal opportunity for experience to those who dare avail themselves of it, of the no less marvelous potency of vital magnetism, as a restorative of health, a healer of disease, nay a very Messiah who can restore the entranced and semi-dead to life again, who can question that the Alchemists of old were Prophets of the new? and that their labors, veiled mysticism, and occult symbolism, only hovered on the threshold of those sublime truths, which Mesmer and Franklin have since demonstrated, and that even now, modern science is applying the philosopher's stone to every act of simple electrotyping, and modern magnetizers are administering draughts of the Elixir Vitae with eery wave of their life-bringing hands.

It boots not now to rehearse the names and exploits of the many wise and patient scholars, whose heretical beliefs were necessarily hidden under the jargon of alchemical discourses, and pretended researches into physical science. The Alchemists started upon metaphysical propositions, and arguing from the original sacredness of fire, the Deific principle hidden away under every atom of matter, they proceeded to physical experiments, in order to utilize this divine fire, and obtain a perfect command over all the elements of nature.

They discovered in the course of their varied wanderings, from the visible to the invisible, many useful chemical combinations. Roger Bacon, for example, eliminated many profound truths in Astronomy, and improved upon, if he did not actually invent the telescope, burning-glasses and gunpowder. Arnold de Villeneuve, Raymond Lulli, Albertus Magnus, Thomas Aquinas, and many others more or less renowned, preserving faith in the wonders of chemistry, added constantly to the sum of human knowledge in this direction, besides advancing step after step into those realms of power and achievement which enabled Swedenborg, Mesmer, Franklin, Galvani, Volta, and even the scoffing Faraday, to found upon the experiments of unknown and despised builders, those triumphant galleries and corridors of mesmeric, magnetic and electrical science, of which the Ancient Alchemists and Rosicrucians laid the foundation stones.

Supplement to Section XVIII
Alchemists and Philosophers
--

It would be impossible in a work of this limited nature to cite all the names, much less the opinions, of that numerous class distinguished either as Alchemists, Rosicruicians, Astrologers, or Philosophers, who formed the ranks of Mysticism during the seventeenth and eighteenth centuries. Amongst the most distinguished of these ill-understood classes, were Nostradamus, a celebrated astronomer, and an expert Astrologer; Paracelsus, an excellent Physician and a scholar, who either accidentally, or as the result of research, discovered those truths concerning mineral and animal magnetism which Mesmer subsequently reduced to a system; Van Helmont, a truly prophetic person, but one who cultivated his gifts of Seership by the study and practice of magical arts; Albertus Magnus, Thomas Aquinas, Artephius, Arnold de Villeneuve, Raymond Lulli, Roger Bacon, Nicholas Flammel, George Ripley, and many other practical chemists, who perceived the possibilities of Alchemy, and who distinguished themselves from the thirteenth to the eighteenth centuries in writing on this subject and awakening the terror of the ignorant, and the denunciations of the bigoted.

In the early part of the fifteenth century, the study of Alchemy and the practices of Magic became at once famous and infamous, through the influence of the celebrated Gilles de Laval, a marshal of France, whose wealth, unbridled luxury and shameless debaucheries led him to the practices of magical art, for the sake of administering to the vilest of passions, and the replenishment of his exhausted coffers, drained by his unparalleled extravagance. As this monster in human form supplied to the fiction mongers of later times the original of the famous drama of "Blue Beard," some idea may be formed of the vast notoriety to which his crimes attained.

Neither the historical facts, nor the exaggerated tales which combined to render the name of Marshal de Retz memorable through all time, belong to this record; it is enough to add that the magical practices to which he resorted in aid of his unholy purposes, contributed greatly to deepen the horror with which this art was regarded - especially in an age too ignorant and priest-ridden to distinguish the nature of occult science from its worst abuse.

It was during the fifteenth century that Henry Cornelius Agrippa flourished, an adept in physical science, scholarly attainments, as well as occult art, which made him the honored officer of Kings and Princes, the friend, adviser and Physician of Queens and Princesses, and the Paragon of Magicians, in all ages. It is from a compendium of his occult practices that we are enabled to present our readers in the following section with a complete Arbatel of Magic, or full directions for the performance of those curious rites in which Agrippa and many of his contemporaries claimed to be able to control the legions of Planetary Spirits.

It must be remembered that this distinguished Knight and great Adept was a devout Roman Catholic, hence he employed those sacred names, garments and forms, which belonged to his Church, just in the same manner as the Arabians, Greeks, Chaldeans and

Egyptians employed the names and formulae of belief peculiar to their time in their magical rites. Let it be borne in mind, however, that such features of each system are but the exoteric forms in which the esoteric principles are wrapped up. They have no real potency beyond the satisfaction they procure to pious minds, that they are engaged in no ceremonials displeasing to their Gods, or contrary to their forms of worship.

Provided always that the magician is duly prepared by fasting, abstinence, prayer, and contemplation - provided that his magnetism is potent and his will all-powerful - the spirits will obey and answer him, whether he conjures them in the name of Buddha, Osiris, Christ or Mahomet. The true potency resides in the quantity and quality of the Astral fluid, by which the operator furnishes means for the use of the spirits, and the power of the will, by which he compels beings less potent than himself to obey him. With these premises we shall only add, that after a careful study of the occult works of Cornelius Agrippa, we found it wholly impossible to reduce their quaint and involved style to the comprehension of the nineteenth century reader, without infringing upon the integrity of the text. Happily for our purpose, the same idea occurred to a distinguished philosopher said to have been a pupil of the great Agrippa's - one who, with much more perspicuity of style, undertakes to reduce the magical elements of his renowned prototype into much plainer language. As there is not the slightest shadow of difference between the systems of Agrippa and Abano, except in the superior clearness of the latter's style, and as both were translated into English in 1664 by the same scholarly editor, Robert Turner, of London, England, we select Abano's version as the one which cannot fail to prove the most acceptable to our readers.

All the signs, sigils, names of angels, etc., have been faithfully copied with the utmost care.

Section XIX
Heptameron, or Magical Elements of Peter D'Abano
--

In the former book of Agrippa, it is sufficiently spoken concerning Magical Ceremonies and Initiations.

But because he seemeth to have written to the learned, and well experienced in this Art; because he doth not specially treat of the Ceremonies, but rather speaketh of them in general, it was therefore thought good to adde hereunto the Magical Elements of Peter de Abano: that those who are hitherto ignorant, and have not tasted of Magical Superstitions, may have them in readiness, how they may exercise themselves therein. For we see in this book, the distinct functions of spirits, how they may be drawn to discourse and communication; what is to be done every day, and every hour, and how they shall be read (as if they were described syllable by syllable).

In brief, in this book are kept the principles of Magical conveyances. But because the greatest power is attributed to the Circles; (for they are certain fortresses to defend the operators safe from the evil Spirits). In the first place we will treat concerning the composition of a Circle.

OF THE CIRCLE, AND THE COMPOSITION THEREOF

The form of Circles is not always the same; but useth to be changed, according to the order of the spirits that are to be called, their places, daies, and hours. In making a Circle, it ought to be considered in what time of the year, day, and hour you make the Circle; what Spirits you call, to what Star and Region they do belong, and what functions they have. Therefore let there be made three Circles of the latitude of nine foot, and let them be distant one from another a hand's breadth; and in the middle Circle, first, write the name of the hour wherein you do the work. In the second place, write the name of the Angel of the hour. In the third place, the sigil of the Angel of the hour. Fourthly, the name of the Angel that ruleth the day, and the names of his Ministers. In the fifth place, the name of the present time. Sixthly, of the Spirits ruling in that part of time, and their Presidents. Seventhly, the name of the head of the Signe ruling in that part of time wherein you work. Eighthly, the name of the earth, according to that time. Ninthly, and for the completing of the Middle Circle, write the name of the Sun and Moon, according to the said rule of time, for as the outermost Circle let there be drawn in the four angles, the names of the presidential Angels of the Air, that day wherein you work; to-wit, the name of the King and his three ministers. Without the Circle, in four angles, let Pentagones be made. In the inner Circle, let there be written four divine names with crosses interposed in the middle of the Circle; to-wit towards the East let there be written Alpha, and towards the West let there be written Omega; and let a cross divide the middle of the Circle. When the Circle is thus finished, according to the rule now before written, you shall proceed.

212

Of the names of the Angels and their Sigils, it shall be spoken in their proper places. Now let us take a view of the names of the times. A year is fourfold, and is divided into Spring, Summer, Harvest, and Winter; the names whereof are these:

The Spring, Taloi. The Summer, Casmaran. Autumne Adrael. Winter, Earlas.

The Angels of the Spring: Caracasa, Core, Amatiel, Commissoros.

The head of the Signe of the Spring: Spugliguel.

The name of the Earth in the Spring: Amadai.

The names of the Sun and Moon in the Spring: The Sun, Abraym. The Moon, Agusita.

The Angels of the Summer: Gargatel, Tariel, Gaviel.

The head of the Signe of the Summer: Tubiel.

The name of the Earth in Summer: Festativi.

The names of the Sun and Moon in Summer: The Sun, Athemay. The Moon, Armatus.

The Angels of Autumne: Tarquam, Gnabarel.

The head of the Signe of Autumne: Torquaret.

The name of the Earth in Autumnae: Rabianara.

The names of the Moon in Autumne: The Sun, Commutaff. The Moon Affaterium.

THE CONSECRATIONS AND BENEDICTIONS, AND FIRST OF THE BENEDICTION OF THE CIRCLE.

When the Circle is ritely perfected, sprinkle the same with holy water and say, "Thou shalt purge me with hysop, O Lord, and I shall be clean; thou shalt wash me, and I shall be whiter than snow."

THE BENEDICTION OF PERFUMES

"The God of Abraham, God of Isaac, God of Jacob, bless here the creatures of these kindes, that they may fill up the power and vertue of their odours; so that neither the enemy nor any false imagination may be able to enter into them, through our Lord Jesus Christ, &c." Then let them be sprinkled with holy water.

THE EXORCISME OF FIRE UPON WHICH THE PERFUMES ARE TO BE PUT.

The fire which is to be used for fumigations is to be in a new vessel of earth or iron, and let it be exorcised after this manner:

"I exorcise thee, O thou creature of fire, by him by whom all things are made, that forthwith thou cast away every phantasme from thee, that it shall not be able to do any hurt in anything. Then say, "Bless O Lord this creature of fire, and sanctifie it, that it may be blessed to set forth the praise of they holy name, that no hurt may come to the exorcisers of Spectators, through our Lord Jesus Christ, &c."

OF THE GARMENT AND PENTACLE.

Let it be a Priest's garment if it can be; but if it cannot be had, let it be of linen and clean. Then take this Pentacle made in the day and hour of Mercury, the Moon increasing, written in parchment made of a kid's skin. But first let there be said over it the mass of the Holy Ghost, and let it be sprinkled with water of baptism.

AN ORATION TO BE SAID WHEN THE VESTURE IS PUT ON.

"Ancor, Amacor, Theodonius, Anitor, by the merits of they Angels, O Lord, I will put on the garment of Salvation that this which I desire may bring to efect, through thee, the most holy Adonay, whose Kingdom endureth forever and ever, Amen."

OF THE MANNER OF WORKING.

Let the Moon be increasing and equal, if it may then be done, and let her not be combust.

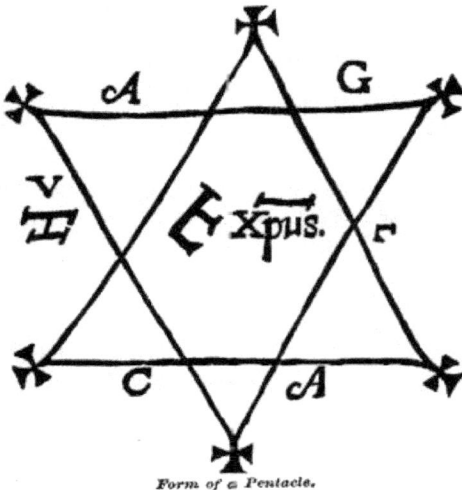

Form of a Pentacle.

The Operator ought to be clean and purified for the space of nine days before the beginning of the work, and to be confessed and receive the Holy Communion. Let him have ready the perfume appropriated to the day wherein he would perform the work. He ought also to have holy water from a Priest, and a new earthen vessel with fire, a Vesture and Pentacle; and let all these things be rightly consecrated and prepared. Let one of the servants carry the earthen vessel full of fire and the perfumes, and let another bear the Book, another the Garment and Pentacle, and let the Master carry the Sword, over which there must be said one Mass of the Holy Ghost; and on the middle of the Sword let there be written this name: Alga; and on the other side therof, the name On. And as he goeth to the consecrated place, let him continually read Litanies, the servants answering; and when he cometh to the place where he will erect the Circle, let him draw the lines of the Circle as we have before taught; and after he hath made it, let him sprinkle the Circle with holy water, saying: Asperges me Domine, etc.

The Master, therefore, ought to be purified with fasting, chastity and abstinency from all luxury the space of three whole days, before the day of the operation; and on the day that he would do the work, being clothed with pure garments, and furnished with Pentacles, perfumes and other things necessary hereunto, let him enter the Circle and call the Angels, from the four parts of the world, which do govern the seven Planets, the seven dayes of the week, Colours and Metals, whose name you shall see in their places, and with bended knees invocating the said Angels particularly, let him say: "O Angeli supradicti, estate adjutores mea petitioni, et in adjutorium mibi, in meis rebus et petitionibus."

Then let him call the Angels from the four parts of the world that rule the Air the same day wherein he doth the work; and having implored specially all the names and Spirits written in the Circle, let him say: "O vos omnes, adjuro atque contestor per sedum Adonay, per Hagios, Theos, Ischyros, Athanatos, Paracletos, Alpha et Omega, et per hos tria nomina secreta, Agla, On, Tetragrammaton, quod bodie debeatis adimplere quod cupio."

These things being performed, let him read the Conjuration assigned for the day wherein he maketh the experiment; but if they shall be pertinacious, and will not yield themselves obedient neither to the Conjuration assigned to the day, nor to the prayers before made, then use the Conjurations and Exorcisms following.

AN EXORCISM OF THE SPIRITS OF THE AIR.

We being made after the Image of God, endued with power from God, and after his Will, do exorcise you by the most mighty and powerful name of God, El, strong and wonderful (here he shall name the spirits he would have appear, of what Order soever they be), and we command you by him, who said the word and it was done, and by all the names of God, and by the name Adonay, El, Elohim, Elohe, Lebaoth, Elion, Escerchie, Jah, Tetragrammaton, Saday, Lord God most high: We powerfully command you, that you forthwith appear unto us, here before this Circle, in a fair humane shape, without any deformity or tortuosity; come ye all such, because we command you by the name of God;

and by these three secret names, Agla, On, Tetragrammaton, I do adjure you; and by all the other names of the living and true God, I exorcise and command you, that you appear here before this Circle to fulfill our will in all things which shall seem good unto us; and by this name Primeumaton, which Moses named, and the earth opened and swallowed up Corah, Dathan and Abiram; and we curse you and deprive you from all your office, joy and place, and do bind you in the depth of the bottomless Pit, there to remain until the day of the last Judgment; until you forthwith appear before this Circle to do our will; Therefore come ye, come ye, come ye, Adonay commandeth you; Saday, the most mighty and dreadful King of Kings, whose power no creature is able to resist, be unto you most dreadful, unless ye obey, and forthwith appear before this Circle, let miserable ruin and fire unquenchable remain with you; therefore come ye in the name of Adonay Lebaoth, Adonay Amioram; come, come, why stay you? hasten! Adonay, Saday, the King of Kings commands you; El, Aty, Azia, Hin, Jen, Achaden, Vay, El, El, El, Hau, Hau, Hau, Va, Va, Va.

A PRAYER TO GOD TO BE SAID IN THE FOUR PARTS OF THE WORLD, IN THE CIRCLE.

"O my most merciful heavenly Father, have mercy upon me, although a sinner, make appear the arm of they power in me this day (although thy unworthy child) against these obstinate and pernicious Spirits. I humbly implore and beseech thee, that these Spirits which I call may be bound and constrained to come, and give true and perfect answers to those things which I shall ask them, and that they may declare and shew those things which by me shall be commanded them." Then let him stand in the middle of the Circle, and hold his hand towards the Pentacle and say: "By the pentacle of Solomon I have called you, give me a true answer." Then let him say: "By the most mighty Kings and Potentates, and the most powerful Princes, Ministers of the Tartarean Seat, chief Prince of the Seat of the ninth Legion; I invoke you, and conjure you, and strongly command you, by thim who spoke it was done, and by this ineffable name Tetragrammaton Jehoah, which being heard, the Elements are overthrown, the Air is shaken, the Sea runneth back, the fire is quenched, the Earth trembleth, and all the Hosts of Celestials, Terrestrials, and Infernals do tremble, and are confounded together; wherefore forthwith and without delay, do you come from all parts of the world, and make rational answers unto all things I shall ask of you; and come ye now without delay manifesting what we desire, being conjured by the Name of the eternal, living, and true God Helioren and fulfill our commands, intelligibly and without any ambiguity."

VISIONS AND APPARITIONS.

These things duly performed, there will appear infinite Visions and Phantasms, beating of Organs and all kinds of Musical Instruments, which is done by the Spirits, that with the terror they might force the Companions to go out of the circle, because they can do nothing against the Master. After this you shall see an infinite Company of Archers with a great multitude of horrible beasts, which will so compose themselves as if they would devour the follows: nevertheless, fear nothing.

Then the Priest or Master, holding his hand towards the Pentacle shall say, "Avoid hence these iniquities by virtue of the Banner of God;" and then will the Spirits be compelled to obey the Master, and the Company shall see no more.

Then let the Exorcist, stretching out his hand to the Pentacle, say, "Behold the Pentacle of Solomon which I have brought before your presence. Behold the person of the Exorcist in the middle of the Exorcism, who is armed by God, and without fear, and well provided, who potentially invocateth and calleth you, come therefore with speed, in the virtue of these names, Aye, Seraye, Aye, Seraye; defer not to come by the eternal Names of the living and true God, Eloy, Archima, Rabur, and by the Pentacle here present, which powerfully reigns over you, and by virtue of the Celestial Spirits your Lords, make haste to come and yield obedience to your Master." This being performed , there will be hissings in the four parts of the world, and then immediately you shall see great motions; and when you see them, say, "Why stay you? wherefore do you delay? prepare yourself and be obedient to your Master."

Then they will immediately come in their proper form; and when you see them before the Circle, shew them the Pentacle covered with fine linen; uncover it and say, "Behold your conclusion, if you refuse to be obedient;" and suddenly they will appear in a peaceable form and will say, "Ask what you will, for we are prepared to fulfill all your commands, for the Lord hath subjected us hereunto;" and when the Spirits have appeared, then you shall say, "Welcome Spirits, or most noble Kings, because I have called you through him to whom every knee doth bow, both of things in Heaven and things in Earth, and things under the Earth, in whose hands are all the Kingdoms of Kings, neither is there any that can contradict his Majesty. Wherefore I bind you, that you remain affable and visible before this Circle, neither shall you depart without my license, until you have truly and without any fallacy performed my will, by virtue of his power who hath set the Sea her bounds, nor go beyond the law of his Power, the most high God, who hath created all things, Amen. In the name of the Father, and of the Son, and of the Holy Ghost, go in peace unto your places; peace be between us and you, be ye ready to come when ye are called.

THE FIGURE OF A CIRCLE FOR THE FIRST HOUR OF THE LORD'S DAY IN SPRING-TIME.

THE FIGURE OF A CIRCLE FOR THE FIRST HOUR OF
THE LORD'S DAY IN SPRING-TIME.

These are the things which Peter de Abano hath spoken concerning Magical Elements.

But that you may the better know the manner of composing a Circle, I will set down one scheme; so that if any would make a Circle in Spring time, for the first hour of the Lord's day, it must be in the same manner as in the preceding illustration.

It remaineth now, that we explain the Week, the several days thereof, and the first of the Lord's day.

CONSIDERATIONS OF THE LORD'S DAY

The Angel of the Lord's day, his Sigil, Planet, Sign of the Planet, and the name of the fourth Heaven.

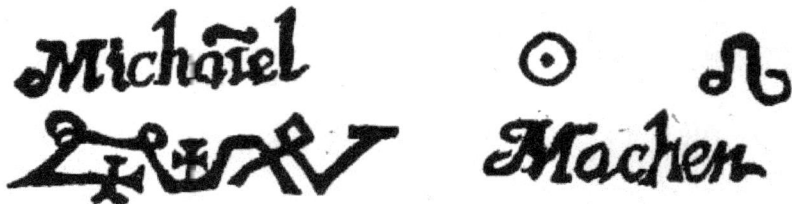

The Angels of the Lord's day: Michael Dardiel, Huralapal.

The Angels of the Air ruling on the Lord's Day: Varcan, King

His Ministers: Tus, Andas, Cynabal.

The winde which the Angels of the Air above said are under: The North-winde.

The Angel of the fourth Heaven, ruling on the Lord's day, which ought to be called from the four parts of the world.

At the East: Samael, Baciel, Atel, Gabriel, Vionatraba.

At the West: Anael, Pabel, Vstael, Burshat, Suceratos, Capabili.

At the North: Atiel, Auiel, vel Aquiel, Masgabriel, Sapiel, Matuyel.

At the South: Haludiel, Machasiel, Charsiel, Vriel, Naromiet.

The perfume of the Lord's day: Red Sanders.

THE CONJURATION OF THE LORD'S DAY.

"I conjure and confirm you, ye strong and holy Angels of God, in the name Adonay, Eye Eye, Eya, which is he who was and is, and is to come. Eye Abray, and in the name Saday, Cados, Cados, Cados, sitting on high upon the Cherubin; and by the great Name of God himself, strong and powerful, who is exalted above all Heavens, and by the name of his Star, which is Sol; and by his Sign; and by all the names aforesaid, I conjure thee, Michael, oh, great Angel, who art chief Ruler of the Lord's day; That thou labor for me, and fulfill all my petitions, according to my will and desire, in my cause and business."

And here thou shalt declare they cause and business, and for what thing thou makest this Conjuration.

The Spirits of the Air of the Lord's day are under the Northwinde; their nature is to procure Gold, Gemmes, Carbuncles, Riches; to cause one to obtain favor and benevolence; to dissolve the enmities of men; to raise men to honors; to carry or take away infirmities. But in what manner they appear, it's spoken already in the Book of Magical Ceremonies.

CONSIDERATIONS OF MUNDAY.

The Angel of Munday, his Sigil, Planet, the Sign of the Planet, and the name of the first heaven.

The Angels of Munday: Gabriel, Michael, Samael.

The Angels of the Air ruling on Munday: Arcan, King

His Ministers: Bilet, Missabu, Abuzaha.

The winde which the said Angels of the Air are subject to: The West winde

The Angels of the first Heaven ruling on Munday, which ought to be called from the four parts of the world.

From the East: Gabriel, Gabrael, Madiel, Demiel, Janael.

From the West: Sachiel, Laniel, Habaiel, Bachannel, Corabael.

From the North: Mael, Uvael, Valuum, Baliel, Balay, Humastrau.

From the South: Chrauiel, Dabriel, Darqueil, Hanun, Anayi, Vetuel.

The perfume of Munday: Aloes.

THE CONJURATION OF MUNDAY.

"I conjure and confirm upon you, ye strong and good Angels, in the name of Adonay, Adonay, Eye, Ey, Eye, Cados, Cados, Cados, Achim, Achim, Ja, Ja, strong Ja, who appeared in Mount Sinai with the glorification of King Adonay, Saday, who created the sea and all lakes and waters in the second day, and sealed the sea in his high name, and gave it bounds beyond which it cannot pass; and by the names of the Angels, who rule in the first Legion, who serve Orphauael, a great and honorable Angel, and by the name of his Star, and by all the names aforesaid - I conjure thee, Gabriel, who art chief Ruler of Munday, that for me thou labor and fulfill," &c., as in the Conjuration of sunday.

The Spirits of the Air of Munday are subject to the West winde, which is the winde of the Moon; their nature is to give silver, to convey things from place to place; to make horses swift, and to disclose the secrets of persons both present and future; but in what manner they appear, you may see in the former book.

CONSIDERATIONS OF TUESDAY.

The Angel of tuesday, his Sigil, his planet, the sign governing that planet, and the name of the fifth Heaven.

The Angel of Tuesday: Samuel, Satael, Amabiel.

The Angels of the Air ruling on Tuesday: Samax, King.

His Ministers: Carmax, Ismoli, Paffrau.

The winde to which the said Angels are subject: The East winde.

The Angels of the fifth Heaven ruling on Tuesday, which ought to be called from the four parts of the world.

At the East: Friagne, Guael, Damael, Calza, Arragon.

At the West: Lama, Astagna, Lobquin, Sencas, Jazel, Isiael, Irel.

At the North: Rahumel, Hyniel, Rayel, Seraphiel, Mathiel, Fraciel.

At the South: Sacriel, Janiel, Galdel, Osael, Vianuel, Laliel.

The Perfume of Tuesday: Pepper.

THE CONJURATION OF TUESDAY.

"I Conjure and confirm upon you, ye strong and holy Angels, by the name of Ya, Ya, Ya, He, He, He, Va, Hy, Hy Ha, Ha, Va, Va, An, An, Aie, Aie, Eloim, Eloim; and by the name of that high God who made the dry land appear, and called it Earth, and brought forth herbs and trees out of the same; and by the name of the angels ruling in the fifth Heaven, who serve Acimoy, a great Angel, strong and honourable; and by the name of his Starre, which is Mars, and by the names aforesaid, I Conjure upon thee, Samael, who art a great Angel and chiefe ruler of Tuesday; and by the name Adonay, the living and true God, that for me thou labour and fulfill," &c., as in the Conjuration of Sunday.

The Spirits of the Air of tuesday are under the East-winde; their nature is to cause wars, mortality, death and combustions, and to give two thousand Souldiers at a time; to bring death, infirmities or health. The manner of their appearing you may see in the former book.

CONSIDERATIONS OF WEDNESDAY.

The Angel of Wednesday, his Sigil, Planet, the Signe governing the Planet, and the name of the second Heaven.

The Angels of Wednesday: Raphael, Miel, Seraphiel.

The Angels of the air ruling on Wednesday: Mediat or Modiat, Rex.

Ministers: Suquinos, Sallales, Blaef.

The winde to which the said Angels are subject: The South-west-winde.

The Angels of the second heaven governing Wednesday, which ought to be called from the four parts of the world.

At the East: Mathlai, tarmiel, Barabo.

At the West: Jerescus, Mitraton.

At the North: Thiel, Rael, Jeriabel, Venabel, Velel, Abniori, Veirnuel.

At the South: Miliel, Nelapa, Babel, Caluel, Vel, Laquel.

The Fumigation of Wednesday: Mastick.

THE CONJURATION OF WEDNESDAY.

"I Conjure and confirm upon you, ye strong, holy and potent Angels in the name of the most dreadful and blessed Ja, Adonay, Eloim, Saday, Sady, Eie, Eie, Eie, Asamie, Asaraie; and in the name of Adonay, the God of Israel, who created the two great lights to distinguish the day from the night, and by the name of all the Angels serving in the second host, before Tetra, a great and powerful Angel; and by the name of his Star, which is Mercury; and by the name of the Seal, which is sealed by God most mighty and honourable; by all things before spoken, I Conjure upon thee, Raphael, a great Angel, who art chief ruler of the fourth day; and by the name of the seat of the animals having six wings, that for me thou labor," etc., as in the Conjuration of Sunday.

The Spirits of the Air of Wednesday are subject to the South-west winde; their nature is to give all Metals; to reveal all earthly things, past, present and to come; to pacifie Judges, to give victories in war, to re-ediie, and teach experiments and all decayed Sciences, and to change bodies mixt of Elements conditionally out of one into another; to give infirmities or health; to raise the poor, or cast down the high ones; to binde or loose Spirits; to open locks or bolts; such kind of Spirits have the operation of others; but not in their perfect power, but in virtue or knowledge. In what manner they appear it is before spoken.

CONSIDERATIONS OF THURSDAY.

The Angel of Thursday, his Sigil, Planet, the Signe of the Planet and the name of the Sixth Heaven.

The Angels of Thursday: Sachiel, Castiel, Asasiel.

The Angels of the Air governing Thursday: Suth, Rex.

Ministers: Maguth, Gutrix, Pacifer.

The winde which the said Angels of the Air are under: The South-winde.

But because there are no Angels of the Air to be found above the fifth heaven, therefore on Thursday say the prayers following in the four parts of the world.

At the East: "O great and most high God, honored world without end."

At the West: "O wise, pure, and just God, of divine elemency, I beseech thee, most holy Father, that this day I may perfectly understand and accomplish my petition. Thou who livest and reignest world without end, Amen."

At the North: "O God, strong and might from everlasting."

At the South: "O mighty and merciful God."

The perfume of Thursday: Saffron.

THE CONJURATION OF THURSDAY.

"I conjure and Confirm upon you, ye holy Angels, and by the name Cados, Cados, Cados, Eschereie, Eschereie, Eschereie, Hatim, Ya, strong founder of the worlds, Cantine, Jaym, Janie, Auie, Calbot, Sabbac, Berisay, Alnaym; and by the name Adonay, who created Fishes, and creeping things in the waters, and Birds upon the face of the earth, and by the names of the angels serving in the sixth host, before Pastor, a holy Angel, and a great Prince; and by the name of his Star, which is Jupiter, and by the name of his Seal, and by the name Adonay, the great God, creator of all things; and by the name of all the Stars and by their power, and by all the names aforesaid, I conjure thee, Sachiel, a great Angel, who art chief ruler of Thursday, that for me thou labor," etc., as in the Conjuration of the Lord's day.

The Spirits of the Air of thursday are subject to the South-winde; their nature is to procure the love of women, to cause men to be merry and joyful; to pacifie strife and contentions; to appease enemies; to heal the diseased, and to disease the whole; and procureth losses, or taketh them away. Their manner of appearing is spoken of already.

CONSIDERATIONS OF FRIDAY.

The Angel of Friday, his Sigil, his Planet, the Signe governing that Planet, and the name of the third heaven.

The Angels of Friday: Anæl, Rachiel, Sachiel.

The Angels of the Air reigning on Friday: Sarabotes, King.

Ministers: Amabiel, Aba, Abalidoth.

The winde which the said Angels of the Air are under: "The West-winde.

Angels of the Third Heaven, ruling on Friday, which are to be called from the four parts of the world.

At the East: Satchiel, Chedusitaniel, Corat, Tamael, Tenaciel.

At the West: Turiel, Coniel, Babiel, Kadie, Maltiel, Huphaltiel

At the North: Peniel, Penael, Periat, Raphael, Rainel, Doremiel.

At the South: Porna, Sachiel, Chermiel, Samael, Santanael, Famiel.

The perfume of Friday: Pepperwort.

THE CONJURATION OF FRIDAY.

"I Conjure and Confirm upon you, ye strong Angels, holy and powerful; in the same On, Hey, Heya, Ja, Je, Adonay, Saday, and in the name Saday, who created four-footed beats, and creeping things, and man in the sixth day, and gave to Adam power over all creatures; and by the name of the Angels serving in the third host, before Dagiel, a great Angel and powerful Prince; and by the name of the Star which is Venus, and by his Seal which is holy, and by all the names aforesaid, I conjure upon thee Angel, who art chief ruler of the sixth day, and thou labour for me." etc., as before in the Conjuration of Sunday.

The Spirits of the Air of Friday, are subject to the West-winde; their nature is to give silver; to excite men, and incline them to luxury; and to make marriages; to allure men to love women; to cause or take away infirmities; and to do all things which have motion.

CONSIDERATIONS OF SATURDAY, OR THE SABBATH DAY.

The Angel of Saturday, his Seal, his Planet, and the Signe governing the Planet.

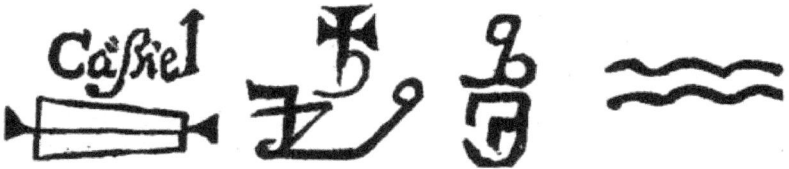

The Angels of Saturday: Sassiel, Machatan, Uriel.

The Angels of the Air ruling on Saturday: Maymon, King.

Ministers: Abumalith, Assaibi, Balidet.

The winde which the said Angels of the Air aforesaid are under: The Southwest-winde.

The fumigation of Saturday: Sulphur.

It is already declared in the Consideration of thursday, that there are no Angels ruling the Air, above the fifth heaven; therefore in the four angles of the world, use those Orations which you see applied to that purpose on Thursday.

THE CONJURATION OF SATURDAY.

"I Conjure and Confirm upon you, Caphriel or Cassiel, Machator, and Seraquiel, strong and powerful Angels; and by the name Adonay, Eie, Achim, Cados, Lord and Maker of the world, who rested on the seventh day; and by the names of the angels serving in the seventh host, before Booel, a great Angel, and powerful Prince; and by the name of his Star, which is Saturn; and by his holy Seal; and by the names before spoken, I Conjure upon thee Caphriel, who art chiefe ruler of the seventh day, which is the Sabbath day, that for me thou labor," etc., as it is set down in the Conjuration of the Lord's day.

The Spirits of the Air of Saturday, are subject to the South-west-winde; the nature of them is to sow discords, hatred, evil thoughts and cogitations; to give leave freely to slay and kill everyone, and to lame or maim every member. Their manner of appearing is declared in the former book.

OF THE NAMES OF THE HOURS AND THE ANGELS RULING THEM.

It is also to be known, that the Angels do rule the hours in a successive order, according to the course of the Heavens and Planets unto which they are subject, so that that spirit which governeth the day, ruleth also the first hour of the day; the second from this governeth the second hour; the third, the third hour, and so consequently; and when seven Planets and hours have made their revolution, it returneth again to the first which ruleth the day; therefore, we shall first speak of the names of the hours.

Hours of the day: 1. Yain, 2. Janor, 3. Nasmia, 4. Salla, 5. Sadedalia, 6. Thamur, 7. Ourer, 8. Thamic, 9. Neron, 10. Jayon, 11. Abai, 12. Natalen.

Hours of the night: 1. Beron, 2. Barol, 3. Thami, 4. Athar, 5. Methon, 6. Rana, 7. Netos, 8. Infrac, 9. Sassur, 10. Aglo, 11. Calerva, 12. Salam.

TABLES OF THE ANGELS OF THE HOURS ACCORDING TO THE COURSE OF THE DAYES.

Sunday - Angels of the hours of the day: 1. Michael, 2. Anael, 3. Raphael, 4. Gabriel, 5. Cassiel, 6. Sachiel, 7. Samael, 8. Michael, 9. Anael, 10. Raphael, 11. Gabriel, 12. Cassiel.

Angels of the hours of the night: 1. Sachiel, 2. Samael, 3. Michael, 4. Anael, 5. Raphael, 6. Gabriel, 7. Cassiel, 8. Sachiei, 9. Samael, 10. Michael, 11. Anael, 12. Raphael.

Munday - Angels of the hours of the day: 1. Gabriel, 2. Cassiel, 3. Sachiel, 4. Samael, 5. Michael, 6. Anael, 7. Raphael, 8. Gabriel, 9. Cassiel, 10. Sachiel, 11. Samael, 12. Michael.

Angels of the hours of the night: 1. Anael, 2. Raphael, 3. Gabriel, 4. Cassiel, 5. Sachiel, 6. Samael, 7. Michael, 8. Anael, 9. Raphael, 10. Gabriel, 11. Sassiel, 12. Sachiel.

Tuesday - Angels of the hours of the day: 1. Samael, 2. Michael, 3. Anael, 4. Raphael, 5. Gabriel, 6. Cassiel, 7. Sachiel, 8. Samael, 9. Michael, 10. Anael, 11. Raphael, 12. Gabriel.

Angels of the hours of the night: 1. Cassiel, 2. Sachiel, 3. Samael, 4. Michael, 5. Anael, 6. Raphael, 7. Gabriel, 8. Cassiel, 9. Sachiel, 10. Samael, 11. Michael, 12. Anael.

Wednesday - Angels of the hours of the day: 1. Raphael, 2. Gabriel, 3. Cassiel, 4. Sachiel, 5. Samael, 6. Michael, 7. Anasel, 8. Raphael, 9. Gabriel, 10. Cassiel, 11. Sachiel, 12. Samael.

Angels of the hours of the night: 1. Michael, 2. Anael, 3. Raphael, 4. Gabriel, 5. Cassiel, 6. Sachiel, 7. Samael, 8. Michael, 9. Anael, 10. Raphael, 11. Gabriel, 12. Cassiel.

Thursday - Angels of the hours of the day: 1. Sachiel, 2. Samael, 3. Michael, 4. Anael, 5. Raphael, 6. Gabriel, 7. Cassiel, 8. Sachiel, 9. Samael, 10.1 Michael, 11. Anael, 12. Raphael

Angels of the hours of the night: 1. Gabriel, 2. Cassiel, 3. Sachiel, 4. Samael, 5. Michael, 6. Anael, 7. Raphael, 8. Gabriel, 9. Cassiel, 10. Sachiel, 11. Samael, 12. Michael.

Friday - Angels of the hours of the day: 1. Anael, 2. Raphael, 3. Gabriel, 4. Cassiel, 5. Sachiel, 6. Samael, 7. Michael, 8. Anael, 9. Raphael, 10. Gabriel, 11. Cassiel, 12. Sachiel.

Angels of the hours of the night: 1. Samael, 2. Michael, 3. Anael, 4. Raphael, 5. Gabriel, 6. Cassiel, 7. Sachiel, 8. Samael, 9. Micael, 10. Anael, 11. Raphael, 12. Gabriel.

Saturday - Angels of the hours of the day: 1. Cassiel, 2. Sachiel, 3. Samael, 4. Michael, 5. Anael, 6. Raphael, 7. Gabriel, 8. Cassiel, 9. Sachiel, 10. Samael, 11. Michael, 12. Anael.

Angels of the hours of the night: 1. Raphael, 2. Gabriel, 3. Cassiel, 4. Sachiel, 5. Samael, 6. Michael, 7. Anael, 8. Raphael, 9. Gabriel, 10. Cassiel, 11. Sachiel, 12. Samael.

But this is to be observed by the way, that the first hour of the day, of every country, and in every season whatsoever, is to be assigned to the sun-rising when he first appeareth arising in the horizon; and the first hour of the night is to be the thirteenth hour, from the first hour of the day; but of these things it is sufficiently spoken.

[The worthy "pupil," or rather student and admirer of the great Cornelius Agrippa, in his introduction to the Magical Elements of peter d'Abano conveys the impression to the reader's mind that the "heptameron" given above was written after the time of Agrippa, as a digest of that great Sage's magical method. Those who are versed in the lives and chronological appearances of the Alchemists are aware that Peter D'Abano flourished some two hundred years earlier than Agrippa, whilst Robert Turner's Compendium of the philosophy of both was ' done into English" nearly two centuries later than the period of Agrippa's birth. Though Abano's method is decidedly the same as Agrippa's, the Translator has wisely given the former credit for superior perspicuity of style, hence the above selection of Abano's Heptameron]

Section XX
Cornelius Agrippa's Philosophy
--

Although there are many remarkable features of interest in the writings of Cornelius Agrippa, we deem it unnecessary to give farther citations of magical practices. The reader, desirous to accomplish himself in the Magician's art, would derive but little encouragement from a study of Agrippa's works, especially as he repeatedly affirms that "a man must be born a Magician from his mother's womb." This passage, with others of a kindred character, plainly imply the great Magician's belief, that what we have so often termed naturally prophetic, or Mediumistic endowments, are far more available to procure communion with, and control of spirits, than any arts which he can recommend. Again and again, too, Agrippa enlarges on the potency of the will to produce magical results. His opinion of this great instrument of power is conveyed in the following quaint passage:

"Notwithstanding the use of all these signs, and whether or not the Magician shall make every pentacle duly, and write every name in order, even if he do speak all which is here set down in every circumstance; yet, when no spirit cometh, it is the mind of the invocant which doth fail him, for all these things are but as winds, which do blow on the temper of the mind, to stir it up to action." "Unless a man be born a Magician, and God have destined him even from his birth to the work, so that spirits do willingly come of their own accord - which doth happen to few - a man must use only of these things herein set down, or written in our other books of occult philosophy, as means to fix the mind upon the work to be done; for it is in the power of the mind itself that spirits do come and go, and magical works are done, and all things in nature are but as used to induce the will to rest upon the point desired."

Agrippa, like Dee, Lilly, and other professors of the astrological art, teaches that it is an exact science, which can be learned and practiced independently of other magical formulae. In this as in his ceremonial directions, the great philosopher's language is too involved to be available to the general reader.

Next to Cornelius Agrippa, one of the most famous of all the middle age Mystics, was Paracelsus, a Physician, Philosopher and writer, whose usefulness and practical sense justly entitle him to the high rank assigned him as the founder of a new and revolutionary system of practice in the curative art. Whilst his voluminous works form a perfect storehouse of suggestive thought and ideality in the realm of metaphysics, our space will only allow us to notice the remarkable uses which he claimed to have discovered by the application of the magnet and the potency of the human will in the cure of disease. Paracelsus himself affirms, that he relied chiefly on those two elements of power for effecting the many extraordinary cures attributed to him.

The famous "weapon salve," by which he was said to heal the most dangerous wounds, simply through anointing the weapons which had inflicted them, - was no doubt only a means of psychological effect analogous to those now so familiarly in use amongst

Electro-biologists. Being as the narrative of his life proves a powerful magnetizer and still more potential psychologist, the efects he produced through these supreme agencies, naturally enough seemed miraculous in the eyes of an ignorant and superstitious community, hence it would be difficult to credit all the extraordinary achievements and magical performances attributed to him without an understanding of the true secret of his power. Paracelsus wrote many elaborate treatises on the occult virtues of herbs, precious stones, gems, and crystals. he himself was a fine clairvoyant and accomplished in the faculty of crystal seeing. hence arose the belief that he kept a familiar spirit imprisoned in a splendid crystal which he wore in the hilt of his sword, and that from this demon he derived his theurgic powers and remarkable gifts of healing.

Paracelsus was a bitter opponent of the then popular system of drug medication, and as his denunciations of Apothecaries nostrums, and medical charlatanism, were fulminated with all the unsparing violence of an impulsive and fearless opponent, it is no wonder that he was loaded with opprobium by the rival practitioners of his time, fiercely denounced by one party, and as extravagantly eulogized by another, hence his real claims to consideration as a bold and scientific innovator and an original discoverer, have scarcely received justice at the hands of posterity. The following brief excerpts from his treatise on the Magnet, and his views of the potency of the human will, afford some insight into the basic ideas of his philosophy.

He says:

"The magnet has lain before all eyes, yet no one has ever thought whether it was of any further use than that of attracting iron. The sordid doctors throw it in my face that I will not follow the ancients. But in what should I follow them? All that they have said of the magnet is nothing save what every peasant sees; namely, that it attracts iron. But a wise man must enquire and experiment for himself, and thus it is that I have discovered that the magnet possesses quite another, though concealed, power, from that visible to every one.

"In sickness you must lay the magnet in the centre from whence the sickness proceeds. The magnet has two poles - an attracting and a repelling one. It is not a matter of indifference how these poles are applied; for instance: where the attack affects the head, it is proper to lay four magnets on the lower part of the body, with the attracting pole turned upwards, and on the head place only one with the reflecting pole downwards, and then you bring other means to your aid." "I cure by this means: epilepsy, defluxions of the eyes, ears, nose, and all manner of diseases." ...."I find such secrets hidden in the magnet that without it I could in many cases have effected nothing."

The religious and magical philosophy of Paracelsus, is essentially that of the Cabala, from which he derived, not only his views of Creation, Deity, angelic essences, the doctrine of emanations, etc., but hints concerning the occult secrets of nature, which he, as a practical and scientific Physician, utilized in his system of cure, by herbs, magnetic crystals, and psychological impressions.

Although often quoted in fragmentary sketches of Paracelsite philosophy, we deem the following opinions concerning the power of the human will eminently worthy to be noted in a book of magic, and more illustrative of the real mind of the philosopher than the vague and shadowy speculations of so many of his followers. In the Strasbourg edition of Paracelsus' voluminous writings, he says:

"It is possible that my spirit, without the help of my body may through a fiery will alone, and without a sword, stab and wound others.

"It is also possible that I can bring my adversary's spirit into an image (wraith), then double him up, and lame him at pleasure. You are to know that the will is a most potent operator in medicine. Man can hang a disease on man or beast through curses, but it does not take effect through an image of virgin wax, but by means of the strength of fixed will." .... "Determined imagination is the beginning of all magical operations. It is a spell from which there is no escape but by reversing the operator's intent." .... "The imagination of another may be able to kill me or save me." .... "No armor protects me against magic, for it injures the inward spirit of life." .... "The human spirit is so great a thing that no man can express it. God himself is unchangeable and almighty, so also is the mind of man." "If we rightly esteemed the power of man's mind, nothing on earth would be impossible to him."

It would be needless to offer further quotations from the writings of the numerous mystics who flourished from the thirteenth up to the beginning of the nineteenth centuries. The doctrines of the famous Rosicrucians have already been sufficiently noted. Of their existence or even origin as an order, we do not feel called upon to dilate, neither would we have shown in former sections to be dependent upon natural endowments, or methods of culture sufficiently defined for all practical purposes. It only remains now for us to analyze somewhat more in detail than formerly, the characteristics of that wonderful and mysterious drama which occupies such a prominent place during the middle ages under the title of Witchcraft.

Although the narratives on this subject are so numerous, and accounts of the trials in various countries so fully set forth in the writings of many eminent authorities, that any reiteration of them in this place would be superfluous, still we feel that more attention has been given to the details of events than to the elimination of a philosophy, the attempts at explanation rendered by the Savants of the time being limited to the universal solvent of the Devil and his Imps, and those of the modern Spiritualists to the sole agency of the spirits of deceased persons.

WHen can we obtain a fair statement and a scientific classification of the phenomena exhibited in this weird movement, we shall assuredly find a broad field of action left untouched by either of these inefficacious attempts of explanation.

In the first place a large mass of the accusations were fictitious, especially in the case of those victims of the popular fury, whose age, helplessness, and ignorance, rendered them fit subjects for superstitious dread. Still another class were unconsciously and perhaps involuntarily, the victims - not of benefit or even undeveloped human spirits - whose intelligence and humanity would have led them to manifest their presence in human modes - but of Elementaries, whose sub-mundane propensities were exhibited in animal actions, and deeds of folly and malignity, which favored the popular idea of Satanic origin. It must be remembered that there is as much irrationality in wholesale and obstinate skepticism, as in credulity. The trials for Witchcraft and the numerous narratives put forth concerning it, prove that there existed a certain family resemblance amongst its details which suggests a basis of facts even for the most exaggerated accusations, For example: The "spectres" or "wraiths" of the accused were frequently seen apart from their bodies. The modern Psychologist must be aware that the phenomenon of the "doppel ganger," or the apparition of the "living spirit," is too well established a phenomenon to be denied.

Many of the accused confessed to the practice of anointing their bodies with the famous "witch salve," largely composed of Napellus, Aconite, Belladonna, Henbane, and other herbs which notoriously produce the sensation of flying through the air.

Many we not here find a clue to the universal idea, that these self-deluded beings - who, in come instances at least, flattered themselves that they could communicate with occult powers by occult practices - actually indulged the sensations and visions they related by the narcotics they indulged in? None can deny that the aspirations after the unknown, and the longing to communicate with the invisible world, to say nothing of the attempts to improve upon miserable human conditions by the aid of internal or any available arts that could be arrived at - have stimulated humanity at every age; hence let us be just, and whilst we may and must admit that a fearful amount of superstitious error prevailed on the subject of witchcraft, and an incalculable sum of cruelty and sacrifice of human life was the consequence, we must still allow that there was a substratum of truth in the universal belief, which the ignorance of the age could not separate from malevolent accusations against innocent persons, and which the superstition of time could not reduce into the application of true occult powers.

It was clearly proved that some of the accused persons did at times make use of charms, spells, amulets, ungents, talismans, invocations, and other magical arts.

The part of true philosophy should be to consider whether any of these practices contain elements of potency - not to dismiss them all as idle and baseless superstitions. Is it possible to suppose that such arts should have been handed down from the days of Moses, and perhaps for thousands of years previous, and surviving all the changes of time, and humane opinions, continue to crop out in every age and country, unless they originated in some foundation of natural law? As we shall devote the next section to a review of possibilities that belong to this occult and ill-understood subject, we close this necessarily brief review of the Witchcraft mania, by presenting one illustration of that most common of all its phenomenal phases, which proves the unconscious, yet potential action of Magnetism and Psychology. Although the narrative we select is one which the zeal of Glanville, from whose writings we quote it, has made familiar, doubtless, to most of our readers, we deem it the best illustration we can offer of a majority of the cases for which so many unfortunates suffered the horrors of the rack and stake.

Glanville, Chaplain to Charles II., of England, writing in defense of the truth of Witchcraft, or rather its actuality, as it occurred in the seventeenth century, says:

"On Sunday, 15th of November, 1657, about three of the clock in the afternoon, Richard Jones, then a sprightly youth about twelve years old, son of Henry Jones, of Shepton Mallet, in the county of Somerset, being in his father's house alone, and perceiving some one looking in at the windows, went to the door, where one Jane Brooks of the same town (but then by name unknown to this boy) came to him. She desired him to give her a piece of close bread, and gave him an apple. After which she also stroked him down the right side, shook him by the hand, and so bid him good-night. The youth returned to the house, where he had been left well, when his father and one Gibson went from him; but at their return, which was within the hour, they found him ill and complaining of his right side, in which the pain continued the most part of that night. And on Monday following, in the evening, the boy roasted the apple he had of Jane Brooks, and having eaten about half of it, was extremely ill, and sometimes speechless, but being recovered, he told his father that a woman of the town on the Sunday before had given him that apple, and that she stroked him on the side. He said he knew not her name, but should her person if he saw her. Upon this Jones was advised to invite the women of Shepton to come to his house upon the occasion of his son's illness, and the child told him, that in case the woman should come in when he was in his Fit, if he were not able to speak, he would give him an intimation by a jogg, and desired that the father would lead him through the room, for he said he would put his hand upon her if she were there. After this, he continuing very ill, many women came daily to see him. and Jane Brooks, the Sunday after came in with two of her sisters, when several other women of the neighborhood were there.

"Upon her coming in, the boy was taken so ill that for some time he could not see nor speak; but having recovered his sight, he gave his father the Item, and he led him about the room. The boy drew towards Jane Brooks, who was behind her two sisters among the other women, and put his hand upon her, which his father perceiving, immediately scratched her face and drew blood from her. The youth then presently cried out that he was well, and so continued seven or eight days; but then meeting with Alice Coward, sister to Jane Brooks, who passing by, said to him: 'How do you, my Honey?' he presently fell ill again. And after that, the said Coward and Brooks often appeared to him. The boy would describe the clothes and habit they were in at the time exactly, as the constable and others have found upon repairing to them, though Brooks' house was at a good distance from Jones'. This they often tryed and always found the boy right in his descriptions.

"On a certain sunday about noon, the child being in a room with his father and one Gibson, and in his fit, he on the sudden called out that he saw Jane Brooks on the wall, and pointed to the place, where immediately Gibson struck with a knife; upon which the boy cried out: 'O father, Coz. Gibson hath cut Jane Brooks' hand and 'tis bloody.' The father and Gibson immediately repaired to the constable, a discreet person, and acquainting him with what had passed, desired him to go with them to Jane Brooks' house, which he did. They found her sitting in her room on a stool with one hand over the other. The constable asked her how she did? She answered, not well. He asked again why she sate with one hand over the other? She replied, she was wont to do so. He enquired if anything were amiss with her hand? Her answer was, it was well enough. The constable desired that he might see the hand that was under; which, she being unwilling to show him, he drew out and found it bloody, according to what the boy had said. Being asked how it came so, she said, I was scratched with a great pin."

"On the 8th of December, 1657, the Boy, Jane Brooks and Alice Coward, appeared at Castle Cary, before the Justices, M. Hunt and M. Cary. The Boy having begun to give his testimony, upon the coming in of the two women, and their looking on him, was instantly taken speechless, and so remained till the women were removed out of the room, and then in a short time, upon examination, he gave a full relation of the mentioned particulars.

"On the 11th of January following, the Boy was again examined before the same Justices at Shepton Mallet, and upon sight of Jane Brooks was again taken speechless, but was not so afterwards when Alice Coward came into the room to him.

"On the next appearance at Shepton, which was on the 17th o February, there were present many gentlemen, ministers and other; the Boy fell into his fit upon the sight of Jane Brooks, and lay in a man's arms like a dead person; the woman was then willed to lay a hand on him, which she did, and he thereupon started and sprung out in a very strange and unusual manner. One of the Justices, to prevent all possibilities of Legerdemain, caused Gibson and the rest to stand off from the boy, and then the Justice himself held him. The youth being blindfolded, the Justice called as if Brooks should touch him, but winked to others to do it, which two or three successively did, but the boy appeared not concerned. The Justice then called on the father to take him, but had privately before desired Mr. Geoffry Strode to bring Jane Brooks to touch him, at the same time as he should call for his father; which was done, and the boy immediately sprang cut after a very odd and violent fashion. He was after touched by several persons and moved not; but Jane Brooks being caused to put her hand upon him, he started and sprang out twice or thrice, as before. All this while he remained in his fit, and sometime after; and being then laid on a bed in the same room, the people present could not for a long time bow either of his arms or legs."

"Between the mentioned 15th of November and the 11th of January, the two women appeared often to the Boy, their hands cold, their eyes staring, and their lips and cheeks looking pale. In this manner on a Thursday about noon, the Boy being newly laid into his bed, Jane Brooks and Alice Coward appeared to him, and told him that what they had begun, they could not perform, but if he would say no more of it, they would give him money, and so put a two-pence into his pocket. After which they took him out o his bed, laid him on the ground, and vanished; and the boy was found by those that came next into the room, lying on the floor, as if he had been dead. The two-pence was seen by many, and when it was put into the fire, and hot, the boy would fall ill; but as soon as it was taken out, and cold, he would be again as well as before. This was seen and observed by a minister, a discreet person, when the boy was in one room and the two-pence (without his knowledge) put into the fire in another; and this was divers times tried in the presence of several persons.

"On the 25th of February between two and three in the afternoon, the boy being at the house of Richard Isles at Shepton Mallet, went out of the room into the garden; Isles's wife followed him, and was within two yards when she saw him rise up from the ground before her, and so mounted higher and higher, till he passed in the air over the garden wall, and was carried so above ground more than 30 yards, falling at last at one Jordan's door at Shepton, where he was found as dead for a time. But coming to himself, told Jordan that Jane Brooks had taken him up by the arm out of the Isles's garden and carried him in the air, as he related.

"The Boy at several other times was gone on the suddain, and upon search after him found in another room as dead, and at sometimes strangely hanging above ground, his hands being flat against a great beam in the top of the room, and his body two or three feet from ground. There he hath hung a quarter of an hour together; and being afterwards come to himself, he told those that found him that Jane Brooks had carried him to that place and held him there. Nine people at a time saw the boy so strangely hanging by the beam.

"From the 15th of November to the 10th of March following, he was by reason of his fits much wasted in his body, and unspirited; but after that time, being the day the two women were sent to Gaol, he had no more of these fits.

"Jane Brooks was condemned and executed at Charde As sizes, March 16th, 1658.

"This is the sum of M. Hunt's narrative, which concludes with both the justices' attestation, thus: - 'The aforesaid passages were some of them seen by us, and the rest, and some other remarkable ones not here set down, were, upon examination of several credible witnesses, taken upon Oath before us.

"'ROBERT HUNT.
"'John Cary.'"

Thousands, and tens of thousands of narratives have been already published on the subject of Witchcraft, some colored by the wildest exaggeration, others circumstantial in detail, and as matter-of-fact as the one quoted above - all tend to prove the existence of unknown and occult forces pervading human history, equally influential upon individuals and communities, and perpetually challenging the attention of the wise and philosophic for a classification of the facts, and the evolvement of some basic principles of spiritual science by which to explain, govern and control them.

Section XXI
The Magic Mirror - Its Composition

--

The following mode of preparing and using a Magic Mirror, is recommended by Alphonse Cahagnet, author of the Celestial Telegraph, and, as the methods prescribed are simple, and the results obtained are generally efficacious, they are submitted to the reader in the words of Cahagnet himself:

MAGIC MIRROR

"I promised not to reserve to myself anything I had learned from spirits; I will keep my word by giving the secret of the magic mirror, revealed to me by the Spirit of Swedenborg, who himself, possessed one, and of which I have already spoken. I made two in the way recommended to me, one of which I presented to my friend, M. Renard, who after several experiments, gave a favorable report of it; mine was equally good. This is how we should go to work: Produce a piece of glass as fine as possible, cut it in the required size, place it over a slow fire, at the same time dissolving some very fine black lead in a small quantity of pure oil to give it the consistence of a liquid pomade, which may easily be spread over the glass when well diluted.

"The glass being hot, incline it on both sides, in order that the mixture may spread of itself all over alike; then, the glass being placed on something quite straight and flat, let the mixture dry without disturbing it; in a few days it will become as hard as pewter, presenting a very fine dark polish; put your glass in a frame, and after well wiping its surface, hang it up on a wall, as you would a looking-glass, but always in a false light. Place the person who desires to see a spirit, or scene before this mirror, station yourself behind him, fixing your eyes steadily on the hinder part of the brain, and summon the spirit in a loud voice in the name of God, in a manner imposing to the individual looking in the mirror.

"It may be naturally supposed that this kind of experiment requires certain conditions, the first of which is to find an individual endowed with this kind of vision. Nothing in general in psychological facts. There was much talk at one time of the magic mirror of Dr. Dee, which was sold, in 1842, among the curiosities in the possession of Horace Walpole, at Strawberry Hill, for the enormous sum of three hundred and twenty-six francs. It was simply a bit of sea-coal, perfectly polished, cut in a circular form, with a handle. This curiosity formerly figured in the cabinet of the Earl of Peterborough. In the catalogue it was thus described: 'A black stone, by means of which Doctor Dee evoked spirits.' It passed from the hands of the Earl into those of Lady Elizabeth Germaine, then became the property of John, last Duke of Argyll, whose grandson, Lord Campbell, presented it to Walpole. The author of the 'Theatrum Chemicum,' Elias Ashmole, speaks of the same mirror in the following terms.

"'by the aid of this magic stone, we can see whatever persons we desire, no matter in what part of the world they be. and were they hidden in the most retired apartments, or even in the caverns in the bowels of the earth.' John Dee, born in London, in 1527, was the son of a wine-merchant; he studied the sciences with success, and devoted himself, at an early period, to judicial astrology; Queen Elizabeth took him under her protection; he composed several useful works, employed much of his time in the science of magic, conjured spirits, made predictions, and beheld the invisible; when he had discovered his mirror he returned thanksgivings to God. He was occupied during his whole life in the search for the philosopher's stone, and died in London at the age of eighty-four, in a state of abject poverty.

"The Count de Laborde brought us a somewhat similar secret from Egypt. The Baron Dupotet communicated a like one to his subscribers, in his Journal de Magnetisme; one is much more simplified than the other, and succeeds equally as well. M. de Laborde evokes; makes use of perfumes and stands in need of the cooperation of spirits. M. Dupotet seems only to employ the magnetism of thought. Cagliostro also employed a magnetism, but little suspected, by placing on e hand on the head of his pupils. The Sorcerers of our country places proceed in like manner, with the first mirror met with, imploring the assistance of the spirits that facilitate such experiments.

"M. de Laborde makes use of a brilliant ink which he puts in the hollow of the looker's hand, and stimulates his nervous system by perfumes. M. Dupotet makes use of a piece of coal with which he describes a circle on the floor with the intention of making perceptible to the person operated upon, such picture as the latter desires; he keeps the subject inclined for this experiment by thought. Sorcerers have their reputation, which is of great assistance to them. Certain prepossessions against such or such a person suspected of theft or aught else, their imposing air, their supplication to spirits, without knowing positively the meaning of what they say, this suffices, and they operate!

"Leon, of whom I have spoken, followed in their steps. Prayer, faith and a disposition of the visual organs facilitated his experiments. Cagliostro, preceded by his reputation as an incomprehensible man, was often successful in consequence of the fact he displayed in selecting his pupils, the occult magnetism he employed, etc.; but if I ask Messrs. de Laborde, Dupotet, Cagliostro, the sorcerers, Leon and others, whether they themselves saw in their mirrors or reflecting body, they will reply no; therefore, there must be a disposition for this kind of experiment; we must be influenced by an imposing display, an occult magnetism, or the aid of invocations and perfumes. Wherefore, in order to profit by my mirror, I would advise the ceremony to be performed with a certain dignity, and to have recourse only to what may act on the imagination or nerves, as much by a normal or spiritual magnetism as by the assistance of perfumes. All those that bear or shed a sweet, pleasant smell, are suitable for the good spirits; such as incense, musk, gum-lac, etc., and for evil spirits, the seeds of henbane, hemp, belladonna, anise, or coriander, etc. Each seeks his own atmosphere, or one akin to it; but, above all, shun the assistance of evil spirits. Let the spirit of justice, discretion, humanity predominate in you; or otherwise, woe betide you!

"It will not, perhaps, be comprehended why I should recommend shunning the invocation of evil spirits, and yet make known the perfumes they delight in. I presume that I shall be thought sufficiently consistent to speak here only of the apparitions we desire to obtain, on the score of thefts, or other crimes, committed to your prejudice. It is the spirits of such culprits who will obey your command to present themselves, and seek the nauseous smell of these perfumes. You have nothing to fear from them, since, on the contrary, they have everything to fear from you. What I recommend you avoid, when demanding apparitions of those you desire to see is pronouncing words, the meaning of which is unknown to you, that invite baneful spirits to your assistance. This is true Magic."....

When M. Cahagnet informs his readers that the distinguished operators whose experiences he cites do not themselves see aught in their mirror, he omits to add that the assistance of one predisposed to magnetic seership is essential, in fact a magnetized subject is necessary to the success of these methods, unless the operator is himself a Medium or Seer. It will be asked by the intelligent reader if a Medium or Seer is essential to the success of experiments by the mirror or crystal, why may not the said Medium or Seer behold in vision, and without the aid of the instruments, all he desires? To this we answer the magnetism of the operator, the psychological influence of the invocation and the fixidity of the gaze riveted upon the shining surface of the mirror are aids to lucidity - though not its primal source - but our opinions on the subject of Magic and natural mediumship have already been given in detail and we only add accounts of the methods recommended and practiced by celebrated modern Experts to supplement our views of ancient - with modern magic. For this purpose we subjoin the following communication given to a successful Adept of the present generation by a Planetary spirit - the guardian of his mirror - when questioned concerning the best method of divination, also of receiving communications from spirits. The words appeared on the mirror inscribed therein by the spirit, and were read off by the Adept:

"The best and most ancient method of divination was by the Crystal, or Urim and Thummim.

"It's origin was divine, and the inspiration, visions and communications received through this source, when man was pure and holy, were free from all human agency, wholly divine. The use of the crystal in modern times, is almost as potent as the Urim and Thummim of the Jews, and provided it is in the hands of one gifted with clear sight, its revelations are infallible.

"Spirits do not actually appear in the crystal, but the seer is magnetically assisted to look through its pellucid depths into the spirit world. In this way he or she is brought in such near contact with spirits that they can readily converse with mortals." ....

Another planetary spirit, questioned on the same subject, said:

"Whenever guardian spirits, or angels of the higher orders move in the spirit world, the air that surrounds them is cleared of everything that is, in any degree, more gross than themselves.

"Thus, if an atmospheric spirit meet a more heavenly spirit, the atmospheric spirit yields to the pressure of the air that surrounds the other, and retires to let him pass. In this way spirits visit the atmosphere, and the spheres lower than their own, also the earth, without once coming in contact with those below him, unless he wishes to do so. Thus, too, when he is 'called' to converse with human beings, the Invocant's thoughts, or rather will, immediately reach him, and he appears separating and sending before him all influences less angelical than his own.

"Guardian spirits and angels of high degree are only seen in the Urim and Thummim, the crystal and the mirror, the other modes of divining, by vessels of water, by circle work, by shades, by bands, or black fluids, are only available for seeing deceased persons, atmospheric spirits, wandering spirits, evil or undeveloped spirits."

The following method, especially commendable for its simplicity, has been frequently employed with success in magical evocations of Planetary or other spirits by Adepts in the nineteenth century.

It is selected from hundreds of others in the author's possession, chiefly from the perspicuity of its wording, and the absence of mystic assumptions.

Its composition is attributed to the celebrated Astrologer and Crystal Seer, Nostradamus.

DIRECTIONS FOR CRYSTAL SEEING.

"Having procured a good, clear stone, one that no spirit has been called into before, the Seer must determine to use it for no bad purpose. I do not say determine to use it only for good purposes, because many frivolous and trifling things might occur that would induce one to use it for the knowledge of things appertaining to the world; but, having determined to use it for no bad or unholy purpose, he should dedicate it first with a fervent prayer to God.

"Do not make use of a mediator, but firmly, yet humbly, trust that God will put you in possession of a Guardian Spirit that will show you the visions you may thereafter wish."

"Having done this, inspect the Crystal, and before asking to see any vision, ask first to see the name of your Guardian Spirit; having done this, ask to see him; when he appears, ask him to give you any advice he may deem fit in using it. Ask him to name the days and hours that he will appear, and also those on which you may call other spirits. Ask him to become the Guardian Spirit of your Crystal; to prevent any evil spirit from appearing, and to give you timely notice of anything about to happen to you, that you may prevent it, or that he may prevent it for you.

"This done, you must discharge him. He should not be kept more than half an hour at the first meeting.

239

When you invoke him the next time, exorcise with a strong and determined will three times before you ask him any questions; if at those three times he does not vanish, you may perfectly rely upon him.

"After the first time, you may keep him as long as it may suit yours and his convenience; if he wishes to leave, he can do so without a discharge; but be careful that you always use a discharge after having finished of a night.

"When invoking any Atmospheric Spirit, or a spirit of any inferior degree, such as those of living as well as dead people, always use the term 'if convenient and agreeable,' etc.; or, 'at your pleasure;' but more particularly of a living person; to your Guardian Spirit, or a Spirit of a High order, it is not necessary.

"But above all, do not use it in any way, or make it directly or indirectly an object for the gaining of money. It may appear to go on smoothly for a few times. You may have the information and the visions you wish for; but in the end the consequences are lamentable, and they come sooner or later.

"When you have got used to a Crystal, feel confidence in it, and assured in many ways of the Truth of it, then you can use a Mirror, which is by a very great deal the best.

"The Mirror is to be used the same as a Crystal, but from seeing visions so large and life-like, and from the size of the aperture which is made by that into the spiritual world, it enables you to come more closely in contact with the spirits you address.

"Of all modes of divining, this is the easiest and the best, the information is given slowly at first, then gradually more and more, until you reach the grand height of all human knowledge upon spiritual matters, until you know as much as the human mind can in any way comprehend of what passes beyond its own World."

THE CALL

"In the name of the Almighty God, in whom we live and move and have our being, I humbly beseech the Guardian Spirit of this Mirror or Crystal to appear.

"When appeared you can ask your questions, and obtain instructions as to Calling - asking when he will allow you to call him again, and fix his time for appearing.

FOR A VISION.

"In the name, etc., I humbly beseech the Spirit of this Mirror to favor me with a Vision that will interest or instruct us (or favor us with a Vision of such and such a place or event, etc.).

TO SEE A PERSON.

"In the name, etc., Then say, R. B. be pleased to appear in this Mirror if convenient and agreeable. (Never fail in this.)

EXORCISM.

"In the name of the Almighty God, in whom we live and move and have our being, I dismiss the Spirit now visible in this Mirror if he is not" - "or if he is not a good and truthful Spirit.

"This must be said very intently and strongly three times, with the finger upon the Crystal, whenever a Spirit is from any cause suspected.

DISCHARGE.

"In the name, etc., I dismiss from this Mirror all Spirits that may have appeared therein, and the peace of God be between them and us forever.

"This must be said three times upon closing, even if Spirits are not seen, as they may have entered, and its neglect will soon spoil the Mirror or Crystal."

Section XXII
History of Magnetism
--

Those who would write the true history of Magnetism must seek materials in that of magic, for the one is just as surely a record of the other, as the principles of Astrology are derived from the science of Astronomy.

We have written to little purpose if we have failed to impress our readers with the fact that the relations between the worlds of invisible and visible being, are only made known through the occult forces which enable the visible to penetrate into the realms of the invisible - also that the means by which Spirits, Angels, and even Tutelary Deities, communicate with mortals, depend wholly upon these same occult forces. Whether we call this all-pervading motor of being, "divine fire, astral light, electricity, magnetism or life," it is, as we have before shown, the eternal, indestructible, universal and infinite element of force. Magic. Deific relations. Angelic ministry, and spirit communion, are but applications of this force operating upon man, and the visible Universe is only a magnificent chess-board, on which Force is playing the eternal game of creation and destruction, with Suns and Satellites for its chess-men. Whilst it becomes evident that the ancients obtained a wide control over this stupendous motor power by long study and painful initiations, the men of the middle ages in a great measure lost the clue to its guidance, and the apparitional demonstrations of its eternal activity, revealed by glimpses from the worlds of invisible being, only served to startle them into superstitious terror, without instructing them concerning the potential agency at work.

Slowly but surely the veil of mystery is again lifting, and again men see the Cyclops at work forging hemispheres and earths, Angels and Men, out of matter and spirit by the motor power of this same life-lightning. The revelation now so slowly yet surely stealing in upon human consciousness, has not been heralded by the roar of the tempest, the boom of the thunder, or the throes of the quaking earth.

Like the still small voice that spoke to the Prophet Elijah when the Lord passed by - it has come in the low whispers of two new sciences - the science of Life or magnetism, and the science of Soul, or psychology. Only the very first elements of these two magical revelations have as yet dawned upon our age, but they have shown us enough to be assured that when they are fully understood and scientifically applied, they will afford a clue to all the mysteries of the past, and enable man to achieve by natural law, all those phenomenal demonstrations which in ancient times were termed miraculous.

To trace the advent of these phases of spiritual science, it will be necessary to recall the bold claims of Paracelsus for the almost miraculous powers of the magnet, and though most of his followers were dreamy and impractical mystics, who failed to apply the comprehensive ideas which he suggested, they served to keep alive the flame of occult fire which he kindled, until the appearance on the scene of the noble and illuminated Swedenborg, who presented as a Seer of unequalled lucidity, that glorious element of psychological science, which completely supplemented the opinions of Paracelsus concerning magnetism. It remained for Anton Mesmer to combine these two supreme soul forces into their correlative relations, and demonstrate by the practical application of magnetism, the possibility of emulating the natural endowments of Seership, through the revelations of the magnetic sleep.

It must not be supposed that we attribute to that illustrious triad of modern philosophers, Paracelsus, Swedenborg and Mesmer, any new discoveries in nature.

They only rekindled lights of divine science which ignorance and superstition had sought to stifle if they could not extinguish them.

Magnetism the life principle and psychology the soul power of the Universe, had been as we have constantly alleged, the motors of all magical operations, and the knowledge of this fact, and an understanding of how to apply these sublime forces, constituted "the wisdom of the Ancients," and the arcanum of all their mysteries. But the master spirit of antiquity had been slain by the destroying demons of time, change and revolution. The Master's word was lost, and for ages the building of the grand Temple of Spiritual Science waited for the key-stone necessary to complete the arch of the entrance gate. The Alchemists of the twelfth and thirteenth centuries perceived the existence of a "philosopher's stone," but dared not declare that it was to be found only in the universal life force of magnetism. The Rosicruicians of two centuries later realized the true nature of the "Elixir Vitae" in the imperishable quality of Soul essence, but how could they venture to reveal to a scoffing, yet superstitious age, the stupendous fact that this Soul essence could be controlled, imparted, and utilized even without the agency of death to liberate it from the body? It was because Paracelsus bravely and openly taught of this philosopher's stone, giving its true name as Magnetism, and Swedenborg as fearlessly displayed the latent possibilities of spiritual communion and Seership in the human Soul, that these noble philosophers stand confessed as the Fathers of the new dispensation.

The position of Mesmer in this great unfoldment is not less triumphantly defined, but that the momentous revolution he effected in spiritual science may be the more clearly understood, we shall proceed to give a brief compendium of the theorems by which his methods of practice were explained.

It is from Dr. Justinius Kerner's clear yet reverential notices of his life of this inestimable man, so little appreciated in his own time, so ill understood even yet by the cold world upon which he opened up such a realm of spiritual sunshine, that we extract the following items:

Anton Mesmer first saw the light at Weiler, on the Rhine, May the 23d, 1734. As quite a young child, he is said to have exhibited a remarkable predilection for running water, delighting to follow up the course of streams and brooks to their source, and frequently neglecting his scholastic duties for the pleasure of hovering on the banks of the mighty Rhine, gathering stones, shells, and disporting, with a strange joy, in the falling rain, the wild wind, the howling tempest, and the balmy sunshine. He was passionately addicted to the study of nature, and an insatiable yearning led him to explore her recesses, even at an age when his childish mind failed to command language for the expression of the great thoughts that possessed him. During his initiatory studies for the medical profession, he noticed and his associates were accustomed to comment on the strange manner in which the blood of a patient under the operation of the knife or lancet would immediately change the course of its flow as soon as he approached. Sometimes, it is said, it would cease instantly, and where the flow was sluggish, its increase would be immediately promoted by his touch, receding or suspending altogether when he withdrew. A thousand petty incidents, commented on at the time as "very curious," but subsequently remembered as tokens of his ever-present and spontaneously magnetic influence, were constantly occurring from his early childhood up to the time when his unerring instincts led him into the arcanum of his great discovery.

How this occurred will be best rendered in the language of Kerner, who says:

"During his fifteen years' medical practice in Vienna, he came upon his new art of healing through observing the origin, the form, and the career of diseases, in connection with the great changes in our solar system and the universe; in short, in connection with what he termed Universal Magnetism. He sought for this magnetism originally in electricity and subsequently in mineral magnetism. He made use of the magnet for healing at first in 1772, led to this discovery by the astronomer, Father Hel; using the magnet, however, simply as a conductor from his own organism through his hands, and by this means brought forth remarkable cures. A year subsequently, experience showed him that without touching the magnet, through his hands alone, he could operate much more powerfully upon the human organism, and thus originated through him the discovery of Animal Magnetism, which he developed into a science.

"It was after this manner that Mesmer reasoned: 'There must exist a power which permeates the universe, and binds together all the bodies upon earth, and it must be possible for man to bring this influence under his command.' This power he first sought for in the magnet; he pondered upon it with regard to man, and immediately applied it to the cure of diseases. The remarkable operations which were produced, and the cure of the sick, would, in another investigator, have brought him to an end of his experiments. Mesmer, however, went forward. Ever accompanied by the idea of the primary power which must permeate the universe, and is ever active within it, the thought occurred to him that the influence must exist yet more powerfully in man himself than in the magnet; since, he argued, if the magnet communicates to the iron the same polarity which causes itself to be a magnet, and organized body must be able to produce similar conditions in another body. He thus perceived that he could not ascribe alone to the magnet which he held in his hands the effects which he had observed produced, since he also must in turn influence the magnet. Upon this he cast aside his magnet, and with his hands alone brought forth similar and unadulterated effects."

No great discovery has ever yet convulsed the world that has not subsequently brought forth its cloud of claimants to share in its honors. One says: "Why, this is nothing new! I always knew it, and have observed it a hundred times." This cry is echoed and re-echoed until a hundred, a thousand - aye, half the age, perhaps, insists they always knew it was so; it is nothing new. Nothing can be truer than this in relation to magnetism; yet, with all the wise world's perception of its truth, it required the genius of a Mesmer to practicalize, and above all, to reduce it to scientific theorems.

Kerner gives some narratives of Mesmer's methods of treatment in his earliest stages of magnetic practice, which, although very striking, are not sufficiently germain to our purpose to admit of quoting here; we, therefore, omit them, and proceed to present the conclusions they caused the narrator to draw from them. He writes this:

'He ascertained that the principal agent in his cures dwelt within himself, and that its power increased by use. Nevertheless, the idea was never combated by Mesmer, that persons upon whom animal magnetism exercises but a slight influence, are rendered more susceptible to this influence by the assistance of electricity and galvanism.

"Seifart remarks that he had observed that Mesmer wore beneath his linen shirt another of leather-lined with silk, and supposes that Mesmer sought by this means to prevent the escape of the magnetic field. He believes that Mesmer also wore natural and artificial magnets about his person, with the intention of strengthening the magnetic condition in himself.

"At all events it is certain that at a later period he employed for the strengthening of the magnetic condition, an apparatus, the Baquet, or, as he called it, the Magnetic Basin, or Paropothus. This receptacle, as it was originally formed by Mesmer, was a large pan or tub, filled with various magnetic substances, such as water, sand, stone, glass bottles filled with water, etc. It is a focus within which the magnetism finds itself concentrated, and out of which a number of conductors proceed; these conductors being bent, somewhat pointed parallel iron wands, the one end of each wand being in the tub, whilst the other end could be applied to the seat of the disease. This arrangement might be made use of by a number of patients seated around the tub. Any suitably-sized receptacle for water - a pond or a fountain in a garden - would serve a patient as a baquet so soon as the patient made use of an iron wand to conduct the magnetism towards him or herself."
....

"In vain did Mesmer endeavor to convince his medical contemporaries of the truth and importance of his discovery; in vain was his announcement of it to the scientific academies. With but a single exception, he received no answer from them. This exception was the Academy of Berlin, which passed the following judgment: - It would in nowise enter upon an inquiry into a matter which rested on such entirely unknown foundations.

"Upon this Mesmer brought all his discoveries into the form of twenty-seven aphorisms, which he sent to the scientific academies in the year 1775. These aphorisms contain Mesmer's doctrine clearly and briefly expressed, and it is important to become acquainted with them, since his ideas are here given in his own words:

"'1. There exists a reciprocal influence between the heavenly bodies, the earth, and all living things.

"'2. A fluid which is spread everywhere, and which is so expanded that it permits of no vacuum, of a delicacy which can be compared to nothing besides itself, and which, through its nature, is enabled to receive movement, to spread and to participate in it, is the medium of this influence.

"'3. This reciprocal activity is subject to the operation of mechanical laws, which until now were quite unknown.

"'4. From this activity spring alternating operations, which may be compared to ebb and flow.

"'5. This ebb and flow are more or less general, more or less complex, according to the nature of the origin which has called them forth.

"'6. Through this active principle, which is far more universal than any other in nature, originates a relative activity between the heavenly bodies, the earth, and its component parts.

"'7. It immediately sets in movement - since it directly enters into the substance of the nerves - the properties of matter and of organized bodies, and the alternative operations of these active existences.

"'8. In human bodies are discovered properties which correspond with those of the magnet. Also various opposite poles may be distinguished, which can be imparted, changed, distributed and strengthened.

"'9. The property of the animal body, which renders it susceptible to the influence of the heavenly bodies, and to the reciprocal operation of those bodies which surround it, verified by the magnet,, has induced me to term this property Animal Magnetism.

"'10. The power and operation thus designated as Animal Magnetism can be communicated to animate and inanimate bodies; both, however, are more or less susceptible.

"'11. This power and operation can be increased and propagaged through the instrumentality of these bodies.

"'12. Through experience it is observed that an efflux of matter occurs, the volatility of which enables it to penetrate all bodies without perceptibly losing any of its activity.

"'13. Its operation extends into the distance without the assistance of an intermediate body.

"'14. It can be increased and thrown back again by means of a mirror, as well as by light.

"'15. It can be communicated, increased, and spread by means of sound.

"'16. This magnetic power can be accumulated, increased, and spread.

"'17. I have observed that animated bodies are not all equally fitted to receive this magnetic power. There are also bodies, although comparatively few, which possess such opposite qualities that their presence destroys the operation of this magnetism in other bodies.

"'18. This opposing power permeates equally all bodies; it can also in the same manner be communicated, accumulated and propagated; it streams back from the surface of mirrors, and can be spread by means of sound. This is not alone occasioned by a deprivation of power, but is caused by an opposing and positive power.

"'19. The natural and artificial magnet is equally, with other bodies, susceptible to animal magnetism, without, in either case, its operation upon iron or upon the needle suffering the slightest change.

"'20. The system will place in a clearer light the nature of fire, and of light, as well as the doctrine of attraction, of ebb and flow, of the magnet, and of electricity.

"'21. It will demonstrate that the magnet and artificial electricity, with regard to sicknesses, possess simply qualities possessed in common with other active forces afforded by nature; and that if any useful operation springs from their instrumentality, we have to thank animal magnetism for it.

"'22. From instances deduced from my firmly established and thoroughly proved rules, it will be easily perceived that this principle can immediately cure diseases of the nerves.

"'23. Through its assistance the physician receives much light regarding the application of medicaments, whereby he can improve their operation, call forth more beneficial crises, and conduct them in such wise as to become master of them.

"'24. Through communication of my method, I shall, in unfolding a new doctrine of disease, prove the universal use of this active principle.

"'25. Through this knowledge the physician will be enabled to judge of the origin, the progress, and the nature even of the most intricate diseases. he will be enabled to prevent the increase of disease, and bring about the cure without exposing his patient to dangerous effects or painful consequences, whatever be the age, sex or temperament of the patient.

"'26. Women during pregnancy and in childbirth receive advantage therefrom.

"'27. The doctrine will, at length, place the physician in such a position that he will be able to judge the degree of health possessed by any man, and be able to protect him from the disease to which he may be exposed. The art of healing will by this means attain to its greatest height of perfection.'

"Thus deeply convinced of the truth of his doctrine, it was natural that Mesmer should feel keenly pained by the misconception and contempt of men, for whom, in other directions, he entertained esteem. He expresses his bitter sorrow in various of the writings left behind him.

"'This System, which led me to the discovery of animal magnetism,' he writes, 'was not the fruits of a single day. By degrees, even as the hours of my life accumulated, were gathered together in my soul the observations which led to it. The coldness with which my earliest promulgated ideas were met filled me with astonishment as great as though I had never foreseen such coldness. The learned (and physicians especially) laughed over my system, but quite out of place, however, for although unsupported by experiment, it must have appeared fully as reasonable as the greater portion of their systems, on which they bestow the grand name of principles.

"'This unfavorable reception induced me again to examine my ideas. Instead, however, of losing through this, they gained a higher degree of manifestation, and, and in truth everything convinced me that in science, besides the principles already accepted, there must still be other, either neglected or not observed.'" ....

As our work is imply an attempt to elucidate philosophy from facts, we shall pursue the history of Mesmer no farther. His followers, some few of whom were indeed worthy successors to so great an original, added many valuable experiences to his, but failed to evolve any ideas more thoroughly comprehensive than those given in his twenty-seven aphorisms. To show why the mine of rich treasure opened up by Mesmer has been so slowly and reluctantly transferred to the mint of national currency in human practice, we have only to remember the bitter persecutions, cruel ingratitude and misrepresentation, which followed the good and amiable Anton Mesmer through his life, and pursued his followers after his decease.

The narrow conservatism of the age, too, and the pitiful jealousy of the Medical Faculty, rendered it difficult and even dangerous, to conduct magnetic experiments openly in Europe within several years of Mesmer's decease. Still such experiments were not wanting, and to show their results, we give a few excerpts from the correspondence between the famous French Magnetists, M. M. Deleuze and Billot, from the years 1829 to 1840. By these letters, published in two volumes in 1836, it appears that M. Billot commenced his experiments in magnetizing as early as 1789, and that during thsi space of over forty years, he had an opportunity of witnessing facts in clairvoyance, ecstasy, spiritual mediumship, and Somnambulism, which at the time of their publication transcended the belief of the general mass of readers. On many occasions in the presence of entranced subjects, Spirits recognized as having once lived on earth in mortal form - would come in bodily presence before the eyes of an assembled company, and at request, bring flowers, fruits, and objects, removed by distance from the scene of the experiments.

M. Deleuze frankly admits that his experience was more limited to those phases of Somnambulism in which his subjects submitted to amputations and severs surgical operations without experiencing the slightest pain, also they could disclose hidden things, find lost property, detect crime, predict the future, speak in foreign languages, and describe distant places with great eloquence and power.

In a letter dated July, 1831, M. Billot writing to Deleuze, says:

"I repeat, I have seen and known all that is permitted to man. I have seen the stigmata arise on magnetized subjects; I have dispelled obessions of evil spirits with a single word. I have seen spirits bring those material objects I told you of, and when requested, make them so light that they would float, and, again a small boiteau de bonbons was rendered to heavy, that I failed to move it an inch until the power was removed."

Alfonse Cahagnet, to whose invaluable work, the "Celestial Telegraph," allusion has already been made, published a series of experiments with a vast number of lucid subjects who by virtue of his magnetism became Clairvoyants.

At first their lucidity only sufficed to discover the things of earth, and trace earthly scenes and persons. As the magnetic sleep took deeper hold on their senses, however, it became apparent that a new world opened up before them.

Without any mental direction from the magnetizers - they one and all persisted in describing the spirits of those whom the world deemed dead. They discoursed with them, sometimes personated them, gave truthful accounts of their lives on earth, and described their appearances so accurately that scores of enquiring mourners, attracted by the fame of Cahagnet's Lucides, came thither to find their dead restored to them. It was as if a gate had suddenly been opened into the realms of paradise, and poor, suffering, bereaved humanity might be seen crowding upon each other to gaze through these golden portals and discover there all they had loved, all they had lost, and as in a mirror behold the delightful panoramas of being where their own tired feet were to find rest when their bodies should sleep the last sleep of humanity.

To those who enjoyed the unspeakable privilege of listening to the "somnambules" of Billot, Deleuze, and Cahagnet, another and yet more striking feature of unanimous revelation was poured forth. Spirits of those who had passed away strong in the faith of Roman Catholicism, often priests and dignitaries of that conservative church, addressing staunch and prejudiced believers in the faith, too, always asserted "there was no creed in Heaven," no sectarian worship, no remains of dogmatic faiths.

They taught that God was a grand Spiritual Sun - life on earth a probation; the spheres different degrees of compensatory happiness or states of retributive suffering; each appropriate to the good or evil deeds done on earth. They described the ascending changes open to every soul in proportion to its own efforts to improve.

They all insisted that man was his own judge, incurred a penalty or reward for which there was no substitution. They taught nothing of Christ, absolutely denied the idea of vicarious atonement - and represented man as his own Savior or destroyer.

They spoke of arts, sciences, and continued activities, as if the life beyond was but an extension of the present on a greatly improved scale. Descriptions of the radiant beauty, supernal happiness, and ecstatic sublimity manifested by the blest spirits who had risen to the spheres of paradise. Heaven, and the glory of Angelic companionship, melts the heart, and fills the soul with irresistible yearnings to lay down life's weary burdens and be at rest with them.

"O to be there!" must be the cry of every tired spirit who listens to these enchanting pictures of an enchanting hereafter; one, too, which so reasonably and harmoniously meets the aspirations of that human nature we yet bear about with us, which whilst longing for the unimaginable glories of Heaven, shrinks back appalled from the incomprehensible mysticism of theology. Such were some of the original and startling revealments poured forth by the French Clairvoyants, who, during the first half of this century, led in their somnambulic hands whole legions of arisen spirits and teaching angels, all eivdently builders, flocking into the great workshops of modern spiritual science, to take their places in the erection of the new Church of humanity. We cannot close this necessarily brief summary, without quoting a few words from that philosophic herald of Magnetism's new morning, Baron Dupotet. This brave and skillful Scientist says:

"No one can conduct magnetic seances with patience and fidelity, without coming to the conclusion which bursts upon my own mind, namely: that in Magnetism I rediscover the Spiritology of the ancients. Let the Savant reject the doctrine of spiritual apparitions as one of the great errors of the past, the results of the Magnetic seance re-affirms them all. They do more. They prove that the healing of the sick, the ecstasy of the Saints, all their miraculous works are ours. Is the knowledge of ancient magic lost? - we have all the facts on which to reconstruct it."

The learned Magnetist then recites a vast number of the phenomena produced through his own subjects and those of Puysegur, Seguin, Bertrand, and many others, which fully equal in marvel any of the magical histories of past ages.

And these discoveries multiplying in number every day, and increasing in marvel as the Adepts became more and more accomplished in their art, clustered to their meridian point before the year 1840, nearly ten years before the outbreak of modern Spiritualism in America, a movement from which many date the advent of spiritual revelation in this generation.

As a matter of phenomenal wonder, the latter class are right in their definition; but as the glorious triad of Masters through whom the lodges of ancient mystery are transformed into the temples of modern science, Paracelsus, Swedenborg and Mesmer take rank in unapproachable honor and unrivaled distinction. To their determined spirit of inquiry, to the patience, fidelity and acumen with which they conducted their extensive researched, and the unparalleled courage with which they dared to assail the prejudices of the age in which they lived, the generations to come will owe the fact that magnetism and psychology have rediscovered the lost art of ancient magic, and transmuted the visionary stone and elixir of mediaeval mystics into the pure gold of modern spiritual science.

Section XXIII
Spiritualistic Literature

--

We have reached that point in our review when we find ourselves at the final stage of our journey, standing face to face in fact with the last great spiritual dispensation of the ages, commonly termed "Modern Spiritualism."

In touching upon this part of our record the task resolves itself chiefly into the duty of cataloguing the many lucid and valuable expositions of the subject which are already extant, rendering the least attempt to add to this vast collection of special literature, a work of supererogation. In England, "The Two Worlds," by Thos. Shorter; "From Matter to Spirit," by Mrs. De Morgan, the admirable spiritualistic works of Wm. Howitt, and Mrs. Crowe's "Night Side of Nature," offer more food for reflection than it would seem the public mind has as yet been able to assimilate, whilst hosts of tracts, pamphlets, able magazines and newspapers, furnish continual streams of information from which no thirsting soul need go away empty. France is equally rich in the literature of Spiritism, although the general tone of its later writers is deflected to sustain the peculiar opinions of that body of believers known as "Reincarnationists." It would be as useless as impertinent to cite German literature in support of Spiritualistic doctrines or point to its phalanx of immortal writers whose affirmations of the Spiritual side of man's nature have never failed since the advent of the printing press to this hour. Holland in its excellent periodicals, and Russia in its liberal patronage of spirit media are also contributing their quota to the general storehouse of occult knowledge. In the meantime brave, unflinching defenders of these truths, writing in Spain from amidst the ghostly shadows of the grim old Inquisition, devoted bands of Spiritualists, writhing under the proscriptive ban of Priestcraft in South America, scattering forces from the Sandwich Islands, New Zealand, the East and West Indies, Australia, California, and indeed wherever civilization has a foothold, all contribute to fill up the columns of a world-wide Spiritual Almanac, and record the ceaseless irruptions of spirit people into this mundane world of ours.

There are many circumstances which combine to fix the era of this great modern movement at or about the date assigned to what has been popularly termed "the Rochester knockings." Whilst it would be far more difficult to name any period of human history where Spiritism was not, rather than when it commenced to act, there is much propriety in assuming that the first systematic effort to reduce the telegraphic signals made by spirits to a method of direct and continuous communication between themselves and mortals occurred at Rochester, in the State of New York, America, and commenced in the years 1847 and '48.

The first public exhibition of Spiritual power, too, occurred at this place and time, conducted under the direction of Spirits, and terminating in reports of COmmittees elected by the people, alleging a Spiritual cause for the disturbances, that these public meetings were convened to inquire into. In America, also, was presented, for the first time in history, a petition to the Government of the country, signed by many thousands of the most respectable of its citizens, praying for a scientific commission to inquire into a purely Spiritualistic movement.

It is from these causes, together with the immense surfaces of country embraced in the American manifestation - their power, variety, force and phenomenal wonder, the enormous masses of its believers, and the profusion of its literature, that mankind seem to have combined, with one accord, to yield the palm of all potency, number and influence to American Spiritism.

Before entering upon a final summary of this movement, it behooves us to render another reason why we should concentrate upon the Modern Spiritism of the United States the deepest emotions of respect and gratitude which mankind can render to the movers and founders of the great spiritual outpouring.

On American soil was born, and under American skies were first poured out, the vaticinations of a Seer, who stands second to no prophet, religious teacher, reformer, writer, or phenomenal wonder-worker, that the page of history has ever borne witness of. That Seer is Andrew Jackson Davis. During a brief residence in America, some few years since, the author, being on a visit to a friend in a charming country-seat, found himself made free of a noble library of several hundred volumes. In one portion of that enchanting study, just where the beams of the sinking sun would fall most favorably through the softened lustre of the stained-glass windows, stood a rich ormulu table, where, in singular contrast to the luxurious objects surrounding them, were piled up a large mass of plainly bound volumes, most of them large and evidently sufficiently popular with their possessor, for they bore more conclusive marks of wear than any other of the gorgeously bound volumes that the room contained. On opening with some curiosity the most ponderous of these books, the eye fell upon the following passages somewhere about the 142d page:

"As it was in the beginning, so the vast and boundless Uniercoelum, the great sun and centre from which all these worlds emanated, is still an exhaustless fountain of chaotic materials and living inherent energy to drive into existence billions and millions of billions of suns, with all their appendages more than have yet been produced! For it has eternal motion and contains the forms that all things subsequently assume; and it contains laws that are displayed in its geometrical and mechanical structure, combinations, laws, forces, forms and motions that have produced, and will still produce, an infinitude of systems, and systems of systems, whose concentric circles are but an expanse from the great germ of all existence, and are incessantly acting and re-acting, changing, harmonizing, organizing, and etherealizing every particle of chaotic and undeveloped matter that exists in the vortex!" ......

Struck with the peculiarity of these strange and high-strung words, and their analogy with the opinions that the had himself imbibed from the study of the Universe, and its laws, the author proceeded to turn other pages of this volume, and found astounding and deeply occult descriptions of God, man, creation, the Solar and Astral systems, the mystery of force, life, being, the order of creation, in fact, eloquent, burning words, and thoughts

253

almost beyond earthly comprehension for their sublimity, in every line. Hours swept on like seconds. The wonderful volume was glanced through, then others were opened.

The same writer's mind glowed through all those plain, cheap books - books which should have been bound in rubies and sapphires - and the reader became at least almost paralyzed at the breadth of information, the intense insight into being, and the majesty with which some mind more than mortal had swept creation, and reduced its vast research into the holiest and most elevated language.

Hours passed on. The early morning that had invited the student into that choice retreat now deepened into the gray mists of evening; yet still the straining gaze roamed through the wonderful stack of shabby books, until it fell upon the passage:

"The great original ever-existing omniscient, omnipotent and omnipresent productive power, the Soul of all existence, is throned in a central sphere, the circumference of which is the boundless universe, and around which solar, sidereal and stellar systems revolve, in silent, majestic sublimity and harmony! This power is what mankind call Deity, whose attributes are love and wisdom, corresponding with the principles of male and female, positive and negative, sustaining and creative." ....

At this point the master of the mansion, opening the library door, uttered an exclamation of surprise to find the guest whose presence he had missed for upwards of twelve hours, still at home.

The next words spoken were, "Who is the author of these wonderful books?"

"Oh, those," replied the host, with seeming indifference, "those books are all written by a poor shoemaker's boy of Poughkeepsie. That one" - pointing to the largest, the one which had first attracted the attention and awakened the astonishment of the reader - "was written, or rather spoken, when the lad was about sixteen years of age; He was too ignorant to write it, he could not have even spelled the words."

"In what school was he brought up, for heaven's sake?"

"Utter destitution."

"Who taught him all these wonderful things?"

"God and the angels. He never had any human teachers. Of that I am a living witness."

"But how in the name of all that is weird and wonderful were these volumes written?"

"Oh, at first they were taken down as he spoke them by a Scribe; because I tell you, he who discoursed of sun, stars, systems, astronomy, geology, physiology, and every other known science, was too uneducated to be able to write down the words he spoke, and

254

then, after graduating in the schools of - God alone knows where - but no college or seat of learning on this earth - he wrote the rest himself, every line of them."

"But if God and angels taught him, is there no record as to how he learned?"

"Yes, one which scores of living men and women will testify to. He was magnetized as a little shoemaker's lad of the humblest and poorest condition, and then he became an independent clairvoyant."

"Aye, indeed! Magnetism, and then Psychology. God's psychology poured into the soul, when it becomes clairvoyant, and ascends to the spheres of Deific knowledge! Why, this is ancient magic! The secret of all spiritualistic powers and possibilities; yet, when did any ancient Magian, any mind however aspiring, vast, or illuminated, assume such a depth, height, and breadth of comprehension as this? Answer me, my friend. Has such a paragon ever existed as the author of this library?"

"Swedenborg, perhaps. You forgot him."

"But these revelations are more human, more comprehensible and nearer to man's estate than Swedenborg's. They might be breathings of Swedenborg's spirit, correcting the shortcomings of his earthly career."

"Perhaps they are. This man believes in spirits."

"Can this wonder of the age exist and the world not know of it?"

"Yes; people know all about him, but they don't care for him now. He is living in great obscurity somewhere in Jersey, I believe."

"But the Spiritualists - surely those immense bodies of thinkers who have disclaimed the false assumptions of creeds and unscientific absurdities of ecclesiastical dogmas - do not those people so wonderfully taught of the spirit, accept him as their prophet, their leader, their heaven-inspired teacher?"

"Hold, hold, my friend! you know not what you say. The Spiritualists are all 'individuals.' They are their own Gods, their own Prophets, leaders and teachers; what! present any human leader, teacher, or Prophet, to the great bulk of the American Spiritualists! You will find you are treading on dangerous ground, and will soon be warned back with the phrases, 'we want no Popes, Cardinals, Bishops, or Priestly Leaders here.'"

But Leaders and Teachers they must have. Do they not sustain great mass meetings where the public gather together to hear their opinions discussed?"

"Aye, but each one presents his own opinion, and none but his own. Sometimes these opinions are as widely divergent as the heavens and the earth; and sometimes not unlike in essence, light and darkness, still their pride is to maintain 'a free platform,' and under this appellation, the Angels of darkness are as free to have their say as those of light."

"But this is chaos, disorder, not Spiritism, much less the sweetness, grace and dignity of this Harmonial Philosophy!"

"The time was when Davis' revelations, startling materialism out of its blank negations, and compelling attention from the wonderful and unprecedented methods of their delivery, drew around him a large class of admiring friends and elevated thinkers, who were not ashamed to call themselves after him. 'Harmonial Philosophers,' but in the revolutionary spirit of this great movement Spiritualism, thousands have rushed into its ranks, glad to escape from creeds, dogmas, and ecclesiastical despotism. The memory of this dethroned tyranny is still too strong upon them to admit of any present attempts to organize a new religious system. The swing of the pendulum has carried the soul from despotism into license, and until the revolutionary elements of thought can subside into equilibrium, depend upon it even the amiable and unassuming 'harmonial philosopher's[' leadership cannot be tolerated."

"But in the meantime were these stupendous revelations given in vain? Surely so noble a philosophy, received through an inspiration so unmistakably divine, so free from human bias or moral intervention, ought to commend itself to every civilized nation of the present age!"

"My friend, you forget the elements of which this generation is composed. Setting aside the scientists who scoff out of notice every idea connected with spiritual existence, or outside the known routine of science, who do you expect in Catholic and Protestant Europe to sympathize with the revelations of the Poughkeepsie Seer? Some few there are in every country where these plain, black volumes have made their way, who regard them as we do. Many who even believe they are the voice of the earth's Tutelary Angel, speaking from between the Cherubim and Seraphim of past and future ages, but they like us, must wait until the age is more receptive of these sublime truths. At the present day, the great majority of European religionists hold up their hands with holy horror at the name of A. J. Davis, and cry, 'Pantheist! Heathen Philosopher! This is the man who denies the Trinity, disbelieves in the awful Jehovah with his great white throne! This is the hard-headed moralist who would take away our Savior from us, deny us the consolation of the vicarious atonement, and compel us all to do personal penance for our sins, and even abandon them altogether! This is he who calls God a Spiritual Sun, Jesus an amiable young man, creation an evolution, and flies in the face of Genesis and the thirty-nine articles!'"

In after years, when the author had time and opportunity to study out the vast stores of spiritual thought and profound philosophy, displayed in the voluminous writings of this great modern Prophet, the admiration they excited, determined him, if he ever more visited America, he would seek out this marvel of the age, even as the Disciples of classic Greece sat at the feet of her master spirits to learn wisdom.

The time for the fulfillment of this cherished purpose, came, and in company with an ardent Disciple of the Harmonial Philosophy from a distant land, the author commenced his search.

Few Spiritualists seemed to know even the whereabouts of the Poughkeepsie Seer. Surely, we thought he must be at the head of some great Church, Temple, Synagogue, a mechanic's institute at the least, or a popular lecture hall; some place, where spiritually starved souls could feed upon the Divine revelations of nature as taught by one of her purest and most faithful interpreters! But no! the great Alchemist who had transmuted the Magic of early ages into the gold of spiritual science, the Seer, Philosopher, and greatest phenomenon of this or any age, had to be sought for in a little shop in an obscure street, where, without followers, disciples, admirers, and to judge from appearances with but very few customers, amidst his neat, well ordered collection of books, ranged on their shelves in curious little delicate curves, and tastefully adorned with illuminated mottoes, and Autumn leaves - stood the great Seer, selling his books for a livelihood.

The placid mein and gentle tones of the unassuming salesman betrayed none of the pangs of grief, indignation and humiliation which two foreigners felt for him, as they made their silent purchase, with hearts too full for utterance, and withdrew.

"That man is nobler far in the quiet, cheerful dignity with which he accommodates himself to the sordid necessities of a petty trade, than when he stood as the interpreter of Angels, dictating 'Nature's Divine Revelations.'" Thus spoke one of the deeply-moved visitors.

"The age is not worthy of him; he lives a century before his time," rejoined the other.

"Aye! but his works will live with him. The truths he reveals are eternal, and the revelator will yet become immortal," was the reply. Even so. Time, the touchstone of truth, will do justice to him - to all; and so, Andrew Jackson Davis, farewell! But, whilst the 'Magic Staff' - Penetralia, Stellar Key, Arabula, Harmonia and Divine Revelations - are in print, or even in memory, never let American, English, French, German, or 'critic' of any other land, presume to say: 'Spiritism has no philosophy.' In the volumes enumerated above, it has the best, broadest, holiest and yet most practical philosophy that was ever enunciated since God said: 'Let there be Light, and there was Light!'"

We are not informed whether Mr. Davis ranks himself before the world as a Spiritist or not. Few of his brethren of that order seem to know or care much about him now; but the mode in which his philosophy was produced, justifies a stranger's claim for him, to-wit: that of all the children of the Spirit that have illuminated this great modern movement called Spiritism, one of the best, truest and most honorable of them all is he who, in deep obscurity, illustrates so thoroughly the proverb, "A Prophet is not without honor, save in his own country."

Our sketch of supermundane Spiritism would not be complete without this humble tribute to one who forms its noblest illustration - to one with whom the writer has never exchanged a word on earth, and in all human probability never will, but who rejoices to believe that name, so coldly slipping out of human remembrance and appreciation now, will be enshrined in the hearts of unborn generations, and in the shining roll of immortality be held sacred as the Founder of a Divine and natural Harmonial Dispensation.

In commenting on American and European Spiritism, we recognize no right to add items of history to the immense stores already extant, nor weary our monthly periodicals have never failed to chronicle from the opening of the movement to this day. Deeming a work published under the peculiar limitations which herald forth this volume will only render it an ephemera of the day, our closing remarks will be addressed to those who must already be informed upon every point of the passing Spiritualistic movement. If they are not so, the works of Robert Dale Own, Judge Edmonds, Epes Sargent, Eugene Crowell, but, above all, Emma Hardinge's inimitable "Twenty Years' History of Modern Spiritualism," will bring every student face to face with the entire details of all that has been effected by Spirits communicating to mortals on American soil. Here, too, as in Europe, there are vast numbers of tracts being continually issued, representing all the various phases of the movement, besides many which do not belong to it, but which persons, who believe in its facts, availing themselves of its popularity, thrust before the public as Spiritualistic.

Books of poems, novels, treatises, some with rare merit, others less than mediocre, flood the age from Spiritualistic sources. A great many newspapers and magazines have been published in the interests of the movement, lived their time, served their period of usefulness, and died out, others still maintain their hold upon the world's attention and command, a full share of patronage. The oldest, the "Banner of Light," commenced in the earliest days of the American movement, and now (1876) occupying the distinguished place of its leading organ, is in itself a compete repertoire of all the astounding phenomena, passing events, and celebrated personages, who constitute the history of Spiritism.

The more detailed sources of information thus indicated, it only remains for use to notice some of the principal characteristics of the modern movement.

In America these are strikingly tinctured by the national idiosyncrasies of the people, but the methods of signaling by spirit power are alike all over the world. They consist first, of the production of sounds by knocking; table-tilting, lifting of heavy bodies, the transportation of small articles, such as fruits, flowers, jewels, etc., etc., through the air, and their production at points of distance from their scene of departure. The execution of music by spirits playing upon instruments furnished by mortals, and still more rarely, music sung or played by spirits, without any visible means of its production. The voices of spirits are also heard clairaudiently and externally, sometimes uttering words only, at others, long addresses. Spirits display their hands, feet, faces, and sometimes the whole form "materialized" out of the emanations of the mediums and human beings surrounding them. In this fleshy masquerade the spirits dance, sing, disport with the persons around them, and perform like players on the mimic stage of a theatre. Other demonstrations consist of resisting fire, the extension of the body, also its elevation into the air, and floating around the apartment. Spirits also exhibit feats of strength, tying and untying their Media when bound with ropes, and executing just such sleight-of-hand tricks as are common to jugglers. Many higher phases of spirit power are exhibited, such as trance speaking and writing; Seership, or the power of seeing and describing spirits, or personating their peculiarities so as to be recognized; also the impressions which the mind receives from spirits, to declare names and other signs of identity by which mortals can be assured their spirit friends are present. Many photographic likenesses of Spirits are said to have been produced through Media, whilst others are impelled to draw portraits of Spirits, or flowers and allegorical scenes, others to behold visions, prophetic, descriptive, or symbolical.

Many are impelled to describe diseases, prescribe remedies, or effect cures by the laying on of hands. This movement has also brought to light a great many latent powers of the soul, which spring up under the sympathetic contagion of the time, and exhibit themselves in psychometric delineations of character by touch, clairvoyance, magnetic virtue and prophetic intuition. ANother striking and curious phase is the frequent apparition of the spectre, or astral spirit, disengaged from the still living body, and manifesting its presence at a distance, with or without the consciousness of the subject.

Now the great marvel and special interest which attaches to all these manifestations of spirit power in the nineteenth century is their original spontaneity, and the fact that they have in most instances fallen upon the media through whom they are produced, without solicitation or any form of preparation.

It is in this spontaneity, and the vast abundance of the phenomena, that the modern movement differs so widely from all preceding examples, where - except in rare cases - years of preparation, initiation, and magical processes have been required for the performance of occult works. Modern Spiritism also is more characteristic of human spirit agency than that of any other era.

Up to the close of the last century, when the German and French magnetizers so widely popularized the practices of Mesmerism and the powers of Psychology, a belief prevailed that occult works were effected by Planetary, Elementary, and Tutelary Spirits chiefly, and that the apparition of deceased persons was rare and exceptional. The experiments of the magnetizers, and the cloud of witnesses who poured in through their subjects from the realms of spirit land, bringing indisputable proofs of their identity with the souls of deceased ancestors, completely reversed this opinion, and induced a prevalent belief that all manifestations of a spiritualistic character originated with the liberated souls of humanity. The author has, in previous sections, adduced sufficient reason for assuming a middle ground between these opinions; and whilst there is abundant evidence to prove the constant interposition of human spirits in human affairs, and the identity of such spirits with a vast amount of the occult phenomena produced in every age of the world, we may also rest assured that the realms of the Elementaries can and do exercise considerable influence upon humanity, especially in relation to animal propensities and earthly things; also that Planetary Spirits rule, guide and interpose in human destiny, and that Tutelary Spirits take charge of and govern nations, planets, and all bodies in space.

That all these spirits can be seen, communed with and invoked, is also sufficiently proved in the course of this work.

When we consider the stupendous and revolutionary changes of opinion that this great Spiritual outpouring induces, we are driven to accept of three manifest conclusions; the first is, that we cannot be too grateful for these demonstrations, nor too careful to sift them from all taint of human folly, impurity, hallucination or imposture.

Next we should recognize it as our incumbent duty, even an urgent necessity, to preserve to ourselves and posterity, the high privileges of this beneficent and instructive intercourse by studying its laws, and endeavoring scientifically to master its methods, so as to control the communion and be enabled to conduct it at pleasure.

Next, it must strike every reasonable mind with indignation, to perceive that those who have assumed the high position of leaders either in science or ecclesiasticism, should go far abandon their trust as to permit the people to grope their way blindfold through the mists, obscurities, and difficulties of this vast outpouring, without lending their aid to sole its mysteries, proving its errors if it had any, conserving its truths if they exist, and demonstrating whatever is true or false, valuable or pernicious in its action.

It is an acknowledged axiom in logic, that abuse is no argument, ridicule is no proof. And yet to these petty arms - pop-guns worthy only of pugnacious school-boys - have many of the most eminent scientists of the day descended, when compelled by the force of public opinion to deal with the subject of Spiritism.

High ecclesiasticism has done worse, for it has falsified the very basis of its own pretensions, the corner-stone of its authority being miracle. By denouncing the modern power or right to work what has been unscientifically termed "miracle," the Church work what has been unscientifically termed "miracle," the Church has virtually undermined its own foundations and either proved itself impious enough "to fight against the living God," or hypocritical enough to maintain an institution founded upon myth and falsehood.

From these positions there is no escape, and though we have no intention in these brief remarks to wage war upon materialistic Science, or atheistic Ecclesiasticism, we point out the position to our readers to show them why they must rely on themselves, and cease to utter vain appeals to any human leaders to help them, or continue their humiliating efforts to convert great men who don't want to be converted.

Many very eminent scientists and excellent members of ecclesiastical bodies have - as individuals, not as official members of an organization - taken hold of Spiritualism and hazarded name and place in its advocacy, but it must be obvious even to these illuminated thinkers, that the formulae of material science and the influences of credal faith have no connection with this great independent movement.

The Scientist finds that a new set of laws, and those purely psychological, must be studied and obeyed, before he can make headway with Spiritism, and the Ecclesiastic continually proves that the Spirits do not respond to the invocations or exorcisms of Credal faiths, nor can the broad and unconservative revelations of Spiritism be accommodated to the narrow dogmas of sects.

Once again, then, we recommend the study and adoption of those principles which Spiritism itself discloses, and as these are in the strictest relations to good order, good morals, purity of life, and the spirit of universal brotherhood, we can do mankind no better service than to recommend a profound study both of the science and religion of Spiritism.

To illustrate our meaning all the more forcibly, we will revert to the three aforesaid conclusions, which the study of Modern Spiritism, especially the American phase of the movement, compels the observer to come to: "We cannot be too grateful for these demonstrations, nor too careful to sift them from all taint of human folly, impurity, hallucination, or imposture.

The author has taken the opportunity of making three visits to America, and that for the sole purpose of studying the spiritual manifestations produced on her soil.

On the last two occasions he has observed with more regret than surprise, a gradual but evident decadence in the general feeling of grateful appreciation which these manifestations at first awakened. Some believers have become accustomed to what was at first an exciting wonder, and their curiosity satisfied, they need no more. Others have slackened in zeal because they have been disappointed in some special results they anticipated; but a still larger number have withdrawn their public support from a movement where the taint of human folly and impurity has become so evident as to brand every lass of believers with the evil reputation fastened upon it by the few. Hallucinations and imposture, too, have prevailed to an alarming extent in the ranks of Spiritism, and these two last elements combining with the before mentioned causes, have shaken the faith of many, and repelled still more from this cause.

It is as a corrective to the errors which so prominently force themselves into notice in connection with the first conclusion we draw, that we recommend a careful consideration of the second, namely: "That we should recognize it as our incumbent duty, even an urgent necessity, to preserve to ourselves and posterity the high privileges of this beneficent and instructive intercourse, by studying its laws, and endeavoring scientifically to master its methods, so as to control the communion, and be enabled to conduct it at pleasure."

On this point let it be remembered that all the magical arts and possibilities detailed in previous sections, are as open to mankind to-day as ever they were. Whether it be expedient to seek them or no, is not the question. We simply reiterate they are attainable, and with the lights of science we now enjoy, especially in our improved knowledge of magnetic, psychologic and physiological laws, they can be arrived at with far less severe

261

probationary efforts, and with far milder methods of culture than those formerly exercised.

Superficial commentators on this subject, talk of the "lost art of magic," and describe as impossible achievements for modern Europeans or American, the marvels enacted by Hindoo Fakeers, Egyptian Derishes, and Arabian Santons, Mediaeval Ecstatics, Witches and Wiards; but what marvels are much greater than the talking Spirits whose truth and spiritual origin were so clearly demonstrated at Koon's spirit rooms, even as early as 1850? (vide Hardinge's Modern American Spiritualism). What revelations of Zoroaster, Buddha, Pythagoras, Plato, or other great philosophers of antiquity, have ever rendered a better code of morals, purer life, or more scientific demonstration of creative order, and the mysteries of the Univercoelum, than the entranced Mystics, Swedenborg and Andrew Jackson Davis? Does M. Jaccoloit give one single marvel of Hindoo Spiritism that has not transpired in equal force and greater abundance through the physical force Mediums of England and America?

The Ecstatics of the Monasteries were canonized as Saints, because the stigmata appeared on their bodies; their forms were elevated in the air, and they could read the thoughts of other, prophesy the future, etc., etc.

It is not our purpose to detract from the value of the abundant literature now before a very unappreciative age, by repeating the authentic and well attested narratives they contain. Any unprejudiced reader will find the marvels reported of the Asiatic Mystics equaled, and in many instances transcended by the illustrations of spirit-power given in Hardinge's "Modern American Spiritualism" alone.

Let it suffice to say, that the stigmata of names, figures, dates, and signs, which have convinced thousands of darkened minds of the Soul's immortality, have appeared on the persons of numerous mediums of this century, and are still appearing to those who care to seek for such evidence; that the levitation of the body is a common occurrence; the power of prophecy has been amply demonstrated in thousand of well-attested instances. The capacity to resist fire has been abundantly shown.

The vaticinations of the Greek and Roman Sybils never exceeded many of the eloquent utterances of unlettered boys and girls in the modern Spiritual movement, and if shameful imposture and very bad reputations had not intervened so frequently to destroy faith or even patience with the modern manifestations, they exceed in use, wonder, beauty and number, a thousand fold, all the marvelous tales recited of Greek, Roman, Hindoo, Egyptian, Persian, Chaldean, or Hebrew Spiritism, that is, when the latter are sifted down to well proven narratives, Cabalistic sentences are translated into plain sense, and allegorical flights of fancy are reduced to actual fact.

The failures of modern Spiritism, its degradation, lack of organic power, evil repute, and gradual but sure decadence, all proceed from the human side of the movement. It may be difficult, perhaps impossible, to repair the errors committed by a fast fading generation, but it is for us to lay the foundation of improved conditions, by dealing with the rising generation, and for this purpose, the wisest course we can now pursue to show our devotion to the interests of truth, and our duty to posterity, would be to found a new "School of the Prophets."

In these, young, fresh, susceptible organisms should be selected as Neophytes to fill a future order of Mediums, Priests and Ministers. Their food should be plain and simple, their habits pure and orderly, their lives spotless, their morals regulated by the most exalted and dignified standards of truth, justice, piety, and goodness. They should be under the regulation of a company of holy women and scientific men. Good, pure-minded healthful magnetizers should be received into fellowship with them, and one and all should be magnetized to determine who were operators, and who subjects. The first should be set apart as Physicians to the sick and operators for mediumistic and clairvoyant development. The second as Media, Prophets, and Ministers.

As soon as the aforesaid powers were discovered, they should be classified and the magnetizations continued until the subjects felt impressed to discontinue them and stand alone. Periodical seances should be established, at which scientific order should strictly prevail. The floors of the circle room should be intersected with plateaus of glass, to prevent the escape of the magnetic fluid. The air should often be purified with streams of ozone; the walls surrounded with graceful forms of art and well selected colors. Those destined to become Magnetizers or Physicians should sit in rooms well-supplied with powerful magnets. Tender, susceptible media should never commence their sittings without first holding the poles of a good electro-magnetic battery in their hands, closing their exercises in the same way. No drugs, narcotics, or stimulants should be used under any circumstances, but all other legitimate appeals to the senses should be put into requisition, the most potential of which should be healthful exercises, bathing, the performance of exquisite music, and the sight of beautiful forms of art.

Those sensitives manifesting tendencies towards clairvoyance should practice gazing steadily into the crystal or mirror. Those susceptible of psychometrical delineations, should practice their power, remembering that this, and all other Spiritual gifts, are as much the result of culture and exercise, as are the developments of muscular strength, or intellectual achievement. No seances should ever be attempted without a solemn preparatory invocation to good and wise Spirits, and to any Tutelary, Angelic Guardian, or Deific power, in which the Invocant places faith, and this not only for the purpose of stimulating the mind to aspiration and soliciting the presence and influence of the good and wise, but also for the purpose of banishing evil and mischievous spirits from interfering. The same ceremonial of discharge or dismissal should be used on breaking up a seance, in fact we would recommend at least as much courtesy in the treatment of Angelic essences, as the usages of society demand for ordinary acquaintances.

A "School of the Prophets" conducted on some such principles as we have thus briefly outlined, would certainly do as much for this generation as the mysteries and Temple services of antiquity effected for the nations in which they were practiced - in a word - it would provide a class of duly qualified Magnetic Physicians, Prophets, Mediums, Clear Seers, and Spiritualistic persons, whose morals, characters, and gifts being cultured and superinduced into religious and scientific methods, would fill the world with blessing and usefulness instead of as now, desecrating high and holy gifts to base and sordid purposes, or disgracing them with characteristics which we do not care to dwell upon in this volume.

All the public exercises of Spiritualism should be conducted in decency and order. A general basis of principles should unite all persons who believe in Spiritual existence and Spiritual gifts, and well-qualified expounders of these subjects should be the officiating ministers. In these gatherings, as in the process of scientific culture, the sweetest melodies, the noblest harmonies, the purest flowers and fragrance, and the most pleasing association of artistic sights with sounds should be employed. All that could contribute to elevate, purify and exalt the Soul's noblest powers should be resorted to, as legitimate means of influence, and nothing low, degrading, slang, or impure, should be associated with Spiritual ideas.

In private families, the practice of heterogeneous, disorderly or idle gatherings to seek Spirit communion, should be sternly discountenanced. The whole subject has been shamefully secularized; treated either as a common-place method of spending an idle hour; sought for the mere purposes of curiosity, fun, fortune-telling or marvel-seeking.

If the theories propounded in this volume be correct, and spirits of various grades, from the very highest to the very lowest, hover around us, seeking to minister or pander to the motives which impel the seekers, or the characteristics of mind which pervade the assemblage, then what class of SPirits must inevitably attend nine-tenths of the spirit circles now in vogue, and what results of good, use, individual or collective elevation, can be expected to grow out of them? In the present heterogeneous condition of human society, we dare not recommend the endeavor to obtain personal communion with the spirit world to every individual. The merchant, trader, mechanic, operative, seamstress, shop-keepers and laborers, whose time must be nearly all consumed in the routine of perpetual drudgery, and whose over-taxed minds and bodies cannot be properly attuned to such exercises, should not attempt to deplete their systems, or risk the integrity of mental and physical balance, by seeking to culture Spiritualistic endowments.

Spiritism, like every other calling, demands it votaries, its devotees, and its peculiarly-prepared ministers. Persons having time to devote to the culture of their gifts and steady enthusiasm to sustain them during their probationary training, are the only classes who should attempt to teach, preach, or tender service publicly as Mediums between the better world of Spirits, and the much-darkened world of poor humanity.

Far be it from the author of these pages to discourage the sweet and loving practice of family circles, meetings together in the pleasant and sacred seclusion of home, or the social relations of friendship, to invoke the dear household deities who have passed on before, or who would be so certain to respond to the appeal of those whom they have best loved on earth.

They will surely be there, those loving spirit friends; aye, wherever two or three are gathered together in the name of the spirit, whatever spirit they summon will be there, be it God or the Adversary; spirits of the heart's dearest affections, or goblins from the metal crypts of earth, which avarice would fain rob of its hidden treasures. In the meantime, in order to systematize even these innocent home communings, good order and strict conformity to scientific principles should be observed. We are not now undertaking to lay down the exact methods in which each circle for development or communion should be conducted. We can only touch upon the generalities of the subject, and would recommend well wishers to these great truths if they desire their rapid and orderly promotion, to abandon the childish and egotistical fear that now paralyzes them, lest some competent adviser or highly inspired person should assume leadership amongst them, and remember that to every organism there must be a head as well as organs, to every circumference a centre, and in every nation a governmental combination for the protection of the governed, no less than for the restraint of the lawless. Having disposed of this poor, envious phantom which so troubles the peace of such Spiritists, and convinced themselves that it is not necessary that a well-qualified adept in spiritual things should require those whom he counsels to place a triple crown on his head, kiss his slipper, and pronounce his dictum infallible - let Spiritists come together in reverent deliberation, and decide which methods of scientific investigation they can or ought to pursue so as to evolve the basic principles upon which spirits communicate.

Let them appoint qualified persons to prepare reports and verify their opinion by successful experiments, and until such reports, conjoined with such experiments, be accepted by the sense, reason and convicted judgment of the deliberators, let the reports be peremptorily rejected, and the investigation continue, if it be necessary, from generation to generation, until results are achieved. But such a council, animated by such a spirit, would not have to wait long. Magnetism is the pabulum by which spirits communicate, Psychology the influence. These are the secret virtues of Magic, Witchcraft and Mediumship in every age, and human nature changes not. If the founders of home circles will carefully study out the rules briefly suggested as indications in forming a school for the education and training of Media, they will surely become, in part at least, successful enough to reward them for some time consumed, and some sacrifices consummated.

If possible a room should be set apart, consecrated and held consecrated to spiritual science.

No unholy thing should enter there, no unholy thoughts be invited.

The circle should meet at least once, but better twice or thrice each week. None should enter there until they had fasted at least four hours previously, and assemble together with clean face and clean hearts. Let them come as to a holy place; and if neither vocal nor instrumental music of a sweet and harmonious character can be procured, a small but finely toned chime of bells, glass harmonica, or good musical box should invariably be provided; - thus the atmosphere will be arranged into harmonious strata, according to the suggestions upon music contained in a previous Section. Let the chamber be adorned with all the little stores of beauty and pleasant forms possible. Flowers are sometimes injurious to media, their strong perfume causing too much excitement to the senses, but where ozone can be procured, it is well to pass streams through the air, and the use of the electromagnetic battery held by two persons placed at each pole, the rest forming a chain, ever strengthens the force, and benefits all present. Ten minutes' use of this machine should open and close each seance. Also, we would enforce the same rule of opening with an invocation, and closing with a courteous discharge to the spirits, suggested above. Family gatherings might experiment with magnetization as before suggested, the strongest, healthiest and most worthy of the party being selected as the operator. Crystals and mirrors should be laid on the circle table, also writing materials and slates.

A large circle beneath the table, sufficient to insulate all the sitters assembled, and prevent even their garments from touching the ground, should be formed of glass, and this would greatly conduce to aid the manifestations by preventing the too rapid efflux of vital force.

It should forever after be prohibited to sit in totally darkened apartments. Spirits come to earth in their own Astral light, and to this element material light is opposed; still the unqualified abuses that have arisen from the prevalence of total darkness at spiritual seances should induce every wise investigator to discountenance them utterly.

The fact that many of the most stupendous evidences of spirit power have been given in semi-lighted apartments, should be a sufficient answer to those who plead for darkness as a necessary condition for strong demonstrations; besides, the wise and faithful investigator can better afford to dispense with strong demonstrations, than good morals, decency, or spiritual agency without human interference.

Let dark circles be abandoned to Elementary Spirits, in and out of earthly encasements, and the impostors will find much of their occupation gone.

For more detailed instructions in this and all forms of spiritual culture, we commend a careful perusal and reperusal of these pages. Attempts should be made to elaborate the many suggestions it contains, by the aid of a council selected from experienced media and philosophic thinkers - but whilst the aim in view should be to perfect those methods by which Spiritism can be organized into a religion and cultivated as a science, both Church and Lyceum should be left free to expand in every direction, open to new light, new conditions of society, and the progress of human opinion. Basic principles should be sought for and laid down as fundamental rules from which there can be no departure; powers of growth and advancement should be just as liberally provided for, ever remembering that mind grows, but writings do not, and that whilst the Universe is a stupendous organism whose centre - the grand man - the Spiritual Sun - the Unknown and Unknowable - changes not, - the manifestations of his infinity, his variousness, his beauty, and goodness, are out-wrought in eternal series of changes. Light and Heat, - Truth and Love, are eternal and unchanging principles. Their manifestation in created being are infinite. All are tending outward from a grand central heart to an illimitable circumference, yet all are held in the gravitating arms of immutable law; all are moved in the expanding grooves of inevitable progress, - and all are sent forth on Sun-like paths of ascending glory to model after God. Study him, honor him, glorify him in thyself. Thou canst not misunderstand or fail to know him. In Heaven, in the boundless Universe, he is the Macrocosm, the infinitely large; on earth and in thyself, He is the Microcosm, the infinitely little. In the understanding of the mystery of God lies all the secret potency of Art Magic.

In the apprehension of his scheme, his glorious harp of creation, on which his master hand is striking tones from the lowest bass to the highest treble; you hear the majestic symphony whose notes are suns, systems, worlds, earth, men; - Mundane, Sub-Mundane and Super-Mundane Spiritism.

Epilogue to the Drama of Art Magic

Some readers there be whose chief aim is - unconsciously to themselves, perhaps - but greatly to the detriment of their higher natures - to search into what they read rather for the discovery of errors in orthography, and innovations upon conservative methods of typography, than for the elimination of ideas, or the enjoyment of soul intercourse with their author. To this class of readers our pages will doubtless present a fruitful soil for their special methods of criticism, and to such, we have no other apology to offer, than that contained in the few choice and pointed words of the Editor's Preface.

There is still another class whose methods of study have received the peculiarly significant soubriquet of, skimming. The chief delight of such persons is in an elaborately prepared Index, over the columns of which they rejoice to pore, industriously picking out just the particular words they have sympathy with, glancing at these - for Index worshipers only glance, do not read - and abandoning the rest of the volume to more patient and capable students than themselves.

The author's life-long experience with a variety of readers, has induced him to look upon Index worshipers, as the most superficial of all book owners, and finally determined him not to spend time in writing for them at all. In the compilation of Historical, Legal, Statistical or Biographical works, an Index is not only useful, but absolutely essential. In a book of these ideas only, such an appendix offers a premium to the unworthy habit of "skimming," and therefore, rejecting the courteous offer of our patient and untiring Editor, to satisfy the hypercritical, by the addition of an Index, we submit the foregoing pages for study - study which cannot master the ideas presented in one superficial reading, much less in Index skimming.

We ask a careful perusal and reperusal of these pages, not for their literary merit, nor the exactitude of their methods, but for the sakes of the high themes discussed, and the weighty subjects which fill up each column. When our readers have bestowed this much study upon the volume, they will not need an Index; until they have done so, we have written it for them in vain. Neither have we followed the well-beaten track of custom, in giving a list of authorities cited in this volume. Whenever possible we have given the names of such authors as have supplied us with felicitous quotations; but we feel no impulse to burden our work with the abomination of such signs as "vols., vers., chaps.," etc., etc., any more than we recognize the propriety of harassing our readers by foot-notes, or references to literature, perhaps unattainable to all but special seekers into occult lore. And now that our work - not of apology, but of sturdy resistance to conventional habits in book-making - is done, what remains, save to tender everlasting thanks to our gentle, faithful and long-suffering Editor; most kindly greetings to the brave "Banner of Light," the "Spiritual Scientist," "London Medium," and "Spiritualist," who have so generously and courteously sustained her, and a potential psychologic, heartfelt God-speed to the noble five hundred who, in the face of scorn, contumely, ridicule and blatant ignorance, have dared to registered their honored names as subscribers to Art Magic, four hundred, at least, of them paying their subscriptions before they were due, trusting gallantly to the good faith and honesty of Emma Hardinge Britten that they should not be robbed of their due, and the rest signifying their insight and recognition of the divine in humanity, with an absence of all sordid motive or fear of public opinion, which forever protests against the doctrines of "human depravity, original sin," or aught but the sublime truth that the world is made flesh, and dwells amongst men now and evermore!

CPSIA information can be obtained
at www.ICGtesting.com
Printed in the USA
BVHW070810021120
592326BV00014B/2059